The Age of Enlightenment COOKBOOK

miriam kasin

ARCO PUBLISHING, INC.
219 PARK AVENUE SOUTH, NEW YORK, N.Y. 10003

Dedicated to the unbounded, pure Being within us:
the true source of all nourishment and fulfillment.

Published by Arco Publishing, Inc.
219 Park Avenue South
New York, N.Y. 10003

Copyright © 1980 by Miriam Kasin

All rights reserved. No part of this book may be
reproduced, by any means, without permission in
writing from the publisher, except by a reviewer
who wishes to quote brief excerpts in connection
with a review in a magazine or newspaper.

Library of Congress Cataloging in Publication Data

Kasin, Miriam.
    The age of enlightenment cookbook.

    Includes index.
    1. Vegetarian cookery. I. Title.
TX837.B43   641.5   79-264
ISBN 0-688-04539-6

Printed in the United States of America

Contents

Acknowledgments

I would like to express my deepest gratitude to the following people:

Tom Bell, whose assistance and encouragement helped guide the entire project.

My parents, Gerald and Edith Kasin, for their assistance and encouragement.

Barbara Meyer and Aaron Neely, for providing the first impulses.

Carolyn Kelly, for transcribing my notes.

The many people who contributed information and ideas for recipes, including Eva Lundgren, E. Michael Buckley, Henny Nielsen, Diana Brewer, Susie Raymond, Penelope Winslow, Rosie Witherspoon, Edward and Janice Fox, Marilyn Karnaze, Terry Shaw, and again, my mother (the *best* cook).

Introduction

Cooking is a game of creation. It is played with a few tools, ingredients, and rules that contain within them an infinite number of possibilities for different creations. Once a basic mastery of the game is achieved, that which is produced is simply a matter of the desire of the cook. *The Age of Enlightenment Cookbook* has been created to assist those interested in vegetarian cooking to gain such mastery, so that whatever they wish to create falls within the range of their capabilities.

However, all cooks would agree that there is far more to the art and science of cooking than simply reading some instructions in a book. As an ancient proverb states, "Knowledge that is in the book remains in the book." Indeed, the words on the pages of a cookbook are of no practical significance until they are put into *action* by the cook.

Ultimately a meal is the expression of the love, intelligence, and creativity of the person who prepares it. It is the amount of these inner qualities exercised in the preparation of a meal that determines its quality and life-supporting effects—in some ways far more than the nutritional content or the sensory impact of the food itself. The *cook* is the most important basic "ingredient" in any recipe.

The framework of the diet presented here is that of a meatless, eggless cuisine based on fresh foods. Emphasis is placed on fresh fruits and vegetables, dairy products, grains, legumes, nuts, and seeds—with the use of herbs and spices to enhance their flavors. No preserved, artificially flavored, or fermented foods are included. The quality of the food we eat has a bearing on the quality of our life and health, and the life-value available in fresh foods is highly beneficial. The flavor of fresh foods is also more lively.

The recipes in *The Age of Enlightenment Cookbook* are adaptable to the many variations within a vegetarian diet, from that of the vegan (a person who eats no animal products whatsoever) and the health-food enthusiast to the preferences of the traditional gourmet cook. Basic instruction is given for the novice, while a wide range of international recipes offer fresh inspiration and challenge to the experienced cook. The non-vegetarian who wishes to reduce the amount of meat and eggs in his or her diet—or is simply looking for new ways to serve vegetables, grains, etc.—will find new ideas to add to the repertoire.

Enjoy!

STAPLE INGREDIENTS

Many novice vegetarian cooks, particularly those making a transition from another type of diet, are a bit confused as to what to shop for. The following is a list of foods and beverages that we feel are important to a well-stocked kitchen. Some are obtainable from supermarkets; others are found only in health-food stores. Check the index for the commentaries on the individual items (the word "about" indicates a commentary and description). Often, descriptions of what to look for when selecting a product or which type of product to purchase (i.e., stone-ground yellow cornmeal instead of de-germed white cornmeal) are included. Important notes on storage of the items are also provided—fresh foods must often be stored in a manner quite different from that of their preservative-loaded counterparts.

Tailor the list to suit individual preference and the weekly budget—we certainly don't intend that everything on the list be purchased in one shopping trip! One way to begin would be to consult the menu plans provided in this book, select some of the recipes to be prepared during the week, and purchase the ingredients for those recipes. An asterisk next to the ingredient indicates that it is found in many of the recipes.

Grains, Cereals and Pasta

Purchase in bulk and store. Include grains and cereals for dinner, hot breakfast cereals, and for making granola and müesli breakfast cereals.

  rice, white and/or brown*
  rolled oats*
  cracked wheat and/or bulgar wheat*
  millet
  barley
  buckwheat
  wheatberries
  rye
  farina or semolina
  cous cous (for special occasions)
  wild rice (for special occasions)
  whole wheat spaghetti
  whole wheat macaroni
  noodles (See index for homemade pasta
    recipes.)

Flour for baked goods and for binding and breading

  whole wheat flour*
  unbleached white flour*
  whole wheat pastry flour*
  soy flour* (often used for binding egg-
    less foods)
  wheat germ*
  arrowroot and/or cornstarch* (for bind-
    ing and thickening)

Flour for bread-baking and specialty cooking

  rye flour
  rice flour
  barley flour
  millet flour
  chick-pea flour
  bran

Beans

Have at least two or three varieties in the house. Buy in bulk and store—beans last a long time, and one can have many varieties on hand and use them as desired.

  lentils* (for sprouting, too)
  garbanzos*
  split peas, yellow and green
  pinto beans*
  kidney beans*
  black beans
  aduki beans
  soybeans
  mung beans (for sprouting, too)
  navy beans
  lima beans
  dhal: mansoor, urad, chana, split moong
    (mung), etc.

Oils, all-purpose

  safflower
  sunflower
  soy
  corn germ

Oils for specialty cooking and salads
ghee*
olive*
sesame
walnut
coconut

Nuts and Seeds
Have nuts and seeds for main dishes, baking and for snacks, at least one or two types.

walnuts*
almonds*
cashews*
sesame seeds* (dozens of uses)
sunflower seeds* (dozens of uses)
pumpkin seeds
poppy seeds (for baking and cooking)
pecans, hazelnuts, pine nuts (for occasional use)
dried, grated coconut*
alfalfa seeds (for sprouting)

Dried Fruit
Have raisins and at least one other type of dried fruit in the house, for snacking and baking.

raisins*
currants
figs
dates*
dried apricots*
prunes

Fruit for desserts and snacking
dried cherries
dried pineapple
dried peaches
dried pears

Sweeteners
Have honey for uncooked foods, and sugar or another sweetener for cooked foods, on hand.

white sugar*
dark brown sugar*

honey* (Keep a light honey for mixing with foods, and a stronger type for beverages)
blackstrap molasses*
unsulphured molasses*
maple syrup

Herbs and spices
Almost all herbs and spices are featured in *The Age of Enlightenment Cookbook*. Purchase many, in small amounts.

basil
dill weed
thyme
marjoram
oregano
sage
cumin
ground ginger
cloves
allspice
anise or fennel
fenugreek
turmeric
cinnamon
nutmeg or mace
saffron
dill seeds
asafoetida
coriander
cardamom
black and yellow mustard seeds
caraway seeds
celery seeds
curry powder
fresh ginger (store in bags in the refrigerator—it can last for months)
mint (buy mint tea rather than the tiny amounts sold with the herbs)

Seasonings
rosewater
seasoned salt*
sea greens (kelp, dulse, nori, etc.)

Beverages
  herb teas
  grain beverage coffee substitute
  kefir culture

Baking needs
  baking powder*
  baking soda*
  yeast*

Miscellaneous
  non-instant milk powder
  agar agar flakes

Fresh foods to be purchased weekly or biweekly
  fruits in season*
  vegetables in season, for cooking and
    salads*
  fresh parsley for seasoning*
  fresh lemons for seasoning*
  milk*
  butter*
  cottage cheese*
  ricotta*
  cheese*
  sour cream (occasionally)
  cream cheese (occasionally)
  heavy and light creams (occasionally)
  yogurt for culture (as needed, or yogurt*)
  buttermilk for culture (as needed, or
    buttermilk*)
  bean curd

(See index for homemade recipes for seasoned salt, grain beverage coffee substitute, binding powder, and bean curd.)

NOTE TO THE NEW COOK

If cooking is a new experience, read the sections on kitchen organization, utensils, cooking terms and procedures, basic ingredients, and so forth. They were written for you. Also read and memorize the tables of United States measurements—it saves time to know the basic equivalents by heart.

Before trying a recipe:

1. Read the beginning of the recipe section; i.e., before preparing "herb biscuits," read the paragraphs concerning biscuits in general—they contain information that applies to the preparation of all biscuits.
2. Read the recipe through once. Check to see if there are any ingredients that need advance preparation, such as beans which must be soaked overnight. Also make sure that the time involved in the preparation is compatible with your schedule, and that all the ingredients listed are in the house.

It is best to follow recipes exactly until a feel for cooking develops. After confidence is gained and the cooking procedures become more automatic, you can begin to improvise and experiment with a better chance of success. Most recipe sections include lists of suggested variations and alternate ingredients to aid in successful improvisation. Where the word "variations" appears at the bottom of a recipe, specific ingredients and alternate cooking methods that work well are listed. These are only suggestions—there are many other possibilities that would also work.

Finally, when a recipe advises the addition of an ingredient "to taste," or no specific measurement is listed, proceed cautiously. Start with a pinch or two of the ingredient, sample, and let taste be your guide. A good method of sampling foods is to keep a small bowl and a spoon handy. You can then place a little of the food in the bowl with the mixing spoon and sample it with the separate spoon.

NOTE TO THE VEGAN

Almost every recipe in *The Age of Enlightenment Cookbook* can be prepared without the use of dairy products. We do not advocate the elimination of dairy products from the diet except for those people who cannot digest them, have an allergic reaction to them, or have otherwise been advised against their use by a doctor.

People who fall into the above categories should read the section on dairy substitutes in the Basic Ingredients chapter. Included are suggestions for replacements and simple recipes for dairy substitutes that can be made in the home.

To locate substitutions for dairy products in the recipes:

1. Look at the bottom of the recipe, for "Vegan Variation."
2. There are entire sections of recipes which follow the same methods of dairy-free preparation. Read the discussions at the beginning of each section for instructions to the vegan.
3. Wherever butter appears in a recipe, unless otherwise indicated, use margarine as the substitute.

In some recipes, an alternate ingredient that produces an equally good result is listed. For instance, it is suggested that lentil sauce be used to replace the cheese in lasagna.

KITCHEN SAFETY

The most important factor in kitchen safety is careful attention to the activity at hand. Most kitchen accidents can be traced to lack of attention. The cook was watching TV, talking on the phone, and keeping an eye on the kids while cooking, or, in general, the mind was just on other things at the time the accident occurred. For safety, as well as for enjoyment when cooking, try *just cooking*. Everything will flow more smoothly and effectively, and accidents should never occur.

A few basic tips for kitchen safety are:

1. Keep pot handles turned to the side of the stove rather than facing front.
2. Keep long-cooking foods, such as soups and stews, on the back burners to avoid an upset.
3. When removing the lid from a pot that contains boiling or steaming food, partially open the lid toward the back of the stove first. This allows the steam to escape away from the body and you avoid a steam burn. After the cloud of steam has dispersed, remove the lid entirely.

4. Read the special instructions for safety during deep-frying.
5. Keep a first-aid kit handy with materials for cuts and burns.
6. In the event of a burn, place the affected area under ice-cold water *immediately*, and keep it there until the pain subsides. If there is more than superficial damage to a small area of the body, call a doctor immediately.

The Basics

The Kitchen: Stage for the Drama of Creation

Organizing the kitchen is setting the stage and arranging the props for the drama of creation which takes place two or three · times each day. The amount of orderliness and the care given to maintaining the stage set, be it the most primitive campfire arrangement or a sophisticated, professionally equipped kitchen, can greatly affect the quality of the cook's performance. Finding dirty or broken equipment, or having to stop and hunt for a misplaced utensil, will result in interruptions and missed cues that break the spontaneous flow of creating a meal. Appreciation for the art of cooking is shown by organizing the work space and tools in an efficient and convenient arrangement, and taking loving care to keep them clean and well maintained.

THE KITCHEN ENVIRONMENT

A room that is bright, airy, and clean is a pleasure to work and create in. Brightly painted walls, a few plants, and some favorite pictures on the wall can do a lot to create an uplifting atmosphere. Most kitchens have a triangular arrangement of the stove, refrigerator, and sink, each being about equal distance from the other two. The preparation and storage areas are most convenient if within the reach of all three items.

Much time and energy can be saved by analyzing one's most frequent movements and arranging the kitchen to harmonize with those work patterns. For instance, if nut butter is made daily, keeping the nuts, grinder, and jars together in one place will save time and energy.

Cleanliness is absolutely essential to a healthy and wholesome environment. Clean up the kitchen while you are cooking by putting away utensils and ingredients as soon as they have been used. Washing the preparation area and, if possible, the pots immediately after the cooking is finished allows you to avoid facing an overwhelmingly chaotic kitchen right after a pleasant and relaxing meal. Mop the floor and clean the surfaces as necessary. A periodic washing of all surfaces with a solution of lemon juice and salt dissolved in water helps keep the environment and atmosphere fresh.

1

STORAGE

Store foods in bags or containers that will maximize their preservation. Keep a space to store jars and paper and plastic bags for later use.

The most frequently used foods and utensils can be kept near the front of the shelves, with the less frequently used items toward the back and in the less convenient spaces. The same principle can be applied in the refrigerator by keeping the foods that should be used first toward the front. Utensils and pots can be hung from hooks near the stove and preparation area, or stored in nearby drawers.

GARBAGE

Even a small commitment to "waste not, want not" can result in an amazingly small amount of material actually being thrown out as garbage. Many communities have glass and paper recycling centers or pick-up services. If yours does not, bottles and jars can be reused, as can paper and plastic bags. Food scraps that can't be fed to the animals (be they pets, farm animals, or just passing birds) can go into a compost heap. Paper garbage that can't be recycled can be burned at home in the fireplace.

Neighborhood cooperation goes a long way in minimizing waste. If your house doesn't have a garden or a fireplace, there may be a neighbor who would actually be grateful for compost or kindling materials.

THE KITCHEN "FURNITURE"

The Stove

Gas ranges are heated by natural gas, which feeds into a pilot light that lights the burners. The burners emit a flame that can be instantly increased or reduced, allowing maximum temperature control. Gas ranges need frequent cleaning. Remove the grills from the burners and scrub the trays underneath. Clean the stove surface as necessary.

Electric stoves have burners made of electrically heated coils. The coils are thermostatically controlled to give a choice of temperatures. However, they heat and cool somewhat slowly, giving a less than instant control over the heat. One can reduce the temperature instantly by removing the pan partially or completely from the burner, but there is no way to instantly increase the heat.

Clean the surface of the stove with a sponge or scour as necessary. The area beneath the coils needs infrequent cleaning unless there is a spill, and if it is lined with foil, you need only replace the foil occasionally.

The Oven

A good oven heats accurately to the temperature desired and maintains the heat at that temperature throughout the entire oven. All ovens vary in their performance and you must become familiar with the particular personality of your own. To insure the most even and accurate heating possible, make sure that the door shuts tightly. Have the thermostat checked every one or two years for accuracy, or keep a separate oven thermometer and check it against the thermostat. Have the thermostat adjusted if it is very inaccurate.

Cleanliness of the oven is also important for optimum heat circulation. Besides interrupting the flow of heat, old, burned food that has collected on the floor and sides of the oven produces smoke and odors that can affect the taste of the foods being baked. Clean up spills immediately when the oven is cool enough, and clean the entire oven periodically with an oven cleaner.

The Broiler

The broiler may be a separate unit below the oven, or broiling is accomplished inside the oven itself with the heat coming only from the top. Clean the broiler pan after each use. You can avoid having to clean the entire pan by placing food on a smaller baking sheet on top of the pan. Clean the rack as necessary.

The Refrigerator and Freezer

The best refrigerators have plenty of room to store fruits, vegetables, and dairy products. If the program of using only fresh foods is followed, a small freezer unit will be adequate for ice cubes and occasional ice creams and frozen desserts. Make sure that the doors to both refrigerator and freezer close tightly.

Check the fruit and vegetable bins daily for wilting leaves and rinds. Wash the refrigerator as necessary with mild soapy water or warm water mixed with baking soda. Remove the trays, wash them, and then wash the refrigerator walls and floor; rinse and wipe dry.

To defrost the freezer: When ice has collected in the freezer and on the refrigerator coils too heavily for convenience, choose a day when perishable items can be safely removed from the freezer and refrigerator—perhaps the day before shopping, when the supplies are depleted. Turn off the current, remove the food, and leave the door open. Pans of boiling water can be placed near the icy sections so that the steam will melt them more quickly. When the ice has melted sufficiently, gently scrape it off with a knife, being careful not to damage the coils. Wash the refrigerator and freezer and wipe dry. Turn on the current and replace the food.

The Sink

Sponge out the sink after each use and scour as necessary. Avoid putting large pieces of food or large amounts of heavy oils down the drain. Always have the drain guard in place, and keep a drain cleaner and plunger available for occasional stop-ups. Have the trash and compost garbage cans near the sink. It is also good to keep a supply of hand lotion nearby for use after cleaning and dishwashing.

Preparation Area

A cheerful area with plenty of counter space is ideal for preparation. Keep the cutting board, knives, and utensils handy. Sponge off the counters after each use and scrub as necessary with a soft sponge or brush and cleaning liquid.

TOOLS AND UTENSILS

Investing in high-quality, well-made utensils pays off in ease, efficiency, and, in some cases, in increased health value in food preparation. The following are some of the tools of the trade for a modern kitchen. An asterisk (*) indicates that the tool is convenient but not absolutely necessary, or that it is useful for a specialized purpose only.

The hands are undoubtedly the best tools. As long as they are clean, don't be afraid to use them for mixing, stirring, forming, and so forth. The food is an expression of the inner state of the cook, and a cook's loving touch can only enhance it. Also, the hands are far more sensitive than any other instrument for detecting lumps and other textural qualities.

*Apple Corer**

Baking Pans and Sheets: Stainless steel or glass pans and stainless steel baking sheets are the best for all-around use. Glass pans retain more heat than metal ones, and suggested baking temperatures should be lowered by 25 degrees when they are used. Have at least:

2 8-inch or 9-inch round pans
1 9-inch square pan
1 or 2 rectangular pans
1 or 2 baking sheets
2 loaf pans
1 muffin tin
1 or 2 9-inch pie pans

Wash baking pans and sheets in hot soapy water. If food is baked on, soak them for a few hours in soapy water.

*Basting Brush**

Blender: Look for a blender that is powerful enough to crush ice, so that it will be able to purée fruits, vegetables, and beans, make nut butters, and do dozens of other things. Whether it has three speeds or twenty is unimportant, but if the motor is not strong enough to crush ice the blender will probably only be able to mix liquids, and maybe do some other jobs with a great deal of prodding.

When hot foods are blended, the hot air may rise and push off the top of the blender. To avoid accidents, blend hot foods in small amounts, or place a towel over the lid and hold it down firmly while blending.

Wash the blender top and lid in hot soapy water. The blades of most blenders can be removed and washed separately. Sponge off the base containing the motor, and do not immerse it in water.

Casserole Dish: Look for a heavy pottery or glass dish with a tight-fitting lid. A 1- or 2-quart casserole is adequate for family meals; have a larger one for company dishes.

Citrus Juicer: Hand or electric.

Cleansing Powder: Lemon juice and salt can also be used as a cleanser.

Colander

*Cookie Cutters**: The rim of a glass can cut out round cookies.

Cutting Board: A heavy, level, smooth, unfinished board. Some cutting boards are built into the cabinetry. Sponge off the cutting board after each use. Scrubbing occasionally with mild soapy water and a brush helps prevent germ growth. Sand down the surface every one or two years for continued cleanliness and a smooth surface.

*Deep-Frying Basket**: If deep-frying is done often, a frying basket aids in efficiency and safety. Otherwise, a slotted spoon is sufficient.

Dishtowels: At least two or three.

Dishwashing Brush

*Eggbeater**: Good for whipping cream.

*Food Mill**

FOOD MILL

*Food Processor**: Home models of the machines used in restaurant kitchens. They grate, grind, blend, and do many other things more effectively than a blender. Food processors are expensive and nice to have, but they are not necessities.

Frying Pans: Have at least one large and one small frying pan. Cast-iron pans with cast-iron handles can double as baking pans. (See *pots and saucepans* for discussion of cast iron.)

Grater

*Griddle**: A soapstone griddle is the original oil-free cookware. A soapstone or cast-iron griddle is ideal for preparing pancakes, tortillas, chapatis, etc., but frying pans also serve the purpose.

Grinder: Grinders are available for grinding nuts, seeds, beans, and grains. A blender or mortar and pestle can grind with varying degrees of success, and a food processor can also do the job. Old-fashioned meat grinders will find many uses in a vegetarian kitchen.

Hand Lotion

Knives: A good, sharp knife is the most important single kitchen utensil. Some professional chefs keep their own personal knives and carry them in a special case to wherever they are cooking. Look for knives with carbon steel blades and strong, tight-fitting handles. Store knives where the blades will not touch other metal objects and chip, and wash knives separately from other utensils, both for maintenance of the blades and for safety. Have at least one paring knife, one chopping knife, and one bread knife. A Chinese chopping cleaver is excellent for chopping the food and then scooping it up into the bowl with the wide, flat blade. Have a whetstone or knife sharpener to keep knives in top shape. Repair loose handles immediately.

Ladles

Juicer*: Fresh juices can be used for soup bases and as liquid for cooking and baking. However, the delight and the nutritive values of fresh juice alone are enough to make a juicer a highly desirable and practical appliance. The best juicers extract the juice and separate it from the pulp. Have a separate citrus juicer for citrus fruits.

Lettuce Basket*: For washing and drying salad greens. Lettuce baskets are inexpensive, and very practical for those who serve salad daily.

Measuring Cups and Spoons: Have a metal 1-cup dry measure and a glass 4-cup liquid measuring cup. Avoid plastic, which can melt and also absorb oils and take on a rancid taste. Look for measuring cups and spoons with both American and metric measures on them.

Mixing Bowls: Stainless steel or pottery bowls that can double as serving bowls are the most useful. Plastic bowls are undesirable as plastic absorbs oil, which may become rancid. Have a variety of sizes—at least one large, one medium, and one small bowl.

Nutcracker*: A hammer and a hard surface can also do the job.

Oven Cleaner

Paper Towels: For ecological reasons, use a sponge or cloth whenever possible and reserve the paper towels for only the jobs that require a disposable absorber, such as draining deep-fried food.

Pastry Bag and Tips*: Pastry bags are used mostly for cake decorating, and are a lot of fun. A canvas pastry bag is the best. The bag should be turned inside out and washed with warm soapy water after each use.

Pastry Board*: A pastry board is desirable only if pastry and pie doughs are prepared often. A marble slab is ideal for keeping the dough cold while it is being worked. A smooth wooden board reserved for pastry-making only—never cutting—is also suitable.

Pastry Cutter*: A pastry cutter cuts butter into the flour for pastry, pie, and biscuit doughs. The fingers or two knives also accomplish the task perfectly well.

Plastic Gloves: For scrubbing and dishwashing.

Plastic Wrap

Plunger

Pots and Saucepans: Choose pots that have tight-fitting lids and strong handles, fit well on the burners, and are large enough to accommodate the amount of food that will be cooked. It is good to have several pots and saucepans of various shapes and sizes, including a double boiler arrangement. The amount of food usually cooked and the cooking processes used most frequently will help determine the proper sizes. For instance, in steaming vegetables, the pot should be no more than two-thirds full for optimum effectiveness; if five cups of vegetables are usually cooked, a two-quart pot is necessary for that purpose.

It is best not to use pots and lids made of different metals. Chemical interactions can take place which release unhealthy substances into the food. The occurrence is most frequent when cooking acid foods. Never put an aluminum lid or aluminum foil on a copper pot.

Stainless steel pots never release any chemicals into the food. They are easy to keep clean and are lightweight. However, stainless steel does not conduct heat particularly well. A copper-clad stainless steel pot or a copper pot lined with stainless steel gives the ideal combination of healthful cookware that conducts heat efficiently. Wash stainless steel pots in hot soapy water. They may be scoured occasionally. Scour the copper with copper cleaner, as necessary.

Copper pots are the most effective heat conductors. They are very heavy, as they must be lined with another metal. Most copper pots are lined with tin, but some can be found with stainless steel linings. The lining should be checked once a year for damages or wearing down, and any broken or worn spots repaired immediately, to prevent harmful substances from entering the food. Wash copper pots in hot soapy water. Scour the copper with copper cleaner, as necessary.

Cast-iron pots are heavy and slow-heating. They introduce iron into the food, which is good for health. Acid foods may become discolored when cooked in cast-iron pots.

Cast-iron pots have to be seasoned after purchase and after the first few uses until a protective coating builds up. To season, smear the inside of the pot with a mild-flavored vegetable oil and place in a 400° oven for half an hour. Wash cast-iron pots in mild soapy water and dry immediately with paper towels to prevent rusting. Never scour with a cleaner, or the seasoning will be removed. If the pot begins to rust, wash off the rust and rub the pot with oil. The rust is not dangerous to health, so don't worry if it appears.

Teflon and other stickless coatings are intended for cooking without the use of oil. They are also good for foods that tend to stick to the pan, such as potatoes. If Teflon coating becomes chipped or scratched it will release unhealthful substances into the food, and the pot should be discarded. Teflon should thus be treated very carefully. Use only soft wooden spoons and spatulas in Teflon pans, and wash in warm soapy water with a soft sponge. Store the pans where they will not be chipped.

Aluminum should be avoided for all pots and pans. Aluminum poisoning could result from the aluminum that is inevitably released into the food.

Potato Masher*

Potholders

Rack for cooling baked goods*: A cutting board or the top of the stove can also be used.

Rolling Pin: A bottle will do in a pinch, but takes more work to use than the real thing.

Salad Bowl: Wooden salad bowls are aesthetically beautiful, and a well-seasoned salad bowl is a treasured item. The wood is seasoned and protected by the oils that dress the salads. However, the cold-pressed oils suggested in this book become rancid after awhile, and occasionally this will happen to the seasoning on the salad bowl. Store the salad bowl in a cooler area to deter rancidity, and after the bowl is well seasoned, wash it in mild soapy water and wipe dry after each use. Until the bowl is seasoned, however, simply wipe the bowl clean with paper towels after each use. Stainless steel, pottery, and glass bowls may also be used for salads.

Scale: A kitchen scale that weighs up to 1 or 2 kilos is essential for metric measuring.

Scouring Pads

Sieve or Strainer: Apart from straining, a sieve can be used to purée soft foods by forcing them through the mesh. It is also the best flour sifter available. Pour the flour into the sieve and shake it gently over a bowl.

Sifter*: See above note on sieves.

Spatula

Spice Grinder*: A small electric coffee grinder makes an excellent spice grinder. A mortar and pestle may be used, and a blender can be used in a pinch.

Sponges: One for the floor, one for the counters, and one for the dishes.

Steamer*: A steaming basket holds food over boiling water so that it may be cooked by the steam. Small steaming baskets are quite inexpensive. Also available are pots

in a sort of double boiler arrangement, with holes in the top pot to allow the steam to enter. Food can also be steamed in a colander or sieve that fits into a larger pot, if the lid can still fit tightly.

Spoons: Have at least two or three wooden spoons, a large stainless steel spoon, and a slotted spoon. (Chinese skimming spoons are practical and aesthetically beautiful slotted spoons.)

Vegetable Brush*: For scrubbing root vegetables.

Vegetable Peeler*: A paring knife also does the job.

Wax Paper

Whisk: Excellent for making sauces, stirring, beating, and a variety of other uses.

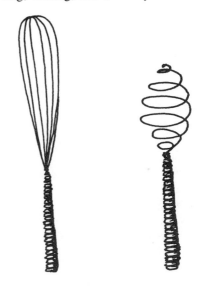

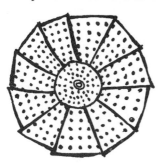

The first kind pictured has a wider range of uses than the second.

Wok: Woks, used extensively for Chinese and Japanese cooking, are indispensable for stir-frying, and can also be used for steaming, preparing soups and stews, and for deep-frying. Their shape allows the use of less oil for deep-frying than conventionally shaped pots use. Heavy rolled steel woks are best for deep-frying and stir-frying. Keep a heavy rolled steel wok exclusively for frying, and a lightweight stainless steel wok for preparing soups and stews. Buy a wok with a lid. Season the wok by rubbing with oil after each use until a protective coating builds up. Always wash the wok immediately after use in warm soapy water. Never scour it.

Cooking Terms and Procedures

Following are definitions of terms used in the preparation and cooking of food. Practice makes perfect—follow the instructions and diagrams until proficiency, and efficiency, naturally develop.

CHOPPING

PREPARATION

BASTE: To pour or brush liquid over food.
Tools: Spoon or basting brush.

BEAT: To stir very fast and hard. Used to mix, incorporate air into a batter, or to remove lumps.
Tools: Large spoon, whisk, or sometimes a fork.
Method: Stir vigorously in a clockwise direction. If beating is meant to add air, lift the spoon slightly out of the mixture at the beginning of each rotation, giving a slight up-and-down motion to each stroke.

BLEND: To mix separate ingredients until they are totally combined.
Tools: Spoon, fork, or hands; blender when indicated.

CHOP: To cut into small, odd-shaped but uniform pieces. "Coarsely" chopped indicates pieces only slightly smaller than sliced bits. "Finely chopped" indicates very small pieces—almost ground.
Tools: Large knife or curved chopper; occasionally the blender.

Method: Spread the food out on a cutting board. To use a chopper, roll the blades back and forth over the food until the desired size is reached. To use a knife, place the knife point on the cutting board, and, never raising the point from the board, raise and lower the blade over the food. Another method is to hold the knife handle in one hand and the top of the blade in the other, and chop with the blade held level.

To chop dry foods, such as nuts, in a blender, place a small amount of the food in the blender and turn it on for one second. Repeat until the food is the desired size. To chop vegetables, slice them and place them in the blender. Cover them with water. Turn the blender on for one second. Repeat, if necessary, until the food is the desired size. Strain the water out. Some nutrients will be lost by this method.

CREAM: To mix butter until it is smooth and creamy in consistency. Usually the process involves blending the butter with another ingredient, such as sugar.

Tools: The back of a wooden spoon, or the hands.

Method: Have the butter at room temperature. Place it in a bowl, along with the other ingredient, if applicable, and press it against the sides of the bowl and spread it out with the back of the spoon. Repeat until it is soft, and then beat the mixture until smooth. When using the hands, squeeze and work the butter until soft and then beat with a spoon until smooth and creamy.

DICE OR CUBE: To cut into cubes.

Tool: A small, sharp knife.

Method: If ½-inch cubes are desired, slice off a ½-inch-thick piece of the food, and then cut it into lengthwise and crosswise pieces ½-inch wide to

form cubes. An easy method of cubing vegetables is to make vertical lengthwise and crosswise cuts in the vegetable, not quite cutting through, and then to horizontally slice off the cubes.

FOLD: A gentle method of mixing ingredients into a light, airy batter.

Tools: A large spoon or rubber spatula.

FOLDING

Method: Pour the food over the batter. Slide the spoon or spatula gently down along the side of the bowl to the bottom, and with a scooping motion bring the batter from the bottom of the bowl to the top, along the opposite side of the bowl. Turn the spoon or spatula over to release the batter onto the top, and gently repeat the process over and over in a continuous circular motion until the ingredients are sufficiently blended.

GRATE: Use of a grater to shred food into tiny pieces.

GRIND: To pulverize dry foods to a powder, or to crush moist or oily foods to a paste.

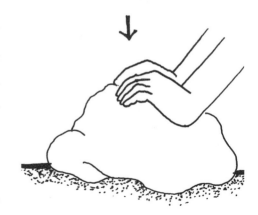

> *Tools:* Grinder, blender, or mortar and pestle.
>
> *Method:* Grinder: Follow instructions for the particular type of grinder being used.
>
> Blender: Place a small amount of food in at a time and blend until pulverized.
>
> Mortar and pestle: Pound and crush foods against the bottom and sides of the mortar with the pestle.

KNEAD: A procedure used to blend the ingredients in a dough or to help develop the gluten in the flour.

> *Tools:* The hands. Kneading machines are available for large amounts of kneading. It is fun to knead by hand, however, and a machine is unnecessary unless it is truly preferred by the cook.
>
> *Method:* Place the dough on a floured board. Using both hands, fold the dough toward the body. Without breaking the motion, push it down and away from the body with the heels of the hands, bearing down with the weight of the body. Turn the dough to a different angle and repeat the pro-

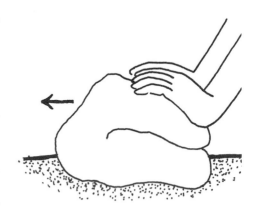

cess. "Light kneading" means to knead only a few times. Longer kneading can mean repeating the process for as long as ten minutes. Perform longer kneading in a continuous rhythm—it is enjoyable and soothing.

To knead with a machine: Place the hook attachment on a mixing machine, and mix at a low speed until the dough is the proper consistency.

MASH: To beat semi-soft cooked foods, such as carrots or potatoes, to a smooth pulp.

Tools: Fork, potato masher, or food mill.

Method: Press down and pound with a fork or potato masher until smooth. A fist can also be used. Put soft foods through a food mill to mash.

MINCE: To chop very fine. See "chop" above.

PARE OR PEEL: To remove the skin or rind from a fruit or vegetable.

Tools: Vegetable peeler or knife.

Method: Vegetable peeler: Peel away from the body in short strokes, or use it in the same manner as a paring knife.

Paring knife: Grasp the knife and brace the food with the thumb of one hand, while cradling the food in the other hand. Peel off a strip carefully toward the thumb, turning the vegetable or fruit over during the process to peel both sides in one continuous motion. Repeat until it is fully peeled.

Note: Much of the vitamin content in fruits and vegetables lies close to the skin, so peel very carefully, to remove just the skin itself.

PURÉE: To blend soft foods to a smooth pulp.

Tools: Food mill, sieve, or blender.

Method: Put the food through a food mill, press it through the mesh of a sieve using the back of a wooden spoon, or whirl it in the blender.

SHRED: To grate coarsely or to cut into long, thin bits.

Tools and Method: Grate all foods on a coarse grater, except for cabbage and lettuce, which may be sliced across the leaves to make thin strips.

SLICE: To cut foods in a uniform pattern.

Tool: Sharp knife.

Method: Hold food firmly on a cutting board with one hand and slice off uniform pieces with the other. The French slicing method is to hold the food down with one hand in a cupped position. Guide the knife by moving the side of the blade close to the fingernails, moving the hand along the food to expose the next portion. (Also see index for Japanese vegetable slicing methods.)

SLIVER: To cut into thin, matchstick-shaped pieces.

Tools: A small sharp knife.

Method: Slice food very thin. Cut the pieces again into matchstick shapes.

Note: To sliver nuts, shave off very thin slices with a knife.

STIR: To mix ingredients together in a circular motion.

Tools: Mixing spoon.

Method: Grasp the spoon firmly in one hand, hold the bowl firmly on the table or cradled in the crook of the arm with the other, and move the spoon through the batter in a circular motion. Scrape down food which has collected along the sides of the bowl as necessary.

TOSS: To lightly mix loose ingredients, such as salad greens.

Tools: Salad servers, two forks, or two spoons.

Method: Take a utensil in each hand and insert to the bottom of the bowl. Grasp some of the ingredients between the utensils and scoop up, bringing them just over the ingredients on the top, and drop them over the top. Repeat until the ingredients are mixed.

WHIP: A mixing method used to incorporate air into the batter.

Tools: Whisk or eggbeater.

Method: The batter should only half fill the bowl, to allow for expansion. To use a whisk, hold the bowl firmly in one hand and the whisk in the other. Beat in a diagonal circular motion, so that the whisk is brought out of the mixture at the beginning and end of each stroke, to incorporate air into it. To use an eggbeater, beat very fast to create a froth.

COOKING

Cooking is the application of heat to raw ingredients that transforms them into better-tasting, easily digested foods. Knowledge of the variety of cooking methods gives the cook the ability to produce many different flavors and textures from the same foods. Some nutrients will be lost during any cooking process. However, in the final analysis the foods are rendered more digestible by cooking, and a greater amount of nutrients will be absorbed by the body. In Japan, a nutritionally balanced meal contains foods cooked by a variety of methods (along with some uncooked foods), with the assumption that what is taken out by one cooking method will be left in by another.

Cooking techniques are divided into two categories with two opposite methods:
  1. direct or indirect heat
  2. moist or dry heat
In direct heating, the flame is applied directly to the food, while indirect heat is applied to another medium which then cooks the food. Moist or wet heat cooks food in liquid, whereas with dry heat the food must contain its own moisture.

BAKE: Baking is a dry heat which is both direct and indirect. The heat of the oven cooks the exposed portions of the food and also heats the cooking vessel, which cooks the unexposed portions.

Method: Preheat the oven to the desired temperature before introducing the food. Ten minutes is about average for a home oven, though ovens vary. The middle rack of the oven is best for circulating heat, and if many dishes are being baked at once, make sure that there is ample space between the pans and racks for the heat to circulate. Avoid opening the door too often, which lowers the temperature. Heat rises, and foods on the higher rack will bake more quickly than those on the lower. Some ovens will bake food in the back more rapidly. Check to make sure the door closes tightly if this characteristic becomes very noticeable.

High-Altitude Baking: The atmospheric conditions starting from about 3500 feet change the formulas for baking. Carbon dioxide expands more rapidly, which increases the leavening. Water boils at a lower temperature, so foods cook more slowly. Water evaporates more quickly, tending to dry out some foods, particularly flour.

The varying altitudes and climatic conditions in different geographical areas will produce these differences in varying degrees. To develop recipes that work in your area, experiment with the general principles that follow and keep a record of which adjustments bring good results. Friends and neighbors who have developed their own adjustments will be helpful. You might also check with the home economics department of a local college or university, or with an extension of the state agriculture department.

General principles for high-altitude baking:

1. Use larger baking pans to accommodate the increased leavening.
2. Baked goods tend to stick to the pans. Butter pans generously or line with waxed paper. Spring form cake pans are very helpful.
3. Reduce the amount of baking powder and soda by one-quarter to one-half.
4. Reduce the amount of sweetening by 1 to 4 tablespoons.
5. Increase the amounts of flour and liquid by 1 to 2 tablespoons each. (Buttermilk, yogurt, or sour cream may not need any adjustment.)
6. Yeasted doughs may double in bulk in one-quarter to three-quarters the suggested time. Check frequently to insure that they do not rise longer than necessary.

The higher the altitude, the more adjustments may have to be made. Try the minimum adjustments first, or try only one or two of them at a time, until the right combination is reached.

BLANCH: Use of moist, direct heat in which foods are dropped into boiling water and cooked for 1 to 2 minutes. Generally used to remove the skins easily from fruits and nuts.

Method: Bring to a boil enough water to completely cover the food. When it is bubbling furiously, drop the food in and cook for 1 to 2 minutes. Drain immediately.

BOIL: To use an indirect, moist heat, either to cook a food by immersing it in boiling water, or to cook a liquid by boiling it. The boiling point is characterized by bubbles coming to the surface of the liquid and breaking, while the liquid itself moves vigorously. This is sometimes referred to as a ''rolling'' boil, as opposed to a ''low'' or ''slow'' boil, where bubbles appear and break but the liquid does not move very much.

Method: To cook foods in boiling water, make sure that there will be ample water to cover them and that the pot will not be more than about ⅔ full. Bring the water to a boil and add the food slowly, to prevent lowering the temperature of the water. Rapidly boiling water may need to be replenished from time to time as it evaporates. If the heat is too high it might boil over, so watch carefully and reduce the heat immediately if it starts to bubble up.

When cooking a liquid by boiling it, in the case of milk or other thick liquids, care must be taken not to scorch or burn it. Stir frequently and scrape down the sides of the pot as the liquid evaporates. Simmering is usually a better procedure unless boiling is specifically indicated.

Boiling and altitude: The boiling point at sea level is 212° Farenheit or 100° Centigrade, and recipes that call for boiling water refer to this temperature. At higher altitudes water boils at lower temperatures and evaporates more quickly. Greater care must be taken that liquids do not scorch or burn and that water is replenished more often. The temperatures at higher altitudes are:

2000 feet	208°F.	98°C.
5000	203°	95°
7500	198°	92°
10,000	194°	90°

BRAISE: To first sauté foods in butter or oil, and then complete the cooking in a covered pot with a little water.

BROIL: Broiling is the use of a direct, dry heat, where food is exposed, one side at a time, to a very high temperature from an overhead heat source in the broiler. Some units allow broiling to be done in the oven.

Method: Place foods on the broiler pan while it is still cold. If the pan is hot, it should first to smeared with butter or oil to prevent sticking. Set the thermostat on broil or 550°, and place the pan on the broiler rack. The rack should be at least 3 inches below the heat source—in the case of most vegetarian foods, even lower is advisable. Check the food frequently and turn it over as soon as one side is done to cook the other side.

DEEP-FRY: Deep-frying is an indirect heat which is neither moist nor dry. Foods are cooked by immersing them in hot oil or ghee. Deep-frying imparts a unique texture to foods, crisp outside and tender inside. With proper attention, deep-fried foods need not be greasy at all, and can be healthful and delightful.

Method: To prepare non-greasy deep-fried food, have the oil very hot and the food very cold, and then cook it quickly and drain it well. Use a wok or a pot with high sides to hold the oil. Because of its shape, the wok requires less oil. In either case, the pot should sit firmly on the burner, with no chance of jiggling or slipping. Keep the handle to one side so that the pot will not be knocked over accidentally.

A slotted spoon, tongs, or a deep-frying basket will be necessary to insert and remove the food from the oil. Have a tray covered with paper towels for draining. For safety, keep all water and moisture away from the pot and the utensils, and make sure that all the utensils are completely dry.

Use ghee or an oil that can be heated to a high temperature, such as safflower or soy. Olive oil may be used if its flavor is compatible with the food being cooked. The oil should be at least 2½ to 3 inches deep in the pot, but should not fill the pot more than halfway to allow room for it to bubble up. Heat the oil slowly to evaporate any moisture that might be present. The average temperature for deep-frying is 350° to 375°F. If the oil begins to smoke, its structure has broken down and it can no longer be used effectively. Cool the oil and discard it. If the oil is too hot, the food will burn on the outside and remain raw on the inside. If it is too cool, the food will be very greasy and may fall apart during the cooking. Test one piece of food before adding the whole batch. The heat may have to be adjusted once or twice during the cooking.

Have the food as dry as possible, and cut it into uniform pieces for equal frying time. If the food is to be coated with batter, it should be dry before it is dipped into the batter. (Remember that if a batter is rich in butter and sugar, it will absorb more oil during the frying.) Lower the food into the oil with the chosen utensil. The food should sink to the bottom and then rise to the top with the oil bubbling energetically around it. If it sticks to the bottom, the oil isn't deep enough. The oil may bubble up to the top during the cooking. If it begins to bubble toward the rim of the pot, immediately turn off the heat and pour in some oil that is at room temperature. If the oil bubbles over and starts a fire, pour salt or baking soda on the flame—if the flame is isolated it will go out quickly. *Do not* pour water on the flames—it will only spread them.

Cold food will lower the temperature of the oil, so fry only a few pieces of food at a time to maintain the high heat. Leave the oil free for a minute between batches to heat up again. Add more oil as necessary during the cooking and allow the temperature to rise again.

When the food is done, drain it on paper towels and serve immediately. Deep-fried food cannot be successfully prepared in advance.

DOUBLE BOILER COOKING: Double boiler cooking is an indirect, dry heat that is used for delicate foods that burn or curdle easily, such as sauces.

Method: A pot containing the food sits in a larger pot that contains boiling water, and the gentle heat from the water cooks the food. A double boiler with a wide bottom gives the best overall heat. The water in the lower pot should come halfway up the sides of the upper pot, except in recipes which call for the food to be cooked "over, not in, boiling water." In that case the water should not touch the upper pot at all. Bring the water to a low boil so that it will not upset or jiggle the upper pot.

FRY: To cook foods in a skillet containing ½ to 1 inch of hot oil. Also see "sauté."

SAUTÉ: The word "sauté" comes from the French "sauter," meaning "to jump." Food is sliced thin and cooked in a small amount of butter or oil. Also see "stir-frying" and "kinpura cooking" for variations on sautéing for vegetables.

Method: Slice food into thin, uniform pieces for uniform cooking. Coat a skillet with butter or oil. Two tablespoons is sufficient for four to six cups of most foods. Heat the oil and then add the food. Cook on a medium flame, stirring constantly. Each piece of food should be touching the bottom of the pan at all times—do not attempt

to sauté a mound of food at once. If the food sticks to the pan, add a little more oil. Eggplant especially absorbs a lot of oil, and replenishing may be in order. However, do not add large quantities—sautéed foods are delicate, never greasy.

SCALD: To bring a liquid to the boiling point and then remove it from the heat. Usually this is done to milk to destroy enzymes that could affect yogurt cultures or yeast.

SIMMER: To cook at a heat just below the boiling point. Tiny bubbles rise to the surface of the liquid and the liquid moves very slightly. Also see "boiling," above.

Method: Bring the liquid to a simmer and turn the heat on low to maintain the temperature.

STEAM: Foods are cooked in a pot by the steam produced by a small amount of water. Steaming is used to cook vegetables and fruits. For the method of steaming breads and puddings, see the index for "steamed puddings" and individual recipes for steamed breads.

Method: Place water ½ to 1 inch deep in a pot or saucepan. Bring the water to a boil and add the food. The pot should be no more than ⅔ full for optimum heat circulation. Cover with a tight-fitting lid and reduce the heat so that the water is just simmering. Cook until the food is tender, and drain it in a colander.

If you are using a steaming basket, the water should not touch the underside of the steamer and should be kept at a low boil during the cooking. Food cooked in a steaming basket will take a few more minutes than food cooked directly in water.

STIR-FRY: Stir-frying originated in the orient as a method of conserving oil and fuel while retaining a maximum amount of the vitamins and flavor of the food.

Method: A wok is the only effective pot for stir-frying. A flat-bottomed skillet can be used in a pinch but will not produce results as successful. Use sesame-flavored oil or an oil that can be heated to high temperatures, such as safflower or soy. Use two tablespoons of oil for four to six cups of food. Heat the oil on a medium-high flame. Have the vegetables ready, sliced into very thin, uniform pieces. Add the longest-cooking foods first, then the shorter-cooking foods. Stir rapidly until the food is done. The classic Chinese time allotment for stir-frying is two minutes. If a few more minutes of stir-frying is desired, it is perfectly acceptable, as long as the final product, in the case of vegetables, is crisp and fresh. For longer-cooking vegetables, try the kinpura method (see page 76).

Weights and Measures

UNITED STATES MEASUREMENTS

In the United States measuring system, the liquid and dry measurements are very different. Do not attempt to use the liquid ounces marked on the measuring cup to measure dry weights. A measured 8-ounce cup of parsley will be much less in dry weight than a measured 8-ounce cup of mashed potatoes!

How to measure

Measuring spoons, dry cup measures, and liquid cup measures are used.

Liquid: Fill the measuring spoon or cup to the desired mark. Hold a measuring cup at eye level to check accuracy—the measurement will appear to be different when you are looking down at a cup on a table.

Dry: Fill the cup or measuring spoon to the top and then level it off with the flat side of a knife blade.

To measure butter: One stick of butter equals ½ cup, or 8 tablespoons, or 4 ounces. Slice the appropriate amount off the stick.

To measure by displacement: if ¼ cup of butter is desired, fill a liquid

DRY MEASURING

measuring cup with ¾ cup of water. Add butter a little at a time until the waterline hits one cup. Drain, and ¼

cup of butter remains. Displacement measuring must always be done so that the butter floats in the water— don't try to measure ¾ cup of butter by displacing ¼ cup of water.

Note: When butter is melted, it will total slightly more than its unmelted measurement. Re-measure melted butter for accuracy.

Equivalents: Memorize these for ease in measuring.

pinch	= less than ⅛ teaspoon
1 teaspoon	= ⅓ tablespoon
1½ teaspoons	= ½ tablespoon
3 teaspoons	= 1 tablespoon
4 tablespoons	= ¼ cup
5 ⅓ tablespoons	= ⅓ cup
8 tablespoons	= ½ cup
16 tablespoons	= 1 cup
½ cup	= 1 gill
1 cup	= ½ pint
2 cups	= 1 pint
1 pint	= ½ quart

4 cups	= 1 quart
2 pints	= 1 quart
4 quarts	= 1 gallon

Fluid ounces

2 tablespoons	= 1 fluid ounce
16 fluid ounces	= 1 pint
32 fluid ounces	= 1 quart

Dry Volume Measurements

Dry volume measurements are used for raw fruits and vegetables and may be applicable if one is buying for a food co-op or for a large institution. They are $\frac{1}{6}$ larger than the fluid measurements given the same names.

1 quart	= 2 pints
1 peck	= 8 quarts
1 bushel	= 4 pecks

METRIC SYSTEM MEASUREMENTS

The metric system employs fluid measurements for volume only, and uses weight for dry measurements. It is an exceedingly accurate measuring method for cooking. Metric measuring is accomplished with measuring spoons, a measuring cup marked with deciliters and liters, and a kitchen scale that weighs in kilos.

How to measure

Liquid: Use a measuring cup. Small measurements are made with measuring spoons.

Dry: Measure on a scale according to weight. Place powdery ingredients on a piece of paper on the scale, after first weighing the paper and then subtracting its weight from the final result. Small measurements will be made in measuring spoons.

Metric Measurements and Equivalents:

Liquid:

100 milliliters	= 1 deciliter
100 deciliters	= 1 liter

Dry:
100 grams = 1 kilo
Metric Equivalents of United States Measurements:
Liquid:
1 cup	= approximately ¼ liter
1 pint	= .4732 liters (a little under ½ liter)
1 quart	= .9463 liters (a little under 1 liter)
1 gallon	= 3.785 liters (approximately 3¾ liter)

Dry weight:
1 ounce	= approximately 30 grams
1 pound	= approximately 454 grams
1.10 pounds	= ½ kilo
2.20 pounds (1⅕ pounds)	= 1 kilo

Dry volume:
1 pint	= .551 liters
1 quart	= 1.101 liters
1 peck	= 8.81 liters
1 bushel	= 35.24 liters

Temperature conversions:
To convert Fahrenheit into Centigrade:
1. Subtract 32;
2. multiply the result by 5;
3. divide by 9.
To convert Centigrade into Fahrenheit, perform the reverse:
1. Multiply by 9;
2. divide the result by 5;
3. add 32.

Commonly used temperature equivalents:
Water freezes	32°F	0°C
Water boils (sea level)	212°	100°
Soft ball stage	234–238°	112–114°
Slow oven	268°	131°
Medium oven	350°	177°
Hot oven	450°	232°
Broiling	550°	288°
Deep-frying	375°	190°

ENGLISH OR IMPERIAL MEASUREMENTS

The weight measurements of the United States and England are identical, and convert into metric measurements identically. The liquid measurements are completely different, even though some go by the same names!

Equivalents of United States measurements for English or Imperial Measurements:
1¼ U.S. teaspoon	= 1 English teaspoon
1¼ U.S. tablespoon	= 1 English tablespoon
1 U.S. gill (½ cup)	= 5/6 English teacup
1 U.S. cup	= 5/6 English breakfast cup
1 U.S. pint	= 5/6 English Imperial pint
1 U.S. quart	= 5/6 English Imperial quart
1 U.S. gallon	= 5/6 English Imperial gallon

Menu Planning and Menus

When a cook prepares a meal, he or she takes on the responsibility of contributing to the health and well-being of those who eat it. It is a privilege to be allowed to care for people (or oneself) in such a manner, and it can be done with great dignity and creativity.

There is an art to planning meals that help bring the mind and body into increased harmony by pleasing the senses while nourishing the body. A well-planned meal has enough variety to be interesting, but not so much as to be overwhelming; it has portions large enough to satisfy everyone without encouraging overeating; and it provides nutritious combinations which harmonize for easy digestion.

Planning menus ahead of time for a few days or a week can be helpful in providing a variety of foods over a given period. The plan can be a specific list of dishes or just a rough suggestion for foods to be used each day. Flexibility is important—schedules and preferences may have changed when the day of a planned meal arrives. When planning menus, remember:

1. Combinations of complementary but contrasting elements create graceful, harmonious meals. Balance a heavy, filling dish with a light one, a complex dish with a simple one, a spicy food with a bland or cooling food, a crisp texture with a soft texture, a light color with a bright color.

2. If you are serving a new and unusual dish to the family for the first time, perhaps the rest of the meal can be composed of old favorites.

3. Plan a meal that can be prepared in the time available. If preparation of one dish takes most of the available time, the other dishes should be those which can be assembled quickly. Keep this in mind when foods need advance preparation, such as soaking beans, making yogurt, and so forth.

4. Use fruits and vegetables that are in season and are available at reasonable prices.

5. Plan dishes that will not need the same equipment at the same time; i.e., bake the apples at 350° earlier in the afternoon so that the pizza can go in later at 500°.

7. Serve the more perishable or riper foods on or just after the day they are purchased (or picked), and plan dishes containing the longer-lasting foods for later in the week.

MENUS

Each of the following menus contains a vegetable, a grain, and a protein consisting of beans, nuts, or dairy products. A salad is included with each dinner and fruit is served many times a week, with desserts being featured once or twice each week.

Obviously, the preferences and nutritional needs of families differ, and the menus can be rearranged, added to, and subtracted from, *ad infinitum*. For additional menus, see the daily and party menus for the foods of different countries under "Enlightened International Cooking."

A 28-Day Main Meal Menu Plan

SUNDAY:
nutloaf with almond
gravy
steamed barley
steamed peas
carrot-raisin salad
fruit

MONDAY:
dhal
zucchini curry
pilau rice
cucumber-tomato raita
fruit

TUESDAY:
soyburgers on burger
rolls
steamed green beans
coleslaw
berry smoothies

WEDNESDAY:
Boston baked beans
cornbread
spinach-sprout salad
with lemon and honey
dressing
blueberry pie

THURSDAY:
eggplant parmagiana
steamed millet
green salad with lemon-
tomato dressing
fruit

FRIDAY:
shepherd's pie
green salad with slivered
almonds and cottage
cheese dressing
Swedish rye bread
fruit

SATURDAY:
borscht with sour cream
stuffed cabbage rolls
steamed broccoli
green salad with
watercress dressing
baked bananas

SUNDAY:
mixed vegetable tempura
steamed rice
mung sprout salad with
tahini dressing
bliss balls

MONDAY:
broccoli casserole
Swedish potatoes
green salad with lemon-
and-oil dressing
carrot cake

TUESDAY:
dhal
eggplant-potato curry
chapatis
pineapple chutney
avocado raita
fruit

WEDNESDAY:
corn chowder
zucchini burgers
Parkerhouse rolls
green salad with lemon-
honey dressing
fruit

THURSDAY:
latkes with hung yogurt
and applesauce
steamed peas
marinated cucumbers
and beets
frozen yogurt

FRIDAY:
spaghetti with tomato
sauce and cheese
salad with lemon-herb
dressing
French-style bread
fruit salad

SATURDAY: Lentil loaf with nut
gravy
steamed carrots
anadama bread
green salad with
avocado-tomato
dressing
baked apples

SUNDAY: minestrone
melted cheese
sandwiches
green salad with lemon-
herb dressing
fruit salad

MONDAY: Hiranya garbanzoes
steamed rice
green salad with French
dressing
sautéed zucchini
fruit

TUESDAY: spinach pie with millet
crust
steamed cauliflower
sprout salad with tahini
dressing
carrot cake

WEDNESDAY: carrot crumble
whole wheat bread
green salad with cubes
of cheese and lemon-
tomato dressing
steamed green beans
baked pears

THURSDAY: Chinese-style stir-fried
vegetables with
almonds
spring rolls
steamed rice
fruit salad with yogurt
dressing

FRIDAY: vegetable soup
stuffed eggplant
rye bread
salad with lemon-herb
dressing
nut-butter cookies

SATURDAY: guacamole
cheese enchiladas
salad with lemon-and-oil
dressing
fruit

SUNDAY: potage St. Germain
spinach crepes with
béchamel sauce and
almonds
marinated tomatoes
French-style bread
coffee crunch ice cream

MONDAY: cauliflower burgers with
cheese
baked zucchini
biscuits
coleslaw
fruit

TUESDAY: lentil soup
wheatberry bread
steamed green beans
Greek salad
fruit

WEDNESDAY: vegetables Stroganoff
over soy noodles
salade Niçoise
steamed broccoli
apple tart

THURSDAY: vegetable paella
artichokes with cashew
mayonnaise
spinach salad with
sesame seeds and
avocado dressing
fruit

FRIDAY: cauliflower-nut loaf
               tomato aspic on greens
               granola bread
               steamed chard
               stuffed dates

SATURDAY: spinach-yogurt dip
               moussaka
               cous cous
               pita
               green salad with tahini
                 dressing
               fruit salad with mint
                 leaves

Menus for Holidays and Celebrations

Party Menu I:
cream cheese-walnut spread
wheat germ sticks
nut loaf with tomato sauce
spinach salad with avocado dressing and
  croutons
steamed peas
cheese-herb swirls
carob cake with carob fudge frosting

Party Menu II:
golden avocado-carrot soup
crepes filled with ratatouille
cheese sauce
steamed green beans with sauce noisette
cracked wheat bread
mango ice cream with fresh fruit sauce

Party Menu III:
antipasto tray
tomato aspic with herbed cashew mayonnaise
lasagna
tossed green salad with slivered Jerusalem
  artichokes
basic bread
cantaloupe halves filled with strawberry ice

Buffet for a Large Group:
homos with celery sticks for dipping
tomatoes stuffed with guacamole
borscht with sour cream (cold)
spinach-cheese tarts—pre-sliced
vegetable pies—pre-sliced
sliced whole wheat bread
pineapple fruit salad served in scooped-out
  pineapple shells
salade Niçoise
zucchini bread
lemon cake with lemon-cream cheese icing
nut butter cookies
urn of herb tea
urn of grain coffee
cranberry-orange punch

Breakfasts

I
yogurt and fruit sprinkled with toasted
  wheat germ
English muffins with butter
lemon grass tea

II
hot oatmeal with milk
oranges
grain coffee

III
bagels
baked apples with cream or yogurt
grain coffee

IV
corn muffins
canteloupe halves filled with yogurt or cottage cheese
mint tea

V
dosa pancakes
stewed fruit with yogurt
rose hip tea

VI
müesli with strawberries
orange juice
grain coffee

VII

granola cereal with milk and bananas
broiled grapefruit
chamomile tea

VIII

sticky buns
melon halves
hot carob drink

IX

pancakes with fruit sauce and ricotta
red clover tea

Lunch at Home

I

tomato soup
toast
Greek salad

II

melted cheese sandwiches on potato bread

creamed spinach
apple slices

III

cottage cheese
salade Niçoise
herb biscuits

IV

corn on the cob
green salad
smoothies

V

vegetable pancakes with cheese sauce
spinach salad

VI

fruit salad with ricotta
oatmeal bread toast
verveine tea

VII

nutburgers on rolls
carrot-raisin salad
fruit frappé

International Cooking

Rather than adhering to absolute authenticity, the recipes in this book present the essence of the flavors, characteristics, and cooking methods used in different parts of the world, adapted to fit the context of a fresh foods vegetarian diet. A few of the recipes have also been altered to include more widely available ingredients than the completely authentic dish would contain. On the other hand, we do not subscribe to the theory that "if it's got tomato sauce it's Italian, if it's got soy sauce it's Chinese," and so on, and we think you will be pleased with the happy medium that

allows vegetarians to enjoy the styles of cooking and the dishes that are gifts of the many unique and special cuisines of the world.

The following section briefly outlines some of the characteristics, serving methods, and ingredients of the major cuisines covered in this book. Complete listings of the recipes of each country covered below, plus a few more, can be found in the index.

CHINA

A wide variety of dishes in the Chinese style are available to vegetarians, as a highly developed vegetarian cuisine prevailed in Buddhist monasteries for centuries.

One of the major culinary contributions of China is the technique of stir-frying. Chinese vegetables are quickly cooked in a wok and then served plain or with a light cornstarch- or arrowroot-thickened sauce. Chinese soups are clear and light. Salads are not usually found in the Western style, as the Chinese generally dislike the flavor of uncooked vegetables. Desserts are rarely served.

In the Chinese home, meals are served in mid-morning and in mid-afternoon. Breakfast, if any, is apt to be rice gruel. Four or five dishes, none considered a "main" dish, are placed on the table. Each family member has his or her own bowl of rice, and they bring the food from the communal dishes to their rice bowls. Chinese banquets are famous for their va-

riety—many dishes will be served, with the rice brought out last.

Food is eaten with chopsticks. To use chopsticks, balance one chopstick with the thumb and the second or third finger as shown in the diagram. This chopstick stays stable and does not move when grasping food. The second chopstick, which moves to pick up and release food, is held between the thumb and index finger.

Special Ingredients in Chinese Cooking

Oil: Soy oil or a light-flavored oil. Sesame oil is used as a garnish. Classical Chinese cooking employs only flavored oils, such as ginger-flavored oil and sesame-flavored oil.

Vegetables and fruits: Bok-choy, mustard greens, mung sprouts, bamboo shoots, lotus root, winter melon, and snow peas are some of the vegetables unique to the Chinese cuisine. Tomatoes and cucumbers were introduced in the twentieth century. Eggplant, green beans, celery, green peppers, and broccoli are used often. Turnips are the basis of the many meat substitute dishes invented by the Buddhist monks. Lichee nuts are a unique Chinese fruit.

Dairy products are not found in Chinese cooking.

Beans: Soybeans and soybean products, such as bean curd and soy milk, are used.

Nuts: Almonds, pecans, and sesame seeds are common.

Grains, breads, and noodles: Rice is the staple of the Yangtze valley and southern China. Wheat, millet, and barley are found in the north. Wheat and bean thread noodles are served in broth. Leavened, steamed buns are the only form of bread usually served in China.

CHOPSTICKS

Beverages: Tea, without milk or sweetening.

Spices and flavorings: Cinnamon, Szechuan pepper (a hot red pepper used in Northern and Szechuan cooking), fennel, cloves, star anise, and "five spice powder" made of a mixture of the preceding spices, are common, as well as fresh ginger root and cilantro. Soy sauce is a major flavoring (sattvic sauce is suggested in this book as a non-fermented substitute). A pinch of sugar is often added to vegetable dishes to enhance flavors.

Chinese-style Menus

scrambled bean curd
stir-fried vegetables with almonds
steamed rice
spring rolls

won ton soup
sweet-and-sour vegetables
Chinese-style fried rice
tea

Holiday or Party Menu
sizzling rice soup
turnip cakes
stir-fried mixed vegetables over puffed bean
 threads
stir-fried gluten strips with sweet-and-sour
 vegetables
Chinese-style fried rice
steamed buns filled with aduki paste
mandarin apples and bananas
tea

FRANCE

There are two traditional mainstreams of French cooking; the "Cuisine Bourgeois," or home cooking derived from peasant cooking, and the "Haute Cuisine," the artistic and elegant cooking now popular in restaurants and homes throughout the world.

The Cuisine Bourgeois reflects the regional styles, while the Haute Cuisine has become a style unto itself, for centuries setting the standard for the highest quality food for all the western world.

In recent years, the two styles have become more integrated and the overall cuisine is tending toward a lighter, yet elegant fare. Today, a typical urban middle-class meal might consist of an hors d'oeuvre served at the table, a soup followed by a main course, a vegetable and/or salad course, and a dessert. On weekdays the dessert would consist of fruit and cheese, and on Sundays it might be a cake or pastry. Crusty French bread remains on the table throughout the meal.

Special Ingredients Used in French Cooking

Oil: Butter and ghee; for Mediterranean dishes, olive oil.

Vegetables and fruits: All varieties common in Europe.

Grains and breads: Rice and barley are common grains. White, crusty French bread is a mainstay. For the completely authentic recipe for French bread, see *Mastering the Art of French Cooking, Vol. 2,* by Julia Child (Alfred A. Knopf, publisher). Two hundred fifty tests were performed to perfect the recipe, a labor of love for which this author expresses humble admiration.

Dairy products: France is famous for its cheeses. A wide variety of soft, fresh cheeses is available; however, cottage cheese is generally not found.

Beans: Lentils and white beans are particularly common.

Nuts: Almonds, walnuts, and hazelnuts are used frequently.

Beverages: Bottled mineral water, tisanes, or herb tea mixtures. Grain coffee substitutes may be served.

Spices and flavorings: Green herbs and most dessert spices are used frequently.

French-style Menus:

Provençal stuffed tomatoes
ratatouille
steamed rice
green salad with lemon-herb dressing
French bread
fruit and cheese

II

potage St. Germain
crepes stuffed with creamed spinach and covered with mornay sauce
apricot tart

Party or Holiday Menu
cream of watercress soup
asparagus quiche
julienne green beans with noisette sauce
celeriac salad on greens
coupe melba
French bread

GERMANY

German cooking is highlighted by an imaginative tradition of baking. Varied cakes, cookies, breads, and pastries from Germany are known throughout the world. At Christmastime the windows of the ''backerei-conditorei'' are filled with highly decorated confections: pretzel-shaped cookies, gingerbread houses, large flat gingerbread cookies with pictures and messages inscribed in white icing, and a profusion of fruit- and nut-filled cookies and braided breads.

Of the general cooking, the hearty peasant fare is most adaptable to vegetarian kitchens. Thick soups, whole-grain breads, and many dishes featuring cabbage and potatoes are found. Yogurt is used frequently in light meals and as a salad dressing.

German-style Menus

lentil soup
German spicy red cabbage
mashed potatoes
salad with yogurt dressing
rye bread
German apple torte

Christmas Treats
speculatius
gingerbread people
kranzkuchen
Weihnachtstriezel
butter cookies

GREECE AND THE MIDDLE EAST

The cooking of Greece and the Middle East ranges in its origins from monks and philosophers to palace courts to desert nomads carrying their supplies in their saddlebags and cooking them over an open fire. The history of the cuisine begins with some of the first evidence of crop cultivation in Mesopotamia, one of the ''cradles of civilization.'' The Old Testament contains references to the foods eaten by the tribes of ancient Israel. The Greek philosopher Archestratus wrote one of the first treatises about cooking and eating, *Gastrology,* in 350 B.C. The chef's hat is reputed to have originated in the Greek monasteries, where the cooks, feeling themselves to be a cut above the ordinary monks, wore white hats to distinguish themselves!

Vegetarian food is eaten in Greece during Lent, when the Greek Orthodox Church forbids the consumption of all animal products. Vegetables and fruits are served only in season, so that they will be fresh. Wild greens and herbs are often used in salads and cooked foods.

The main meal is served very late in the evening in Greece and many Middle Eastern countries, giving rise to a famous element of the cuisine, ''meze'' or ''mezethakia'' in Greek and ''mazza'' in Arabic. Meze or mazza consists of various tidbits which are served in the hours before the meal to allay hunger. Large arrays of these appetizers (mezethakia literally means ''opens the appetite'') almost comprise a meal in themselves.

The cuisines of the Middle Eastern countries are integrating and evolving at a rapid rate, as the countries themselves are undergoing enormous economic and agricultural changes, and we can look forward to new contributions from them.

Special Ingredients in Greek and Middle Eastern Cooking

Oil: Olive oil is common, particularly in Greece and Turkey. Otherwise use a mild-flavored oil.

Vegetables and fruits: Eggplant, tomatoes, and green peppers are common throughout the Middle East. Spinach and wild greens in season are used in Greek cooking. Fresh and dried figs, dates, and apricots are common. Pomegranate seeds are added to both desserts and main dishes as a decorative effect.

Grains and breads: Rice and wheat, particularly cracked wheat and bulgar. Couscous is used in North Africa. Farina is employed in desserts. In Greece a crusty white bread is served, and pita, a flat leavened bread, is found in Israel and the Arab countries.

Dairy products: Cultured milk products, notably kefir and yogurt. Goat's milk and goat's milk cheeses, particularly feta cheese, are found in Greece.

Beans: A wide variety of beans is used, particularly garbanzos, white beans, and lentils.

Nuts: Pine nuts, pistachios, and walnuts are common. Sesame seeds and tahini are found in Arab and Israeli cooking.

Beverages: Fruit juices, kefir, and yogurt drinks. In Morocco, mint tea highly sweetened with sugar accompanies social occasions and business transactions.

Flavorings and spices: Lemon juice, olive oil, and parsley are major flavorings. Green herbs are used frequently in Greece. Cumin, saffron, cinnamon, cardamom, and coriander are found in North Africa and the Middle East. Orange flower water and rosewater are used to flavor desserts.

Greek and Middle Eastern-style Menus

Middle Eastern:

I

borani
pita
moussaka
steamed bulgar wheat
green salad
fresh figs

II
falafel sandwich on pita
taratoor sauce
baba ganooj
tabouli
Greek:
fasolada
spanakopita
green salad with lemon-and-oil dressing
basic bread
loukoumathes

Greek Holiday or Party Menu
marinated vegetables a la Grecque
cacik
dolmathes
vegetable kebabs
pilau-style rice
Greek salad
baklava

INDIA

The *Ayurveda,* the most ancient medical treatise in the world, outlines a thorough science of nutrition which is successfully practiced to this day. Vegetarianism is widely practiced in India, making it the home of perhaps the most complete vegetarian cuisine.

All the dishes are served simultaneously at an Indian meal. The meal is served on a

thali, a large metal tray with little bowls to hold the more liquid foods. Sometimes food is served on banana leaves—the forerunners of paper plates. A mound of rice will be placed in the middle of the thali in southern India, and in the north, flat, unleavened breads will be served. Dishes of vegetables, beans, yogurt, chutneys, and sweets (sometimes eaten in the middle of the meal rather than at the end) are arranged around the rice or bread.

Food is eaten with the hands (the right hand only for Hindus), either scooped up with pieces of the bread or mixed with the rice. In the south, more rice and yogurt are served at the end of the meal. All over India, paan, a mixture of betel leaf with spices, coconut, nuts, lime, and other ingredients, is chewed as a digestive aid. Sweets are prevalent at festivals and holidays. They are sometimes covered with silver or gold leaf—finely powdered real gold and silver that is pressed into an edible paper-thin foil.

Special Ingredients Used in Indian-style Cooking

Oil: Ghee is the preferred cooking oil. One may also use a mild-flavored vegetable oil. Mustard oil is sometimes used, particularly in chutneys, as a hot addition.

Dairy products: Milk, buttermilk, and yogurt (called "curd," and incubated only a few hours, so that it is still sweet and runny) are common. Panir, a fresh cheese, and khoa, a condensed milk paste, are two uniquely Indian dairy products.

Vegetables and fruits: Many Indian fruits and vegetables are rare or unavailable outside of Asia. Of the available produce, potatoes, eggplant, peas, okra, green beans, cabbage, cauliflower, carrots, and pumpkin are used frequently. Tomatoes, avocadoes, papayas, pineapples, and mangoes are common. Apples are available in the north.

Beans: Beans are part of the staple diet of India. Lentils, yellow split peas, mung beans, and red lentils are common. Of the uniquely Indian beans, chana, urad, split mung and toor can sometimes be found in Indian specialty stores.

Nuts: Pine nuts, pistachios, almonds, and cashews are common. Coconuts are used in all stages of development, from unripe green to mature brown.

Grains and breads: Rice is the staple of southern India. Basmati is a superior rice grown in India. Wheat, barley, and millet are found in the north, where unleavened flatbreads and a lightly leavened bread, nan, are served.

Beverages: Tea, mixed with milk and sugar or honey. Yogurt-based drinks, buttermilk, and fruit juices are common.

Flavorings and spices: See garam masala, page 59.

Some of the common spices used in Indian cooking are:

asafoetida
black mustard seed
black pepper
cardamom
cinnamon
cloves
coriander
cumin
fenugreek
fresh ginger
green chilies
nutmeg
red chilies
saffron
turmeric

Other flavorings include tamarind, which is soaked and the soaking water used, and rosewater for desserts. A pinch of sugar is added to vegetable dishes to blend flavors.

Indian-style Menus

I

dhal with lentils
zucchini curry
saffron rice
eggplant raita
shrikhand
tea

II

dhal with yellow split peas
peas and panir
puris
Mysore pak
spice tea

Holiday or Party Menus:

I

dhal with red lentils
pilau rice
mint chutney

kofta
samosas
avocado raita
gulab jamuns
spice tea

II

biryani
zucchini and cauliflower pakoras
peach chutney
parathas
cucumber raita
carrot halva
tea

ITALY

Italy has given to the world one of the best known and best loved cuisines. Some Italian dishes, such as polenta, can be traced to ancient Roman times. An Italian meal could consist of soup, antipasto, a pasta dish, main course, green salad, dessert, and beverage, with crusty Italian bread on the table throughout. A completely satisfying meal, however, can be simply an Italian main dish served with salad and bread.

Special Ingredients in Italian-style Food
Oil: Butter is used in the north and olive oil in the south.
Vegetables and fruits: Zucchini, eggplant, spinach, and green peppers are prevalent. Tomatoes, in the form of tomato sauce, are a signature of Italian cooking. There are many varieties of tomato-based sauces with a great range of subtleties besides the standard spaghetti-and-pizza sauce found outside of Italy. Melons, fresh figs, and strawberries are some of the many fruits served.
Dairy products: Italy produces many cheeses. Ricotta and mozzarella are used widely.
Beans: Many varieties are used, notably garbanzos and kidney beans.

Nuts: Almonds and pistachios are common.
Grains, cereals, and pastas: Pasta is immediately associated with Italy, where it is produced in literally hundreds of shapes and sizes. In northern Italy, rice and polenta, a coarsely ground cornmeal, are served instead of pasta. Crusty white Italian bread is common.
Beverages: Bottled mineral water, and sweet fruit syrups mixed with carbonated water, are common. Grain coffee substitutes can be used to create facsimiles of the many Italian coffee drinks.
Spices and flavorings: Oregano, basil, thyme, and marjoram are used so frequently in Italian cooking that they are referred to as "Italian herbs." Olive oil and lemon juice add flavoring. Anise is added to some baked goods.

Italian-style Menus
I

baked polenta with tomato sauce
sautéed zucchini
green salad with lemon-and-oil dressing
fruit and cheese

II

minestrone
fried mozzarella
green salad with herb dressing
fruit salad

Party or Holiday Menus
I

antipasto
fettucine
eggplant parmigiana
green salad with tomato dressing
ricotta spumoni

II

lasagna
green salad with lemon-and-oil dressing
basic bread
strawberry ice in cantaloupe halves

JAPAN

Harmony of flavors, colors, and nutrients is the hallmark of a well-prepared Japanese meal. Japanese dishes are light and simple. A variety of cooking methods and a way of slicing the vegetables at many different angles allow as much of the nutritional value as possible to remain in a meal. Only fresh fruits and vegetables in season are served, for optimum freshness.

Woks are used for stir-frying and kinpura frying. A large pot called a nabe is used for a style of cooking in which food is cooked in broth at the table.

Japanese meals are decoratively arranged on the plate. Raw vegetables may be cut into elaborate flower shapes for a decorative garnish. The Japanese table is very low, and the family takes kneeling positions to eat. The food is eaten with chopsticks. For some holidays the food is served in boxlike containers with little compartments to hold the different foods.

Special Ingredients in Japanese-style Cooking

Oil: Soy or sesame-flavored oil.

Vegetables: Various sea greens, such as nori (laver) and kombu (kelp), are unique to Japanese cooking. Burdock or gobo root, snow peas, daikon radish, and mung sprouts are among the vegetables used. Carrots, celery, squash, green beans, and cabbage can be incorporated into Japanese-style meals.

Dairy products: Not found in Japanese cooking.

Beans: Soybeans and soybean products, such as bean curd (called tofu in Japanese); aduki or azuki beans are also common.

Nuts: Almonds, cashews, and sesame seeds.

Grains and noodles: Rice is the staple grain. Glutinous rice—a sticky, slightly shiny variety—and a sweet rice are two varieties used. Bean thread noodles and wheat and buckwheat noodles are served in broth.

Beverages: Unsweetened tea. Mu tea and bancha, or twig tea, come from Japan and are available in health-food stores.

Flavorings and spices: Sattvic sauce can be used as an unfermented substitute for soy sauce (called shoyu sauce in Japan). Gomasio is a Japanese table seasoning. Sea greens give flavor to soups and vegetable dishes.

Japanese-style Menus

I

mixed vegetable tempura
aduki beans and rice
kinpura-fried carrot and burdock slivers
bancha tea

II

sushi
noodles and bean curd
stir-fried mixed vegetables
mu tea

JEWISH

There is no one country that can claim Jewish food as its own. An international cuisine has developed which is served in Jewish homes around the world. Eastern European influences dominate. The Jewish communities of the U.S.A. have contributed and adapted many foods. Some dishes are served for specific holidays and have religious or historical significance. For instance, matzoh, an unleavened cracker, is traditionally served during Passover to signify the Biblical period in which the Jews, fleeing from their enslavement in Egypt, had no time to leaven their bread, and baked it unleavened before their exodus.

Many vegetarian main dishes have been developed because of the ''kashrut'' or "kosher" dietary laws. One of the laws, based on a Biblical injunction interpreted to mean that meat and dairy products may not be served at the same meal, has given rise to exclusively "dairy" dishes. A vegetarian who refrains from eating dairy products containing rennet maintains a kosher diet.

Jewish-style Menus

I

blintzes
coleslaw
tea

II

piroshki
kasha varnishkas
steamed cabbage
green salad

Hanukkah Menu

borscht with sour cream
latkes with applesauce
steamed peas
tzimmes
green salad
honey cake

MEXICO

Mexican cuisine is a mixture of influences, including the foods of the native Indians and those which the Spanish conquistadores adapted to the native crops. Mexican foods are quite varied, but many of them are variations on a theme of tortillas, rice, beans, and cheese. A Mexican main dish served with a salad and a steamed vegetable can make a more than adequate meal.

Special Ingredients Used in Mexican-style Cooking

Oil: Light-flavored oil or butter.
Vegetables and fruits: Corn, tomatoes, and green peppers are common. Avocadoes and (in southern Mexico) tropical fruits such as mangoes, papayas, and guavas are common.
Dairy products: Milk, hard cheese, and sour cream.
Beans: Pinto, kidney, and black beans.
Grains and breads: Rice. Tortillas, unleavened flat breads made of cornmeal or sometimes of wheat flour, are a signature of Mexican cooking. Leavened breads and rolls and sweet dessert breads (pan dulce) are commonly served.
Spices and flavorings: coriander, cumin, cinnamon, cloves, cilantro, chilies and jalapeño peppers.
Beverages: Fruit juices. A hot carob drink sprinkled with cinnamon can be served.

Mexican-style Menus

tostadas
green salad with avocado-tomato dressing
Mexican cornbread dessert
bocoles
steamed green beans
green salad
basic bread
banana ice cream

Party or Holiday Menu

guacamole with tostaditas
tamale pie
flautas
Mexican-style corn
green salad
tropical fruit salad

SCANDINAVIA

Perhaps the most widely known element of Scandinavian cooking is the smorgasbord, a buffet containing dishes for an entire meal. An adapted smorgasbord focusing on one course of a meal, such as hors d'oeuvres or desserts, can also be served.

Scandinavian-style Menus

latkes
creamed spinach
green salad with sour cream dressing
orange rice

Smorgasbord of Scandinavian Desserts
koldskål (punch)
fruit soup
cardamom tea cake
Danish rice pudding
apple crisp
ra æblekage
Swedish pancake cake

SWITZERLAND

Switzerland is the home of supreme dairy products. Swiss yogurt, cheeses, and creamy milk are unsurpassed, and an ample cuisine has developed around them. A traditional Swiss "soup" is a mixture of bread, cheese, butter, and milk or cream in which a spoon can stand straight up! Switzerland is also the birthplace of the health-food revival. The foods and recipes used at the Bircher-Benner clinic in the nineteenth century sparked a reform movement in which the use of fruits, nuts, whole grains, and yogurt found a place in the European diet. Today a reformhaus, or health-food store, can be found in almost every city in Switzerland.

Swiss-style Menus

cheddar cheese soup
rösti
steamed broccoli
green salad
cottage cheese doughnuts

Swiss Breakfast
müesli
orange juice
hot carob drink

UNITED STATES OF AMERICA

"As American as mom and apple pie"
Though the influence of the native American Indians can be seen in some of the foods of New England, the cuisine of the U.S.A. largely consists of dishes brought by immigrants from their native countries and adapted to the crops available where they settled. English and German influences are felt in the Northeast (the Pennsylvania Dutch, so famous for their cooking, are German—"Dutch" coming from "Deutsch"). French and Spanish cooking, combined with West Indies influences, has created Creole cooking of the South. Mexico has contributed to the foods of the Southwest. Many other ethnic foods are found throughout the United States.

U.S.A.-style Menus

Northern Menu
Boston baked beans
Boston brown bread
steamed green beans
green salad
Indian pudding

Southern Menu
gumbo
rice
biscuits
green salad
ambrosia salad

Thanksgiving Menu
nutloaf
breadcrumb stuffing
cashew gravy
candied yams
steamed peas
cranberry sauce
pumpkin pie with whipped cream
roast chestnuts

"Fast Food" Menu   coleslaw
lentil burgers on burger rolls   milkshake
french fries

Entertaining

Bringing a large group of people together for a meal provides a wonderful opportunity to shower friends with the best of one's hospitality and creativity. Careful planning and organization provides a smoothness of service that gives guests optimum comfort and enjoyment. It also helps the host or hostess relax as well when everything is "well and wisely put."

Begin by considering the time available for shopping, preparation, and clean-up, and if there will be any help available. Make sure that there will be enough silverware and plates for both eating and serving, refrigerator and shelf space for storage and pots, and oven and stove space for cooking the amount of food needed.

Preparing large quantities of food takes much longer than cooking for a few people. Some of the individual touches one can add to a dinner for six just may not be possible if the meal is for fifteen. Depending on the schedule, it may be more practical to plan a large casserole or similar dish which does not require the preparation of individual servings.

A guide for large amounts can be made by multiplying the recipe to serve the number of guests expected. However, do not try to multiply the salt, pepper, or spices—they must be added to taste. Also, most recipes expand only to a certain point, after

which their accuracy breaks down. Most of the recipes here can be multiplied up to eight times. If more food is required, it is better to prepare the multiplied recipe twice. Consult cookbooks for institutional cooking to get a feel for large-scale proportions. It is quite an experience to be throwing in handfuls of basil for the first time when you are used to doling it out in teaspoonfuls, but it is only a matter of enlarging your perspective, and the adjustment can be made quite quickly.

PREPARATION

Either mentally or on paper, work out a time schedule for preparing the meal. Baked goods can be made the night before. Chutneys, marinated foods, and some other dishes can be prepared in the morning. Preparation procedures can be combined: i.e., if celery is to be used in both the salad and the casserole, amounts for both can be sliced at the same time. Set the table and arrange the house well in advance, leaving time for a shower and changing clothes after the major cooking and housework have been accomplished.

SERVING

There is an art to timing the serving of a meal so that no one feels rushed through eating, or is kept waiting longer than necessary. During the meal, timing is necessary to insure that the hot dishes are served hot and the cold dishes cold. The main course can be baking while the soup is being served.

Serving a meal to guests should be done in a way that will make them feel most comfortable. It is a very fulfilling experience to present a meal to the people who sit at your table *in the way that you know they will enjoy the most*. This is the true meaning of etiquette—whether it means eating with the hands from a banana leaf in India or serving an eight-course meal with full regalia of silverware and plates in France.

The "correct" way to serve and eat varies from culture to culture, and also varies according to the people we are dining with. We may act differently depending on whether we are serving our family, close friends, distinguished visitors, people newly arrived from a foreign country, and so forth. The point is obvious, but it is truly a mark of the skill of the host or hostess to present food that is most appropriate and will put everyone at ease. Sometimes a person who is accustomed to formal service will most enjoy an informal help-yourself family meal, while another type of guest may feel shy in such a situation and would appreciate being served by the host or hostess. In any case, over and above the way that the meal is served, it is the attitude of the host or hostess—the love and caring that is shown to the guests—that shines through and makes the atmosphere enjoyable and comfortable.

The following is an outline of some of the traditional ways of serving meals. Also see "International Cooking" for some of the serving methods used in different cultures. If a situation arises where the formal rules of etiquette are necessary and appropriate, consult a book on etiquette.

Food is usually served at the table in one of three ways. The first two are considered family-style, while the third is used for formal dinners. It can be applied to less formal occasions as well.

1. The food is brought to the table in serving bowls, which are passed around to allow the guests to serve themselves.
2. The food is brought to the table in serving bowls. The plates are stacked in front of the host or hostess, who then serves the food and passes the filled plates to the guests.
3. The food is arranged on individual plates in the kitchen and then is served to each guest at the table. Later courses are served either by walking around the table and placing food on each guest's plate, or by clearing the plates from one course and bringing in the next course on fresh plates. For a formal meal, the food is traditionally served from the right and the plates are then cleared from the left.

Serving in courses is a European phenomenon, introduced by King Louis XIV of France to his court. The classical order of courses is hors d'oeuvres, soup, salad (in France the salad is served after the main course), main course with accompanying dishes, dessert, and hot beverage. The bread remains on the table until the dessert is served.

Courses may be rearranged or dispensed with, as long as the food is served in attractive and digestible combinations, in a manner that everyone present will be comfortable with.

Buffets have the advantage of ease and efficiency in service for a large group of people, and allow the guests to select what and how much they will eat. The food is placed on a large table and the guests help themselves. They can then take their plates to a pre-set table and dine together. Dessert can be included on the buffet table or served later at the dinner table.

Arrange the buffet table with an attractive tablecloth, and place any flowers, candles, or other decorative effects toward the back of the table and out of the way of the serving line. Have the necessary plates, bowls, and cups available first in the line. (The silverware should already be set on the dinner table.) Have the bowls and trays of food within easy reach and equipped with plenty of serving utensils. If possible, keep the hot foods on warming trays. Dishes of cold foods can be placed in large bowls filled with crushed ice for an attractive and practical cooler. (Drain off the water from the melting ice once or twice if the dinner is a long one.) Foods such as breads and pies should be pre-sliced to be individually served. For very large groups, urns containing herb teas and grain coffees can be used. Cups and spoons, cream, honey, and sugar should all be nearby.

For smaller buffets, the warming trays, coolers, and tea urns may not be necessary at all, and the planning may be much simpler.

TABLE SETTING AND DECORATION

A beautiful dining environment does much to enhance the meal and the general atmosphere of the gathering. Simplicity and practicality should be kept in mind when creating decorative effects. Harmonize the colors of the place mats or tablecloth with the table service. Simple centerpieces can be made from flowers, leaves, potted plants, fruits, and nuts (the latter to be eaten with the meal)—anything attractive and appropriate. The centerpiece should

be low enough for guests to see over it, and should leave enough room on the table for the necessary bowls and dishes. Candles provide a beautiful soft light for dining—but check first to make sure that they provide enough light for guests to see what is on the end of their forks and who is across the table!

The Western method of setting a table is:

a. salad fork
b. fork
c. napkin
d. plate
e. knife
f. soup spoon
g. spoon
h. bread-and-butter dish
i. butter knife
j. water glass
k. beverage

The hors d'oeuvre plate may be placed on top of the dinner plate. Salad may be served in a bowl to the left, or in a plate placed on the dinner plate, after the hors d'oeuvre or main course has been cleared. A hot beverage can be set in the place of the cold beverage when dessert is served. The utensils farthest from the plate are used for the first courses, working inward for each succeeding course. Separate utensils may be brought out for dessert.

Basic Ingredients

WATER

Pure H_2O serves two purposes in cooking: to add moisture, and, when heated, to cook foods. However, any type of water other than distilled water is not pure H_2O. It contains the minerals and salts of the geographical area of its origin, and probably also contains man-made additions which either purify the water or pollute it. It is these additions, both natural and man-made, that give the water different cooking and health properties.

Soft water, or water containing a minimum of salts and minerals, is ideal for cooking. It adds nothing of any consequence to the food other than moisture. *Hard water,* water that contains large quantities of natural minerals and salts, may be healthful, but it can affect food in a number of ways:

1. White and light-colored foods may take on a yellowish color. Adding a teaspoon of lemon juice to the cooking water can solve this problem in most cases. Some foods can be cooked in milk instead of water to help retain their color.
2. Most hard waters strengthen the gluten in flour, tending to make baked goods tough. Highly alkaline waters, however, dissolve the gluten and cause baked goods to shrink.
3. Legumes and fruits cooked in hard water may become tough.
4. Some hard waters, particularly those containing sulphur compounds, can have an unpleasant taste that affects the flavor of foods and beverages.

The local water company has analyses of the water supply if you are unsure about the contents or purity of the water. If your water comes from a private well, have it analyzed. Inexpensive water filters that will remove minerals and pollutants are available through health-food stores. A more expensive solution is to purchase bottled spring water. There are companies that will deliver weekly supplies to the house.

If you want mineral water to drink for health reasons, bottled mineral spring waters can be purchased. These are popular in Europe, where they are drunk instead of tap water in some countries.

OIL

Vegetable, nut, and seed oils: Cold-pressed, unrefined, preservative-free oils are the most wholesome and flavorful cooking oils. They are available in health-food stores. Store cold-pressed oils in the refrigerator, as they do not contain preservatives and will go rancid faster than the "cooking" oils and "salad" oils found in ordinary stores. Olive oil and coconut oil should be stored in a cool dark place, as they become semi-solid when stored in the refrigerator.

Some of the mild-flavored oils which can be used for general purposes are soy, safflower, sunflower, and corn or corn germ. They each have a characteristic, but light, flavor. Olive, sesame, walnut, and mustard oils have more pronounced flavors and will make their presence known in the food. Olive oil may be heated to high temperatures, but nut oils are sensitive to heat and are best used for salads and other uncooked foods. Walnut oil is found in fine French cooking as a salad dressing. Mustard oil is used in India as a very hot addition to chutneys and vegetable dishes.

Flavored oils were originally the only oils used in classical Chinese cooking. Today they are found in oriental cuisine, and can be used in many other dishes as well.

Sesame-flavored Oil (China)

1 cup mild flavored oil
½ cup toasted sesame seeds

Combine the oil and sesame seeds in a blender until smooth. Strain the oil through a fine strainer, pressing it out of the remaining sesame paste. Store in the refrigerator. The sesame paste may be served as tahini.

Ginger-flavored Oil (China)

Peel a piece of fresh ginger and slice. Place in a pot with a mild-flavored oil. Heat until the ginger turns brown. Strain out the ginger slices and store the oil in the refrigerator.

SWEETENERS

Fruits can be employed to give natural sweetness to foods without the use of a concentrated sweetener. They generally will not provide as much sweetness as sugar or honey. Sweet fruit juices or crushed ripe fruit may be added to foods. Mashed ripe bananas also add sweetness. Pureed dried fruits give a concentrated sweetness. Pureed raisins and dates are very effective. Date sugar, dried pulverized dates, may be used in the manner of cane sugars except in recipes where the sugar must melt or caramelize. Date sugar will not dissolve. Carob pods and carob powder contain natural sweetness and a light chocolaty taste that combines well with dried fruit and baked goods.

Honey has long been praised for its wonderful flavor and its health-giving properties. However, honey loses its nutritional value and much of its flavor when heated to high temperatures, and it is actually more healthful to use sugar in cooked or otherwise heated foods. Honey has been included as an alternative to sugar in the recipes for those who insist on using it as their only sweetener, but it is not recommended. One can add honey to cooked foods, such as rice pudding, after they have been removed from the stove and allowed to cool for a while.

The highest-quality, most wholesome honey is pure, unheated, and untreated. The variation of flavor in honeys is largely a result of the types of flowers from which they were made. Darker honeys contain more acid, and generally have a more intense flavor, than the lighter ones. Select honeys that will harmonize with the foods they are used with—perhaps a mild honey to mix with foods and a stronger variety to spread on bread or stir into tea.

When using honey in place of sugar in a recipe, substitute ¾ cup honey for 1 cup of sugar, and reduce the liquid in the recipe by 3 or 4 tablespoons per cup. Substitute honey cup-for-cup for molasses or maple syrup.

Maple sugar and *maple syrup* were used extensively by the native American Indians in the New England area. Maple sugar comes in blocks and must be grated to a powder. Substitute ½ cup of maple sugar for 1 cup of cane sugar. Because it is so expensive, maple sugar is best used in recipes where its flavor will be dominant. Maple syrup is produced by boiling down the maple sap—35 to 40 gallons of raw sap are necessary to produce a gallon of syrup. Maple syrup is available in three grades: A, B, and C. The grade-A syrup is lighter and more refined than B and C, but the flavor of the others is very good as well. Store maple syrup in the refrigerator. If it crystallizes, immerse the jar in warm water. Substitute maple syrup in the same proportions as for honey.

Molasses: Use unsulphured or blackstrap molasses. Unsulphured molasses is made from the juice of sun-ripened sugar cane, and adds the flavor usually associated with molasses. Blackstrap molasses is a byproduct of sugarmaking. It is very dark and contains quantities of iron and B vitamins. It also has a very strong flavor. Use it in small amounts, or tone it down by combining it with brown sugar. Store molasses at room temperature in a cool dark place. Substitute molasses in the same proportions as for honey.

Sorghum is a syrup produced in the United States from a grain similar to corn. It has a flavor resembling molasses and may be used in the same manner as molasses.

Sugar is a refined product derived from sugar cane and sugar beets. For many years sugar has been overemphasized and overused as a substitute for foods with higher nutritional value. Now there is an overreaction in the other direction, with some people giving up sugar entirely. We feel that the solution is *moderation*. A little sugar goes a long way, and will not be harmful in the diet of most people. When we prepare fresh foods ourselves, we control the situation. It is when a sugary dessert tops off a meal of sugar-loaded washed-out canned vegetables, enriched, bleached, preserved, sugar-loaded bread, and a sugar- and chemical-loaded soda, that the situation is out of hand. Having a dessert with a little sugar after a meal of fresh vegetables, whole grains, and other nourishing non-sugared foods is an entirely different matter, and has entirely different consequences. It is with this very moderate picture in mind that we feel that sugar does have a place in the diet.

Granulated white sugar adds sweetness but not taste to foods. Store it in a container away from moisture.

Brown sugar is white sugar with molasses added for color and flavor. Brown sugar is measured by packing it firmly into the measuring cup. One cup of packed brown sugar is equal to one cup of granulated white sugar. Store brown sugar in airtight containers to preserve its moisture. A few slices of apple placed in the brown sugar will help keep it moist.

Raw sugar, some varieties of which are called *turbinado sugar,* contains the unrefined crystals left after the molasses has been extracted. Nutritionally there is little difference between raw sugar and white sugar, and it usually is more expensive. Raw sugar will add a very slight molasses flavor to foods.

Powdered sugar is also a form of granulated sugar, but ground much finer.

Confectioner's sugar is a powdery grind of white sugar that contains a little cornstarch. It is used in frostings and uncooked foods, or sprinkled over baked goods for a decorative effect. Confectioner's sugar cannot be substituted for granulated sugar in baked goods. It may have to be sifted before use. Store confectioner's sugar in airtight containers.

To substitute white or brown sugar for honey, molasses, or maple syrup, increase the amount by one-fourth and add 3 to 4 tablespoons of liquid per cup.

Cinnamon Sugar

3 tablespoons sugar
1 tablespoon cinnamon
   Mix together well and sprinkle on hot buttered toast.

DAIRY PRODUCTS

Milk is a highly nourishing and beneficial food. In some areas of the world, cow's milk is considered sacred. Milk is highly perishable and must be kept under constant refrigeration. Ideally, milk should be used within about three days of purchase.

Pasteurized and raw milk: Pasteurization involves heating milk to high temperatures to destroy any disease-causing bacteria. The pasteurization process also removes the vitamin C content and destroys the enzymes necessary for natural souring. Pasteurization was a life-saving breakthrough when there were no methods of preventing disease in cattle and the milk was often contaminated. Raw milk, or unpasteurized milk, is relatively safe to drink if it comes from herds which are inoculated against and regularly tested for disease. Such quality-controlled raw milk is available in health-food stores.

Whole milk is fresh milk, either raw or pasteurized. If left undisturbed, the cream will rise to the top. The cream can be either skimmed off or shaken back into the milk before drinking.

Homogenized milk has been subjected to a process that breaks down the fats and distributes them throughout the milk, so that the cream is permanently mixed in.

Skim or *nonfat milk* has the fat removed—along with the vitamins. The protein and mineral content remain intact.

Powdered milk is made from either whole or nonfat milk in one of two ways:

1. The milk is condensed and then sprayed into a heated chamber to dry.
2. Milk is forced into a chamber in which circulating heated air both condenses and dries it.

Instant and non-instant powdered milks offer the same nutritional value. However, the non-instant variety is recommended for many of the dessert recipes and also for making yogurt. It can be found in health-food stores.

To reconstitute powdered milk, use one part powdered milk to three parts water. Instant milk dissolves in the manner that its name suggests. Non-instant milk may be mixed in a blender, or else add just a little water at first to make a paste, and then stir in the rest. Never try to add non-instant milk powder to hot water. Chill the milk for best flavor.

Dry powdered milk may be added to the dry ingredients of baked goods for extra enrichment.

Goat's milk is slightly richer than cow's milk and is easy to digest. People who have an allergy to cow's milk often can drink goat's milk without problems. Goat's milk should be very fresh and well chilled for best flavor. Use in the same manner as cow's milk for cooking and drinking.

Sour milk is used extensively in baking to increase the leavening action with its acidity.

Sour Milk Method #1

Add 2 teaspoons lemon juice to 1 cup of fresh milk. Let sit 1 minute to clabber.

Sour Milk Method #2

Let *raw* milk stand at room temperature overnight to sour naturally. (Do not attempt this with pasteurized milk, which will simply spoil and smell bad if left unrefrigerated.)

Khoa is a thick, condensed milk paste used in preparing Indian desserts.

Khoa

Bring ½ gallon of whole milk to a boil, being careful not to scorch. Cook at as high a boil as is possible without the milk boiling over for 1 to 1½ hours, stirring frequently. When the milk begins to thicken,

stir constantly until it forms a thick paste that pulls slightly away from the sides of the pot. Cool to thicken completely. This recipe makes about ¾ cup.

If the khoa is slightly yellowish, it was not boiled at high enough heat, but the flavor will be all right. Khoa will last for a few days in the refrigerator. For a simple dessert, mix it with sugar or honey and flavor with a little cardamom, rosewater, and chopped pistachios.

Cultured milk products are the result of specific bacteria cultures being added to milk at an optimum temperature to feed and multiply. It is important to have these bacteria in the intestines to help in the digestion of food. Cultured milk products are also very nourishing and easy to digest, as they are "pre-digested," with the structure already broken down by the cultures. People who have trouble digesting milk can often eat cultured milk products.

Yogurt: Homemade yogurt is quite economical, and one can add one's own fresh fruit to sweeten it. Yogurt can be prepared with everything from nonfat powdered milk to light cream, depending on the richness desired. Since fresh milk must be boiled to destroy an enzyme which hinders the yogurt culture, nonfat powdered milk, which has been heat-treated, is a practical and economical base for yogurt-making. Non-instant powdered milk gives a much better result than the instant type.

Yogurt

1 cup unflavored yogurt (make sure it has *active* cultures)
1 quart milk

If using whole milk, scald and cool to 100°. If using powdered milk, heat to 100°, or lukewarm.

Mix the yogurt thoroughly into the milk. A blender works very well; otherwise, use a whisk or eggbeater.

Pour into a glass container (not a metal one). Cover and let sit in a warm place for 4 to 8 hours or overnight. 100° is the ideal temperature for incubation. Heat by any of the following methods:

1. Place the mixture in a Thermos and wrap a towel around it.
2. Turn the oven on for a minute or two until it is just warm. Place the container of yogurt in the oven and turn it off. Do not open the oven door for at least 4 hours.
3. Set a heating pad on medium and cover it with a towel. Place the container with the yogurt mixture on it and cover with a few towels for insulation.

For a mild flavor, incubate for 4 to 6 hours. For a tart flavor, incubate 6 to 8 hours or up to 10 hours. Yogurt does not like to be jiggled or disturbed while it is incubating. When the yogurt is done, refrigerate immediately. This recipe makes a little over 1 quart.

The whey that collects on the top of the yogurt can be either poured off or stirred back into the yogurt. Nonfat milk will produce slightly more whey than whole milk. If the yogurt is disturbed during incubation it will produce more whey.

If a thick yogurt is desired, ⅓ cup of powdered milk can be stirred into the prepared mixture before incubating.

If the yogurt does not turn out, maybe:

- the temperature was too low.
- the powdered milk wasn't fresh enough.
- the yogurt starter did not contain active cultures. (Some commercial yogurts, particularly "Swiss style"—which incidentally contains gelatin and has nothing to do with the wonderful yogurt made in Switzerland—have inactive cultures which cannot produce more yogurt.)

- If there is a tremendous amount of whey and the milk solids seem to have separated and look grainy, the temperature was too high. Never fear—you have made panir, or fresh cheese. See the recipe on page 44 and complete the preparation.
- If the taste seems a little off, the jars may need to be sterilized.

Save one cup of the yogurt to start the next batch. Yogurt is often more successful if you use a fresh commercial yogurt as a starter once a week.

Hung Yogurt

Hung yogurt is thick and creamy, with a consistency somewhere between that of sour cream and cream cheese. It can be used as a cheese spread, as a substitute for sour cream, or, sweetened, to make a frosting or dessert.

1 quart thick yogurt

Place the yogurt in a muslin cloth or in a clean pillowcase. Tie shut to enclose the yogurt in a "bag," and hang it over a sink or receptacle to catch the whey as it drains off. Let it hang overnight. In the morning, squeeze out the last drops of whey, and then untie the bag and remove the thick hung yogurt. Store in the refrigerator and use the same day. This recipe makes about 1½ cups.

Buttermilk: The true and original buttermilk is the whey left over from butter-making. The cultured milk product we all know as "buttermilk" is made by an entirely different process. Because of its high lactic acid content, buttermilk is used in baking to facilitate rising. Buttermilk can be made from either whole, nonfat, or reconstituted powdered milk. If unhomogenized milk is used, a thin layer of sour cream will form on the top.

Buttermilk

1 quart fresh milk
¼ cup cultured buttermilk

Mix the milk and buttermilk together thoroughly. Cover and place in a draft-free dark place at room temperature for 24 to 36 hours. Store in the refrigerator. Reserve ¼ cup of each batch to start the next batch. If the buttermilk seems to be getting too strong after a number of batches have been made, procure a fresh starter. This recipe makes 1 quart.

Sour Cream

1 pint heavy cream
¼ cup cultured buttermilk

Stir the buttermilk thoroughly into the cream. Let sit in a dark, draft-free place at room temperature for 36 hours, until thick. Store in the refrigerator. This recipe makes one pint.

Kefir has been drunk in the Middle East and in the Caucasus mountains for centuries. It was carried in the saddlebags of wandering tribes in the Middle East, where it could incubate and be transported without refrigeration. Kefir can be served plain, or can be used as a substitute for yogurt or buttermilk in beverages. Mix kefir with fruit juice or serve in smoothies for a sweet drink.

Kefir

3 tablespoons kefir grains
1 quart milk

Mix the kefir grains into the milk. Let stand at room temperature for 24 hours, until it seems to gel. There may be some slight separation.

Pour the mixture through a strainer, and stir and mash with a spoon to separate the milk curds from the kefir grains. Store the kefir in the refrigerator. This recipe makes one quart.

Rinse the kefir grains in running water, and start the next batch of kefir. Kefir grains can be stored up to ten days, held in water or milk in the refrigerator, if they are not going to be used immediately for a new batch of kefir.

The strength of kefir will depend on the amount of grains used and the time that they are left to incubate. The above recipe is a general one for making kefir; the situation is somewhat flexible, and may be changed according to individual preference.

The kefir culture will double about every two months, so one may have a nice gift to give to friends, or go gradually into mass production.

Cream is the fatty part of the milk. If whole, unhomogenized milk is left undisturbed, cream will rise to the top. Heavier grades of cream are produced by letting the milk stand for longer periods of time. "Light cream" is suitable for use on cereals, in beverages, or wherever a rich base is desired. "Heavy cream" or "whipping cream" is suitable for whipping, and for making ice cream and butter. Avoid "sterilized cream" for whipping or "ultra-pasteurized cream" if possible. They have been loaded with preservatives to benefit the grocer—not the consumer.

Butter is fun to make at home occasionally, particularly for children. However, butter-making is generally not practical for daily preparation unless one has access to large amounts of cream and a good churn.
Shake heavy cream in a tightly closed jar for about 15 to 20 minutes, until the butter forms and separates from the whey in a lump. (The whey is the original butter-

milk.) Alternately, the cream can be whipped until it turns to butter, or a combination of the two methods can be used. Squeeze out all the remaining whey and rinse the butter briefly in cold water. Any remaining whey will turn the butter rancid. Squeeze the butter into a ball or press into a mold.

Ghee, or clarified butter, has been used in fine French and Indian cooking for centuries, and is the finest cooking oil in the world. Ghee can last for months unrefrigerated (though it is best to keep it refrigerated and to use it while fresh), can be heated to very high temperatures for cooking, and can substitute for butter in all cooking and as a spread for bread, vegetables, and so forth. It has a wonderful nutlike flavor that enhances all foods it is added to. Ghee is also used as a cosmetic oil, and can be rubbed into the skin. Like butter, ghee is solid when chilled, liquid when melted, and semi-solid when kept at room temperature.

Ghee

1 pound unsalted butter

Bring the butter to a boil in a heavy pot with high sides. Continue to cook the butter on a medium heat so that it is bubbling constantly. The impurities will rise to the top. As they do, skim them off with a spoon and discard. Continue until the butter is completely clear, about 40 minutes. The ghee can be cooked further, until it darkens, or can be left at a yellow-gold color. Strain the ghee through a muslin cloth, being careful not to pour in the impurities that have sunk to the bottom of the pot.

Cheese: There are three basic categories of cheese: soft, semi-soft, and hard. The soft and semi-soft varieties are generally aged less than the hard cheeses, which are sometimes aged for as much as two years.

Many cheeses from all three categories are made with rennet, a non-vegetarian stabilizer. If a cheese is labeled "kosher," "made from kosher enzymes," or "pareve," it is free of rennet. Many health-food stores carry rennetless cheeses. In most stores, if the cheese label does not specify its ingredients, check with the store or company to find out whether or not the product contains rennet.

Soft cheeses are generally the freshest. These include cottage cheese, ricotta, gervais, cream cheese, and a number of other soft white cheeses. Of the semi-soft cheeses, those which have been aged the least include mozzarella ("aged" 24 hours), feta (aged 3 to 4 days), and teleme (aged 8 to 10 days). If a cheese is coated with wax, it probably has been aged several months. If it is covered with or includes mold in its ingredients, well . . . .

Panir is a fresh cheese made in India. Depending on how long it is drained and at what temperature the acid ingredient is added to the milk, it can be soft and crumbly or hard and firm. Panir can be made with whole milk or with reconstituted powdered milk. The following recipes make a little over 1 cup each.

Panir

Method #1 *(for a soft panir)*

½ gallon milk
½ cup lemon juice

Bring the milk to a boil. Add the lemon juice. The curds and whey should separate almost immediately. Strain through a muslin cloth or a fine strainer. For hard panir, let drain for a few hours or overnight.

Method #2 *(makes slightly harder panir)*

½ gallon milk
1 cup yogurt

Bring the milk to a boil. Add the yogurt and boil again. When the curds and whey separate, drain as in Method #1.

Hard panir can be cut into cubes and pan-fried or deep-fried until brown and crispy. Panir can be used as a substitute for bean curd.

For a softer panir, add the acid ingredient to the milk while it is warming, and heat just until the curds and whey separate. Drain as described in Method #1.

Cream Cheese (a rich, buttery version)

1 pint heavy cream

Let the cream stand at room temperature for 3 to 5 days until thick, heavy clots have formed. Place in a muslin cloth or clean pillowcase, and tie it shut; hang it over the sink to drain for 3 hours. Store in the refrigerator and use soon after making. This recipe makes a little over 1 cup.

DAIRY SUBSTITUTES

Milk is a complete food, and there is no complete substitute for all its good effects. Dairy substitutes are recommended only for occasional use, or for use by people who cannot digest dairy products. A variety of dairy substitutes can be purchased in health-food stores. Some can be made at home.

Milk substitutes are as perishable as milk and should be stored in the refrigerator. Nut milks are heat-sensitive.

Soy Milk

from soybeans:

1 cup soybeans
4 cups water

Soak the soybeans overnight. Drain. Combine with the water in a blender until

the beans are pulverized. Strain through a muslin cloth. Store in the refrigerator. This recipe makes 1 quart.

from soy flour:

1¼ cups soy flour
4 cups water

Mix the soy flour and water together. Let stand for 2 hours. Place in a double boiler. Simmer for 20 minutes. Strain through a muslin cloth. Store in the refrigerator. This recipe makes 1 quart.

If preparing soy milk for drinking, mix in a tablespoonful of mild-flavored oil and a tablespoonful or more honey to improve the flavor. The Chinese serve soy milk as a meal, garnished with a little sesame oil.

Coconut Milk

Coconut milk is not the liquid from the coconut. The milk can be prepared with either fresh or dried coconut.

2 cups water
1 to 2 cups grated coconut (depending on desired richness)

Combine the water and coconut in a blender until fairly smooth. Strain through a muslin cloth. Store in the refrigerator. This recipe makes 2 cups.

Nut Milk

½ cup blanched almonds or raw cashews
2 cups water

Combine the nuts and water in a blender until smooth. Let sit in the refrigerator for 1 to 2 hours. Strain through a muslin cloth. This recipe makes 2 cups.

Butter substitutes: Use margarine for all recipes calling for butter except for making ghee. Commercial margarines are generally loaded with additives and preservatives. There is a soybean margarine available at health-food stores that is delicious and preservative-free. For bread and cracker spreads, try using mashed avocado, nut butters, tahini, and cashew mayonnaise. Coconut butter can be made by chilling Coconut Cream (recipe follows) until hardened.

Cream substitutes: Try a rich milk substitute, thin tahini, or the following recipe:

Coconut Cream (An Indonesian method)

4 cups grated fresh coconut
1 quart combined coconut liquid and water

Bring the coconut and water to a boil. Simmer, covered, for 20 minutes. Puree in a blender, 2 cups at a time. Strain. Let the liquid sit undisturbed at room temperature to cool. The cream will rise to the top; carefully skim it off with a spoon.

Serve the same day at room temperature. This recipe makes about ⅔ cup.

Cheese substitutes: Bean curd can be used to substitute for panir, and in some cases for ricotta or cottage cheese. Tahini and taratoor sauce add flavor to dishes calling for melted cheese, but do not give an equivalent flavor or texture. Lentil, tomato, and pesto sauces can be used where melted cheese or milk-based sauces are called for.

NUTS AND SEEDS

Nuts are an excellent source of protein and oil (with the exception of chestnuts, which contain mostly starch). For optimum freshness, purchase nuts raw in their shells. Otherwise, purchase raw, unsalted nuts available in health-food stores. The toasted varieties found in supermarkets are often loaded with oil, salt, and preservatives, and because of their salt content will not be appropriate for cooking. Store unshelled nuts in a cool, dark place and store shelled nuts in jars or plastic bags in the refrigerator.

Roasted or toasted nuts: Roasting nuts brings out their flavor to the fullest. The fragrance and flavor of nuts roasted at home is a delight. Besides roasting almonds and cashews, try roasting walnuts and hazelnuts as well.

Roasted or Toasted Nuts

Oven-roasted (Dry): Scatter raw or blanched nuts on a baking sheet. Place in a 350° oven for about 15 to 20 minutes. Stir and shake the pan every five minutes. Remove immediately when the nuts are browned. Salt very lightly according to taste, if desired. The nuts may be lightly coated with a mild-flavored oil before roasting, if desired.

Pan-toasted: Melt 1 tablespoon of butter or oil for every 2 cups of nuts in a heavy skillet. Add only enough nuts to cover the bottom of the skillet and stir often until they are browned. The nuts won't brown evenly, as only part of their surfaces will touch the pan at any given time. Repeat the process until all nuts are done. Sprinkle lightly with salt, if desired.

Blanched Nuts

Nuts such as almonds and pistachios are blanched in order to remove their skins. Drop the nuts into boiling water. Let sit for one minute. Drain. Slip the skins off by squeezing at one end.

Deep-fried Nuts

To brown nuts in a hurry, deep-fry them in oil or ghee until browned. Drain well on paper towels.

Ground Nuts

For a dry powder, a European crank grater or the finest grater on a food processor does a good job. For an oily paste, crush the nuts in a grinder or with a mortar and pestle. A blender tends to produce a result somewhere between a powder and a paste. Blend small amounts of nuts at a time.

Nut butter: Homemade nut butters can be made from raw, blanched, or roasted nuts, depending on the flavor desired. Almonds, cashews, walnuts, and hazelnuts make delicious nut butters. Try mixing different types of nuts together for new flavors. Store homemade nut butter in the refrigerator. Nut butters made with melted butter or ghee will harden slightly when chilled.

Nut Butter

2½ cups nuts (raw, blanched, or roasted)
½ to ¾ cups melted butter, ghee, or mild-flavored oil (the nuts may be toasted first in the oil)

Blend the nuts and oil together in a blender to form a smooth paste, adding only as much oil as necessary. Blend in a little salt if desired. This recipe yields 2½ cups of butter.

Nut butter may also be made by grinding nuts to a paste in a grinder.

Mix a little honey into homemade nut butter for a wonderful candy. If the sweetened nut butter is thick and firm, the mixture can be pressed into a pan, hardened, and cut into squares. Add raisins if desired.

Almonds are versatile and subtly flavored, and are ideal for nut milk, nut gravy, and nut halvah. Almonds may be used raw, blanched, blanched and roasted, or roasted.

Golden Almonds

For beautifully colored almonds to decorate desserts, soak a little saffron in water until the water is a bright yellow. Immerse blanched almonds in the water and soak overnight. Drain. Cashews and pine nuts may also be dyed in this manner.

Brazil nuts are generally used raw, but may also be blanched and roasted. Because of their size, it is best to sliver them before adding to other dishes.

Brazil Nut Curls

Blanch brazil nuts. When dry, scrape a knife blade along the wide edge of the nut to slice off thin curls. Gently spread the curls on a baking sheet and roast in a 350° oven until golden brown. Use for decorating desserts or garnishing soups.

Cashews may be either blanched or roasted to remove a slightly toxic chemical. They may be used in the same manner as almonds, and have a particularly wonderful flavor when roasted. Blanched cashews may be ground to an almost creamy consistency.

Chestnuts have properties that are completely different from other nuts. They are soft and starchy, and must always be cooked. Chestnuts are used frequently in European cooking as a substitute for potatoes. Chestnuts may be added to soups and stews or may be tossed with vegetables and grains. Chestnuts are available fresh in the autumn, and are also available dried. To reconstitute dried chestnuts, soak them overnight and then simmer in water to cover until tender.

Steamed Chestnuts

Make deep cross-cuts in the flat side of the shell. Simmer in water to cover for 15 to

CHESTNUT
CROSS-CUT

25 minutes. Drain and remove the shells and the brown inner skin as soon as the chestnuts are cool enough to handle. The inner brown skin is difficult to remove once the chestnuts have cooled.

Roasted Chestnuts

Make deep cross-cuts in the flat side of the shell. Coat the chestnuts with oil. Roast in a 375° oven or over an open fire until the shells can be removed easily. Peel off the shells and inner brown skin as soon as the chestnuts are cool enough to handle.

Coconuts are used in tropical countries in all stages of their development, from green and unripe to brown and mature. In the west they are usually found in their mature stage only. Dried grated coconut (sometimes called desiccated coconut) and coconut chips can be found in health-food stores. Use only the unsweetened, dry, flaky type. The moist, sweetened variety is chemically treated to stay soft.

To open a fresh coconut, pierce or drill holes in the "eyes," the round indented marks on one end. Drain out the liquid. The liquid may be added to other cooking liquids, and must be stored in the refrigerator. To remove the meat most easily from the shell, place the coconut in a 250° oven for 30 minutes. Break the coconut open with a hammer, or smash against a hard surface, or cut with a saw. Pry out the meat with a knife. The shells of evenly sawed-open coconuts can be polished and used as planters or decorative bowls.

Toasted Coconut

Scatter fresh or dried grated coconut on a baking sheet or skillet. To bake, place in a 350° oven for 5 to 10 minutes, stirring frequently. In a skillet, place on a medium flame for a minute or two, stirring constantly until light brown. Remove immediately from the pan or baking sheet.

Coconut Chips

Slice off wafer-thin chips from the meat of a fresh coconut. Toast in a 350° oven, stirring frequently until golden brown.

Hazelnuts or filberts are usually served raw, but can also be blanched and are delicious roasted. Hazelnuts may be used for nut butter and nut gravy. They have a strong characteristic flavor that tends to dominate the foods to which they are added.

Pecans have a high fat content, making them very rich. Pecans are usually eaten raw, but also may be lightly roasted. Pecans can be used interchangeably with walnuts.

Pine nuts, or *pignolas,* or *piñons,* are found in the pine cones of the piñon tree. Though usually eaten raw, they may be lightly roasted. Pine nuts add excellent flavor and texture to grains and desserts. Try using pine nuts in a fruitcake for a wonderful change.

Pistachios are distinguished by their bright green color. They are beautiful when split in half for decorating desserts. They also make a dramatically colored nut halva and nut gravy. Pistachios are usually found raw or roasted in their shells. Choose pistachios with undyed (beige not red) shells. Pistachios may be blanched to remove their skins, if desired.

Walnuts may be eaten raw or lightly roasted. They can be used for nut butter and nut gravy, and may be used interchangeably with pecans.

Seeds: Many small seeds serve as spices, seasonings, and teas, but there are a few seeds that have a life of their own, eaten plain or as the basis for other dishes. Sesame, sunflower, and pumpkin seeds may be toasted in an oven or in a *dry* pan in the same manner as nuts.

Chia seeds are high in protein and may be sprinkled on salads and added to casseroles and grains. Chia seeds produce a type of gelatin when they are boiled in water, which may be sweetened, mixed with fruits, and served as a dessert.

Pumpkin seeds can be added raw or toasted to salads, grains, casseroles, and baked goods, or may be eaten plain as a snack. The pumpkin seeds available in health-food stores have been shelled. Seeds removed from pumpkins and squashes may be rinsed clean, roasted in the oven, and lightly salted as a snack.

Sesame seeds were baked into cakes with honey to serve as emergency rations for the Roman legions. They may be eaten raw or toasted and added to almost all types of dishes. Buy sesame seeds in bulk in health-food stores—the tiny jars of them found in supermarkets are very expensive and the amounts are far too small for most of the recipes in this book.

Sunflower seeds were first brought to Europe from Central America by the Spanish explorers. Representations of sunflowers are found in the art of the ancient Aztecs. Sunflower seeds can be served raw or roasted. They can be ground into meal to enrich baked goods and thicken sauces. See "Thickeners" for sunflower meal as a filler for sauces.

Poppy seeds may be sprinkled into bread doughs and cake batters, and sprinkled on rolls for accent.

FLOUR

Flours containing the whole grain are "live"—they contain the germ of the grain and are perishable. Store in jars or tightly closed plastic bags in the refrigerator. Other flours, such as refined grain flours and bean flours, may be stored in a dry place.

Baked goods made with whole wheat flour or large amounts of non-wheat flours tend to be heavy and sometimes crumbly. On the other end of the spectrum, baked goods made exclusively from bleached white flour will rise unevenly, if they do not contain eggs. For general use, mixtures of whole wheat and other flours with unbleached white flour are recommended for a balance of lightness and good nutrition.

Bleached, all-purpose white flour and its even more refined version, *cake flour,* contain additives. If they must be used in a pinch for baked goods, make sure that at least ½ cup or more of whole wheat flour is added (for a standard cake recipe) to facilitate even rising.

Unbleached white flour has been refined but not bleached or otherwise chemically treated. It gives a light color and delicate texture to baked goods, and serves as a good basis for the addition of heavier flours.

Whole wheat pastry flour is a fine grind of whole wheat flour. It produces a darker color and slightly heavier texture than unbleached white flour, and is good for cakes, pastries, biscuits, and so forth. Since whole wheat pastry flour has little gluten in it, regular whole wheat flour is preferable for breads and yeast-rising doughs.

Whole wheat flour and its less refined version, *graham flour* (named for Dr. Sylvester Graham, an American health-food crusader and innovator), contains the whole wheat kernel and gives a delicate flavor and brown color, along with a somewhat heavy texture, to baked goods. It is excellent for use in crackers and breads, and can be mixed with unbleached white flour in other baked goods for a lighter texture.

Barley flour has an outstanding flavor when lightly roasted. Well-roasted barley flour can be used as a coffee substitute. Add small amounts of barley flour to bread and other baked goods.

Carob, or *St. John's bread,* is ground from the pod of the tamarind, or locust tree. It is claimed by some that St. John really subsisted upon this in the desert, when he was eating "locusts and wild honey." Carob is frequently used as a chocolate substitute in desserts, and its flavor also blends well with dried fruits. The quality of carob flour varies—try different brands for one that brings satisfactory results. For best flavor, use carob powder for only $1/5$ to ¼ the total amount of flour in a recipe. The sweetening may have to be slightly increased, as well. Specially treated carob flour is available for mixing with milk.

Chick-pea or garbanzo flour, or *besan,* is used frequently in Middle Eastern and Indian cooking for both vegetable dishes and desserts. Chick-pea flour can also be used to replace soy flour in baked goods. Lightly roasting garbanzo flour helps to remove its "raw" taste.

Millet flour is fairly bland, but adds a pleasant crunchy texture when added in small amounts to breads and crackers.

Rice flour can be found made from either brown or white rice. It adds a special delicate texture that is both fine and dense when added to baked goods. Rice flour is also used to thicken puddings.

Rye flour has a distinctive flavor that lends itself best to breads and crackers. Rye flour is dry and heavy, and contains no gluten. For best results, use rye flour for no more than one-third of the total flour in a bread recipe.

Soy flour is milled in three varieties: "full-fat," the all-purpose soy flour usually found in health-food stores; "minimum fat," used in the production of soy milk; and "low fat," used in baking. Soy flour can be added to baked goods in small amounts, to sauces and batters, and to other foods for its protein and its binding properties. Because of its strong flavor and heavy texture, ¼ to ½ cup is a sufficient amount to add to a standard cake or bread recipe. Soy flour is used as a binder replacement for eggs (see "eggless baking") and also to make soy milk and bean curd.

Buckwheat flour has a strong flavor and can be used in the same manner as rye flour.

Oat flour can be added in small amounts to baked goods.

EGG SUBSTITUTES AND BAKING WITHOUT EGGS

Eggs provide four things in baked goods: liquid, leavening, binding, and lightness. When another food is substituted for eggs, all four qualities must be taken into account.

Liquid: One grade-A egg contains approximately ¼ cup liquid. However, eggless cake batters should be slightly thicker than ordinary batters, so add extra liquid cautiously. Eggless baked goods tend to be moist, so butter pans well, and use springform cake pans.

Leavening: Leavening in baked goods prepared with baking powder and soda is caused by the reaction of the baking powder and soda (alkaline) when it meets with the moist milk and other ingredients (acid). Carbon dioxide is produced, which leavens the batter. To give the increase of leavening that is necessary when eggs are not used, the acid-alkaline reaction must be increased. Since baking powder and soda destroy B vitamins when used in large amounts, it is not desirable to increase them. Rather, an acid liquid is used: either sour milk or buttermilk. Yogurt and sour cream can also be used. The use of sour milk or buttermilk without eggs tends to make some batters gluey when baked. A mixture of half water and half sour milk or buttermilk provides a good balance. *Sometimes* the use of sour milk or buttermilk alone works—but for safety it is best to use the diluted mixture, which always works. Consult the index for the recipe for sour milk.

Eggless cakes made with 100 percent bleached white flour rise unevenly. Unbleached white flour, or a mixture of white flour and whole wheat flour, should be used for smooth and even rising.

Binding: A binder is particularly desirable in pancake, fritter, and tempura batters, which must spread out, yet hold together. Binders are not absolutely necessary in all baked goods—our muffin recipes do not contain a binder—but they certainly help in many cases. The following is an inexpensive and very effective homemade binder:

Binding Powder

½ cup soy flour
½ cup arrowroot or cornstarch

Mix the ingredients together well. Store in a closed jar. Makes 1 cup.

Two tablespoons of binding powder substitute for one egg, and are enough to bind most standard cake and quick bread recipes. Oat flour and potato flour could also be mixed into binding powder.

Lightness: In addition to proper leavening, there are a few points that are helpful in achieving lightness:

• Mix batter only enough to blend all the ingredients. Overbeating develops glu-

ten in the flour and toughens the final product.

• The use of baking soda as part of the leavening tenderizes the batter.

• Creaming the butter and sugar together as the first step in preparing a batter helps give a lighter effect.

• The use of milk or a dairy product rather than water alone in the batter makes the final product tenderer.

• Unbleached white flour gives a lighter result than whole wheat or heavier flours.

Egg replacements for vegetable dishes, burgers, and bean and grain loaves: Béchamel sauce, mashed potatoes, sour cream, tahini, and nut butters all help hold foods together. The idea is not to think of a substitute for eggs, but rather to create combinations of foods which will hold their shape. Crumbly ingredients such as whole grains or nuts need a soft and sticky ingredient to hold them together. Look at some of the recipes for casseroles and burgers to see the principle at work.

LEAVENINGS

Leavenings produce carbon dioxide in moist batters or doughs, causing them to rise and lighten during the baking or cooking. Baked goods made without leavening are heavy and somewhat crumbly.

Leavenings may be affected by hard water and by high altitudes. See the sections on "water" and "high altitude baking" for information.

Baking powder is a quick-acting leaven. Use a baking powder that does not contain aluminum, which is harmful to the body. Tartrate baking powders and baking powders made with calcium acid phosphate do not contain aluminum. Such non-aluminum baking powders are characterized by the fact that they start their leavening action as soon as they come into contact with moisture in the batter. For this reason they should be stored away from moisture, and a batter should be cooked immediately after it has been prepared to make use of the full leavening action. The longer the batter stands, the weaker the final leavening will be.

It is best not to handle baking powder batters after they have been placed in the oven. A beautifully rising loaf or cake can collapse if poked or jiggled too enthusiastically, or if the oven door is slammed shut.

Baking soda is another quick-acting leaven. It is highly alkaline and its meeting with an acid liquid causes a strong acid-alkaline reaction, producing the carbon dioxide that leavens the batter. Very little baking soda is necessary to leaven batters. Buttermilk, sour milk, yogurt, and molasses, all of which are highly acid, strengthen the reaction of the baking soda. Baking soda can be used alone in such highly acid batters, but for best overall results use a small amount of baking soda as an assist to baking powder—just to give it a little extra lift.

Yeast: Baker's yeast is made of living microorganisms. They feed on the sugars caused by the chemical changes in the flour and produce carbon dioxide in the process, which leavens the dough. Yeasts die when exposed to high temperatures, so their leavening action ceases when they are baked or cooked.

Yeast may be purchased loose in jars, in packages, or in pressed cakes. Store yeast in the refrigerator to keep it fresh and inactive. Check the date stamped on the package or jar to make sure that it is fresh.

Yeast begins to activate at about 60°F., thrives between 70° and 80°, and dies between 138° and 143°. Use lukewarm liquids in the dough and let it rise in a warm place. A slightly warmed oven, near the pilot light on the range, or the top shelf in a warm room will provide sufficient warmth. Salt and oil retard the growth of yeast. The use of nonfat milk facilitates rising slightly more than the use of whole milk.

Let yeast doughs rise only until "doubled in bulk," or else the yeast will burn itself out. For more information on rising yeast doughs, see the introductory information in the Breads section.

THICKENERS

Thickeners add body to the liquids in soups, sauces, puddings, stews, pie fillings, and gravies.

Agar agar is extracted from red algae, and provides an effect similar to that of gelatin in molded salads and desserts. It also serves as an emulsifier in ice creams and frozen desserts. Agar agar comes in bundles, bars, and flakes; the flakes are very easy to use. Agar agar is a good substance to become familiar with. It can be found in most health-food stores.

The recipes in this book call for agar agar flakes which thicken one quart of liquid with one tablespoon of flakes. Erewhon Trading Company of Boston markets an inexpensive and effective product.

Arrowroot and cornstarch: Arrowroot, or kuzu root, is well-known in China and Japan. Cornstarch is also widely used in the orient, as well as in Europe and the West. Both thickeners may be used interchangeably to thicken sauces, puddings, and pie fillings. They may also be used as emulsifiers for frozen desserts and ice creams and as substitutes for the binding properties of eggs. Arrowroot and cornstarch may be mixed with other non-wheat flours for a wheat flour substitute.

Arrowroot has more nutritive value than cornstarch, and has a neutral flavor as opposed to the slight flavor that cornstarch adds to a dish. On the other hand, cornstarch should be used instead of arrowroot for dishes containing acid foods, and in dishes where the thickening must hold for more than a day.

One tablespoon of arrowroot or cornstarch thickens one cup of liquid. Mix the arrowroot or cornstarch with a small amount of the liquid until free of lumps. Bring the remaining liquid to a simmer. Stir in the arrowroot or cornstarch mixture and continue to simmer—not boil—for 2 to 3 minutes to gain the full thickening effect. The food will be thicker still when it has cooled.

Flour: Unbleached white and whole wheat flours are commonly used to thicken soups, gravies, stews, and sauces. Rice, soy, and chick-pea flours may also be employed in the same manner. The most effective method of thickening liquids with flour is to make a roux, which is considered one of the foundations of western cooking. Memorize the proportions.

Roux

Use 2 tablespoons flour and 1 to 3 tablespoons butter to thicken 1 cup of liquid.

Melt the butter in a saucepan. Stir in the flour with a whisk. Cook over a low flame for a minimum of 1 minute, stirring constantly with a whisk to remove lumps. If a browned roux—which gives the dish a nut-like flavor and has a slightly reduced holding power—is desired, cook the roux, stirring constantly, until the flour turns light brown.

For best results, remove the roux from the heat for a few minutes, though this step may be omitted. Then stir in the liquid and beat with a whisk to remove lumps. Bring to a simmer for a few minutes to thicken. Do not boil.

Tapioca is derived from the root of a plant, and is used to thicken fruit sauces, pie fillings, and its own pudding. Tapioca flour or quick-cooking tapioca should be used to thicken sauces and fruit pie fillings. One or two tablespoons of tapioca thicken four cups of fruit mixture. Let the tapioca soak with the fruit mixture for 15 minutes before cooking.

Powdered milk can be used to thicken everything from dessert candies and puddings to sauces and stews. It is usually used in addition to another thickener, or in dishes that need only a light thickening. Use noninstant powdered milk for best results, and add to cool liquids to avoid lumps. As powdered milk can have a pronounced flavor, use sparingly or use in dishes that contain spices or strong flavors of their own. There is no rule for amounts, as the amount depends on the type of dish to which the milk powder is added. Just pour in and stir until the desired effect is achieved.

Sunflower meal fills in vegetable-based sauces and stews to give a thicker effect. It also adds a slight texture and flavor. Stir a small amount of sunflower meal into a finished dish, and add more until the desired effect is achieved.

Grain and cereal thickeners fill in soups and stews. Grains such as barley and rice also may add a small amount of powdery starch which thickens the liquid as well. Add to soups or stews:

rice	farina
semolina	barley
bulgar	buckwheat
oats	cracked wheat

Simmer for the amount of time that each needs to cook. Remember that grains expand to three times their size, and absorb twice their dry volume in liquid, when cooked for their *minimum* cooking time. If cooked longer, they will expand further and absorb more water: i.e., ½ cup white rice cooked for 20 minutes will absorb 1 cup of water and equal 1½ cups cooked rice. Only a few tablespoons of grains are needed to thicken most soups and stews.

Vegetable thickeners: Soups and stews may be thickened with grated raw potato, sweet potato, yams, winter squash, or other starchy vegetables. The grated vegetables should be cooked in the soup or stew for at least 20 minutes.

Cooked vegetable purees add body, flavor, and color to soups and stews. Use purees as a *replacement* for some of the cooking liquid.

HERBS AND SPICES

The difference between an herb and a spice is more of a culinary distinction than a botanical classification. Herbs are generally regarded as the flavorful leaves of certain plants, and spices as the fragrant roots, seeds, and fruits. Besides flavoring dishes, the original contribution of herbs and spices to mankind was their medicinal value. The most ancient records of almost all cultures contain information about the medicinal values of different plants. It may be of interest to the cook to read some books on herbal medicine and learn about the effects of the ingredients we use to flavor our foods.

The art of seasoning foods is one of the most essential and subtle aspects of cooking. No herb and spice chart can offer more than superficial aid. Experience, coupled with a little knowledge, is the ultimate guide.

Use herbs and spices lightly—they are intended to add just an impulse of flavor that enlivens a dish and enhances its flavors.

Fresh herbs retain the greatest amount of flavor and potency. A small herb garden can easily be grown in a garden plot or a windowbox or flowerpots. Mince, crush, or lightly bruise fresh herbs to release their flavor.

To dry herbs: Tie sprigs of fresh herbs into bundles and hang from their stem ends in a dark, airy place, such as a well-ventilated attic, until they are dry and brittle. Store dried herbs in tightly lidded jars in a cool, dark place. Crumble before adding to dishes. A general rule is that ½ teaspoon of crumbled dried herbs equals 1 tablespoon of minced fresh herbs.

Spices retain the greatest amount of their flavorful oils if purchased whole and ground in a mortar and pestle or a small electric coffee grinder just before using. If only ground spices are available, purchase them in small quantities and store in tightly closed jars.

ALLSPICE *(pimenta officinalis)* was introduced to Europe from Jamaica by Christopher Columbus. Allspice is derived from the berry of the pimiento, and contains flavors resembling those of cinnamon, juniper, nutmeg, and cloves. Allspice is used most successfully in desserts and baked goods.

ANISE *(pimpinella anisum)* is a member of the parsley family. In ancient Greece it was hung over the bed to ward off nightmares. The licorice-flavored seeds may be added to baked goods and Indian-style spiced vegetables, and may be brewed into a sweet, soothing tea.

ASAFOETIDA is the dried resin of a root. The highest-quality asafoetida comes in a hard lump, and the amount needed is scraped off with a knife blade. The unique flavor of asafoetida enhances Mexican and Indian foods. Sauté a small amount of asafoetida in oil before adding it to a dish.

BASIL *(Ocium basilicum)* is a major herb in Italian cooking. It may be added to almost all vegetable, grain, and bean dishes, and is excellent in green salads. There is no comparison between the flavors of the fresh and the dried leaves. If one is going to grow one herb, it should be basil.

BAY LEAVES *(laurus nobilus)* were used in the early Greek ceremonies dedicated to Apollo. They are added whole to soups, sauces, and stews, and are removed before serving. Bay trees grow in the western U.S. and the leaves may be gathered fresh.

CARAWAY SEEDS have been found in the remains of meals consumed 5,000 years ago. In ancient Germany they were placed beneath a baby's crib to protect the child. Today the seeds are commonly found in German and European cooking. They are good in cabbage and potato dishes, and can be sprinkled in or on top of breads, crackers, and rolls. Caraway seeds become bitter if cooked more than half an hour, so add them to vegetable dishes during the last portion of the cooking.

CARDAMOM *(Elettaria cardamomum)* was called "grains of paradise" by the ancient Arabians. Cardamom may be purchased in whole pods, and the seeds are removed and ground just before use. Cardamom is often found in Indian sweets and curries and in Scandinavian baked goods. It also enhances fruits and fruit salads. Cardamom seeds may be chewed as a natural breath freshener.

CAYENNE and CHILI PEPPERS add hotness rather than flavor to foods. They are a matter of taste, and proportions have not been given for their use in recipes. They may be added by those who like them in the preferred amounts.

The hotness of these peppers is increased by sautéing them in oil before adding to foods. Use dried red chilies either whole, crumbled, or ground. Green chilies, some varieties called jalapeños, are found fresh and are somewhat milder than red chilies. They may be sliced or minced. Cayenne is usually found in a powdered form.

Great care must be taken when handling cayenne and chilies not to touch the eyes or other mucous membranes until the hands have been thoroughly washed. The peppers may be prepared and sliced under running water to avoid skin irritation. The seeds are the most potent part and can be discarded if a milder effect is desired. When adding peppers to a dish, remember that the full effect of the hotness will not be felt until about thirty seconds after eating them.

CELERY SEEDS may be added to soups, stews, and vegetable dishes for a celery flavor.

CHERVIL is used largely in France, where it is one of the classic "fines herbes." It can be added to green salads and combines well with spinach.

CILANTRO, or FRESH CORIANDER LEAVES, has a strong distinctive flavor that is found in Mexican and Indian foods, as well as those of Northern China. Use only the leaves and add in small amounts. Cilantro can be served raw or lightly cooked.

CINNAMON *(Cinnamon Zeylanicum)*, or true cinnamon, is usually replaced by its near relative, *cinnamomum cassia*. The Bible mentions cinnamon as one of the spices in the oil with which Moses anointed the tabernacle. Cinnamon is the most widely used and versatile dessert spice. It may be added to almost any sweet dessert or baked food. Cinnamon may be purchased ground or in tight curls of bark. The sticks are an aesthetic addition to beverages, but don't try to grind them into powder; as many wood splinters are produced as powder.

CLOVES *(eugenia caryophyllus):* The word "clove" is derived from the French word for nail. Cloves are the unopened buds of a tree grown mostly in Zanzibar. Ground cloves may be added in small amounts to most sweet baked goods and desserts, and whole cloves may be added where they can later be removed—puddings, beverages, and so forth. Whole cloves may be brewed into a tea. Cloves have long been chewed to freshen the breath. The emperor of China in 26 B.C. declared that each person who came into his presence must have a clove in his mouth!

CORIANDER *(coriandrum satium)* may be added to vegetable and bean dishes for a pungent, slightly sweet flavor. Coriander is most often found in the foods of India and Mexico. Also see cilantro, or fresh coriander leaves.

CUMIN is one of the most frequently used spices in the cuisines of Mexico, India, and the Middle East. The seeds may be used whole or ground. In either case, they are most effective when either dry-roasted in a skillet until fragrant or sautéed in a little oil.

DILL *(anethum graveolens)* is mentioned in ancient Egyptian texts. Dill seeds can be used to flavor burgers, casseroles, and grain dishes. The feathery tops, or dill weed, are used in salad dressings, soups, stews, and vegetable dishes. Dill weed goes very well with potatoes. Sprinkle dill weed over salads and other foods for a decorative effect.

FENNEL, like dill, possesses both seeds and a feathery top which are used to season foods. Fennel seeds may be brewed into a tea, and both the seeds and tops are used to flavor dishes and give them a slight licorice taste.

FENUGREEK or FENOEGREEK *(trigonella foenum-graecum):* These versatile seeds can be sprouted, brewed as a tea, or ground and used as a spice. Fenugreek is often a major ingredient in curry powder, and may be added to Indian dishes. Fenugreek is delicious added to salad dressings in small amounts.

GINGER *(zingiber piperita)* is mentioned both in *The Analects of Confucius* and in the Koran. Fresh ginger is found in almost all the cuisines of South and East Asia. Dried ground ginger is used in baked goods and Western desserts. A candied form of ginger is found in Chinese dishes. The four types do not give an equal effect—fresh ginger can never really replace ground ginger, and vice versa. Nevertheless, in a pinch: 1 teaspoon fresh minced ginger equals ¼ teaspoon ground ginger, *or* 1 teaspoon dried ginger simmered in water for 10 minutes, *or* 2 teaspoons candied ginger with the sugar rinsed off.

Store fresh ginger root in the refrigerator away from moisture. Slice off the necessary amount (a little goes a long way), peel, and mince fine, or leave whole and remove just before serving. A bite into a whole piece of fresh ginger is more than the average person cares to experience. Also see ginger-flavored oil, on page 38.

MACE and NUTMEG come from the same fruit. Mace is the dried ground fruit and nutmeg is the core. Pliny listed both spices as the basis for perfume. The Arabs exported them to Europe in the sixth century, and by the twelfth century they were the costliest spices available. Use ground mace in desserts and sweet baked goods. Grate whole nutmeg kernels on a fine grater for desserts and into warmed, sweetened milk. Nutmeg also goes particularly well with spinach.

MARJORAM and OREGANO *(origanum marjorana):* The name is derived from the words for "joy of the mountains" of the ancient Greeks, and covers a number of similar herbs, including marjoram, sweet marjoram, and oregano. Marjoram and oregano are used largely in the cuisine of Italy, and may be added to vegetables, soups, stews, salad dressings, and sauces.

MINT: There are many varieties of mint, spearmint and peppermint being the most common. Mint needs little care to thrive—it grows and spreads lavishly. It can be brewed into a tea, or sprinkled on peas or fruit salads. Mint is used extensively in the cooking of the Middle East.

MUSTARD SEEDS (*brassica nigra,* black; *brassica alba,* yellow) have been found in the ruins of Harrappa and Mohenjo Daro. The Egyptians used them whole, while the Romans ground them and used them as a table seasoning. Yellow mustard seeds are used whole in chutneys and can be added to salads. Ground mustard is added to sauces and salad dressings. Black mustard seeds are found in Indian cooking. Sauté black mustard seeds in oil until they "dance," or begin to pop, before adding to foods. Also see mustard oil, on page 38.

PAPRIKA was first brought to Europe from Central America. It is derived from tetragonna peppers and comes in mild and hot varieties. The hot varieties contain the stalks and seeds. Paprika is used as much for its fiery orange color as for its flavor. Sprinkle paprika for a decorative effect on vegetables, salads, casseroles, and other foods. Paprika scorches and turns brown if exposed to high temperatures.

PARSLEY (*petroselinum sativam*) is frequently used as a garnish, either in sprigs or minced. Parsley has an excellent flavor that comes into its own when added to soups, stews, and vegetable dishes, or when added raw to salads. Parsley may be juiced and added in small amounts to other vegetable juices.

PEPPER (*piper nigrum*) was long one of the most costly spices in the West. White pepper is preferable to black, as it is simply the ripe berry with its husk removed, while black pepper is both unripe and cured. Use whole peppercorns and grind in a pepper mill.

ROSEMARY (*rosemarinus officinalis*) was once believed to grow only in the gardens of the righteous. It was often burned in place of incense in the churches of early England. Rosemary leaves may be used whole or ground. They are very potent, and a small amount enhances soups, stews, and vegetable dishes. Rosemary may also be brewed into a tea.

SAFFRON (*carthamus tinctorius*) threads are the stigma of a crocus grown largely in Spain and in India. About 7,000 crocuses are required to produce one pound of saffron! Fortunately a little saffron goes a very long way. Soak saffron threads in hot water for about half an hour to produce the delicate flavor and golden color for which saffron is prized. Powdered saffron does not need to be soaked. Add saffron to grains, milk, and desserts. Saffron can also be brewed into a tea.

SAGE was used as a medicine in Arabia, and Charlemagne promoted its cultivation throughout his empire. Fresh sage has a flavor that cannot be matched by the dried, ground product. Add crushed sage to soups, stews, and casseroles. Sage goes nicely with corn. Sage leaves can be dipped in tempura batter and deep-fried. Sage may also be brewed into a tea.

SAVORY: Winter savory is usually added to stews, and summer savory can be used with green beans, potatoes, salad dressings, and bean dishes.

TARRAGON, or ESTRAGON (meaning "little dragon" in French) can be added to vegetable dishes, sauces, and salads.

THYME (*thymus vulgaris*) was added to the baths of Roman soldiers to give them vigor. In the Middle Ages, ladies would embroider sprigs of thyme on decorations they would present to their knights. Thyme is a popular herb in Italian cooking, and in Sweden it is a classic in yellow split-pea soup. Thyme is used largely in American Creole cooking. Thyme may be added to almost any dish.

TURMERIC *(curcuma onga)*, with its golden color and strong flavor, is a major spice in Indian cooking and major ingredient in curry powder. Turmeric requires cooking to bring out its flavor. A pinch of turmeric can add a golden color to crackers and flat breads. A little sugar softens the sometimes harsh taste of turmeric.

FLAVORINGS AND SEASONINGS

SALT has been a major flavor enhancer throughout history. A *little* salt makes the food delicious. Natural sodium already exists in many foods. Besides bringing out flavor, salt also dehydrates foods. A small amount may be added to the cooking water of vegetables to keep them firm, while for the same reason salt should not be added to the cooking water of beans.

Table salt is derived from the chemical compound of sodium chloride, and usually contains additives to keep it free-flowing.

Iodized salt is table salt with the addition of iodine, originally produced to supply people living in inland areas with the small amounts of iodine necessary for maintaining the health of the thyroid gland.

Sea salt is derived from sun-dried sea water, and can be obtained from health-food stores. It has a slightly "saltier" flavor than table salt, so a little less is necessary to flavor foods. While sea salt contains no additives, and contains the natural iodine and minerals from the sea, it also contains whatever polluting substances may be in the sea water.

Coarse or *Kosher salt* is coarse-grained sea salt.

Herb salts and *seasoned salts:* For extra flavor salt can be mixed with powdered herbs, dried vegetables, and nutritional yeast. Read the labels on commercial seasoned salts to make sure that they do not contain monosodium glutamate or other unwanted additives. Powdered broth mixes can also be used as a seasoning.

To make seasoned salts at home, grind herbs, spices, and salt together in a blender or spice grinder. Use approximately 1 part salt for 7 to 10 parts herbs and spices. Try different combinations of the following:

allspice	pepper
basil	rosemary
mace	thyme
oregano	toasted sunflower,
coriander	sesame, or pump-
marjoram	kin seeds
mustard seed	curry powder
nutmeg	nutritional yeast
paprika	celery, caraway, and
dried parsley	dill seeds
kelp or other sea	
greens	

Here is a good combination:

Seasoned Salt

¼ cup sea salt
½ teaspoon each rosemary, basil, sage, curry powder
1 teaspoon each paprika, coriander, celery seed
4 teaspoons toasted sesame seeds

Grind all the ingredients together in a blender or spice grinder. Use as a table and cooking salt.

Gomasio (Japan)

10 parts sesame seeds
1 part sea salt

Dry roast the sesame seeds and salt together in a frying pan. Grind the mixture, a little at a time, in a blender or spice grinder. This is a sesame salt that can be used as a table seasoning. It allows one to use less salt and achieve wonderful flavor, with a little protein thrown in.

Low Sodium and Salt-free Diets

Those who wish to reduce without eliminating their salt intake can use seasoned salts and gomasio. For those who must completely restrict their salt intake, lemon juice is the greatest friend. Lemon juice can be added to the cooking water of foods or sprinkled over them before serving. Also become acquainted with the various herbs and spices. Liberal use of chopped fresh parsley and other green herbs, particularly basil and tarragon, can perk up foods. As fresh herbs have more flavor than dried ones, an herb garden is particularly recommended.

Cooking vegetables by baking, sautéing, stir-frying, or deep-frying in oil or ghee brings out their flavors. If the use of oil is also restricted, try the water-free cooking methods, such as baking, or steaming with a steaming basket. Do not overcook foods. Present contrasts in other ways besides flavor. Contrasts in texture and color can add to the overall effect of producing an interesting meal.

Other Seasonings

KELP, DULSE AND OTHER SEA GREENS are used as seasonings, notably in Japan. They contain sea salt and have a distinctive sea flavor. Kelp can be purchased in a powdered form in health-food stores. Other sea greens can be simmered in water or broth that is to be used in soups, stews, and so forth. See kombu broth, page 139. Dulse can be used to flavor desserts as well as vegetable dishes.

CURRY POWDER is not, as one would expect, used frequently in authentic Indian food. A good curry powder can certainly be added to all types of sauces, vegetable dishes, and salad dressings.

Garam masala is a spice mixture designed to be added to Indian-style vegetable dishes and soups in the last few minutes of cooking. There are many versions of garam masala—cooks may have their own favorite mixture, or a recipe passed down by their mothers and grandmothers. In any case, spices that do not require long cooking to bring out their flavors are usually used.

Garam Masala (India)

2 teaspoons each: coriander, cinnamon, cardamom
1½ teaspoons cloves
1 teaspoon mace
1 teaspoon pepper (optional)
1 tablespoon cumin

Toast the spices separately, then mix together. Store in a tightly closed jar. This recipe makes about ¼ cup.

ROSEWATER and ORANGE FLOWER WATER are subtle flower essences used for flavoring desserts. Rosewater is found in the cooking of India, and both rosewater and orange flower water are found in the Middle East. Add just at the end of cooking to mild-flavored puddings, halvas, ice cream, and sweet sauces, as well as to sweet yogurt and milk beverages. Just a few drops are enough to add a subtle, almost undefinable flavor.

GRAIN COFFEE POWDER gives a lift to stews and sauces that are just lacking in "something." Grain coffee powder may also be added in small amounts to non-fruit baked goods and desserts as a substitute for vanilla. Add about a teaspoon to desserts, and ¼ teaspoon or less to stews and savory dishes.

GRATED LEMON AND ORANGE RINDS, or "ZESTS," may be added to sweet puddings, sauces, and baked goods to add a fresh, tart flavor. Use only fresh rinds from undyed fruits, if possible. Grate the colored part only on a fine grater.

HERB TEAS add fine flavor when used as the liquid in sweet and sour sauces, chutneys, and fruit desserts. Mint, rose hip, and hibiscus teas are especially successful. Experiment cautiously until you have a good idea of what effect the flavors will have on a dish.

The Recipes

Hors D'Oeuvres, Snacks, and Savories

Almost every culture has a tradition of small tidbits that are served as a first course, as snack food, or that go together to comprise a full and varied meal. Call them hors d'oeuvres in France, zakuski in Russia, meze or mazza in Greece and the Middle East, for a first course; or partake of a Scandinavian smorgasbord, a Spanish tapas, or a Chinese dim sum lunch for a full meal. Whatever the purpose or occasion, there are many dishes that are adaptable and few rules to follow.

If the foods are intended as an introduction to a meal, it is best that they be light—enough to provide interest without filling up the stomach. Unless one has warming plates and chafing dishes, it is best to serve hot hors d'oeuvres to small gatherings and cold, longer-lasting foods at large gatherings and on buffet tables.

Presentation is especially important with tidbits. Imaginative decoration and other evidences that care and attention have been bestowed on the food add greatly to the enjoyment of it. Try garnishes of parsley, mint, or cilantro sprigs, lemon and lime slices, strips of attractively cut vegetables, or sprinklings of sunflower, sesame, and poppy seeds. Serving cold foods in platters or bowls set in larger bowls of crushed ice provides a cooling psychological effect as well as practical refrigeration.

Simple foods attractively presented are often the best. Pass two or three of the following, providing napkins, forks, or toothpicks if necessary:

roasted nuts or seeds

roasted, salted garbanzos or soybeans
deep-fried lima beans
chana snack (page 131)
mixed raisins, sunflower seeds, and nuts
dried fruit
thin slices of melon, whole strawberries,
    fresh figs, pineapple cubes
thinly sliced carrot and celery sticks,
    cucumber spears
decoratively cut radishes (the French
    serve them with butter and salt)
celery stalks and seeded cucumber spears
    stuffed with cream cheese or sand-
    wich spreads
slices of avocado and tomatoes
little balls of cream cheese rolled in
    ground nuts or coconut

HORS D'OEUVRE SALADS

Small salads can be served for hors
d'oeuvres on individual plates covered with
lettuce, in sturdy cabbage leaves, or in
other small, pretty containers. Try some of
the following:
    marinated vegetables
    radish salad
    three-bean and five-bean salads
    celeriac salad
    tomatoes stuffed with guacamole
    beet cups
    avocado salads
    raitas
    artichoke heart salad
    artichoke heart salad with yogurt
    cucumbers with yogurt, dill, and mint

DIPS

Dips are quite flexible—basically, they
are mixtures with a consistency that can
easily be scooped up with crackers. Besides bowls, containers in which dips can
be served include large seashells, sturdy
cabbage leaves, coconut shells, and other
decorative items.

Scoops for Dips
tostaditas
wheat germ sticks
chapatis, puris
carrot and celery sticks
firm lettuce leaves
whole radishes with the stems left on
wide green pepper strips
wheat crackers
pita cut into eighths
parathas
cucumber spears
young cabbage leaves

*Suggested Ingredients for Creating Your
Own Dips*
Base:
hung yogurt
cashew mayonnaise
mashed avocado
bean purees
sour cream
cream cheese softened with a little milk
steamed pureed vegetables
Flavorings:
chopped nuts or seeds
chopped avocado, tomato, green pepper,
    cucumber
vegetable and bean purees
minced parsley, watercress, spinach
grated vegetables
green herbs
curry powder and spices
caraway or sesame seeds
seasoned salt or gomasio
grated cheese

Simple Vegetable Dip

Serve raw vegetables with a salad dressing
or cashew mayonnaise for dipping.

Baba Ganooj (Arab countries)

A rich, tasty eggplant-potato dip that is
served with pita. Baba ganooj can also be

used as a filling for falafel sandwiches.

1 large eggplant
2 medium potatoes
½ cup olive oil
½ cup toasted sesame seeds
½ cup lemon juice
salt

Preheat the oven to 350°. Prick the skin of the eggplant with a fork and bake whole, until it is soft when pierced with a knife, about 45 to 60 minutes. Cool slightly, peel, and mash.

While the eggplant is baking, boil the potatoes until tender. Drain and mash. Combine the olive oil, sesame seeds, and lemon juice in a blender until smooth. Add the mashed eggplant and potatoes and blend again. Add salt to taste. Serve at room temperature. This recipe makes about 3 cups.

Variations

Substitute ½ cup prepared tahini for the oil and sesame seeds. Mash the mixture with a fork rather than in the blender, for a rougher texture.

Add cayenne or crushed red peppers.

Baba ganooj is sometimes given a smoky-charred flavor by the following method: Instead of baking the eggplant, spear it whole with a large fork and hold it over a flame or a gas range burner, turning it slowly until the skin is charred and blackened and the eggplant is tender. Peel and proceed with the recipe.

Bean-Cheese Dip

Try this as a topping for tacos and tostadas as well as for dipping.

⅔ cup kidney or pinto beans
2 tablespoons oil
1½ teaspoon roasted cumin
1 teaspoon salt
1 cup sour cream
¾ cup grated jack or cheddar cheese

Soak the beans overnight. Drain and cook in plenty of water until tender. Drain and mash.

Heat the oil in a skillet. Add the cumin and sauté for 1 minute. Add the mashed beans and mix well. Cook for 1 or 2 minutes; then remove from the heat and cool.

Beat in the salt, sour cream, and cheese (a blender may be used). Chill.

Serve with tostaditas. This recipe makes about 2 cups.

Variation

Add cayenne, crumbled red chilies, or chopped jalapeños to the oil when heated.

Borani (Iran)

Spinach puree with yogurt, encountered in different variations from Greece to Afghanistan.

1 pound spinach
¼ cup lemon juice
2 tablespoon olive oil
1 cup yogurt
1 teaspoon salt
½ teaspoon roasted cumin

Wash the spinach well and remove the stalks. Steam very lightly. Drain well and cool. Puree the spinach with the remaining ingredients in a blender. Chill.

Serve with pita. This recipe makes 2½ cups.

Variation

If there is no blender, chop the spinach very well after steaming and mix with the other ingredients.

Cream Cheese Dip

1 cup cream cheese (1 8-ounce package)
½ green pepper
1 teaspoon dill seed
1 teaspoon basil
1 teaspoon salt

¼ teaspoon curry powder
1 medium tomato
2 tablespoons toasted sesame or sunflower seeds

Combine all the ingredients in a blender until smooth. Chill. Makes a litle over 1 cup.

Guacamole (Mexico)

Guacamole is as excellent a sandwich spread and filling for tostadas and enchiladas as it is a dip. Though it is sometimes advised that this classic dip be prepared in the blender, a much better texture is achieved by mashing it roughly with a fork.

2 cups mashed avocado (about 2 large avocadoes)
2 tablespoons lemon juice
¾ teaspoon salt
fresh ground pepper

Mix all of the ingredients. Serve chilled with tostaditas. Makes about 2 cups.

Variations

Add 1 small chopped tomato.
Add cayenne or crumbled red chilies.
Add ¼ cup sour cream, ricotta, or cashew mayonnaise.
Add 1 or 2 tablespoons of minced parsley or watercress.

Homos (Middle East)

A spiced garbanzo puree that also works well as a sandwich spread.

1 cup garbanzos
¼ cup lemon juice
2 teaspoons roasted cumin
⅓ cup olive oil or thin tahini
1 teaspoon salt
pepper
2 tablespoons minced parsley

Soak the garbanzos overnight. Drain, then cook them in plenty of water until tender. Drain well and mash. Stir in the remaining ingredients. Serve at room temperature with pita. This recipe makes 2 cups.

Variation
Add a little chopped tomato or green pepper.

Sour Cream Dips

Sour cream makes a very good base for additions. Here is a simple dip that also works well as a salad dressing or as a dressing for baked potatoes. Hung yogurt can replace the sour cream for a more tart flavor.

2 cups sour cream
2 tablespoons minced parsley
¼ teaspoon paprika
¼ teaspoon celery seed
2 tablespoons toasted, ground sesame seeds
1 teaspoon tarragon
½ teaspoon salt

Mix all the ingredients together. Chill. Before serving sprinkle with paprika. This recipe makes 2 cups.

Variations

Omit the celery seed and tarragon, and add ¼ teaspoon curry powder.
Add mashed avocado, chopped tomato, or green pepper, or steamed, pureed vegetables.

Also see Soy Spread or Dip, page 187.

CANAPES

Canapes, tiny open-faced sandwiches on bread or crackers, often find their place at large gatherings and celebrations. As each canape represents about one mouthful, their flavor and their presentation must be memorable. To assist these little morsels in their cameo role, use whole-grain breads for more substantial flavor. Cut the bread slices into interesting shapes with a knife or cookie cutters. Crackers can be cut into interesting shapes before baking, if homemade ones are used. Apply smooth spreads with a pastry tube for a decorative effect. To create canapes, try using some of the following ingredients:

Spreads	*Toppings*
sandwich spreads	sunflower, sesame, poppy, or caraway seeds
cream cheese	
hung yogurt	
cashew mayonnaise	chopped nuts
firm dips	decoratively cut vegetables
	asparagus tips
	sprigs of parsley, cilantro, watercress
	melted cheese
	paprika
	curry powder
	garam masala
	green herbs

Suggestions for canapes

Crackers topped with guacamole and tomato strips.

Wheatberry bread topped with soy spread and green pepper strips.

Canape crackers topped with cream cheese-herb spread, asparagus tips, and watercress sprigs.

Crackers topped with homos, sesame seeds, and criss-crossed tomato and green pepper strips.

Tiny individual melted cheese sandwiches topped with sunflower seeds.

Tiny individual pizzas.

SAVORIES

While these dishes are not necessarily eaten as a first course in their native lands, they adapt very well to the purpose. They may also be served as a side dish or as part of the meal, or collected to form a full meal. Also try tempura (page 89), kofta (page 87), and falafels minus the pita bread, with a bowl of taratoor sauce for dipping (page 171).

Samosas (India)

Samosas must be one of the most delicious and aesthetically pleasing dishes on earth: a flaky, fluted pastry surrounding a spicy vegetable filling.

pastry:
2 cups unbleached white flour
¼ cup melted ghee or butter
½ cup water (approx.)

Sift the flour. Add the ghee and enough water to form a soft, non-sticky dough. Knead lightly a few times, cover, and set aside to rest while preparing the filling.

filling:
3 tablespoons ghee or butter
1½ teaspoons cumin
2½ cups potatoes, peeled and cut in small pieces
⅔ cup peas
1 teaspoon turmeric
1 teaspoon coriander
¼ teaspoon fenugreek
1 teaspoon salt
½ teaspoon sugar or honey
ghee or oil for deep-frying

Heat the ghee or butter in a skillet. Add the cumin and sauté for 1 minute. Add the potatoes and sauté for 10 to 15 minutes, stirring frequently, until they begin to soften. Add the peas, remaining spices, salt, and sugar or honey. Continue to sauté until the potatoes and peas are tender. Mash to a rough—not completely smooth—consistency. (The filling will be slightly salty to the taste, but when combined with the bland dough in the final result will have the correct seasoning.)

Divide the dough and roll into 1-inch balls. Roll out separately on a floured board with a rolling pin into 3½ inch circles. Cut each circle in half. Place a spoonful of filling on half of each half-circle. Fold the dough in half to form a triangle. Moisten the edges with a little yogurt or water and pinch closed. Be sure they are thoroughly sealed. (For a beautiful touch, along the

curved edge, starting at one end, pinch a little of the dough between the thumb and forefinger and twist over. Continue pinching and twisting along the edge to form a fluted pattern.) Deep-fry just until a pale golden color—do not brown. Drain on paper towels.

Serve plain or with mint chutney. This amount makes 25 to 30 samosas.

Variation
Replace the potatoes with finely cut cauliflower.

The following three dishes are widespread favorites from China—crispy fried noodles filled with vegetables and sometimes bean curd. They may be served as part of a meal or as a first course. Success is achieved by mincing the vegetables very fine before stir-frying them.

Spring Rolls (China)

noodle or soy noodle dough (page 201)
2 cups vegetables, finely minced and stir-fried with a ¼-inch piece of fresh ginger, peeled and minced (measure *after* stir-frying). Use at least 3 of the following: grated carrot, grated turnip, celery, mung

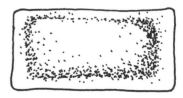

sprouts, green pepper, bok-choy, cabbage, spinach.

½ teaspoon sugar or honey
salt
white pepper
oil for deep-frying

Roll out the dough as for noodles. Cut into 4-by-5-inch rectangles.

Season the vegetables with the sugar, salt, and pepper. Place some of the filling on half of each rectangle. Fold over lengthwise to form a long, thin rectangle. Seal thoroughly. Trim any excess dough from the edges. Deep-fry until golden. Drain on paper towels. Serve plain or with a sweet and sour sauce for dipping. This amount makes 14 spring rolls.

Variation
Add sesame seeds to the noodle dough.

Won Tons (China)

Won tons are described in the soup section of this book, boiled and served in broth. Here they are pan-fried to accompany a Chinese meal or to serve as a first course.

noodle or soy noodle dough (page 201)
1 cup finely cut stir-fried vegetables (prepared as in preceding recipe)
1 cup well-drained, crumbled bean curd
½ teaspoon sugar or honey
salt
white pepper

Mix all the ingredients for the filling. Season to taste with salt and pepper.

Roll out the dough as for noodles. Cut in 3-inch squares. Place a spoonful of the filling on each square. Fold the dough in half and seal the edges thoroughly. Twist the two ends of the dough like a candy wrapper and press to hold their shape. Fry the won tons in ¼ inch of oil on each side until

golden brown and crispy. Drain on paper towels. Serve plain or with a sweet and sour sauce for dipping. This recipe makes 25.

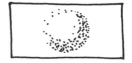

Potstickers (China)

Potstickers, the famous element of the dim sum lunch, are prepared with the ingredients for won tons. Instead of cutting the dough in squares, cut it out in 3-inch circles. Place a spoonful of filling on half of each circle. Fold the dough in half and seal the edge thoroughly. Fry as for won tons. The recipe makes about 25.

Pakoras (India)

Pakoras are spicy little tidbits made from chick-pea flour that may be plain or filled with vegetables or fresh cheese. They are delicious as a first course or served as part of an Indian-style meal. The use of chick-pea flour makes them very nutritious.

POTSTICKERS

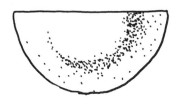

1½ cups chick-pea flour (besan)
¼ teaspoon baking powder
1¼ teaspoons salt
1 teaspoon turmeric
1½ teaspoons cumin
1½ teaspoons coriander
4 cups thinly sliced vegetables, sliced bananas, or cubed panir (use cauliflower, zucchini, potatoes, squash, green beans, or other vegetables)
1 to 1⅓ cups water
ghee or oil for deep-frying

Combine the chick-pea flour, baking powder, salt, and spices. Add water to make a thick batter—use the lesser amount for plain pakoras and a larger amount for filled pakoras. A blender may be used. Heat oil for deep-frying. For plain pakoras, drop spoonfuls of batter into the oil. For filled pakoras, dip the food in the batter, coat it thoroughly, and deep-fry until golden brown. Drain on paper towels.

Serve with chutney. This recipe serves 4.

Variations

Add cayenne or powdered red chilies to the batter.

For an inauthentic variation, dip cubes of mozzarella or cream cheese in the batter and deep-fry.

Prasad Pakoras

Place a generous dab of cream cheese between two thin slices of zucchini and press to hold. Dip in pakora batter and deep-fry.

Spinach-Potato Balls (India)

A tender, spicy filling with a crispy coating.

4 medium-large potatoes
1 tablespoon melted ghee or butter
1 teaspoon cumin
1 teaspoon turmeric
1 cup finely chopped spinach, packed
1 teaspoon salt
¾ cup farina (Cream of Wheat)
ghee or oil for deep-frying

Boil the potatoes until they are tender. Drain and peel. Mash the potatoes with the ghee or butter, cumin, turmeric, salt, and half the farina. Squeeze and roll the potato mixture into 1-inch balls. Roll each ball in the remaining farina to coat it thoroughly. Deep-fry the balls until browned. Drain on paper towels. Serve as part of an Indian meal or as a first course. This recipe makes 30 to 35 balls.

Knishes (Jewish)

A heavy-duty New York food, knishes are often deep-fried; these are baked to lighten the delicious load.

1 recipe pastry pie crust, with the wheat-germ variation (page 256), potato stuffing (page 188), or kasha stuffing (page 188)

Preheat the oven to 375°. Roll out the pie crust ⅛ inch thick on a floured board. Cut out ten circles 5 inches in diameter. Place a large spoonful of filling in the middle of each circle. Bring up the edges of the dough and pinch together to enclose the filling and form a sphere. Place the knishes seam-side down on a buttered baking sheet. Bake for 35 to 40 minutes, until golden brown. Serve hot. This recipe makes 10.

Piroshki (Russia)

Here is a group-sized amount of these rich, filling pastries. The pastry completely encloses the filling in some piroshkis; in this recipe, the dough forms a decorative cradle for the filling.

1¼ cups unbleached white flour
1¼ cups rye flour
1 teaspoon salt
⅔ cup butter
⅔ cup sour cream
a double recipe of potato stuffing (page 188)
1½ cups grated cheese
sesame or poppy seeds

Sift the flours and salt into a bowl. Add the butter and work with the fingers or a pastry cutter until the mixture resembles coarse meal. Add the sour cream. Mix until the ingredients can just hold together in a ball. For best results, wrap in waxed paper and chill for 1 to 6 hours, or prepare the night before and chill.

Pre-heat the oven to 375°. Roll the dough out ⅛ inch thick on a floured board. (If it has been chilled, let it sit at room temperature for 20 minutes first.) Cut out 4½-inch circles. Mix the cheese into the potato filling. Place a large spoonful of the filling in

the middle of each circle. Sprinkle the filling with sesame or poppy seeds. Bring up the dough, making little pinches in it to encase, but not completely enclose, the filling (see diagram). Place on a buttered baking sheet and bake for 30 to 40 minutes, until the crust is lightly browned. Carefully remove the piroshkis with a spatula. Serve hot. This recipe makes 20 piroshkis.

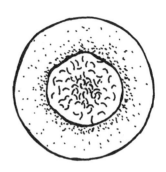

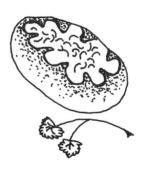

Variations

Use pastry pie crust for a less rich pastry.
Vegan Variation: Omit the grated cheese.

Fried Mozzarella (Italy)

Wonderful melted cheese in a crisp crust.
Other cheeses may be used in place of mozzarella, and this dish may be served either
as a first course or as an accompaniment to
a meal.

1 pound mozzarella or other cheese
tempura batter (page 89)
bread crumbs or breading mixture (page
189)
oil for deep-frying

Cut the mozzarella into cubes or rectangles. Dip the cheese first in the batter to
coat thoroughly; then roll it in the bread
crumbs or breading mixture. The coating
will be very gooey at this point. Gently
drop the cubes into the hot oil. Deep-fry
until golden and remove immediately. Drain
on paper towels and serve. This recipe
makes 4 servings.

Sushi (Japan)

There are many types of sushi—small,
beautifully presented tidbits. For this particular type, in Japan, sushi-makers—flat,
flexible screens of bamboo—are employed
to help roll them up. Nori can be obtained
from a health-food store or Japanese specialty market.

1 cup cooked rice
1 tablespoon lemon juice
2 teaspoons sugar or honey
¼ teaspoon salt
2 teaspoons sesame oil
⅛-inch piece fresh ginger, peeled and
minced
¼ cup each: grated carrot, slivered green
pepper, celery, turnip

8 or 9 strips nori sea greens, 1 inch by 6
inches

Mix the rice with the lemon juice, sugar
or honey, and salt. Set aside. Heat the oil
in a wok. Add the ginger and wait a minute
then add the vegetables. Stir-fry until crisp
but tender. Cool.

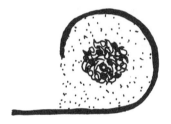

Toast the nori strips by waving them once or twice over a flame or a gas burner. They will crinkle slightly.

To assemble the sushi, lay out a nori strip. Spread a thin layer of rice on it, leaving ½ inch at one end and 1½ inches at the other end bare. Cover the rice with a thin layer of vegetables. Wet the 1½-inch end; roll the nori strip around the filling and tuck the ½-inch end into the wet 1½-inch end. They will stick together. Press in any stray rice kernels or vegetable bits and set upright. Repeat the process with each nori strip. Serve chilled or at room temperature. This recipe makes 8 to 9 sushi.

Variation

Other vegetables may be used, as long as there is an attractive color contrast.

Vadas (India)

Vadas, deep-fried balls of pureed lentils, are served in a variety of ways. They may be added to curries, and are found in Dahi Vada (page 130) in a cooling yogurt sauce. Here they are served in their own right, with perhaps a bowl of chutney for dipping.

1 cup lentils, yellow split peas, or urad dhal
½-inch piece ginger, peeled and sliced
1 teaspoon coriander
2½ teaspoons roasted cumin
1 teaspoon salt
½ teaspoon turmeric
chick-pea or soy flour
ghee or oil for deep-frying

Soak the beans overnight in plenty of water. Drain. Grind them to a smooth paste in a blender with just enough water to facilitate grinding. Grind in the ginger. Add the spices, and just enough chick-pea or soy flour to thicken the mixture enough to be dropped in rough teaspoonfuls from a spoon. Test the batter by dropping a little into a bowl of water. If it does not float, add ¼ teaspoon baking powder to the batter. Drop teaspoonfuls into hot ghee or oil, and deep-fry until they are golden. Check one to see if it is cooked through. Drain on paper towels.

Serve plain or with a fruit chutney. This recipe makes about 30 vadas.

Variation

Add cayenne or powdered red chilies to the batter.

Spinach Vadas: Add ¾ cup finely chopped spinach. Prepare the vadas from yellow split peas for an attractive color contrast with the green spinach.

Dolmathes (Greece)

Also called "dolmadas" or simply "dolmas," these are usually prepared from young grape leaves, but may also be made with large spinach leaves or tender young cabbage leaves.

3 tablespoons pine nuts
2 tablespoons olive oil
¾ cup raw rice
1½ cups stock or water (2¼ cups for brown rice)
3 tablespoons currants
few threads saffron
1½ teaspoons dry crumbled mint
salt
pepper
50 grape or cabbage leaves
2 tablespoons olive oil
lemon wedges

Sauté the pine nuts in the olive oil until golden. Add the rice and sauté for 1 minute. Pour in the stock. Add the currants, saffron, and mint. Bring to a boil. Cover and reduce the heat. Simmer until the water is absorbed. Season to taste with salt and pepper.

Blanch the grape leaves in boiling water for 1 minute. (If using cabbage leaves, blanch for 3 minutes.) Drain. Gently separate the leaves and lay flat, stem side up. Cover the bottom of a wide, heavy pot with 10 of the leaves. Place a spoonful of the

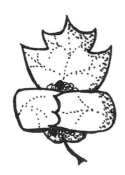

rice on the base of a separate leaf. Tuck in the sides of the leaf to cover the filling and roll up the leaf tightly to make a small,

compact package (see diagram). Continue the procedure with the rest of the leaves.

Place the dolmathes in the pot close together. If necessary, make a second row on top of the first. Pour water about ¼ inch deep in the pot. Drizzle the olive oil over the dolmathes.

Bring the water to a boil, cover, and reduce heat to very low. Simmer gently for 50 minutes. Gently remove the dolmathes from the pot and cool to room temperature. Serve with a wedge of lemon to sprinkle over them before eating.

Serve as a first course or with a Greek meal. This recipe makes 40 dolmathes.

ANTIPASTO (Italy)

Antipasto, or ''before the pasta,'' is, naturally, served as a first course before the pasta course in Italy. It is adaptable as a first course or salad course for any meal, or can be served as a summer lunch or dinner unto itself. To prepare an antipasto, arrange a bed of greens on a large platter, and decoratively arrange a variety of any or all of the following suggested ingredients. Serve with crusty Italian-style bread.

   slices of cheese
   spoonfuls of ricotta
   marinated cucumbers, beets, fennel, green beans, carrots, eggplant, zucchini, artichoke hearts
   marinated vegetables a la Grecque
   marinated kidney beans, white beans, and garbanzos
   3-bean or 5-bean salad
   radish salad
   whole cooked artichokes
   roasted peppers
   fresh sliced cucumbers, tomatoes, radishes, green pepper

Garnish with sprigs of parsley. Provide small plates and plenty of serving utensils.

MEZETHAKIA OR MEZE (Greece)

"Mezethakia," "opens the appetite" in Greek, becomes "Mazza" in the Arab countries—little tidbits that are eaten to allay hunger in the hours before the late dinner. Some restaurants in Greece and the Middle East feature tables with hundreds of these little dishes for the patrons to choose from.

Serve small dishes and bowls with a variety of the following suggested foods. Provide napkins, plates, and forks if necessary.

roasted salted almonds, pine nuts, sunflower seeds, pistachios (the Greeks also serve watermelon seeds)
roasted, salted garbanzos
nuts served with honey
marinated vegetables a la Grecque
marinated white beans and garbanzos
cubes of feta cheese
cucumbers with yogurt, dill, and mint
roasted peppers
fresh figs
dolmathes
melon cubes
steamed pureed vegetables dressed with olive oil
baba ganooj for Middle Eastern meal
homos for Middle Eastern meal
borani

Vegetables

SELECTION

For those without a garden plot, or without time or desire to tend a garden, skill in purchasing vegetables is the first step to successful vegetable cookery. Finding good produce may take a little investigation, but it is well worth the extra attention. If possible, find a store that carries undyed, unsprayed, untreated vegetables grown with natural fertilizers (compost). Since there is no national standard as yet for an "organically grown" or "naturally grown" vegetable, find out what your greengrocer means by such labeling.

Buying locally grown produce *in season* is an ancient and economically sound method of insuring freshness. Select firm, fresh-looking, unwilted, unshrivelled vegetables. Unsprayed vegetables may naturally have some insect marks on the surface, but these will not affect the quality of the vegetable—in one sense, it speaks of its high quality.

Many supermarkets prepackage their produce to speed up the check-out, to discourage customers from buying small amounts, and occasionally to hide a sad story at the bottom of the package with a cheery-looking vegetable or two at the top. Most areas have a produce market that buys directly from the farmers, where one can make one's own selection. Vegetables are stored in supermarkets with the oldest ones toward the front so that they will be bought first, so select from the vegetables toward the back.

STORAGE

All vegetables should be refrigerated, with the exception of potatoes, turnips, and rutabagas, which can be kept in a cool, dark place. Store apples and carrots separately, as the interaction of their chemical compositions may affect their flavors.

Clean the vegetable bin frequently, removing old bits of leaves and vegetables. Snip the leaves off root vegetables before storing, as the sap continues to flow out of the root into the leaves even after picking. (Save beet greens and turnip greens for cooking or salads.)

PREPARATION

The preparation of each vegetable is described under its individual heading. A few general guidelines:

- Wash vegetables just before cooking and just until clean. Soaking, with an occasional exception for eggplant, is not necessary, and leaches away vitamins and flavor.
- When peeling is desired, carefully pare away the skin only, in order to leave most of the vitamins, which lie close to the skin, intact.

- *Cutting:* See the cooking terms "slice," "dice," "chop," and "mince." Also see "knives" under kitchen utensils.

The Japanese have developed many imaginative cutting methods for vegetables, from simple slices to elaborate sculptured flowers. A few of the basic slices are:

DIAGONALS *(namame giri):* Slice vegetables thinly on the diagonal to expose more of the fibers for quicker cooking.

The diagonal cut is an indispensable slicing method for vegetables in all types of dishes.

SLIVERS *(sen-giri):* Slice vegetables on the diagonal, then pile them up four at a time and cut into matchstick-sized slivers.

CRESCENTS *(hangetsu-giri):* Slice rounded vegetables such as carrots or zucchini on the diagonal, then cut each round in half.

TRIANGLES: Slice rounded vegetables on the diagonal, then slice the rounds into quarters.

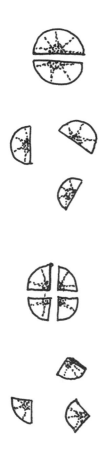

COOKING

As a general rule, light cooking, just to the point of tenderness, retains a maximum of flavors and nutrients. Older vegetables will need longer cooking than young ones.

Vegetables cooked in high-altitude areas will take longer to cook, as the boiling point of water is lower. See "high-altitude baking" (page 12) and "boil" (page 13). Also see the individual headings for various vegetables for approximate cooking times and suggested cooking methods.

Steamed Vegetables (see "steam," page 15). Steaming is perhaps the most widely used and best general method for preparing vegetables. Timing is the key to successfully steamed vegetables—they should be cooked just until done, drained, and served immediately. If steamed vegetables are to be served with a sauce, drain them very well. Vegetables may be steamed in milk, which helps sweeten sulphurous vegetables such as cabbage and cauliflower, but you must be alert for scorching. If steaming directly in water (without the use of a steaming basket), a little salt may be added to the water to keep the vegetable firm. A little lemon juice added to the water enhances the flavor of the vegetable.

Sautéed Vegetables (see "sauté," page 15). Sautéing greatly enhances the flavor of most vegetables. Use ghee, butter, or oil. All the vegetables we list below for stir-frying can be used, as well as tiny cubed potatoes and winter squash. Vegetables can be sautéed with green herbs or curry spices. Mix in sesame seeds or slivered nuts toward the end of the sautéing. Sauté chopped tomatoes to create a tomato sauce. Stir in a tiny drizzle of tahini or taratoor after removing from the heat. Add cubes of fried bean curd, gluten, or panir. Or simply serve sautéed vegetables with a little lemon juice or salt.

Baked Vegetables. A marvelous flavor results when vegetables are baked, as little or no water is added that will remove the natural juices. Most vegetables may be baked whole. However, one may cut them into halves or quarters to reduce the cooking time, which is desirable in the case of rutabagas, beets, turnips, and winter squash. Tomatoes may be halved crosswise, and zucchini, carrots, parsnips, and fennel may be halved lengthwise. All root vegetables, plus tomatoes, summer squash, and fennel (by the oil-free method), may be baked.

METHOD #1: Coat a baking pan and the prepared vegetables with a little oil or melted butter. Bake in a 350° oven until tender. See individual vegetable headings for approximate baking times.

METHOD #2 (Oil-free): Place prepared vegetables in a baking dish with a little water to keep from scorching. Cover and bake in a 350° oven until tender. One may add a little minced parsley, chopped tomatoes, green herbs, and olive oil, butter, and lemon juice when baking vegetables by this method, for better flavor.

Also see potatoes, yams, and sweet potatoes for baking methods.

Boiled Vegetables. Most vegetables fare much better, both nutritionally and in terms of flavor and texture, when steamed rather than boiled. However, boiling is acceptable for the following vegetables: potatoes, sweet potatoes and yams (because they are protected by their skins), artichokes (because they are cooked most evenly), and collard greens (to remove their bitterness). See their individual headings for approximate cooking times.

Deep-fried Vegetables (see "deep-fry," page 14). French-fried potatoes, of course, head the list of favorites. Celeriac, turnips, and rutabagas can also be french fired (page 112). Zucchini slices, cauliflower flowerets, and green beans may be deep-fried, producing a flavorful, if oily, result. Use ghee or a good-quality oil for the purpose. Have the vegetables as dry as possible before frying. Deep-fry until they just begin to brown, and drain them well on paper towels before serving.

Many vegetables may be deep-fried beautifully in batter. See the recipes for pakoras (page 67) and tempura (page 89).

Stir-fried and Kinpura-fried Vegetables (see "stir-fry," page 15). Almost all vegetables lend themselves well to the stir-frying technique. Vegetables which require longer cooking may be prepared by the kinpura technique, developed in Japan to combine steaming and stir-frying in a lightning-quick cooking method.

Kinpura-fried Vegetables

Prepare vegetables for stir-frying and begin to stir-fry. After about ten seconds, sprinkle a little water over the vegetables. The water will create steam, which will further cook them. After the water has been evaporated, sprinkle on a little more water. Continue sprinkling and stir-frying until the vegetables are sufficiently cooked. If desired, one may sprinkle and stir-fry several times, and then add enough water for steaming and cover and steam for the last five minutes. The important point is that the water should never collect in the bottom of the pot during the sprinkling, or it won't produce the necessary amounts of steam.

Vegetables Suitable for Stir-frying or Kinpura-frying

Spinach, bok-choy, cabbage, and other greens
celery
radish
okra
fennel
broccoli
asparagus
water chestnuts
cauliflower
snow peas
carrots
bamboo shoots
eggplant

green beans
lotus root
turnips and parsnips
burdock root
Jerusalem artichokes
peas (cooked with other vegetables)
tomatoes (cooked with other vegetables)
sprouts (mung sprouts are authentic; lentil sprouts also work well)

You will want to stir-fry many of the above vegetables as part of a vegetable mixture rather than by themselves. See the section on Japanese vegetable slicing methods (page 74) to achieve the thin slices and bits necessary for stir-frying.

Additions to Stir-fried Vegetables
sesame or sunflower seeds
blanched almonds or cashews
cubed or crumbled bean curd, stir-fried first
gluten strips, stir-fried first
boiled bean thread noodles

Sauces
Cornstarch- or arrowroot-thickened sauces may be cooked and thickened with the vegetables during the last minute of stir-frying.

sweet and sour sauce
sauce for Chinese-style foods
pineapple sweet and sour sauce

Serve stir-fried and kinpura-fried vegetables over rice, or puffed or boiled bean thread noodles.

Stir-fried Vegetables with Almonds (China)

2 tablespoons soy or sesame-flavored oil
¼-inch piece fresh ginger, peeled and minced
6 cups thinly sliced vegetables (use 8 cups if large amounts of sprouts or greens are included)
⅓ cup blanched almonds
sauce for Chinese-style foods (page 173)

Heat the oil in a wok. Add the ginger and sauté until it begins to brown. Add the vegetables and almonds. Stir-fry until crisp-tender. Add the sauce. Stir until thickened. Adjust the seasoning and serve immediately over rice. This recipe makes 4 servings.

Variations
Omit the sauce.
Replace the sauce with sweet and sour sauce.
Stir-fried Vegetables with Bean Curd: Omit almonds. Stir-fry or deep-fry 1 cup (½ pound) of cubed bean curd and add it to the vegetables just before adding the sauce.

Gluten Strips with Vegetables in Sweet and Sour Sauce (China)

Gluten is a wonderful food to get to know. It is a mainstay of Chinese-style vegetarian cooking. The following is a basic formula. The proportions of gluten to vegetables can be altered.

cooked gluten (page 180), drained well
4 cups thinly sliced vegetables
2 tablespoons soy or sesame-flavored oil
1½ cups sweet and sour sauce (page 173)
salt
white pepper

Cut the gluten into strips. Deep-fry or stir-fry until golden-brown. Set aside. Stir-fry the vegetables in the oil until almost tender. Pour in the sweet and sour sauce, add the gluten, and cook until tender, stirring very gently. Season to taste with salt and white pepper. Serve over rice. This recipe makes 4 servings.

Variation
Substitute sauce for Chinese-style vegetables for sweet and sour sauce.

VEGETABLE PUREES

Most vegetables can be transformed into delightful purees. Besides the familiar pureed potatoes and squash, try pureed peas, carrots, zucchini, cauliflower, Jerusalem artichokes, broccoli, or green beans—it can be like discovering entirely new vegetables.

To puree vegetables, steam twice the amount of vegetables as the desired amount for puree (i.e., 6 cups of peas will produce approximately 3 cups of puree). When the vegetables are very tender, drain, reserving the steaming water. Puree the vegetables in a food mill or food processor, or in a blender with just enough of the steaming water to blend. Add butter, milk powder or a little cream, and salt to taste. Try mixing colors, such as preparing a pea puree and a carrot puree, and serving them side by side. Vegetable purees can also be used to replace part of the water in a soup or stew for more thickness and flavor.

VEGETABLES WITH SAUCES

Vegetables may be served covered with or mixed with a sauce. Serving a steamed vegetable with a bowl of sauce passed at the table is a good idea for families where some members like their foods dressed up and others like them pure and simple. Just remember that a sauce is meant to enhance—not overwhelm—the vegetables it is served with. (Recommended sauces for individual vegetables are listed under the vegetables' headings.)

Creamed Vegetables

4 cups steamed, well-drained vegetables
2 cups béchamel sauce (page 167)

Mix the sauce into the vegetables and serve. This recipe serves 4 to 6 people.

Suggested vegetables: corn, peas, chopped spinach, carrots, green beans, Jerusalem artichokes, Brussels sprouts, mixed vegetables. Zucchini does not work quite as well because it is watery and dilutes the sauce.

Variations

Replace béchamel sauce with cottage cheese cream sauce (page 169).

Mixing a small amount of ricotta into steamed vegetables gives a creamy effect, though a slightly grainy appearance. Mixing ricotta with chopped spinach works particularly well.

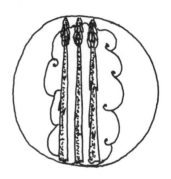

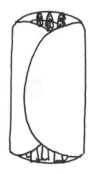

VEGETABLE CREPES

Vegetable-filled crepes make beautiful, light entrees and look very elegant. The ways to fill and top the crepes are endless.

Here are some suggestions for the creation of vegetable crepes.

1. Prepare crepes (page 231).
2. Fill with:

   creamed vegetables
   pureed vegetables
   vegetables Stroganoff
   vegetables Newburg
   ratatouille
   curried vegetables (any type)
   steamed or sautéed vegetables
   vegetables deluxe with rosemary

   and (if appropriate):
   slices of cheese
   ricotta, cottage cheese, sour cream, or yogurt
   taratoor sauce
3. Roll up the crepes, and cover simply filled crepes with:
   béchamel sauce or béchamel variations
   grated cheese
   tomato sauce
4. Sprinkle on top:
   slivered almonds, toasted if desired
   toasted sesame, sunflower, or pumpkin seeds
   chopped roasted nuts
5. If cheese is included in the crepes, place crepes in a 350° oven for 15 to 20 minutes to melt the cheese.
   Serve crepes immediately.

Suggested Combinations for Crepes

Crepes filled with creamed spinach, topped with melted cheese.

Crepes filled with asparagus tips, covered with auroré sauce.

Crepes filled with sliced, sauted artichoke hearts, covered with béchamel sauce and spinkled with roasted slivered almonds.

Crepes filled with ratatouille and covered with cheese sauce.

Crepes filled with eggplant-tomato curry and ricotta.

Crepe Cake

Instead of rolling up crepes in the traditional manner, pile layers of crepes with vegetable fillings, cheese, and anything else you wish between each layer to form cake. Top with a sauce and serve cut in wedges like a cake. For best results, use firm fillings.

INDIAN-STYLE SPICED VEGETABLES AND CURRIES

Indian-style spiced vegetable dishes are surprisingly quick and easy to prepare, in many cases. A wide range of flavors and textures are available, and it is good for the cook to become acquainted with the basic method. Spicing can be subtle—and the dish will certainly not be hot unless cayenne or chilies are added deliberately.

The word "curry" originates from "kadi," a thin sauce sometimes containing vegetables, and all the dishes lumped under the title of "curry" in the West are not considered as such in India. Indian spiced vegetables are usually categorized as being either "wet" or "dry"—that is, containing a liquid sauce or not. The sauces in the "wet" dishes are usually lighter and thinner than Western flour-based sauces.

The spicing of the vegetables is the most distinctive feature of the dishes, and, once mastered, it is the key to unlimited flavor combinations. Spices commonly used in vegetable dishes are:

   black mustard seed (yellow may be substituted in a pinch)
   cumin seeds, whole and ground
   turmeric

coriander
fresh sugar, peeled and minced
ground fenugreek
asafoetida, used in tiny amounts
cloves
cinnamon
cardamom
nutmeg and mace

For hotness, spices used are: cayenne, green fresh chilies, and dried red chilies, either whole, crumbled, or powdered.

Curry powder is not used much in India. However, a good-quality curry powder may be used as a base for other spices.

Garam masala (page 59) is added in small amounts to some dishes at the end of cooking.

Flavorings

Besides salt, a pinch of *sugar* is added to blend flavors. Grated toasted *coconut* is added in small amounts. Chopped *tomato* is added as a flavoring, particularly in North India and Pakistan. *Tamarind* gives a tart flavor to South Indian dishes. Soak in water, drain, and use the *water*. *Lemon* and *lime juice* are added to some dishes.

Vegetables

See list under "Special Ingredients in Indian-style cooking," page 29.

Additions to Curries or Spiced Vegetable Dishes

vadas (add just before serving)
pakoras (add just before serving)
cubes of deep-fried or pan-fried panir (add during last few minutes of cooking)
yogurt (add after cooking)
buttermilk (can be used in place of water)
chick-pea flour (for thickening)

TO PREPARE AN INDIAN-STYLE SPICED VEGETABLE DISH
1. Heat a little mild-flavored oil, ghee, or butter in a pot.

2. Add spices which must be sautéed in oil (cumin, mustard seed, fresh ginger, asafoetida, cayenne, and chilies all must be sautéed to bring out their flavor).
3. If either coconut or tomato is to be used, add it now. Sauté for a few minutes.
4. Add vegetables and remaining spices. Stir to coat with the oil and spices, then pour in just enough water to steam the vegetables, ½ to ¾ cup for 4 cups vegetables.
5. Cover and simmer until the vegetables are tender. If garam masala is to be used, add it just before removing the pot from the heat. If yogurt is to be added, remove the pot from the heat and cool for a few minutes before adding it.

To get acquainted with the spices and the technique, try preparing some of the recipes for Indian-style vegetables. Then try adding one or two of the spices while sautéing vegetables or preparing a stew, to get acquainted with their flavors and effects. Add a little ginger when sautéing spinach, some mustard seeds which have been sautéed in oil to a stew, a little cumin and turmeric (the cumin first sautéed in oil) and tomato to steaming green beans. As always, a light touch is desirable—conservative bravery will bring success—and will open up a whole new world of cooking.

Serve Indian-style spiced vegetables over rice, or with any of the Indian unleavened breads. For a complete meal, serve with a raita, dhal soup, and, if desired, a chutney.

Mixed Vegetable Curry #1 (India)

2 tablespoons ghee, melted butter or oil
¾ teaspoons black mustard seed
1 teaspoon cumin
2 medium tomatoes, chopped
1 cup finely cut cauliflower
⅔ cup finely cubed eggplant
⅔ cup finely cut green beans

⅔ cup peas
1 medium zucchini, quartered lengthwise and sliced
1 medium potato, diced, *or* 1 cup diced winter squash
1 teaspoon turmeric
½ teaspoon coriander
1 teaspoon salt
1 teaspoon sugar or honey
½ cup water

Heat the ghee, butter, or oil in a pot. Add the mustard seed and cumin, and sauté until the mustard seed "dances." Add the tomatoes, and cook for 2 to 3 minutes. Add the vegetables, remaining spices, salt, sugar or honey, and water. Bring to a boil, then cover and reduce the heat. Simmer until all the vegetables are tender, about 20 to 30 minutes.

Serve over rice or with Indian unleavened breads. This recipe makes 4 servings.

Variations
Add cayenne or red chilies to the oil with the cumin. Add vadas (page 71) after removing from the heat. After cooling for a few minutes, add ½ cup yogurt. Other vegetables may be used.

Mixed Vegetable Curry #2 (India)

A rich curry with a pleasant buttermilk base.

6 tablespoons ghee or butter
½ teaspoon salt
½ teaspoon cumin
½ teaspoon turmeric
½ teaspoon cinnamon
½ teaspoon fenugreek
¼ teaspoon cardamom
1 to 3 whole cloves
2 medium tomatoes, chopped
2 tablespoons chick-pea flour (or wheat flour)

2 cups buttermilk or whey
¾ cup each: peas, finely cut cauliflower, zucchini quartered lengthwise and sliced, thinly sliced carrots, finely cut green beans

Heat the butter or ghee in a pot. Add the salt. Add the spices in order at 30-second intervals. When all the spices have been added, add the tomatoes and cook until they have softened slightly. Mash with a fork while cooking. Add the flour; stir to distribute. Cook for 1 minute. Then slowly add the buttermilk or whey, stirring constantly. Add the vegetables. Cover and simmer for 45 minutes. Serve over rice. This recipe makes 4 servings.

Variation
Cayenne or red chilies may be added with the spices.

VEGETABLE STEWS

Stews are prepared in the same way that one would prepare a thick soup. They are great for winter meals and make excellent use of small amounts of vegetables, beans, and grains that remain in the pantry. Stews can be made from any vegetable. Hearty winter stews usually contain potatoes. Tomatoes add flavor to the stew. To prepare a stew:

1. Sauté the vegetables and green herbs for five minutes in a little butter or oil for best flavor.
2. Add broth or water just to cover. Add beans or grains if desired. (Remember that beans and grains will swell to 2 or 3 times their uncooked size. Soak beans overnight first, if necessary.)
3. Bring to a boil, then cover and reduce the heat. Simmer slowly until all the ingredients are tender and the flavors are blended. Adjust the seasoning.

If you are using noodles, add them during the last 10 minutes of cooking (the last

6 or 7 minutes if the noodles are home-made). Stew also may be thickened with a flour-butter roux (see directions for a roux, page 53, and add a few minutes before removing the stew from the heat).

Ingredients to Be Used in Stews

Vegetable mixtures—any that harmonize well.

Additions

any beans
any grains
noodles

Thickeners

Replace part of the cooking water with these toward the end of cooking.

tomato sauce
cream soups
nut or pan gravy
cooked pureed winter squash, potatoes,
    carrots, etc.
béchamel sauce
grated cheese—stirred in during the last
    minute of cooking

Pan Gravy Stew

2 large potatoes, cut in large chunks
2 medium carrots, sliced
¾ cup peas
pan gravy (page 169)

Steam the potatoes and carrots for 10 minutes. Add the peas and continue steaming until the vegetables are tender. Drain well. Add the vegetables to the pan gravy. Heat to serving temperature.

Serve garnished with minced parsley. This recipe makes 2 to 3 servings.

Vegetable Goulash (Hungary)

A robust, unusually flavored stew, with a little impulse of hotness from the paprika.

¼ cup butter
1 green pepper, cut in pieces
2 medium potatoes, cubed
1 stalk celery, sliced thin
2 cups shredded cabbage
1 small carrot, sliced thin
¾ cup water
3 cups chopped tomatoes
1 teaspoon finely grated lemon rind
1 teaspoon caraway seeds
1 teaspoon marjoram or oregano
¼ to ½ teaspoon fresh ground pepper
1 tablespoon sweet paprika (not the hot kind)
salt to taste
2 tablespoons butter
2 tablespoons flour

Heat the butter in a pot. Add the green pepper, potatoes, celery, cabbage, and carrots. Sauté for 5 minutes. Slowly add the water, stir in the tomatoes, and add the lemon rind, caraway seeds, and marjoram. Cover and simmer for 30 to 40 minutes, until all the vegetables are tender. Add the pepper, paprika, and salt to taste.

Melt the 2 tablespoons of butter in a small skillet. Add the flour and cook for 1 minute, stirring rapidly with a whisk to remove lumps. Add to the goulash, stirring constantly, and simmer the goulash for 2 or 3 minutes until thickened.

Serve over noodles. This recipe makes 4 to 6 servings.

Gumbo (USA)

Gumbos are the gift of the South—here is a vegetable version. If you have access to gumbo filé powder, it may be added in place of the coriander and thyme to taste.

3 cups chopped tomatoes
1 bay leaf
½ cup broth or water
2 tablespoons butter

2 tablespoons minced fresh parsley
¼ cup thinly sliced celery
¼ cup chopped green pepper
2 cups okra cut in ½-inch pieces
1 cup green beans, cut in 1-inch pieces
1 cup corn kernels
½ teaspoon coriander
¼ teaspoon sage
½ teaspoon thyme
salt
pepper

Combine the tomatoes, bay leaf, and broth or water in a pot. Simmer for 30 minutes, covered, stirring occasionally. While the tomatoes are cooking, heat the butter in a large skillet. Add the parsley, celery, and green pepper and sauté for 2 to 3 minutes. Add the okra and sauté for 5 minutes, until the okra begins to become tender. Add the okra mixture to the tomatoes. Add the green beans and cook for 10 minutes. Add the corn, coriander, sage, and thyme. Cook for 5 more minutes, until the vegetables are tender. Season to taste with salt and pepper. This recipe makes 4 servings.

Tzimmes (Jewish)

"To make a tzimmes" means to make a fuss or cause excitement. A tzimmes is also a stew made of fruits and vegetables—or sometimes just fruit—with many variations. Tzimmes is traditionally cooked for 2 to 3 hours—this one can be made in about an hour.

3 cups thickly sliced carrots
1 cup pineapple cut into small pieces
10 prunes, pitted and sliced
1 cup water
salt

Combine all the ingredients in a pot. Bring to a boil, cover, and reduce the heat. Simmer very slowly for an hour, until all the ingredients are tender. Add salt to taste.

Sprinkle a little lemon juice over the tzimmes, if desired. This recipe makes 4 servings.

Variations
Replace part of the water with fruit juice.
Tzimmes can be made with sliced sweet potatoes, dried apricots, sliced apples, young turnips, and raisins.
Add a little honey and cinnamon.

Ratatouille (France)

Ratatouille means a stew. Here is the classic vegetable combination from Provence.

⅓ cup olive oil
2 teaspoons basil
1 teaspoon oregano
1 large eggplant, peeled and cubed
2 zucchinis, sliced
1 medium green pepper, sliced thin
3 cups tomatoes, cut in thin wedges
salt
pepper

Heat the oil in a pot. Add the basil and oregano, and sauté for 1 minute. Add the eggplant and sauté on medium heat for 5 minutes. Add the tomatoes and green pepper, and sauté for another 5 minutes. Add more oil if necessary. Add the zucchini. Reduce the heat. Cover and simmer on a low heat for 20 to 30 minutes, until the vegetables are tender. Season to taste with salt and pepper. This recipe makes 4 to 6 servings.

VEGETABLE PIES

A vegetable pie makes an elegant presentation, and is usually very much appreciated. The pie can be made with a pastry crust or with a topping of melted cheese, or it may have no "crust" at all, and appear as layers of vegetables. Here are a few suggested ingredients for vegetable pies:

Crusts

pastry pie crust (plain, wheat germ, or cheese)
oil crust for vegetable pies
millet crust (for a single-crust cheese-topped pie)
filo pastry: 12 sheets each for the bottom and top crusts
a layer of baked eggplant slices or steamed cabbage leaves for a bottom "crust"

Fillings

combinations of finely cut steamed or sautéed vegetables
ratatouille
with:
vegetable purees
grated cheese
tahini or taratoor
nut gravy (small amount)
cheese sauce (small amount)
sesame, sunflower, poppy seeds
ricotta, sour cream, yogurt
cottage cheese
heavy cream and a little butter
bêchamel sauce (small amount)
chopped nuts

Toppings

top crust
sauce or gravy
vegetable puree
grated cheese
bread crumbs

To Assemble a Vegetable Pie

1. Place the bottom crust in a pie pan or rectangular baking pan.
2. Mix ingredients for the filling together, or layer them in the crust.
3. Place the topping or top crust on the pie. Bake in a 350° oven, 45 minutes to 1 hour for pastry crust, 30 minutes for non-pastry crusts.

See the index for a complete listing of vegetable pies.

Vegetable Pie #1 (with millet crust and cheese topping)

millet crust (page 258)
3 tablespoons butter or oil
½ teaspoon each: basil, oregano, thyme
1 potato, diced fine
½ green pepper, chopped
1 carrot, sliced thin
1 large tomato, chopped
3 cups mixed finely cut vegetables
¾ cup cottage cheese
seasoned salt
pepper
cheese slices

Line a 9-inch pie pan or a baking dish with the millet crust. Heat the butter in a wok or large skillet with a lid. Add the herbs, potato, and carrot, and sauté for 7 minutes. Add the tomato; then add the vegetables and cottage cheese. Cover and cook on a low heat, stirring occasionally, until the vegetables are tender. Season to taste with the seasoned salt and pepper.

Pour the vegetable mixture into the crust. Top with slices of cheese. Bake in a 350° oven for 20 minutes, until the cheese is melted.

Variations

Replace millet crust with a partially baked pastry crust.

Vegan Variation: Substitute crumbled tofu for the cottage cheese. Replace the cheese slices with tomato slices drizzled with a little oil and sprinkled with salt, pepper, and bread crumbs.

Vegetable Pie #2 (with a double pastry crust)

pastry pie crust (page 254) with ½ cup grated cheese and 1 teaspoon dill weed added to the dough
filling for vegetable pie #1

Line a 9-inch buttered pie pan with half the dough. Place the filling in the crust and spread evenly. Top with a few slices of cheese. Put the top crust on, seal, and prick in a few places with a fork. Bake in a 350° oven for 1 hour, until golden brown.

Variation

Vegan Variation: Omit the cheese from the crust. Replace the cottage cheese with crumbled bean curd and the cheese slices with tomato slices.

Shepherd's Pie (English)

½ teaspoon basil
½ teaspoon thyme
2 tablespoons butter
1 large tomato, chopped
6 cups finely cut vegetables, mixed
½ cup sattvic sauce (page 173)
¼ cup water
salt
pepper
1 recipe mashed potatoes (page 113)
½ cup grated cheese
paprika

Sauté the herbs in the butter for 1 minute. Add the tomato and cook for 2 minutes. Add the vegetables, sattvic sauce, and water. Cover and simmer until the vegetables are tender.

Adjust the seasoning. Place the vegetables in a buttered baking dish. Spread evenly. Completely cover the vegetables with an even layer of the mashed potatoes. Sprinkle the potatoes with the grated cheese and with a little paprika for decoration. Bake in a 350° oven for 30 minutes. This recipe makes 6 servings.

Cornish Pasties (England)

An adaptation of the classic English savory pastry, embellished with cheese.

pastry pie crust with the wheat germ variation (page 256), with 1 teaspoon basil and ½ cup grated sharp cheese added to the dough
½ teaspoon ground rosemary
2½ cups finely cut mixed vegetables
1 tablespoon oil
½ cup ricotta
salt
pepper

While the pastry dough is chilling, sauté the rosemary and the vegetables in the oil

for 10 minutes, until they are tender. Remove from the heat. Mix in the ricotta and season to taste with salt and pepper. Roll out the dough ⅛ inch thick on a floured board. Cut out 5-inch circles.

Place a large spoonful of filling on half of each circle. Fold over the dough and seal the edges thoroughly. Press the tongs of a fork along each edge and prick the crust once. Place the pasties on a buttered baking sheet. Bake in a 375° oven for 25 minutes, until golden. This recipe makes 10 to 11 pasties.

Variation

Vegan Variation: Omit the cheese from the crust. Omit the ricotta and add ½ cup more vegetables. Sesame seeds may be added to the crust mixture for added protein.

MIXED VEGETABLE DISHES

Vegetables Stroganoff

The creator of this very special dish likes to simmer the sauce for eight hours. We have speeded up the process a bit, and the dish is still outstanding.

½ green pepper, chopped fine
1 cup minced fresh parsley
1 teaspoon basil
½ teaspoon thyme
¼ teaspoon rosemary
2 tablespoons olive oil
1 carrot, grated
1 medium zucchini, grated
3 cups chopped ripe tomatoes
½ cup sattvic sauce (page 173)
1 bay leaf
⅔ cup each: sliced carrots, zucchini, cauliflower
½ cup peas
½ to ¾ cup sour cream
cooked noodles

Sauté the green pepper, parsley, and herbs in the oil for 5 minutes. Add the grated carrot and zucchini and sauté for 5 minutes more. Add the tomatoes, sattvic sauce, and bay leaf. Cover and simmer for 1½ to 2 hours, stirring occasionally, until the sauce is very thick.

Steam the carrots, zucchini, cauliflower, and peas until tender. Drain thoroughly. Add first the sour cream to the sauce, then the vegetables. Add a sprinkling of pepper and adjust the seasoning.

Serve over noodles. This recipe makes 4 to 6 servings.

Variations

Replace the sour cream with yogurt. Add it after removing the sauce from the heat and letting it stand for a few minutes.

Vegan Variation: Though the sour cream is what makes this dish "Stroganoff," it is very good even without it.

Vegetables Deluxe with Rosemary

See the Japanese vegetable slicing methods on page 74 to achieve the shapes suggested for the vegetables.

¼ cup butter
¾ teaspoon rosemary
1½ cups carrots, cut in thin half-moons
1½ cups cauliflower, in small flowerets
2 cups chopped ripe tomatoes
1½ cups zucchini, cut in triangles
¾ cup corn kernels
¾ cup heavy cream
salt
pepper

Heat the butter in a large skillet with a lid. Add the rosemary and sauté for 1 minute. Add the carrots and cauliflower, and sauté for 5 minutes. Add the tomatoes and zucchini. Cover and simmer on a low heat for 10 minutes, stirring occasionally. Add the corn kernels and the cream. Stir, cover, and simmer for 5 minutes, until all the vegetables are tender. Season to taste with salt and pepper. This recipe makes 4 servings.

Variation
Replace the cream with ¾ cup ricotta mixed with 3 tablespoons water. The ricotta will look grainy, but the dish will taste just as good.

Vegetables Newburg

An elegant luncheon or light dinner dish: vegetables in a rosy-pink sauce, served over toast.

4 cups finely cut mixed vegetables: zucchini or summer squash, asparagus tips, peas, carrots, etc.
2 cups auroré sauce (page 168)
½ cup grated Swiss or jack cheese
salt
pepper
toast

Steam the vegetables until tender. Drain very well. Prepare auroré sauce. Add the cheese and stir until it is melted and smooth. Add the vegetables. Adjust the seasoning.

Serve immediately over toast. Garnish with minced parsley or watercress. This recipe makes 4 to 6 servings.

Kofta (India)

There are many varieties of kofta found from Armenia to India. Here is one version, featuring deep-fried vegetable balls in a spicy tomato sauce.

Kofta Balls:
½ head cauliflower
2 medium potatoes, peeled
1 cup peas
1 teaspoon salt
1 teaspoon turmeric
⅓ cup chick pea flour
⅓ cup farina (cream of wheat)

1 tablespoon ghee or butter
ghee or oil for deep-frying

Sauce:
2 tablespoons oil
1 teaspoon salt
1 teaspoon cumin
¼-inch piece fresh ginger, peeled and minced
½ cup water
3½ cups chopped ripe tomatoes
1 teaspoon turmeric
½ teaspoon cinnamon
⅛ teaspoon cloves
1 teaspoon brown sugar or honey

Steam the cauliflower and potatoes for 15 minutes. Add the peas and steam until the vegetables are tender. Drain very well.

While the vegetables are steaming, prepare the sauce: Heat the oil in a pot. Add the salt, cumin, and ginger, and sauté for 1 minute. Add the water, tomatoes, remaining spices, and sugar. Simmer covered, stirring occasionally, for 30 minutes.

While the sauce is simmering, prepare the kofta balls: Mash the drained vegetables with the remaining ingredients for the balls. Deep-fry 1-inch balls of the mixture in ghee or oil until browned. Drain on paper towels.

Place the kofta balls in a serving bowl. Pour the sauce over them and let sit for 1 minute before serving.

Serve over rice. This recipe makes 4 to 6 servings.

Vegetable Burgers

Some wild colors can be achieved—try preparing half the recipe with beets and half with carrots, and, as they say, amaze your family and friends.

2 pounds beets, carrots, turnips, or potatoes
½ cup ground nuts

1 tablespoon butter
½ cup whole wheat flour
1 teaspoon sugar or honey
salt
pepper
bread crumbs or breading mixture (page 189)

Steam the vegetables until very tender. Drain well. Mash. Mix in the nuts, butter, flour, and sugar. Season to taste with salt and pepper. Shape into patties. Roll in the bread crumbs or breading mixture to coat. Fry on both sides in butter until golden brown.

Serve on burger rolls or with a nut gravy. This recipe makes 10 to 12 burgers.

Variations
Replace half of the flour with toasted wheat germ.

Add cooked grains, pureed vegetables, minced parsley.

Upma (India)

In upma, farina comes into its own as a grain.

1 cup farina (Cream of Wheat)
¼ cup ghee or butter
1½ teaspoon cumin
1 cup peas
1 cup green beans, cut in 1-inch pieces
2 cups water
1 teaspoon turmeric
1 teaspoon salt

Toast the farina in a dry pan until it is slightly darkened. Remove from the heat and set aside. Heat the ghee or butter in a pot. Add the cumin and sauté for 1 minute. Add the peas, green beans, water, turmeric, and salt. Cover and simmer until the vegetables are tender. Uncover and add the farina a little at a time, stirring constantly to avoid lumps. Cook until very thick.

Serve immediately. This recipe makes 4 servings.

Variations
Replace the green beans with green pepper or zucchini.

Replace the farina with cracked wheat for an inauthentic but pleasant variation. Do not toast the wheat.

Kebabs

Vegetable (and fruit) kebabs are fun to prepare and flavorful. They may be prepared on a barbecue or in the broiler. The marinade is flexible; here are two ideas for it.

For a delicious marinade, prepare pineapple sweet and sour sauce (page 173); mix in lemon-and-oil dressing (page 165) and a little brown sugar or honey, to taste. Or prepare a double or triple recipe of lemon-tomato dressing (page 165) and sweeten with a little brown sugar or honey to taste.

Soak any of the following suggested foods in the marinade for at least 2 hours:

pieces of green or red bell pepper
cherry tomatoes
partially cooked pieces of eggplant, zucchini, or summer or winter squash
apple slices
pineapple cubes

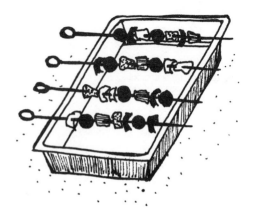

Carefully place the foods on skewers. Barbecue over hot coals or in the broiler, turning once during the cooking to brown both sides. Serve over rice.

Note: If cooking in the broiler, place the skewers over a roasting pan (see diagram) to catch the dripping marinade. Be sure to lower the broiler rack for this method.

If no skewers are available, broil the pieces in a pan—they will taste just as good, even if the presentation isn't quite so dramatic.

Tempura (Japan)

Tempura was invented by the Japanese to please the early Portuguese traders, who liked deep-fried foods. With Japanese artistry, this light, delicate dish was created. Three batters for it, including one that is wheat-free, follow. But first the method:

1 recipe tempura batter
4 to 5 cups thinly sliced vegetables:
zucchini or summer squash
green beans
cauliflower or broccoli flowerets
winter squash
okra
spinach leaves
eggplant
artichoke hearts, steamed
asparagus stalks
sweet potatoes
carrots
cabbage leaves
chard leaves
Jerusalem artichokes
lightly steamed Brussels sprouts

Dip each slice, one at a time, into the batter to coat. Drop the pieces into hot oil. Deep-fry until golden and crisp. Drain on paper towels. For best results, have the oil very hot and the batter chilled—the result will be less oily. This recipe makes 4 servings.

Serve tempura as a main dish or side dish, with rice or Japanese noodles in broth, or with a non-Japanese meal. Tempura can also be served as an hors d'oeuvre.

Basic Tempura Batter

¾ cup unbleached white or whole wheat flour
¾ cup soy flour
1 teaspoon salt
1 cup plus 2 tablespoons water

Combine all the ingredients in a blender or beat until smooth. Chill. Adjust the water if necessary.

Crisp Tempura Batter

This batter does not change color much when deep-fried, and the judgment on doneness must be made according to texture.

1¼ cups unbleached white flour
⅓ cup cornstarch
1½ tablespoons oil
½ teaspoon salt
1 cup water

Combine all the ingredients in a blender or beat until smooth. Chill.

Rice Flour Tempura Batter

This is not an authentic Japanese recipe. It is very good, however, and gives a delicate texture.

1½ cups rice flour
1 teaspoon salt
½ teaspoon turmeric
1 cup milk

Combine all the ingredients in a blender, or beat together well. Adjust the milk if necessary.

Vegetable Kugel (Jewish)

A kugel is a kind of pudding. Here is a puree of vegetables baked until the inside is tender and the outside is brown and crusty. For best results, use a glass baking dish so that the kugel can brown all over.

6 medium potatoes
4 carrots
1½ cups peas
2 cups sliced green beans
2 stalks celery, sliced
1 tablespoon butter
⅓ cup matzoh meal or whole wheat flour
3 tablespoons soy flour
seasoned salt
pepper

Boil the potatoes until tender. Steam the carrots, peas, and green beans until tender. Drain both very well and mash to a rough paste. Sauté the celery in the butter for 5 minutes and add to the vegetable mixture. Add the matzoh meal or flour and the soy flour. Season to taste with salt and pepper. (Add up to 3 tablespoons more butter for a richer kugel.) Turn into a buttered casserole dish. Place in a 400° oven and bake for 1 to 1½ hours, until the top is well browned. This recipe makes 6 servings.

Variations

Sauté green herbs in the butter with the celery.

Add fresh minced parsley.

Individual Vegetables

ARTICHOKES, GLOBE

Artichokes are served either steamed or boiled, and may be eaten hot or cold. They may be added to an antipasto or a summer salad platter, or cooked as for marinated vegetables a la Grecque (page 158).

The delicate flavor of the artichoke is best appreciated with cashew mayonnaise or a simple sauce, such as ghee-and-lemon sauce, for dipping.

Artichoke hearts can be removed from cooked artichokes and dressed with sauces, or sliced into salads, casseroles, stuffings, and fillings for crepes.

When selecting artichokes, look for worm holes. The leaves should be plump and not shrivelled, with mostly green coloring. If they are tightly packed, the artichoke is young and fresh. If they are spread, it is older.

How to eat an artichoke: Have a bowl of sauce for each person, and have an empty bowl on the table for the discarded leaves. Pull off a leaf. Hold the top of the leaf and dip the stem end into the sauce. Scrape off the soft, fleshy part with your lower teeth and discard the leaf. The inner leaves are more tender and more can be eaten of them. When the leaves are gone, the fuzzy "choke" will be revealed in the center. Carefully cut and scrape away the choke. What is left is the heart. Dip it into the sauce and enjoy.

Artichokes, Steamed or Boiled

Slice off the thorny tops of the leaves. *Steam* for 30 to 45 minutes. Or *boil* in water to cover (though the artichokes will float on top) for 20 to 30 minutes. To test for doneness, pull off an inner leaf. If it comes off easily, the artichoke is done.

To add extra flavor, add a little olive oil, lemon juice, and green herbs to the cooking water.

Artichokes a la Grecque (Greece)

4 artichokes
1 cup carrots, quartered lengthwise and sliced thin
1 cup fennel or celery, sliced thin
¼ cup olive oil
¼ cup melted butter
¼ cup lemon juice
½ teaspoon fennel seed
1 teaspoon dill weed
½ teaspoon salt
pepper

Trim the tips of the leaves and cut off the stems so that the artichokes can sit upright. Boil for 15 minutes. Drain. Mix the carrots and fennel or celery. Place in a casserole dish. Place the artichokes upright on top of the vegetables.

Mix the oil, butter, lemon juice, herbs, salt, and a sprinkling of pepper. Pour over the artichokes and the vegetables. Cover, and bake in a 350° oven for 45 minutes.

Serve with rice. This recipe makes 4 servings.

Variation
Substitute tiny cubed potatoes, cut green beans, or other vegetables for part of the carrots and fennel.

ARTICHOKES, JERUSALEM

The name of the Jerusalem artichoke, a root vegetable with a flavor faintly resembling that of the globe artichoke, comes not from Israeli origins, but from a misunderstanding of the Italian word *girasole*—sunflower—given to the flowers of the plant. Jerusalem artichokes grow wild in the United States. They may be eaten raw, sliced into salads, or marinated raw. (See marinated vegetables, page 158.) They may be steamed until crisp-tender, or steamed until tender and pureed. Add Jerusalem artichokes to soups, stews, and vegetable combinations. Use them for tempura. The slices discolor quickly, so sprinkle them with a little lemon juice if they must stand for more than a few minutes.

Jerusalem Artichokes, Steamed

Scrub the Jerusalem artichokes with a vegetable brush. They may be peeled if desired, but it is not necessary. Steam whole for 15 to 20 minutes, until tender but still a little crisp. Or steam them until soft, and mash. Serve plain, with butter and a little lemon juice or salt.

ASPARAGUS

The steaming of asparagus has been a subject of discussion by chefs for centuries—as steaming this delicate vegetable is its major cooking method. Asparagus can also be stir-fried, or marinated by the a la Grecque method (page 158). It may be served hot, with a simple embellishment of lemon juice and butter, or served cold on a

salad platter, with a lemon and oil dressing or with cashew mayonnaise. Add asparagus to Chinese-style stir-fried vegetable combinations, and use the tips for filling crepes and sandwiches. The season for asparagus is so short, however, that it is nice to serve just on its own, in the simplest manner available.

Steamed Asparagus

The methods are many. The challenge is to cook the tougher stalks through without overcooking the delicate tips. Here are two methods that work well.

Method #1: Snap off the white part of the stalks. Pare the end of the stalks lightly. Steam in a wide skillet so that the stalks can lie flat in ½ inch of water for about 10 minutes. If the asparagus is young and thin it may take less time. It should be bright green and crisp-tender.

Method #2: Trim asparagus as above. Tie into bundles. Stand them upright in a deep pot filled with 1 inch of water. Invert another pot over the top to serve as a lid, and cook for 10 minutes—more or less. The water will cook the stalks while the steam cooks the tips.

Asparagus Quiche

A beautiful, rich dish with a delicate asparagus flavor and color. This recipe makes one 9-inch quiche.

1 pound asparagus
½ cup heavy cream
⅛ teaspoon nutmeg
¾ teaspoon salt
4 tablespoons binding powder
3 tablespoons unbleached white flour
1 cup ricotta
1 cup grated mild cheese
1 9-inch pastry pie crust, partially baked

Steam the asparagus until barely tender. Drain. Slice off the tips and set aside. Place the stems in a blender with the cream, nutmeg, salt, binding powder, and flour. Puree thoroughly. Pour the mixture into a saucepan. Heat slowly, stirring constantly with a whisk, until thickened. Remove from the heat and beat in the ricotta and grated cheese. Gently stir in the asparagus tips. Pour the mixture into the pie shell and spread evenly. Bake in a 350° oven for 30 minutes.

BAMBOO SHOOTS

Bamboo shoots are found in Chinese cooking and add a crisp texture to vegetable dishes and Chinese-style soups. They may be steamed or stir-fried lightly.

Prepare fresh bamboo shoots by first washing them and then slicing them very thin. They have an astringent quality which may be removed before stir-frying by blanching for a minute, if desired.

BEETS AND BEET GREENS

Beets may be served raw, grated into salads. They may be juiced for a rich, sweet juice. Beets may be steamed or baked. They may be added to salads cold or served hot. Beets may be marinated (see methods on pages 158–160). When beets are cooked in mixtures with other vegetables, they tend to impart their color to their neighbors, so it is best to cook them separately. Serve steamed beets with lemon juice, sour cream, or yogurt. Beets may also be used to make vegetable burgers (page 87).

Beet greens may be used in the same manner as spinach or other greens, either raw in salads or cooked.

Steamed Beets

Scrub the beets with a vegetable brush. Cut off the stem end and the root. Steam whole for 30 to 40 minutes or longer until tender, or quarter or slice to shorten the cooking time.

Baked Beets

Rub beets with butter or oil, or place in a baking dish with a little water. Cover and bake in a 350° oven for 1 hour or longer, until tender. The beets may be quartered or sliced to reduce cooking time. For extra flavor, add lemon juice, a little butter, and minced parsley before baking.

Beet Cups

Steam or bake beets whole. When they are cool enough to handle, carefully hollow them out to form cups. Fill with sour cream and sprinkle with minced parsley, or fill with a rice stuffing mixture or with finely cut sautéed vegetables and top with a little sour cream. Return to the oven for a few minutes to heat.

BOK-CHOY (CHINESE CABBAGE)

Bok-choy is used extensively in Chinese cooking. It can be added to soups or to Chinese-style stir-fried vegetable combinations. Break off the leaves and cut off the tough ends. Slice across the leaves for thin pieces.

BROCCOLI

Broccoli can be steamed, or cut fine and stir-fried or kinpura-fried. It may be used for tempura or added to vegetable combinations. Broccoli has a very strong flavor which is not so successful when cooked in soups and stews. A variety of textures can be achieved by serving the broccoli cut in spears, in small flowerets, or chopped. It can also be pureed.

Broccoli is best served simply, with butter and a sprinking of lemon. It may be dressed with taratoor sauce, and is a classic served with cheese sauce. Chopped broccoli may be served creamed. Serve broccoli spears cold on a salad platter with a little lemon-and-oil dressing.

Look for broccoli with fresh leaves and an all-green head. There should be no yellow flowers.

Steamed Broccoli

The leaves are edible and nutritious, but peel the broccoli stalk. Steam whole, or cut in spears or flowerets, or chop. Broccoli spears will cook in about 10 minutes. Whole broccoli will take a little longer, and sliced or chopped will take less. Be alert not to overcook. Broccoli retains its bright color just up to the point when it becomes tender, and a minute later will be limp and dull.

Broccoli au Gratin

Steam broccoli spears until tender. Place in a baking dish and cover with grated cheese. Top with a sprinkling of bread crumbs or sesame seeds. Place in the broiler for a minute or two to melt the cheese.

Variation
Cover the broccoli with bêchamel sauce and then proceed as above.

Also see Brussels Sprouts, Broccoli, or Cabbage Casserole, page 96.

BRUSSELS SPROUTS

Serve Brussels sprouts steamed. Brussels sprouts may be steamed lightly, drained well, and used for tempura. Serve Brussels sprouts with a little butter and lemon juice or salt, with a cream sauce, with cream cheese hollandaise, or in tomato sauce. Cheese sauce goes very well with Brussels sprouts.

Select firm Brussels sprouts with tightly packed heads and few yellow or brown leaves.

Steamed Brussels Sprouts

Remove any brown leaves and slice a cross-cut gash in the stem. Steam for about 10 minutes, until tender. Brussels sprouts can be steamed in milk, to soften the flavor, if desired.

Brussels Sprouts au Gratin

Prepare as for broccoli au gratin. Top with chopped roasted almonds instead of sesame seeds.

Brussels Sprouts, Broccoli, or Cabbage Casserole

3 cups washed trimmed Brussels sprouts, or 2 pounds broccoli cut into spears, or 4 cups shredded cabbage
1 tablespoon olive oil
¼ teaspoon rosemary
½ teaspoon sage
½ teaspoon basil
3 cups chopped ripe tomatoes
salt
pepper
1 to 1½ cups grated cheese
½ cup dry bread crumbs

Steam the vegetables until almost tender. Drain well. While the vegetables are steaming, sauté the herbs in the olive oil for 2 minutes. Add the tomatoes and cook for 10 minutes, until they form a sauce.

Mix the vegetables with the tomato sauce. Season to taste with salt and pepper and turn into a casserole dish. Sprinkle first with the cheese, then with the bread crumbs. Bake in a 350° oven for 20 minutes, until the cheese is melted. This recipe makes 4 servings.

BURDOCK ROOT (GOBO ROOT)

Burdock root is used in Japanese cooking. It is peeled, slivered, and stir-fried with other vegetables. A nice flavor and color combination results when slivered burdock root and carrots are stir-fried together. Burdock root may also be steamed, marinated, and added to salads. It is also dried and used as a tea. The sliced root discolors quickly, so sprinkle it with lemon juice if it must stand more than a few minutes.

Steamed Burdock Root

Peel the burdock root and slice. Steam for 20 to 30 minutes until tender.

CABBAGE

"Mon petit chou"—my little cabbage—is a term of endearment in France. Cabbage can be endearing when cooked properly, the first rule of which is never to overcook. The flavor will be delicate when the cooking is delicate. The loose-leafed varieties of cabbage are excellent for stuffed cabbage rolls. The tightly packed heads, either purple or white-green, can be shredded raw into salads (the purple variety adds dramatic coloring) and can be steamed, sautéed, or stir-fried. Cabbage leaves can be used for tempura or pakoras. Sturdy cabbage leaves make decorative "bowls" for salads, hors d'oeuvres, and dips. Add cabbage to Indian-style spiced vegetables, Chinese-style spiced vegetables, and to soups and stews. Cabbage lightly sautéed or steamed and dressed with a little butter is delicious. Cabbage can be served creamed or with cheese sauce. It can be spiced with caraway seeds or with curry spices, or can be cooked in tomato sauce.

Select cabbages with firm, tight heads; in the case of the loose-leafed varieties, look for fresh green leaves.

Steamed Cabbage

Cut cabbage in quarters, or slice or shred it. Young shredded cabbages can take as little as 5 minutes to steam, while older cabbages can take as long as 20 minutes. Add a little lemon juice to the steaming water of purple cabbage to keep its color fresh. Cabbage can be steamed in milk, if desired, to help soften its flavor. Purple cabbage can be steamed in apple juice.

Sautéed Cabbage with Caraway (Germany)

2 tablespoons butter
¼ teaspoon caraway seeds
½ teaspoon salt
3 cups coarsely shredded green cabbage

Melt the butter in a large skillet or wok. Toss in the caraway, salt, and cabbage, and sauté on a medium heat until the cabbage is tender. This recipe makes 4 servings.

Cabbage-Tomato Curry (India)

2 tablespoons oil
1 teaspoon whole cumin seed
½ teaspoon black mustard seed
1 teaspoon salt
1½ cups chopped ripe tomatoes
¾ cup water
1 teaspoon turmaric
dash cloves
4 cups shredded green cabbage

Heat the oil in a pot. Add the cumin and mustard seed and sauté until the mustard seed dances. Add the salt. Add the tomatoes and cook for a few minutes until they begin to become mushy. Add the water, turmeric, cloves, and cabbage. Bring to a boil, cover, and reduce the heat. Simmer for 20 to 30 minutes, until the cabbage is tender. Uncover toward the end of cooking to let a little of the water boil off.

Serve over rice. This recipe makes 3 to 4 servings.

Spicy Cabbage and Apples (Germany)

5 cups shredded purple cabbage
1 apple, chopped
¾ cup apple juice or water
¼ cup lemon juice
2 teaspoons sugar or honey
1 tablespoon oil
1½ teaspoons cumin

½ teaspoon yellow mustard seed
½ teaspoon cinnamon
⅛ teaspoon cloves
½ teaspoon salt

Bring the cabbage, apple, apple juice or water, lemon juice, and sugar or honey to a boil. Cover and reduce the heat. Heat the oil in a small skillet. Add the cumin and mustard seed. Sauté until the mustard seed dances. Add to the cabbage. Add the cinnamon, cloves, and salt. Simmer until the cabbage is tender. Adjust the seasoning. If using water instead of apple juice, another teaspoon of sugar or honey may have to be added. This recipe makes 4 to 5 servings.

Variations
Add ⅓ cup raisins with the cabbage.

Replace the apple juice with fig or prune juice.

After cooking, drain, and stir in a little sour cream or yogurt.

Stuffed Cabbage Rolls (Russia)

Versions of cabbage rolls are served in Russia and Eastern Europe. A loose-leafed variety of cabbage is the easiest to work with.

8 whole green cabbage leaves
potato stuffing (page 188) or grain stuffing (page 188)
8 slices of cheese
2 to 3 cups tomato sauce

Steam the cabbage leaves until tender, but still firm. Drain gently. Place the cabbage leaves, curling upward, on a table. Place an equal amount of the stuffing on the base of each leaf. Place a slice of cheese on top of the stuffing. Roll up the leaves, tucking the edges in, to make a package enclosing the filling. Place the cabbage rolls in a baking pan. Cover with tomato sauce. Bake in a 350° oven for 30 minutes. This recipe makes 8 rolls (4 servings).

Variations
If using a grain stuffing, add a small amount of currants or raisins to it.

Omit the tomato sauce and bake the cabbage rolls in a well-buttered casserole dish, covered, with sour cream.

Vegan Variation: Omit the cheese.

Cabbage Casserole

4 cups shredded green cabbage
¼ teaspoon caraway seeds
2 tablespoons butter
1½ cups béchamel sauce
1 cup grated cheese
¼ cup bread crumbs *or* ⅓ cup chopped nuts

Sauté the cabbage and caraway seeds in the butter until tender. Mix the béchamel sauce with the cabbage. Place in a buttered baking dish. Sprinkle with the cheese, and then with the nuts or bread crumbs. Bake in a 350° oven for 20 minutes, until the cheese is melted. This recipe makes 4 servings.

Variations
Substitute auroré sauce for béchamel.

Vegan Variation: Omit the grated cheese.

CARROTS

Grate carrots into salads, and into cake and quick bread batters. Serve the sticks as hors d'oeuvres, with a salad dressing for dipping. Carrot juice is sweet and good alone, and makes a delicious base for mixed vegetable juices. Use whole young carrots for marinated vegetables a la Grecque. Use carrots for tempura and pakoras. Carrots may be used for vegetable burgers (page 87). Cook carrots by steaming, sautéing, stir-frying, kinpura-frying, or baking. Carrots may be steamed and pureed.

Add carrots to Chinese-style stir-fried vegetables and Indian-style spiced vegetables. Carrots may be served plain, with butter and little parsley, drizzled with honey or maple syrup, creamed, in sweet and sour sauce, with taratoor sauce, or with tahini.

Steamed Carrots

Scrub carrots with a vegetable brush. Steam whole carrots for about 20 minutes, until tender. Young carrots or sliced carrots will take less time.

Baked Carrots

Bake carrots whole, or cut them in half lengthwise and bake by either method described on page 76.

Sesame-Ginger Carrots

3 tablespoons ghee or butter
¼ teaspoon ground ginger
3 cups carrots, sliced thin on the diagonal
¼ cup sesame seeds
2 tablespoons honey

Heat the butter and ginger in a wok or large skillet. Add the carrots and sauté until they start to become tender. Add the sesame and continue sautéing, stirring constantly, until tender. Remove from the heat.

Drizzle with the honey. Stir and serve. This recipe makes 4 servings.

Carrot Crumble

A light main dish. A squash crumble can be made by substituting 3½ cups cooked, pureed winter squash for the carrots. Yams may also be used.

7 cups sliced carrots
3 to 4 tablespoons butter or ghee
½ teaspoon cardamom

½ teaspoon ground ginger
1½ tablespoons brown sugar
salt

Crumble Topping:
¼ cup wheat germ
¼ cup sunflower seeds
¼ cup oats
½ cup whole wheat flour
¼ teaspoon salt
3 tablespoons melted butter
1 tablespoon water

Steam the carrots until very tender. Drain well and mash. Mix in the butter, spices, and brown sugar. Add a tiny amount of salt to taste. Spread the mixture in a baking dish.

Place the wheat germ, sunflower seeds, and oats in a blender. Blend to a powder. Mix with the flour and salt. Add the butter and water, and mix to a crumbly texture with the fingers.

Sprinkle the crumbly topping evenly over the carrots. Bake in a 350° oven for 40 to 45 minutes, until the topping is browned. This recipe makes 4 to 6 servings.

Carrots Vichy

Carrots with a light pan glaze.

1 pound young carrots, or mature carrots cut in half
2 tablespoons butter or ghee
4 teaspoons sugar
¼ teaspoon salt

Trim the ends and lightly scrape the carrots. Place ½ inch of water in a saucepan. Mix in the butter, sugar, and salt. Add the carrots. Bring to a boil. Cover, and reduce heat to medium-high. Cook until the carrots are tender and all the water has evaporated. Watch very closely during the last few minutes of cooking to make certain that the liquid doesn't scorch. A light syrup will remain in the bottom of the pan. Roll the carrots in it to coat. This recipe makes 4 servings.

Glazed Carrots or Parsnips

12 carrots or parsnips
⅓ cup packed brown sugar
3 tablespoons melted butter
½ teaspoon cinnamon
1 tablespoon orange or apple juice

Trim the ends and lightly scrape the carrots or parsnips. Steam until almost tender. Drain. Place in a baking pan. Mix the brown sugar, butter, cinnamon, and juice. Pour over the carrots or parsnips and roll them in the mixture to coat. Bake in a 400° oven for 20 minutes. This recipe makes 6 servings.

CAULIFLOWER

Cauliflower can be steamed, sautéed, stir-fried, or kinpura-fried. Whatever the method, cook cauliflower just until tender and no more—overcooking ruins the delicacy of flavor that a cauliflower can have.

Use cauliflower for tempura and pakoras. Add cauliflower flowerets to Indian-style spiced vegetable dishes, and to vegetable combinations. The flavor of cauliflower can become too strong in soups and stews. Cauliflower may be steamed, pureed, and mixed with mashed potatoes, or served as

a substitute for them. Marinate cauliflower by the a la Grecque method (page 158) and serve on salad platters.

Serve cauliflower with cheese sauce, creamed, with taratoor sauce, with sauce noisette, or plain with butter. In hard water areas, add a little lemon juice to the cooking water to help retain the whiteness of the vegetable.

Select cauliflowers with compact, tight heads and fresh green leaves. Those huge heads may merely be spread out—and old—making the smaller heads often the better choice.

Steamed Cauliflower

Trim off the leaves and part of the stalk. Make cross-cut gashes in the stalk if steaming whole. Steam whole for 15 to 25 minutes until tender, or steam the flowerets for 8 minutes or more. Cauliflower may be steamed in milk, if desired.

Cauliflower au Gratin

Prepare in the same manner as Broccoli au Gratin, page 94.

Cauliflower Burgers

1 head cauliflower
½ teaspoon paprika
¼ cup nut butter
¼ cup minced fresh parsley
1 teaspoon dill seed
½ cup toasted wheat germ
seasoned salt
bread crumbs or breading mixture (page 189)

Steam the cauliflower until tender. Drain well. Mash the cauliflower with the paprika, nut butter, parsley, dill seed, and wheat germ. Add seasoned salt to taste. If the mixture is crumbly, add more nut butter. Gather a handful of the mixture and shape into a ball. Roll in the bread crumbs or breading mixture to coat. Flatten slightly. Fry on both sides in butter until golden.

Serve on burger rolls or with nut gravy. This recipe makes 8 to 10 burgers.

Variation
Put slices of cheese on the finished burgers and place in the broiler for a minute to melt the cheese.

Cauliflower and Coconut (India)

½ cup ghee or butter
½ teaspoon black mustard seeds
½ cup grated coconut, fresh or dried
1 cauliflower, cut in very small pieces
¾ teaspoon turmeric
½ teaspoon salt
water

Heat the ghee or butter in a large skillet. Add the mustard seeds and sauté until they dance. Add the coconut and sauté until golden. Add the cauliflower, turmeric, and salt, and just enough water to steam the cauliflower. Stir, cover, and cook until the water is gone and the cauliflower is tender. This recipe makes 4 to 6 servings.

Cauliflower-Nut Loaf

A main dish casserole loaf. Try preparing it with roasted almonds.

1 head cauliflower
⅓ cup coarsely chopped nuts
½ cup ground nuts
¼ cup breadcrumbs
½ teaspoon paprika
½ cup ricotta or sour cream
¼ teaspoon rosemary (ground, if possible)
2 cups grated cheese
salt
pepper

Steam the cauliflower until tender. Drain well and mash to a rough—not smooth—

paste. Add the chopped and ground nuts, breadcrumbs, paprika, ricotta or sour cream, rosemary, and 1 cup of the cheese. Season to taste with salt and pepper. Press the mixture into a buttered loaf pan. Sprinkle the remaining cheese on top. Bake in a 350° oven for 30 minutes. This recipe makes 4 to 6 servings.

Cauliflower and Peas with Tomato (India)

This dish is a feast for the eyes—red tomatoes and green peas on a field of turmeric-golden cauliflower, with accents of black mustard seed.

⅓ cup ghee or butter
¾ teaspoon black mustard seed
1 teaspoon cumin
¾ teaspoon salt
2 tomatoes, chopped
1 head cauliflower, cut into small pieces
1 teaspoon turmeric
¼ teaspoon fenugreek
½ cup water
¾ cup peas

Heat the ghee or butter in a pot. Add the mustard seed, cumin, and salt, and sauté until the mustard seed dances. Add the tomatoes and cook for 2 minutes. Add the cauliflower, turmeric, and fenugreek. Stir in the water. Cover and simmer for 10 minutes. Add the peas, and more water if necessary. Cover and continue to simmer for 5 to 10 minutes more, until the vegetables are tender. This recipe makes 4 to 6 servings.

CELERIAC, OR CELERY ROOT

Celeriac is a large, knobby root vegetable that has been used in fine French cooking for centuries. If it is available, by all means make use of it. Celeriac can be grated raw into salads, or can be lightly steamed and marinated. Use partially cooked pieces of celeriac for tempura, or prepare celeriac in the same manner as french-fried potatoes. Celeriac can also be steamed or baked.

Steamed Celeriac

Celeriac must be peeled, and it is easier to peel after it has been sliced. Steam slices of celeriac for 20 minutes or longer, until tender. Add a little lemon juice to the cooking water in hard-water areas to help retain the whiteness.

Baked Celeriac

Slice celeriac into ½ inch pieces and peel. Brush both sides with melted butter or oil. Bake 30 to 40 minutes in a 350° oven until tender. Turn over once or twice during the baking.

CELERY

Besides its natural place in salads, celery can be juiced together with other vegetables. The stalks can be stuffed with cream cheese, nut butter, or sandwich spreads. Cooked celery is usually found in combination with other vegetables, steamed, sautéed, stir-fried, or creamed. Celery can be

cooked in tomato sauce. Celery adds wonderful flavor to soups and stews, particularly when the leaves are added as well.

Thinly sliced sautéed celery accents grain dishes and casseroles as well. Celery leaves can be dried, ground, and mixed with salt as a seasoning.

Steamed Celery

Steam celery stalks for 8 to 10 minutes, until tender.

CHARD (SWISS CHARD)

Chard may be prepared in the same way as spinach, after removing the base of the thick stem. It may replace cabbage leaves

in stuffed cabbage rolls, and may be used for tempura. Chard may be added to Chinese-style mixed vegetables as a substitute for bok-choy.

Steamed Chard

Steam chard for 5 to 10 minutes, until the stalk is tender. Do not salt the water.

CHESTNUTS

Chestnuts are used interchangeably with potatoes in some European countries. They may be mixed with vegetable combinations, added to soups and stews, and mashed like potatoes. See recipes for steamed and roasted chestnuts on pages 47–48.

CORN

Corn is a staple of many Central and South American countries, and is prevalent throughout North America as well. Corn produces cornmeal, cornstarch, popcorn, and corn oil. The sugars in corn convert into starch soon after picking; if just-picked corn is available it is by far the best. Eat corn on the cob, or remove the kernels and serve creamed, or add it to soups, stews, and vegetable medleys. For a simple salad dish, mix steamed, cooled corn kernels with cottage cheese and chopped tomatoes. Serve corn on the cob plain and simple, with just butter and salt.

Steamed Corn

Remove the husks and cornsilk. Break off the stem. Steam in unsalted water or in milk for 4 to 10 minutes. For corn-off-the-cob, scrape off the kernels and steam them for no more than 5 minutes. A little sugar or honey may be added to the cooking water to enhance the sweetness, if desired.

Mexican-style Corn

2 tablespoons butter
½ teaspoon ground cumin
1 green pepper, cut in small pieces
1 large tomato, cut in small pieces
2 cups corn kernels
½ cup water
salt

Heat the butter. Add the cumin, green pepper, and tomato and sauté for a few minutes. Add the corn and water. Cover and simmer for 5 minutes. Drain. Add salt to taste. More butter may be added. This recipe makes 3 to 4 servings.

Variation

Sauté green fresh chilies in the butter with the green pepper.

Succotash (USA)

Succotash hails from Rhode Island, where it was the "Misickquatash" of the Narragansett Indian tribe.

1½ cups cooked kidney or lima beans
2 cups corn kernels
2 tablespoons butter
salt
pepper

Steam the corn kernels for 5 minutes. Drain. Mix with the butter and beans, and season to taste with salt and pepper. This recipe makes 4 servings.

Corn Pudding

Very rich—a little goes a long way, and will be fondly remembered.

1¾ cups heavy cream
2½ cups corn kernels
2 teaspoons sugar or honey
4 tablespoons binding powder
½ teaspoon salt
2 tablespoons minced fresh parsley (opt.)

Mix the binding powder with a little of the cream until smooth (a blender may be used). Mix all the ingredients and pour into a buttered baking dish. Dot the top with butter and bake for 45 minutes in a 350° oven, until a light crust has formed. This recipe makes 4 servings.

Bocoles (Mexico)

These corn pancakes are an adaptation of an Aztec dish, or, as the person who described the dish called it, "a Moctezuma dish."

3 cups corn kernels
½ cup cornmeal
2 tablespoons soy flour
½ teaspoon salt
2 tablespoons oil
water to blend

Combine all the ingredients in a grinder or blender, adding just enough water to the blender to puree all the ingredients into a very thick batter. Fry 2-inch pancakes in butter until they are a dark, crusty golden brown on one side, then flip and fry on the other. Do not flip the bocoles until they are completely done on one side, or they will fall apart in mid-air. This recipe makes 4 to 5 servings.

Serve plain, or with the following apocryphal sauce:

2 cups chopped ripe tomatoes
½ teaspoon salt
½ teaspoon basil
butter or oil

When the bocoles are done, add a little more butter or oil to the pan. Sauté the tomatoes with the basil and salt, mashing as they cook, until soft. Serve over the bocoles.

An even less authentic but delicious sauce for bocoles is tomato chutney.

Corn Fritters

1 cup flour
1 teaspoon salt
2 teaspoons baking powder
2 tablespoons binding powder
½ teaspoon thyme
⅛ teaspoon sage
3 tablespoons oil
¾ cup water
¾ cup yogurt
2 cups corn kernels

Mix the dry ingredients together. Add the oil, water, and yogurt. Mix well (a blender can be used). For best results, chill the batter for 1 hour.

Add the corn kernels. Fry 2-inch pancakes on each side in ¼ inch of oil until golden and crisp. Drain on paper towels. This recipe makes 18 to 20 fritters.

Variations

Add a little chopped green pepper or jalapeño pepper to the batter.

Omit the herbs and serve the fritters with maple syrup.

CUCUMBERS

Cucumbers are usually served uncooked, or juiced for a clear, sweet juice. They may be marinated, and in Europe they are sometimes served steamed and tossed with sour cream. The peel of cucumber is edible except when commercially coated with wax.

Steamed Cucumbers

Peel the cucumbers, if desired. Quarter or slice them and steam for about 15 minutes. Drain, and toss with sour cream.

EGGPLANT (AUBERGINE)

The word aubergine is derived from the Arabic word meaning peach. Eggplant is a unique and wonderful vegetable, with qualities and textures unavailable in any other food. Eggplant can be baked, sautéed, or stir-fried. It can be steamed, but its flavor and texture are not best developed by this method. Eggplant has a great affinity for oil, which it absorbs in tremendous amounts, and somehow does not show its best face if cooked without it.

Eggplant slices can be marinated by the a la Grecque method, used for pakoras or tempura, and added to both Chinese-style and Indian-style vegetable combinations. Serve eggplant with tomato sauce or taratoor sauce, or stir-fry it with a sweet and sour sauce.

The peel of the eggplant is very hard to digest, so peeled eggplant is used in many of the recipes. Otherwise we suggest removing the peel before eating. Most of the time eggplant may be eaten without extra preparation. Occasionally it can be bitter. When you seem to have latched onto a bitter crop, soak the slices in cold water for 15 minutes, or salt them and press with a weight for a little while to squeeze out the bitter juice.

Steamed Eggplant

Slice or quarter eggplant and steam for 10 to 15 minutes until tender.

Baked Eggplant

Baked eggplant slices are the basis for many dishes. See the recipes following this one for a few suggestions.

Slice an eggplant lengthwise or crosswise in half-inch pieces. Brush both sides with oil. Place on a baking sheet and bake for 30 to 40 minutes or more in a 350° oven until tender. Turn over once during the baking.

Eggplant au Gratin

Cover slices of baked eggplant with grated cheese. Sprinkle with sesame seeds or bread crumbs. Place in the broiler for 1 minute to melt the cheese.

Eggplant Florentine

Top slices of baked eggplant with mounds of creamed spinach. If desired, top with grated cheese and place in the broiler for 1 minute to melt.

Eggplant Pizza

Top slices of baked eggplant with thick tomato sauce. Sprinkle with grated cheese. Place in the broiler for 1 minute to melt the cheese.

Red-cooked Eggplant with Peppers (China)

Red-cooking is a method of braising foods with soy sauce, which imparts a hint of reddish color. Here we use sattvic sauce as a nonfermented substitute for soy sauce, and the effect is similar.

¼ cup soy oil
¼-inch piece fresh ginger, peeled and minced
1 medium eggplant, peeled, cut into quarters, and sliced thin
1 small green pepper, cut into strips
1 medium tomato, chopped
½ cup sattvic sauce (page 173)
½ cup water
1 tablespoon arrowroot or cornstarch
white pepper

Heat the oil in a wok. Add the ginger and fry for a few seconds. Add the eggplant and stir-fry for a few minutes. Add the green pepper and stir-fry for a minute more. Add the tomato, sattvic sauce, and ¼ cup of the water. Cover, reduce the heat, and simmer until the eggplant is tender. Mix the cornstarch or arrowroot into the remaining ¼ cup water until smooth. Add to the eggplant and cook until the sauce thickens. Season with a little white pepper. This recipe makes 4 servings.

Variations

If bitter, add a little sugar or honey.
The peppers may be omitted.

Stuffed Eggplant

2 eggplants
¼ cup olive oil
1½ teaspoons basil
1 teaspoon thyme
¼ cup minced fresh parsley
1 green pepper, chopped
2 zucchinis, quartered lengthwise and sliced thin
3 large tomatoes, chopped
salt
pepper
1½ cup grated cheese
2 teaspoons sesame seeds

Cut the eggplant in half lengthwise. Carefully hollow out the halves with a knife, leaving 4 shells. Rub the insides of the shells with a little olive oil. Sprinkle lightly with salt and pepper. Place in an oiled baking pan and bake in a 350° oven for 10 minutes.

While the shells are baking, chop the scooped-out eggplant. Heat the ¼ cup olive oil in a wok or large skillet. Add the basil, thyme, and parsley and sauté for 1 minute. Add the eggplant, green pepper, zucchini, and tomatoes. Sauté until tender. Season to taste with salt and pepper. Fill the eggplant shells with the vegetable mixture. Sprinkle with the grated cheese. Sprinkle the cheese with sesame seeds. Bake in a 350° oven for 20 minutes, until the cheese is melted. This recipe makes 4 servings.

Variation

Vegan Variation: Omit the grated cheese.

Eggplant Parmigiana (Italy)

See Eggplant Pizza (page 103) for one method of preparing this famous dish, or try this casserole method.

1 large eggplant
3 large tomatoes
¼ cup olive oil
2 teaspoons basil
1 teaspoon oregano
2 cups grated cheese
salt
pepper

Peel the eggplant, if desired. Cut in half lengthwise, then cut in ¼-inch slices. Cut the tomatoes into thin wedges. Heat the olive oil in a large skillet. Add the herbs and sauté for 1 minute. Add the eggplant, and sauté on a medium heat for 5 minutes. Add the tomatoes, reduce heat slightly, and sauté the mixture for another 10 to 15 minutes, until the eggplant is tender and the tomatoes are mushy. The skillet may be covered

to hasten the process. Season to taste with salt and pepper. Place the mixture in a baking dish. Mix in half the cheese. Spread the mixture evenly and sprinkle the remaining cheese over the top. Bake in a 350° oven for 20 minutes, until the cheese is melted and bubbly. This recipe makes 4 servings.

Variations

Sauté green pepper or zucchini with the eggplant.

Add toasted sesame seeds to the mixture before baking.

Eggplant-Potato Curry (India)

A wonderful curry. The texture of the potatoes and the flavor of the eggplant complement each other beautifully.

1 medium eggplant
2 medium potatoes
2 tablespoons ghee or oil
¾ teaspoon black mustard seed
1½ teaspoons cumin
1 to 1½ teaspoons salt
1 teaspoon turmeric
¾ cup water

Peel the eggplant and potatoes. Cut into tiny cubes. Heat the ghee or oil in a pot. Add the mustard seed and cumin, and sauté until the mustard seed dances. Add the potatoes and the eggplant. Sauté for 5 minutes, stirring constantly. Add the salt, turmeric, and water. Cover and simmer for 20 to 30 minutes, until the vegetables are tender. Stir once or twice during the cooking.

Serve with rice or Indian unleavened breads. This recipe makes 4 servings.

Variations

Add cayenne or red chilies to the oil.

Add 2 chopped tomatoes to the oil after sautéing the spices. Cook for 2 minutes before adding the vegetables.

Eggplant-Tomato Curry (India)

1½ teaspoons cumin
¾ teaspoon black mustard seed
3 tablespoons oil
2 large tomatoes, chopped
1 large eggplant, peeled and diced
1 teaspoon turmeric
1 teaspoon salt
½ teaspoon sugar or honey
¼ cup water

Sauté the cumin and mustard seed in the oil until the mustard seed dances. Add the tomatoes and cook for 2 to 3 minutes. Add the eggplant and sauté for 5 minutes, stirring constantly. Add the turmeric, salt, sugar or honey, and water. Cover and simmer for 20 minutes, until the eggplant is tender.

Serve over rice or with Indian unleavened breads. This recipe makes 4 servings.

Variation

Add cayenne or red chilies to the oil.

Folded-over Eggplant

1 large eggplant
breading mixture (page 189)
olive oil
1½ cups ricotta
½ cup dry bread crumbs
1 cup grated mozzarella
1 tablespoon binding powder
1 teaspoon basil
salt
pepper
3 cups tomato sauce
1 cup grated mozzarella (optional)

Peel the eggplant, if desired. Cut lengthwise in 10 thin slices. Dredge each slice in the breading mixture. Fry on both sides in ¼ inch of olive oil until golden and tender. Drain on paper towels.

To prepare the filling, combine the ricotta, bread crumbs, grated cheese, binding powder, and basil. Season to taste with salt and pepper. Place a generous amount of the filling on half of each eggplant slice. Fold the eggplant over to cover the filling. Place the eggplants in an oiled baking dish. Cover with the tomato sauce. If you wish, sprinkle 1 cup of grated cheese over the top. Bake in a 350° oven for 20 minutes, until the cheese is melted. This recipe makes 4 to 5 servings.

Moussaka (Middle East)

This rich, flavorful moussaka is "a la Turque," as opposed to an "a la Grecque" non-vegetarian version. It is served both in Turkey and in the Arab countries.

¼ cup olive oil
1½ teaspoons cumin
1 large eggplant, peeled if desired, and quartered and sliced
2 cups chopped ripe tomatoes
1 teaspoon cinnamon
½ teaspoon sugar or honey
1 teaspoon salt
1 cup cooked garbanzos

Heat the oil in a skillet. Add the cumin and sauté for 1 minute. Add the eggplant and sauté for 5 minutes. Add the tomatoes and continue cooking for 3 to 4 more minutes. Stir in the cinnamon, sugar or honey, salt, and garbanzos. Place in a casserole dish, cover, and bake in a 350° oven for 1 hour.

Serve with cous cous, bulgar, or rice. This recipe makes 4 servings.

FENNEL OR FINNOCHIO

Fennel, which is technically a fruit, was known in ancient China, India, and Egypt, and was a symbol of success in ancient Greece. The tops and seeds are used as an herb and as a tea. Fennel, with its slightly licorice flavor and crisp texture, may be sliced raw into salads and used in the same manner as celery. It may be juiced in small amounts and combined with other vegetable juices. Fennel may be steamed, sautéed, or stir-fried. It is excellent marinated by the a la Grecque method (page 158) and added to antipasto or salad platters. Fennel can be creamed, cooked in tomato sauce, or, in the Swiss fashion, served with cheese sauce.

Steamed Fennel

Steam fennel whole, cut in half lengthwise, or sliced, for 10 to 15 minutes until tender.

Fennel Baked with Cheese (Switzerland)

Steam fennel stalks cut in half lengthwise until tender. Drain well. Place in a baking pan. Top with grated cheese and sprinkle with chopped, roasted almonds. Place in the broiler for a minute to melt the cheese.

GREEN BEANS
(String or Snap Beans)

Green beans may be steamed, deep-fried, cut fine and stir-fried, or kinpura-fried. They may be marinated and added to antipasto and salad platters. Use green beans for tempura and pakoras. Add green beans to soups, stews, and Indian-style spiced vegetable combinations. Try the recipe for Sesame-Ginger Carrots, page 97, substituting green beans for the carrots and omitting the honey.

Serve steamed green beans with lemon juice and butter, sauce noisette, taratoor, or tahini, or cooked in tomato sauce. Toss green beans with toasted sesame seeds or slivered almonds. Green beans can be cut fine and creamed (see page 78).

Steamed Green Beans

Trim the ends. Green beans can be steamed whole, sliced in 1-inch pieces, cut fine, or cut julienne-style. Steam whole green beans for 10 to 15 minutes, just until crisp-tender. Sliced green beans will take less time.

Green Beans and Coconut (India)

A mild, decorative green-bean side dish.

2 tablespoons ghee or butter
½ teaspoon black mustard seed
¼-inch piece fresh ginger, peeled and minced
¼ cup grated coconut
3 cups green beans, trimmed and snapped in half
¼ teaspoon salt
½ cup water

Heat the ghee or butter in a pot. Add the mustard seed and ginger, and sauté until the mustard seed dances. Add the coconut. Sauté, stirring constantly for 1 minute until lightly browned. Add the green beans, salt, and water. Bring to a boil, cover, and reduce the heat. Cook on a medium-high flame until the water is gone and the green beans are tender. This recipe makes 4 servings.

Green Bean Almandine Casserole

3 cups julienne cut green beans
⅓ cup blanched, slivered almonds
1½ cups béchamel sauce (page 167)
seasoned salt
pepper
1 cup grated mild cheese

Steam the green beans until they are almost tender. Drain well. Place in a buttered baking dish and toss with the almonds. Pour the béchamel sauce over the beans and toss gently. Season with salt and pepper to taste. Sprinkle the grated cheese over the top. Bake in a 350° oven for 20 minutes, until the cheese is melted. This recipe makes 4 servings.

Variations

Substitute cream of celery soup for béchamel sauce.

Vegan Variation: Omit the grated cheese.

Green Bean Curry (India)

A nice meal can be made of green bean curry, lemon rice, and pakoras.

1 tablespoon ghee or oil
¾ teaspoon black mustard seed
2 tomatoes, chopped
1 teaspoon salt
1 teaspoon turmeric
3 cups green beans cut in ½-inch pieces
½ cup water

Heat the ghee or oil in a pot. Add the mustard seed and sauté until it dances. Add the tomatoes and sauté for 5 minutes. Stir in the salt, turmeric, green beans, and water. Cover and simmer for 12 to 15 minutes, until the beans are tender.

Serve over rice. This recipe makes 4 servings.

Variation

Add cayenne or red chilis to the oil.

GREEN AND RED BELL PEPPERS

Green peppers are a crisp addition to salads, and wide slices may be used for dipping. They may be juiced, and small amounts added to other vegetable juices. Try carrot juice with a little green pepper and a small amount of cream for a real treat.

Green peppers can be steamed, sautéed, or stir-fried. Use green pepper strips for pakoras and tempura. Add green peppers to

Indian-style spiced vegetable dishes and Chinese-style stir-fried vegetables. Green peppers add marvelous flavor to soups and stews. Red bell peppers are slightly sweeter than green peppers, being their more ripe version, and may be used in identical ways. Try mixing slices of green and red peppers in dishes for a wonderful color contrast.

Steamed Peppers

Cut green peppers into strips or small pieces. Remove the seedy portion. Steam for about 10 minutes, until tender. (Peppers are rarely served steamed on their own. This is the approximate cooking time when you are adding peppers to vegetable combinations.)

Roasted Peppers

A deceptively simple recipe for the wonderful flavor, texture, and appearance of these peppers. Try preparing with mixed red and green bell peppers, and serve on an antipasto tray or salad platter.

bell peppers, cut in fourths or eighths
olive oil

Place the peppers on a baking sheet. Drizzle with olive oil. Bake in a 350° oven for 30 minutes. The peppers should still be slightly crisp. Serve at room temperature.

Stuffed Peppers

Alternate green and red bell peppers for color contrast.

8 large, firm, unbruised peppers
grain stuffing (page 188)
3 cups tomato sauce
8 slices cheese
bread crumbs

Remove the caps and seedy inside portions of the peppers, forming a case. Steam the pepper cases until almost tender. Drain well. Gently fill the pepper cases with the stuffing. Pour a little of the tomato sauce into a baking pan and place the peppers upright in the pan. Pour the remaining sauce over them. Place a slice of cheese on each pepper. Sprinkle with bread crumbs. Bake in a 350° oven for 15 to 20 minutes, until the cheese is melted and the sauce and peppers are heated. This recipe makes 4 servings (2 peppers each).

Variations
Omit the tomato sauce and place a little water in the bottom of the pan to prevent scorching.
Top with ricotta instead of cheese slices.
Fill with vegetable or bean mixtures.
Vegan Variation: Omit the cheese. Top with bread crumbs, a little tahini, or lentil sauce.

GREENS (Collard, Kale, Dandelion, Turnip, Beet, Mustard, etc.)

Tender young greens may be lightly sautéed and served with a little butter and lemon juice. Collard and mustard greens require longer cooking to remove their bitterness. Greens may be creamed, and most may be used in the same manner as spinach. Greens may be added to salads—dandelion greens are delightful in green salads and may be picked from the garden or fields. Steam greens in the manner of spinach (see page 118).

Collard or Mustard Greens

Wash the greens and trim the stems. Place in water to cover. Simmer for 10 to 20 minutes, until the bitter taste is gone and the greens are tender. Serve with lemon and butter.

KOHLRABI

Kohlrabi may be used in the same manner as turnips. See the section on turnips.

Steamed Kohlrabi

Steam raw kohlrabis whole, but slice the older ones for faster cooking. Trim the ends. Steam for 25 to 30 minutes until tender.

LIMA BEANS

Fresh lima beans may be added to soups, stews and both vegetable and bean combinations. They also may be steamed and marinated or added to salads. Use fresh limas in succotash. They may be pureed. Serve steamed limas with butter or a little cream.

Steamed Fresh Lima Beans

Remove the beans from their pods. Steam for about 20 minutes.

LOTUS ROOT

Lotus root, used in Chinese cooking, is an especially beautiful vegetable, with its delicate, lacy slices. Slice crosswise to reveal the patterns. Slice into salads, stir-fry in Chinese-style vegetable combinations, or add to Chinese-style soups. The slices discolor easily, so sprinkle them with lemon juice to keep them white if they must stand for more than a few minutes.

MARROWS

Mostly found in England and parts of Europe, marrows may be treated in the manner of winter squashes, or as long-cooking zucchinis. They are ideal for serving stuffed. Peel and remove the seeds before cooking.

OKRA (LADYFINGERS)

Okra is found in the cuisine of the American South, and also in India. It may be steamed, sautéed, or stir-fried, and may be used for pakoras and tempura. Okra may be added to soups, stews, and Indian-style spiced vegetable combinations. Okra can develop a somewhat slimy texture when cooked for a long time in water, and it is advised here, though some people like that texture, to otherwise steam okra lightly and then add to a finished soup or stew, or add during the last 10 or 15 minutes of cooking. Okra is delicious cooked in tomato sauce.

Steamed Okra

Trim the ends. Steam whole or sliced for 8 to 10 minutes until tender. Drain immediately.

Okra and Cornmeal (USA)

Deep-fried okra in a crispy coating.

4 to 5 cups okra, sliced on the diagonal in ½-inch pieces
tempura batter (page 89)
cornmeal
oil for deep-frying

Dip the okra slices first in the tempura batter to coat, then roll in cornmeal. Deep-fry until the coating is lightly browned and crisp. Drain on paper towels. This recipe makes 4 to 6 servings.

Variation
Season the cornmeal with a little thyme.

Okra Curry (India)

¼ cup ghee or butter
1½ teaspoons cumin
½ teaspoon black mustard seed
⅓ cup grated coconut
6 cups okra, halved lengthwise and cut in 1-inch pieces
½ cup water
1 teaspoon turmeric
¾ teaspoon coriander
¾ teaspoon salt

Heat the ghee or butter in a pot. Add the cumin and mustard seed and sauté until the mustard seed dances. Add the coconut and sauté, stirring constantly for a minute until lightly browned. Add the okra and sauté for a few minutes. Add the water, turmeric, coriander, and salt. Cover and cook on a medium-high flame until the water is gone and the okra is tender. This recipe makes 4 servings.

Okra and Tomato

Cook 3½ cups sliced okra in 2½ to 3 cups tomato sauce until tender, or:

3 cups chopped tomatoes
½ cup broth or water
1 bay leaf
3½ cups okra, cut in ½" pieces
2 tablespoons butter
¾ teaspoon thyme
¼ teaspoon sage
salt
pepper

Combine the tomatoes, broth, and bay leaf in a pot. Simmer, covered, for ½ hour. Sauté the herbs in the butter for 1 minute.

Add the okra and sauté for 5 minutes. Add the okra to the tomatoes and simmer for 5 minutes or more until tender.

Season to taste with salt and pepper. Both methods make 4 to 6 servings.

Variation
Replace 1 cup okra with 1 cup sliced celery.

PARSNIPS

Parsnips have a strong, sharp flavor when uncooked that mellows to be slightly sweet when cooked. They may be prepared in the same manner as carrots, or even in the same manner as turnips. They may be steamed or baked, and may be served creamed or pureed. They are particularly good baked and served with butter and lemon. See Glazed Carrots and Parsnips, page 98.

Steamed Parsnips

Scrub with a vegetable brush. Trim off both ends. Steam whole for 10 to 15 minutes until tender, or sliced for a little less time.

Baked Parsnips

Parsnips may be baked by both methods for vegetables on page 76. They are especially good split in half lengthwise, rubbed with butter, and baked in a 350° oven until tender and lightly browned.

PEAS

The fresher the peas, the sweeter they will be, and fresh peas are delicious lightly steamed and served with butter and a little cream and sprinkled with mint. Peas add wonderful flavor to soups and stews, and their cooking water itself makes a delicious sweet broth. Add peas during the last 10 or

15 minutes to vegetable dishes and Indian-style spiced vegetables to maintain their bright color. Peas produce one of the most delicious vegetable purees. Two pounds of pea pods yield about two cups of peas.

Steamed Peas

Remove peas from the pods. Steam peas anywhere from 8 to 15 minutes, until they are tender and yet still brightly colored. A little sugar or honey may be added to the cooking water to enhance the sweetness, if desired.

Peas and Lettuce (France)

This treatment brings out all the special flavor and sweetness of the peas.

3 tablespoons butter
2 tablespoons minced fresh parsley
1 stalk celery, with leaves, sliced
2 cups shredded lettuce
½ cup water
1 teaspoon sugar or honey
2 cups peas
1 teaspoon salt

Melt the butter in a saucepan. Add the parsley and the celery. Sauté slowly until the celery begins to become tender. Add the lettuce and sauté for 5 more minutes. Add the water, peas, and sugar or honey. Cover and simmer until the peas are tender. Drain (reserve the cooking water for drinking) and add the salt. More butter may be added if desired. This recipe makes 4 servings.

Variations
Add a little crumbled mint.
Add a little cream after draining.

Peas and Panir (India)

One of the all-time great Indian spiced vegetable dishes, with exquisite flavor and colors.

panir prepared from ½ gallon of milk, hung until firm (see page 44)
2 tablespoons ghee or oil
1 teaspoon fresh minced ginger
2 cups chopped tomatoes
1 teaspoon turmeric
½ teaspoon coriander
2 cups peas
¼ cup water
1 teaspoon salt
large pinch sugar
¼ teaspoon garam masala

Cut the panir into small cubes. Deep-fry until golden. Drain and reserve. Heat the ghee or oil in a saucepan. Add the ginger and sauté for 1 minute. Add the tomatoes and cook until slightly softened. Add the turmeric, coriander, peas, water, salt, and sugar. Cover and simmer for 15 minutes. Stir in the garam masala and the panir. Cook for 1 more minute.

Serve over rice or with Indian unleavened breads. This recipe makes 4 servings.

Variation
Add cayenne or red chilies to the oil.

Peas and Potato Curry (India)

Peas and potatoes are a classic Indian vegetable combination. This curry is used in the preparation of Biryani (page 179), but is also served in its own right.

¼ cup ghee or butter
1½ teaspoons cumin
5 cups potatoes, peeled and cut into small cubes
1 cup water
1 teaspoon turmeric
½ teaspoon coriander
¼ teaspoon fenugreek
1 cup peas
1 teaspoon salt

Heat the ghee or butter in a pot. Add the cumin and sauté for 1 minute. Add the potatoes and sauté, stirring constantly for 5 minutes. Add the remaining ingredients. Cover and simmer for 15 to 20 minutes, until the vegetables are tender.

Serve over rice or with Indian unleavened breads. This recipe makes 4 servings.

Variation
Add cayenne or red chilies to the oil.

POTATOES

Potatoes were used in South America and India for centuries, but it took the creativity of Antoine Parmentier, a French pharmacist in the sixteenth century, to convince Europeans that the potato, which had been brought from the New World over a century earlier as a decorative flowering

plant, actually had great culinary and nutritional potential! He was reputedly lauded by his king for his "discovery," and the French promptly made up for lost time by inventing hundreds of potato dishes.

Potatoes are indeed quite versatile. They may be boiled, steamed, baked, sautéed, or deep-fried. They may be added to soups and stews (where they serve to thicken and also can absorb excess salt), and may be added to Indian-style spiced vegetable dishes. Potatoes may be cubed and used for pakoras, or cooked and added to salads.

Serve potatoes with butter and salt (all that tender new potatoes need), or serve creamed or with cheese sauce. They may be seasoned with dill weed or with curry spices.

Boiled or Steamed Potatoes

Select firm potatoes without any sprouts or green spots. New potatoes, small with reddish skins, are good for steaming and boiling, while mature Idaho baking potatoes may be used for baking and more elaborate cooking methods.

A superior flavor and texture is gained by boiling potatoes, as the skins protect them, but steaming can be done when in a pinch for time. *Boil* whole potatoes in water to cover for 20 to 40 minutes, until completely tender when pierced with a fork. *Steam* quartered or sliced potatoes for 20 minutes or more.

Baked Potatoes

Pierce potatoes with a fork to make air holes in the skin (unpierced potatoes might explode during baking). Bake in a 400° oven for 50 to 60 minutes until tender when pierced through with a fork or knife. To hasten the process, bake with a fork deeply imbedded in each potato—the metal will send heat into the middle of it. Serve with butter, sour cream, or yogurt. Sour cream dip or dressing goes well with baked potatoes.

Roast Potatoes

Peel potatoes. Boil large potatoes for 10 minutes. Coat potatoes with melted butter or oil. Place in a baking pan and bake in a 375° oven for 50 minutes to 1 hour, until tender on the inside and browned on the outside.

Variation
Roll the potatoes in bread crumbs before baking.

Parsley Potatoes

Peel potatoes if desired (do not peel new potatoes) and boil until tender. Drain carefully and serve with plenty of minced fresh parsley sprinkled over them.

Potatoes Parmentier

Sauté tiny cubed potatoes in butter until tender. Sprinkle with salt and pepper and toss with plenty of minced fresh parsley. These potatoes are named for their French saviour.

French-fried Potatoes

The "fries" which the fast-food chains sling out in the U.S. as greasy fillers are the lovingly prepared *pommes frites* of France, a gourmet delight. With a little TLC, french-fried potatoes can be practically greaseless, delicious, and nourishing. Some luxurious day, try preparing them in ghee.

Peel the potatoes and cut them into strips about 2 inches long and ¼ inch wide on all sides. Always dry the potatoes with a towel or paper towel before frying. Leave plenty of room in the pot for the oil to bubble up.

Method #1: Deep-fry in ghee or oil until golden and crisp. Drain well on paper towels.

Method #2: Deep-fry the potatoes just until they are soft and limp. Drain. Raise the temperature of the oil a little. Deep-fry again until golden brown and crisp. Drain on paper towels.

Potato Chips

Potato chips were originally called Saratoga chips, after the spa where they were supposedly invented as a last-ditch effort to please an overly fussy customer.

Peel potatoes and slice off rounds as thin as possible. A food processor or slicer does the best job of achieving the requisite thinness. Deep-fry until golden and crisp. Drain on paper towels.

Mashed Potatoes

6 medium potatoes
2 tablespoons butter
¼ cup milk or cream
salt
pepper

Boil the potatoes until tender. When they are cool enough to handle, remove the peel. Mash thoroughly with the butter and milk or cream. Season to taste with salt and pepper. Beat until fluffy. This recipe makes 4 to 6 servings.

Variations
   Add milk powder for added richness and nutrition.
   Replace the milk with ricotta or yogurt.
   Replace half the potatoes with turnips, rutabagas, or carrots.

Pan-browned Potatoes

These brown, crusty potatoes with tender, buttery centers are real favorites.

6 medium potatoes
¼ cup butter
salt
pepper

   Boil the potatoes until almost tender. Drain, and peel when cool enough to handle. Cut into ½-inch chunks. Heat the butter in a large skillet. Add the potatoes and fry on a medium-high heat, stirring only occasionally so that a crust can form. Sprinkle with salt and pepper. This recipe makes 4 to 6 servings.

Variation:
Add ¼ teaspoon rosemary to the butter.

Oven-browned Potatoes

6 potatoes
3 to 4 tablespoons butter, melted
salt
pepper

   Peel the potatoes and cut them into ½-inch chunks. Place in a baking pan; pour the butter over them. Bake in a 375° oven for 50 to 60 minutes or more, until golden brown. Sprinkle with salt and pepper.

Hash-browned Potatoes (American Fries) (USA)

It is best to prepare hash-browns in a Teflon pan, as they tend to stick.

3 tablespoons butter
3 cups grated potatoes (peeled or unpeeled)
salt

   Melt the butter in a 10-inch skillet. Add the potatoes and sprinkle with a little salt. Fry, stirring, for 1 minute. Press the potatoes down into the skillet and fry very slowly without stirring, until a golden-brown crust has formed. Slice the potato mass into quarters. Carefully turn each quarter over with a spatula and brown the other side. This recipe makes 4 servings.

Swedish Potatoes (Sweden)

These tender, buttery potatoes have a wonderful flavor and texture.

6 medium potatoes
¼ cup melted butter
2 to 3 tablespoons bread crumbs
salt
pepper

Peel the potatoes. Cut slits very close together about ¾ of the way through the potatoes. This can be done by placing each potato in a large, deep spoon and cutting to the edge of the spoon. Place the potatoes, slit sides up, in a baking dish. Pour the

melted butter over them, gently separating the slits to allow the butter to penetrate. Sprinkle the bread crumbs over the tops and into the slits. Sprinkle with salt and pepper. Bake for 45 minutes or longer in a 375° oven, basting with the butter several times during the baking. This recipe makes 6 servings.

Scalloped Potatoes

6 potatoes
2 cups bêchamel sauce (page 167)
butter or ghee
salt
pepper

Peel the potatoes, if desired, and slice in rounds. Place a layer of potatoes in a buttered casserole dish. Cover with some of the bêchamel sauce, sprinkle with salt and

pepper, and dot with butter. Repeat with another layer of potatoes. Pour the remaining sauce over the top and dot with butter. Cover and bake in a 350° oven for 1½ hours. This recipe makes 4 to 6 servings.

Variations

Replace bêchamel sauce with auroré sauce, sauce suprême, or 2 cups cream of celery or cream of spinach soup.

Place slices of cheese between the layers, or uncover for the last 10 minutes of baking and cover with grated cheese.

Potatoes au Gratin

Prepare scalloped potatoes with the cheese variation, or:

4 potatoes
1½ to 2 cups grated cheese
2 to 4 tablespoons bread crumbs
salt
pepper

Boil the potatoes until tender. Cut in rounds. Place the rounds in a buttered baking pan. Sprinkle lightly with salt and pepper, then with the grated cheese, and last with the bread crumbs. Place in the broiler for a minute to melt the cheese.

Stuffed Baked Potatoes

The usual stuffed baked potatoes are filled with mashed potatoes. Here is a version with a vegetable and dairy filling.

6 potatoes
1½ cups pureed vegetables (any or all of these—carrots, peas, green beans, spinach, or broccoli)
1½ cups ricotta, sour cream, or yogurt
2 tablespoons butter
¼ cup minced fresh parsley
salt
pepper
grated cheese (for ricotta version only)

paprika
sesame or caraway seeds

Scrub the potatoes well. Prick with a fork once and bake in a 400° oven until tender. Cool until they can be handled.

Cut each potato in half lengthwise. Carefully scoop out as much of the potato as possible, leaving a firm shell. Mash the scooped-out potato with the vegetable puree and the ricotta, sour cream, or yogurt; add the butter and parsley. Season to taste with salt and pepper. Carefully fill the shells with the potato mixture. Sprinkle with the grated cheese, paprika, and sesame or caraway seeds. Return the potatoes to the oven for 5 or 10 minutes to heat through and to melt the cheese. This recipe makes 6 servings.

Variations

For an elegant touch, pipe a fluted border of fluffy mashed potatoes over the stuffing with a pastry tube after the potatoes have been stuffed.

Vegan Variation: Omit the grated cheese and replace the ricotta with crumbled bean curd or with more margarine.

Potato-Yogurt Curry (India)

A hearty and flavorful curry. A good winter dish.

2 tablespoons ghee or butter
¾ teaspoon black mustard seed
1 teaspoon cumin
¼ cup fresh minced parsley
¼ cup grated coconut
2 cups yogurt
1 teaspoon turmeric
1 teaspoon salt
4 cups potatoes cut in cubes
ghee or oil for deep-frying

Heat the ghee or butter in a large saucepan. Add the mustard seed and cumin, and sauté until the mustard seed dances. Add the parsley and sauté for 2 minutes. Add the coconut and sauté until it is lightly browned. Remove from the heat. Stir in the yogurt, turmeric and salt.

Deep-fry the potatoes until they are soft and slightly golden, but not crisp. Remove each batch with a slotted spoon and transfer to the yogurt mixture. When all the potatoes have been added, heat the mixture just to serving temperature—do not boil. It will already will be quite warm.

Serve immediately. This recipe makes 4 servings.

Aligot (France)

Crusty on the outside and buttery-soft on the inside, Aligot was developed from a description of a dish from the Savoie, in a book about French regional cooking. While it may not be completely authentic, it is certainly everything anyone could wish from a potato dish.

6 large potatoes
3 tablespoons butter
½ cup heavy cream
salt
pepper
1 cup grated swiss or gruyere cheese

Boil the potatoes until tender. Drain and peel. Mash the potatoes with the butter and cream and beat until soft and fluffy. Season to taste with salt and pepper, and beat in the cheese. Spread the mixture evenly in a baking dish. Bake in a 350° oven for 1 hour until golden and crusty. This recipe makes 4 servings.

Variation

Add sautéed, shredded cabbage before baking.

Potato Kugel (Jewish)

Some kugels are made from raw, finely grated potatoes. Here is one prepared from cooked, mashed potatoes. Like a soufflé, it rises, and then retreats after a few minutes out of the oven. Time it to be served immediately.

9 medium potatoes
¼ cup butter
½ cup matzoh meal or whole wheat flour
1½ teaspoons baking powder
1 cup corn kernels or diced carrots and peas
salt
pepper

Boil the potatoes until tender. Drain. When cool enough to handle, peel them and mash with the butter. Mix in the matzoh meal or flour and the baking powder. Add the vegetables, and season to taste with salt and pepper. Preheat the oven to 400° and place a buttered baking dish in it to heat.

Spread the potato mixture evenly in the hot baking dish. Bake for 1 to 1½ hours until well browned. This recipe makes 6 to 8 servings.

Latkes (Jewish)

Latkes, potato pancakes, are traditionally served on Hanukkah. What is less well known is that these traditional Jewish delicacies are also a Swedish tradition!

4 cups finely grated potatoes
¼ cup soy flour
¼ cup whole wheat flour
1 teaspoon salt

Drain the potatoes well. Mix with the flours and salt. Drop handfuls on a well-buttered griddle or skillet. Press and spread out to form thin pancakes. Fry on both sides until golden. (The first batch may stick to the pan, but the following batches won't.)

Serve with applesauce, sour cream, or hung yogurt. This recipe makes 4 servings.

Variation

Add corn kernels and/or sautéed sliced celery to the batter.

Rösti (Switzerland)

6 medium potatoes
¼ cup butter
salt
2 tablespoons water

Boil the potatoes until almost tender. Drain and peel. Slice in rounds and then cut into strips. Melt the butter in an 8-inch skillet. A Teflon skillet will help keep the potatoes from sticking. Add the potatoes, sprinkle with a little salt, and fry, stirring, for a minute or two. Press the potatoes down into the pan. Sprinkle with the water, cover, and cook on a medium heat for about 15 minutes, shaking the pan occasionally to keep the potatoes from sticking. Check the sides to see if they are browned. Uncover the skillet and invert a plate over

it. Turn over the skillet and plate so that the potatoes come out in a cake on the plate. If they have not browned enough, place them in a 400° oven until they are browned.

To serve, cut in wedges. This recipe makes 4 to 6 servings.

RADISHES AND DAIKON RADISHES

Garden radishes are usually eaten uncooked, in salads and on vegetable platters. They taste surprisingly good steamed, and can be added to soups and vegetable mixtures.

Daikon, the Japanese white radish, can be prepared in the same manner as turnips, but it has a stronger flavor. Daikon can be grated fine and served as a condiment similar to horseradish.

RUTABAGAS (YELLOW TURNIPS OR SWEDES)

Rutabagas are of the turnip family, but larger and with milder flavor. They may be prepared in the same manner as turnips, or may be french fried or mashed like potatoes. Mash potatoes with rutabaga, in equal parts, for extra flavor.

Steamed or Boiled Rutabaga

Slice and peel rutabagas. Steam for 30 to 45 minutes until tender. Rutabagas may be boiled whole in water to cover.

Rutabaga with Cheese

4 cups cooked, mashed rutabagas
¼ cup butter
2 cups grated cheese
salt
pepper

Mix rutabagas, butter, and cheese together. Season to taste with salt and pepper. Place in a buttered baking dish and bake for 20 to 30 minutes in a 350° oven. This recipe makes 6 servings.

SEA GREENS

Many varieties of sea greens have been used for centuries, particularly in Japan, for flavoring and seasoning. Sea greens contain salt from the sea, so do not season a dish until after adding them and tasting.

Hijiki is used in Japan for seasoning, and for flavoring soups and stews.

Dulse is found off the coast of Nova Scotia, where the children eat it like candy. It can be used as a tea or in soup stock. Dulse is sweet enough to be used in puddings or other desserts, simmered in milk or cream to add flavor. Simmer 1 tablespoon dulse in 1 cup liquid for 10 minutes.

Nori (Laver) is sold dried in sheets. It can be crumbled into soups or stews or over vegetables. Toast nori by waving it over a flame once or twice. Nori is used as a wrapping for sushi (page 70).

Kelp (Kombu) is found either dried and powdered as a table seasoning, or dried in bunches. It is used to flavor vegetable broths and stews. Add 1 inch of kelp to 1 cup water and simmer for 5 minutes. Remove the kelp before serving, or cut it up and add it to vegetable mixtures.

SNOW PEAS (CHINESE PEA PODS OR SUGAR PEAS)

These delicate pea pods are used extensively in Chinese cuisine. They may be steamed or stir-fried and added to Chinese-style vegetable combinations and soups.

Prepare snow peas by breaking off the stem end and pulling down to remove the string along the side of the pod. Steam or stir-fry for just a few minutes.

SPINACH

Serve spinach uncooked in salads. Try a salad composed of spinach, mung sprouts, and sesame seeds. Pureed uncooked spinach may be added to pasta and bread doughs for color and flavor. Place spinach leaves in a blender with the liquid for the dough and blend. The leaves may be strained out or left in.

Spinach may be steamed, sautéed, or stir-fried. The leaves may be used for tempura or pakoras, or may replace grape leaves in dolmathes. Steamed spinach may be pureed. Serve spinach with lemon and butter, or chopped and creamed. Add to Indian-style spiced vegetable dishes and to Chinese-style stir-fried vegetables. Mix steamed, chopped spinach with ricotta, sour cream, or cream cheese hollandaise.

When cooking spinach by any method, there are two things to remember:
1. Wash the leaves *thoroughly*. Sand gets trapped in the leaves and makes the spinach unpleasantly gritty if it is not fanatically and meticulously rinsed before cooking. Even cleaned spinach from packages still needs some rinsing.
2. What appears to be an enormous amount of uncooked spinach will cook down to almost nothing. Use a large pot and cook two to three pounds of spinach for four to six people.

Steamed Spinach

Wash spinach thoroughly and remove the hard stems. Usually the water clinging to the leaves after washing is sufficient moisture for steaming the spinach—don't add more than a tablespoon or two more. Steam 4 to 10 minutes, until tender. Drain very well. Spinach is easy to chop after cooking; simply run a knife through it while it is draining.

Spanakorizo (Greece)

A flavorful spinach and rice main dish.

2 pounds spinach
1 small green pepper
⅓ cup olive oil
¼ cup minced parsley
½ cup uncooked rice
¾ cup broth or water (1½ cups if using brown rice)
¼ cup lemon juice
1 bay leaf
salt and pepper

Wash the spinach thoroughly. Remove the stems and chop coarsely. Chop the green pepper.

Heat the oil in a pot. Sauté the green pepper, spinach, and parsley for 5 minutes. Add the rice, stock, lemon juice, and bay leaf. (*Note:* if using brown rice, simmer the rice for 15 minutes in the stock before adding to the spinach.) Bring to a boil. Cover and reduce the heat. Simmer about 20 minutes, until all the water is absorbed and the rice and vegetables are tender. Season to taste with salt and pepper. This recipe makes 4 to 6 servings.

Sāg (India)

A simple, tasty way to serve spinach and greens. This dish is traditionally served with cornmeal chapatis (see tortillas, page 220).

1 pound spinach
1 pound turnip greens or other greens
2 tablespoons ghee or butter
1-inch piece fresh ginger, peeled and minced
1 tablespoon coriander
salt

Wash the spinach and greens well; remove the stems and chop coarsely. Shake dry. Heat the butter or ghee in a pot. Add the ginger and sauté for 1 minute. Add the coriander. Add the spinach and greens. Sauté, stirring occasionally, until the greens are tender and the water is gone.

Season lightly with salt. This recipe makes 4 servings.

Variation

Add cayenne or crumbled red chilies to the butter along with the ginger.

Spinach Pie

Here is a recipe which can be altered to make three different pies: one with a pastry crust and a cheese topping, one with a millet crust and a cheese topping, and one with a double pastry crust.

1 pastry crust, partially baked, *or* 1 millet crust without the cheese
2 pounds spinach
½ cup ricotta
½ teaspoon salt
⅛ teaspoon nutmeg
1½ cups grated cheese
1 tablespoon sesame seeds
2 tablespoons wheat germ

Line a 9-inch pie pan with the crust.

Wash the spinach thoroughly and remove the stems. Steam and drain thoroughly. Chop while draining. Mix the spin-

ach with the ricotta, salt, and nutmeg. Place in the crust and spread evenly. Sprinkle the grated cheese on top. Cover with the sesame seeds and wheat germ. Bake in a 350° oven for 30 minutes. This recipe makes one 9-inch pie.

Variations

For a double-crust pie, do not partially bake the crust. Line the pie and fill as above, omitting the sesame seeds and wheat germ, and reducing the amount of cheese slightly. Place the top crust on the pie, seal, and prick in a few places with a fork. Bake in a 350° oven for 50 to 60 minutes, until the crust is browned.

Omit the ricotta.

Vegan Variation: Omit the ricotta and cheese and add 1 pound of spinach. Prepare with a double pastry crust.

Spinach-Cheese Tart

This tart can be served hot or at room temperature. It is nice served at room temperature accompanied by an antipasto platter for a summer lunch or dinner.

1 pastry crust, partially baked
2 pounds spinach
¼ cup heavy cream
2 tablespoons binding powder
1 tablespoon flour
½ cup ricotta
1½ cups grated mild cheese
¼ teaspoon nutmeg
½ teaspoon salt

Line a 9-inch pie pan with the crust.

Wash the spinach and remove the stems. Steam lightly and drain thoroughly. Chop while draining.

Mix the binding powder and flour into the cream. Heat in a saucepan, stirring constantly with a whisk, to form a thick paste. Mix the paste with the spinach, ricotta, nutmeg, and salt. Add the grated cheese. Spread evenly in the pie shell. Bake in a 350° oven for 30 minutes. This recipe makes one 9-inch pie.

Spanakopita (Greece)

The Greek version of spinach pie, using filo pastry.

½ cup butter
½ cup olive oil
3 pounds spinach
salt
1 pound filo pastry (24 sheets)
1 pound feta cheese

Melt the butter and mix with the olive oil.

Wash the spinach and remove the stems. Steam lightly with ¼ cup of the butter-oil mixture. Drain thoroughly, chopping while draining. Add a little salt (remember that filo is quite salty—just a touch will do). Brush a 10-by-14-inch pan with the butter-oil. Lay down a sheet of filo pastry. Brush with butter-oil. Add another sheet and brush again with butter-oil. Repeat until 12 sheets are used. Spread the spinach over the filo evenly. Crumble the cheese over the spinach.

Lay down 12 more sheets of filo, brushing each with the butter-oil. Pour any remaining butter-oil over the top. Score the top few sheets of filo with a sharp knife to make squares approximately 2½ inches wide. Sprinkle the top lightly with water. Bake in a 300° oven for 1 to 1¼ hours, until the filo is lightly browned—just turning golden and no more. This recipe makes 8 to 10 servings.

Variations
Substitute 1½ pounds ricotta mixed with 1 tablespoon dill weed for the feta.

Vegan Variation: Omit the feta and substitute 1 more pound of spinach.

Spinach-Yogurt Curry (India)

3 tablespoons ghee or butter
1½ teaspoons cumin
½-inch piece fresh ginger, peeled and minced
1 teaspoon coriander
2 pounds chopped spinach
1 cup yogurt
salt

Heat the ghee or butter in a pot. Add cumin and ginger and sauté for 1 minute. Add the coriander and spinach. Sauté until tender. Remove from the heat. Drain off any extra water from the spinach. Stir in the yogurt and a tiny dash of salt. This recipe makes 4 servings.

Variation
Add cayenne or red chilies to the ghee or butter.

SPROUTS

Mung sprouts are about the only sprouts regularly served cooked, though lentil sprouts may also be used. Mung sprouts are found in Chinese and Indian cooking. They may be stir-fried and added to Chinese-style vegetable mixtures and soups. For full information on sprouting, see page 153.

Stir-fried Mung Sprouts

2 tablespoons soy or sesame-flavored oil
¼-inch piece fresh ginger, peeled and minced
1 pound mung sprouts (6 cups)

Heat the oil in a wok. Add the ginger and sauté for a minute. Add the sprouts and stir-fry for about 2 minutes, until crisp-tender.

Serve over rice. This recipe makes 4 servings.

Curried Sprouts (India)

2 tablespoons oil
¼-inch piece fresh ginger, peeled and minced
1 pound mung sprouts (6 cups)
½ teaspoon turmeric
1 teaspoon coriander
½ teaspoon salt
½ teaspoon sugar or honey

Heat the oil in a wok. Sauté the ginger for 1 minute. Add the sprouts, spices, salt, and sugar. Sauté until the sprouts are tender.

Serve over rice, or with Indian unleavened breads. This recipe makes 4 servings.

SQUASH, WINTER

Butternut, acorn, hubbard, pumpkin, and other winter squashes may be steamed, baked, cut into tiny pieces and sautéed, or dipped into tempura batter and deep-fried. Steamed or baked squash may be served pureed. Add tiny pieces of winter squash to Indian-style spiced vegetable dishes. Serve squash with butter and drizzle with honey or maple syrup, or sprinkle with brown sugar.

Cooked squash may be used interchangeably with cooked yams or sweet potatoes. Squash seeds may be toasted and eaten in the same manner as sunflower seeds. Look for firm, unbruised squashes with no soft spots.

Steamed Winter Squash

Slice and peel the squash. Cut it into small pieces. Steam for 20 to 30 minutes or longer, until tender. For *spaghetti squash,* boil whole for 40 minutes to 1 hour, until tender on the inside when pierced with a knife. Cut in half lengthwise and scrape a fork lengthwise along the squash to make the ''spaghetti'' strands. Serve with butter and salt—or with tomato sauce and cheese!

Baked Winter Squash

Squash may be baked whole, quartered, or sliced. Bake spaghetti squash whole. If quartered or sliced, remove the stringy portion and seeds. Brush with oil or melted butter. Bake in a 350° oven until completely tender. If the squash is sliced it can take 45 minutes; if whole, it can take from 1 to 1½ hours. Place butter and honey, maple syrup, or brown sugar in the hollows of quartered squashes before serving. Sprinkle a little cinnamon on top, if desired.

Stuffed Winter Squash

Acorn squash is ideal for stuffing.

Cut squash in half. Remove the seeds and stringy portion. Rub the hollows with melted butter and sprinkle lightly with salt and pepper. Fill the hollows with grain stuffing (page 188) or Chinese-style fried rice. Dot the tops generously with butter. Place in a buttered baking dish. Cover and bake in a 350° oven for about 1 hour, until the squash is tender.

Variations

Mix a small amount of tahini or béchamel sauce with the stuffing.

Place decorative pecan halves over the stuffing.

Add sliced roasted chestnuts to the stuffing.

Squash-Maple Casserole

A good Thanksgiving dish.

4 cups cooked, mashed winter squash or
yams (butternut squash gives good color to
the dish)
¼ cup butter
½ cup chopped pecans
½ cup maple syrup
½ cup pecan halves

Mix the squash, butter, chopped pecans,
and maple syrup together. Place in a buttered baking dish and spread evenly. Decorate the top with the pecan halves. Bake
in a 350° oven for 30 minutes. This recipe
makes 4 to 6 servings.

Pumpkin or Squash Curry (India)

¼ cup ghee or butter
2 teaspoons cumin
1 teaspoon fresh minced ginger
¼ cup water
8 cups pumpkin or other squash, peeled
and cut into small pieces
¼ teaspoon nutmeg or mace
¾ teaspoon salt
1 tablespoon or more sugar or honey

Heat the ghee in a pot. Add the cumin
and ginger and sauté for a minute. Add the
pumpkin, water, nutmeg, and salt. Cover
and simmer until the pumpkin is tender.
Add the sugar or honey and mash. Add
more sweetening if desired. This recipe
makes 4 to 6 servings.

Variations
Add cayenne or red chilies to the butter.
Sprinkle on a little garam masala after
cooking.

SWEET POTATOES AND YAMS

George Washington Carver first glorified sweet potatoes and yams in the United
States. Yams have a deeper color and are
slightly more sweet than sweet potatoes.
Both, when cooked, may be used interchangeably with winter squash. They may
be steamed, boiled, or baked, but retain
most flavor when boiled in their jackets.
Slice yams and sweet potatoes very thin
and use in tempura. Pureed yams and sweet
potatoes may be used as a thickener for
soups and stews. Replace the carrots in
Carrot Crumble, page 97, with yams or
sweet potatoes. Serve sweet potatoes with
butter and honey, maple syrup, or brown
sugar.

Boiled Sweet Potatoes or Yams

Boil the sweet potatoes or yams in water to
cover for 20 to 40 minutes, until tender
when pierced with a knife.

Steamed Sweet Potatoes or Yams

Steam sliced sweet potatoes or yams for 20
to 25 minutes. Drain well.

Baked Sweet Potatoes or Yams

Prick the skins and bake in a 400° oven for
50 to 60 minutes, until completely tender.
To hasten the process, embed the tongs of
a fork deeply into each yam, to send heat
into the center of it while baking.

Candied Yams

4 or 5 yams
3 tablespoons butter
1 cup packed dark brown sugar *or* ¾ cup
maple syrup
1 tablespoon lemon juice
1 tablespoon orange juice or water

Boil the yams until almost tender. Drain,
peel, and quarter them lengthwise. Place in
a buttered baking pan. Melt the butter in a
saucepan. Add the brown sugar or syrup

and the juices or water. Bring to a boil. Pour over the yams. Bake in 375° oven for 20 to 25 minutes, basting and turning the yams over once. This recipe makes 4 or 5 servings.

Variation
Sprinkle with ½ cup chopped pecans or walnuts before baking.

Yam-Prune Casserole

4 large yams
¼ cup butter
⅓ cup packed brown sugar
⅔ cup pitted, sliced prunes
⅔ cup chopped walnuts
½ cup apple juice

Boil the yams until amost tender. Peel and slice into ½-inch rounds. Place a layer of the yam rounds in a buttered casserole dish. Sprinkle with half the prunes and ⅓ of the brown sugar and nuts. Dot with butter. Add a second layer of yams and sprinkle with the remaining prunes and ⅓ of the brown sugar and nuts. Dot with butter. Place the remaining yams on top, and pour the apple juice over them. Sprinkle with the remaining brown sugar and nuts. Dot with the remaining butter. Bake in a 350° oven for 15 minutes. Cover and bake for 45 more minutes. This recipe makes 4 servings.

TOMATOES

Though technically a fruit, tomatoes are usually treated as, and combined with, vegetables. Uncooked, they produce a thick, rich juice. Marinate tomatoes for an antipasto tray or salads. Tomatoes add excellent flavor to soups and stews, and in India are used as a seasoning for vegetable dishes. Tomatoes were introduced into China in the twentieth century, and may be added to stir-fried vegetable combinations. They are delicious stir-fried with bean curd and green peppers.

Some people prefer to remove the seeds and skins from tomatoes for cooking. To do so, drop tomatoes into boiling water for 1 minute, drain, and peel off their skins. To remove the seeds, cut in half and squeeze and drain them.

Stewed Tomatoes

Blanch and peel tomatoes if desired. Slice and place in a saucepan with 1 tablespoon water. Simmer covered for 30 minutes, stirring occasionally. Season to taste with salt and pepper.

If desired, add sliced celery, green herbs or minced fresh parsley, brown sugar or honey, or lemon juice before cooking.

Baked Tomatoes, Plain

The flavor of good, rich, ripe tomatoes is beautifully accented by simple baking.

Cut tomatoes in half crosswise. Place in a baking dish, cut side up, with a little water in the bottom of the dish to prevent scorching. Sprinkle lightly with salt and pepper, if desired. Bake in a 350° oven for 10 to 20 minutes until tender. Serve plain, use as a garnish for a nut or bean loaf, or place on toast and cover with béchamel-herb sauce.

Baked Tomatoes, Fancy

4 medium tomatoes
salt and pepper
⅓ cup heavy cream
2 tablespoons fresh minced parsley
1 tablespoon toasted sunflower seeds
1 tablespoon toasted sesame seeds
2 or 3 tablespoons dry bread crumbs

Cut the tomatoes in half crosswise. Place close together in a buttered baking dish (they will fit snugly into a loaf pan). Sprinkle lightly with salt and pepper. Pour the cream over the tomatoes. Sprinkle the parsley, sunflower and sesame seeds, and bread crumbs over the top. Bake in a 350° oven for 15 to 20 minutes until tender. This recipe makes 4 servings.

Variations

Replace the cream with ½ cup grated cheese.

Replace the seeds with toasted chopped almonds.

Sprinkle a little brown sugar or honey on the tomatoes before adding the other ingredients.

Stuffed Baked Tomatoes

Slice the tops off large, firm tomatoes and carefully scoop out the meat inside, leaving a firm case. Drain the cases and sprinkle lightly with salt and pepper. Stuff the cases with grain stuffing, creamed vegetables, or Mexican-style corn. Replace the tops, or sprinkle with grated cheese and/or bread crumbs, chopped toasted nuts, or toasted seeds. Place in a baking pan with a little water to prevent scorching. Bake for 10 to 20 minutes, until the cases are tender and the filling is heated through.

Provençal Stuffed Tomatoes (France)

These elegant tomatoes shine as a first course, or can be served as an accompaniment to a meal. They may be served hot, cold, or at room temperature.

6 large, firm tomatoes
salt and pepper
1 cup finely crushed breadcrumbs
½ cup olive oil
¼ cup fresh minced parsley plus 1 tablespoon dried basil, *or* 3 tablespoons each minced fresh parsley and basil
¼ teaspoon thyme

1 tablespoon finely chopped green pepper (optional)
¼ teaspoon salt

Slice the tops off the tomatoes. Carefully scoop out the insides, leaving a firm case. Drain the cases and sprinkle lightly with salt and pepper. Mix the remaining ingredients together. Carefully fill the tomato cases with the mixture. Place the tomatoes in an oiled baking dish. Bake for 10 to 20 minutes in a 350° oven, until the tomatoes are tender but still hold their shape, and the filling is lightly browned. This recipe makes 6 servings.

TURNIPS

Turnips may be grated uncooked into salads for a sharp flavor. The sharpness of turnips is softened by cooking. Some turnips have a somewhat harsh flavor, and it is good to serve them mixed with other vegetables or with a sauce. Choose young turnips. Turnips may be steamed, baked, or

boiled. They may be pureed. Substitute half the potatoes in mashed potatoes with turnips. Turnips may be used to prepare vegetable burgers (page 87). Add turnips to soups and stews. Serve turnips creamed, or with curry spices. Baked turnips may be served simply, with butter and salt. Turnip greens may be added to salads, or cooked in the same way as spinach. Turnip greens are a major ingredient in Sag, page 118.

Steamed Turnips

Steam young turnips whole, but quarter or slice older ones for faster cooking. Steam 10 to 30 minutes, until tender.

Baked Turnips

Bake whole or sliced by either method for vegetables (page 76), from about 40 minutes for sliced turnips to 1 to 1½ hours for whole ones.

Turnip Cakes (China)

These fritters may be served as a first course, or as part of a Chinese meal.

3 cups finely grated turnips
1 finely grated carrot
¾ cup unbleached white flour
1 teaspoon baking powder
1 teaspoon salt
oil for deep-frying

Mix all the ingredients together well. Spread evenly in an oiled 9-inch square pan. Place a rack, or an inverted bowl, in a large wok or pot and fill with water to ½ inch below the rack. Bring the water to a boil. Place the pan with turnip mixture on the rack and cover the pot. Steam in this manner over a medium heat for 20 minutes.

Allow the turnip mixture to cool, then carefully cut it into 12 rectangular pieces. Deep-fry the cakes until golden. Drain on paper towels.

Serve with sweet and sour sauce or sprinkle with lemon juice. This recipe makes 12 fritters.

WATER CHESTNUTS

Fresh water chestnuts appear on the market occasionally, and are excellent served raw in salads or added to Chinese-style stir-fried vegetable dishes and soups. Their crisp texture is preserved by very light cooking—basically just heating them through. Peel, wash, and slice thin before adding to dishes.

WATERCRESS

Fresh, sharp-flavored watercress can often be found growing in streams. Pick watercress growing in running water, for health. It is served in salads and sandwiches for its sharp flavor. When cooked it loses its sharpness and adds an unparalleled flavor to soups and stews. Though watercress is usually served in combination with other vegetables, it can be creamed and used as a filling for crepes. Prepare watercress in the same manner as spinach.

ZUCCHINI (COURGETTES) AND SUMMER SQUASH

All summer squashes—yellow, Italian, patty pan, and so forth—can be prepared in the manner of zucchini. Grate them into salads. Juice them for a clear, sweet juice. Use zucchini and squash slices in tempura and pakoras. They may be baked, steamed, sautéed, or stir-fried. Sautéed grated zucchini is like an entirely new vegetable. Add zucchini to Indian-style spiced vegetables. Marinate zucchini slices by the a la Grecque method (page 158) and add to antipasto and salad platters. Steamed zucchini can be pureed. Add grated zucchini to sweet bread and cake batters.

Serve zucchini with lemon and butter, with cream cheese Hollandaise, or cooked in tomato sauce. Because it contains a lot of moisture, it tends to thin béchamel sauces a bit.

Choose firm zucchinis and squashes. The smaller ones have been picked when younger and are more tender.

Steamed Zucchini

For best flavor, steam zucchini whole and slice after cooking. Zucchinis may be sliced, however, for shorter cooking time. Steam 7 to 15 minutes, until tender.

Baked Zucchini

Baked zucchini has a wonderful, meltingly soft texture.

Slice zucchini in half lengthwise. Rub with butter or oil and place on a baking sheet. Bake for 40 minutes to 1 hour in a 325° oven, until tender. Be careful not to burn the underside.

Zucchini and Cheese

Grated zucchini is almost like a new vegetable. Here is a simple dish for light lunches or for serving as a side dish.

6 cups grated zucchini
2 tablespoons ghee or butter
1 cup grated cheese
salt and pepper

Sprinkle the zucchini with salt and toss. Let sit for 10 minutes, then drain very well. Melt the butter in a wok or large skillet. Add the zucchini and sauté until tender—about 5 to 7 minutes. If there is more than a tablespoon of water left in the pan, drain it off. Add the cheese to the zucchini, along with a sprinkling of salt and pepper. Stir for a minute until the cheese is melted.

Serve on toast or over rice, or as a side dish. This recipe makes 4 servings.

Zucchini Boats

6 large zucchinis
3 cups tomato sauce
¼ cup olive oil
1½ teaspoon basil
¼ teaspoon rosemary
2 tablespoons fresh minced parsley
1 grated carrot
1 celery stalk, cut fine
1 cup fine dry bread crumbs
½ cup finely chopped walnuts
salt and pepper
1 cup grated cheese

Slice the zucchinis lengthwise and carefully hollow out, removing the seedy portion. Place the zucchini boats side by side in an oiled baking pan. Bake for 15 minutes in a 350° oven.

Chop the seedy portion fine and add to the tomato sauce. Simmer the sauce while preparing the filling. Heat the olive oil in a skillet. Add the herbs and parsley, then the carrot and celery. Sauté until tender. Add the bread crumbs and walnuts. Season to taste with salt and pepper. Fill the hollows in the zucchinis with the bread crumb mixture. Pour the sauce over the zucchinis. Sprinkle the grated cheese on top. Bake for 20 minutes in a 350° oven, until the zucchinis are tender. This recipe makes 4 servings.

Variations

Omit the sauce. Place a little water in the pan to keep the zucchinis from scorching.
Vegan Variation: Omit the cheese.

Zucchini Curry (India)

An unusual, spiced zucchini puree.

¼ cup ghee or butter
½ teaspoon black mustard seed
1½ teaspoons cumin
1 teaspoon salt
½ teaspoon sugar or honey
¼ cup water
8 cups zucchini, peeled, quartered lengthwise and sliced thin
1 teaspoon turmeric

Heat the ghee or butter in a pot. Add the mustard seed and cumin, and sauté until the mustard seed dances. Add the remaining ingredients. Cover and simmer until the zucchini is tender. Mash lightly. This recipe makes 4 servings.

Variations

Cayenne or red chilies may be added to the ghee or butter.

Replace 2 cups of zucchini with 1 medium eggplant, peeled and cubed.

Zucchini Burgers

4 cups coarsely grated zucchini
salt
2 tablespoons sesame seeds
2 tablespoons soy flour
2 tablespoons whole wheat flour
1 cup grated cheese
salt and pepper
bread crumbs or breading mixture (page 189)

Sprinkle the zucchini with salt. Let sit 10 minutes. Drain thoroughly. Mix the zucchini with the sesame seeds, soy flour, whole wheat flour, and cheese. Sprinkle lightly with salt and pepper. Form patties. Coat thoroughly with bread crumbs or breading mixture. Fry on both sides in butter until golden, slowly, taking at least 5 minutes for each side. This recipe makes 8 to 10 burgers.

Zucchini Parmigiana (Italy)

3 tablespoons olive oil
1 teaspoon basil
1 teaspoon oregano
1 teaspoon thyme
5 medium tomatoes, cut in thin wedges
¼ cup water
6 cups thinly sliced zucchini
salt and pepper
2 cups grated mozzarella

Heat the oil in a wok or large skillet. Add the herbs and sauté for a minute. Add the tomatoes and sauté for 3 to 4 minutes. Add the water and the zucchini. Cover and simmer until the zucchini is just tender. Sprinkle with salt and pepper. Add 1 cup of the cheese and stir in. Place in a baking dish and sprinkle the remaining cheese over the top. Bake in a 350° oven for 15 to 20 minutes, until the cheese is melted. This recipe makes 4 servings.

Variations

Bake ratatouille in the same manner as above, with cheese.

Sprinkle toasted sesame seeds over the zucchini before baking.

Vegan Variation: Omit the cheese. Do not bake, but serve as a stew.

Beans

Beans, also called legumes, pulses, and dhal, are a staple protein food in many lands. Pinto beans are prevalent in the Americas, soybeans throughout Southeast and East Asia, various types of lentils in India, and black-eye peas in the southern United States, to name a few. Most types of beans can be sprouted (see page 153).

Beans may be added to most main dishes; combined with rice or other grains, they form a complete protein. Cooked, cooled beans can be added to green salads. Serve beans in tomato sauce, or mixed with vegetable stews and soups.

TO COOK BEANS

One cup of dry beans equals approximately two and a half cups cooked beans.

Before cooking, wash and sort the beans. Sometimes there will be a pebble among the beans. Remove all shrivelled, discolored beans—the bad ones will be quite obvious, but slight variations in color don't matter.

Soaking beans for 12 hours or overnight reduces the cooking time by a half hour or more. With the exception of lentils and split peas, mung beans, and split dhal, beans should be soaked, in about three times as much water as beans.

Though the soaking water contains some nutrients, draining the beans and cooking them in fresh water tends to reduce their flatulence. To drain or not to drain is a matter of personal choice—the soaking water can be used to water plants so that the nutrients will benefit them, if one opts for cooking in fresh water.

Simmer beans in 3 times as much water as beans. Cooking times vary, depending on whether one wants firm beans to add to a salad or tender beans to puree or use in soup.

Cook lentils, split peas, split dhal, and mansoor dhal for 45 minutes to 2 hours.

Cook navy beans, black-eye peas, limas, black beans, and kidney beans for 1½ to 2 hours.

Cook soybeans and garbanzos for 2 to 3 hours or more.

Longer-cooking beans may require addition of more water. Always have the beans covered with water. If a foamy substance forms on top, skim it off. Cook beans uncovered or partially covered.

Marinated Beans

2 cups cooked drained kidney, garbanzo, black beans or firm lentils, or white beans, limas, and soybeans
½ cup oil and lemon juice dressing

Mix together and let sit in the refrigerator for 2 hours or more. Serve on antipasto platters, as mezethakia, on salad platters, or mixed with green salads.

Variation

Add a little chopped green pepper, celery, green herbs, or tomato to the marinade.

Also see Three-bean and Five-bean salads, page 160.

Beans and Rice

Mixtures of beans and rice provide plain, nourishing food in many cultures. The mixture may be embellished with sautéed vegetables, tomato sauce, herbs and spices, and so forth, for more interest.

⅓ cup uncooked beans
½ cup rice

2 tablespoons butter
seasoned salt

Soak the beans overnight, if necessary. Cook until tender. Drain, but retain 1½ cups of their cooking water (2 cups if using brown rice). Return the beans and water to the pot. Bring to a boil. Add the rice. Cover, reduce the heat, and simmer until the rice is tender and all the water has been absorbed. Mix in the butter and season to taste. This recipe makes 3 to 4 servings.

Bean Patties

1⅓ cups uncooked garbanzos, kidney beans, limas, pinto beans, or black beans
1 carrot, grated
1 celery stalk, cut fine
¼ cup butter
1 teaspoon salt
1 teaspoon dill seed
¾ cup grated cheese
bread crumbs or breading mixture (page 189)

Soak the beans overnight. Cook until tender. Drain and mash.

Sauté the carrot and celery in the butter until tender. Add to the beans. Add the salt, dill seed, and cheese. Form into patties. Roll in the bread crumbs or breading mixture. Fry on both sides in butter until golden.

Serve plain or on burger rolls. This recipe makes 8 to 10 patties.

Variations

For a flavor reminiscent of *frijoles refritos,* prepare bean patties with the following alterations:
1. Use pinto, kidney, or black beans.
2. Omit the carrot, celery, and dill seed.
3. Sauté 2 teaspoons cumin in the butter before adding it to the beans.
   Vegan Variation: Omit the cheese.

Deep-fried Beans

Deep-fried limas are served in China with congee (page 196).

Soak lima, garbanzo, or soybeans overnight. Drain well and pat dry. Deep-fry until golden brown. Drain on paper towels. Sprinkle with salt. Garbanzos can be sprinkled with lemon juice and cumin. Serve as a snack or an hors d'oeuvre.

Roasted Beans

Soak garbanzo, lima, or soybeans overnight. Drain well. Scatter on a baking sheet. Toast about 30 minutes in a 350° oven, stirring every five minutes. Be alert toward the end of cooking not to burn them. Sprinkle with a little seasoned salt. The beans may be coated with a little oil before roasting, if desired. Serve as a snack or hors d'oeuvre, or mix into salads.

ADUKI (AZUKI) BEANS

Aduki, small red beans, are used in China and Japan. Serve them mixed with rice, in soups, and in stews. They do not require soaking, and cook in about 1½ hours. Also see Steamed Buns with Aduki Filling, page 217.

BLACK BEANS AND TURTLE BEANS

Black beans are most famous in soup and are used in a sauce in Chinese cooking. Substitute black beans in *frijoles refritos* and other Mexican dishes for the usual kidney or pinto beans. Use black beans for bean patties (above), and in beans and rice. Add to soups and stews.

BLACK-EYE PEAS

These peas are common in the southern United States. Substitute black-eye peas for lentils in Vadas (page 71) for a dish of the South.

Hoppin' John (USA)

A glorified version of beans and rice.

½ cup black-eye peas
3 tablespoons butter or oil
2 stalks celery, sliced thin
¼ teaspoon rosemary
1 teaspoon thyme
2 tomatoes, chopped
1⅓ cups broth or water (use 2 cups for brown rice)
²/₃ cup rice
salt and pepper

Cook the peas until tender. Drain. Heat the butter in a pot. Add the celery, rosemary, and thyme and sauté for 5 minutes. Add the tomatoes and cook for another 2 to 3 minutes. Add the water or broth and bring to a boil. Add the rice, cover, reduce heat, and simmer until the rice is tender and the water is absorbed. Add the black-eye peas. Season to taste with salt and pepper. This recipe makes 4 to 6 servings.

Variation
Cayenne or red chilies can be added to the butter.

DHAL

Dhal is the Indian word for beans, and the special kinds of dhal are available in Indian specialty stores and occasionally in health food stores. Lentils and yellow split peas are used in Indian cooking. Some of the other types are:

Chana: These beans resemble garbanzos. Besan, or chick-pea flour, is ground from chana.

Mansoor: Red lentils. Sometimes these are found in grocery stores. Mansoor is bright orange, and mellows to a bright golden yellow when cooked.

Moong: Mung beans. They are available whole, or husked and split.

Urad: These beans are found with a black husk, or unhusked and split.

For recipes, see Dhal #1 and #2, page 151, and Vadas, page 71.

Dahi Vada (India)

Dahi means yogurt, and vadas are deep-fried balls made of pureed lentils or dhal. It is a flavorful, cooling, and nourishing summer dish.

3 cups cold water
2 tablespoons salt
vadas, page 71
3 cups thin yogurt

Mix the salt and water in a bowl. Drop the vadas into the water, in batches. Let soak for 2 minutes, then drain. Gently squeeze the water out of each vada. (This soaking and draining process removes all the oil from the deep-frying.) Place the vadas in a serving bowl. Pour the yogurt over them.

Stir gently and serve. This recipe makes 4 to 6 servings.

Kedegree (India)

Sometimes called kachadi, kitchri, or kecheree. It is gentle nourishment—soothing and digestible—and very good.

⅔ cup rice
⅔ cup lentils, split peas, mansoor, moong, or urad dhal
5 cups water (use 6 cups for brown rice)
2 tablespoons ghee or butter
¾ teaspoon black mustard seed
1½ teaspoons cumin
1 teaspoon turmeric
¼ teaspoon fenugreek
1 teaspoon salt

Bring the rice, beans, and water to a boil in a pot. Cover, reduce heat, and simmer until all the water is absorbed and the mixture resembles a thick porridge. The cooking will take about 1 hour. Stir occasionally, and be alert toward the end of cooking to make sure the mixture doesn't stick. Heat the butter or ghee in a small skillet. Add the spices and salt, and sauté until the mustard seed dances. Add to the kedegree. Adjust the salt. This recipe makes 4 to 6 servings.

Variations

Add cayenne or red chilies to the butter.

Cook finely cut vegetables in the kedegree. Try potatoes, green beans, carrots, and zucchini.

Omit the spices.

Add more ghee or butter.

Dosas (India)

Dosas are thin pancakes made from dhal and rice. They may be served for breakfast, or wrapped around a filling of curried vegetables and called "masala dosa." A grinder does a better job of preparing the dosas, but a blender can also be used.

1 cup white rice
⅓ cup urad dhal
¼ cup water
½ cup yogurt
½ teaspoon fenugreek (optional)
½ teaspoon salt

Soak the rice and urad dhal separately overnight. Drain. Combine in a blender with the water, or grind in a grinder to a smooth paste. Add the yogurt, fenugreek, salt, and enough water to make a thin pancake batter. Pour a little batter into a well-buttered, heated pan. Starting from the middle of the batter, swirl a spiral motion with a spoon to spread the batter out as thin as possible. Fry like a pancake, turning over when bubbles form on the surface of the batter. The first dosa usually does not come out so well, but the later ones will. This recipe makes about 12 dosas.

Masala Dosa

Place a few spoonfuls of peas and potato curry, eggplant-potato curry, or tiny cubed potatoes sautéed with curry spices on each dosa. Fold like a crepe.

GARBANZOS OR CHICK-PEAS

Garbanzos are found prevalently in the cooking of the Middle East, Greece, Italy, and also in India, where a smaller variety called chana is found. Garbanzos may be added to soups and stews and to grain dishes. They may be deep-fried or roasted, or marinated, and added to antipasto and salad. Use garbanzos to prepare bean patties (page 129). Also see Homos (page 64).

Chana Snack (India)

1 cup garbanzos
3 tablespoons oil
1½ teaspoons cumin
¾ teaspoon salt

Soak the garbanzos overnight. Drain. Sauté in the oil with the cumin for about 10 minutes, until crisp and browned. Sprinkle the salt on top. This recipe makes 2 cups.

Variations

Sprinkle with lemon juice.

Add cayenne while sautéing.

Falafel (Middle East)

Falafel sandwiches are particularly popular in Israel, where they are sold on the street corners.

1 cup garbanzos
½ cup cracked wheat
1 cup water
2½ teaspoons roasted cumin

1 teaspoon salt
¼ cup lemon juice
chick-pea or soy flour
oil for deep-frying

Soak the garbanzos overnight. Cook until very tender. Drain and mash to a smooth paste.

While the garbanzos are cooking, soak the cracked wheat in the water for 1 hour. Drain well. Mix all the ingredients together. Form 1-inch balls with the mixture and flatten each ball slightly. If the mixture does not hold together well enough to form the falafels, mix in a little chick-pea or soy flour. Let the falafels dry for 1 hour. Deep-fry the falafels until they are golden-brown. Drain. Serve with taratoor sauce. This recipe makes about 2 dozen.

To make a sandwich, cut pita breads in half. Fill each half with:

shredded lettuce, sprouts, or salad mix
    (page 155)
2 or 3 falafels
taratoor sauce
tomato slices (optional)

Variations
To make deluxe falafels, add minced parsley to the batter. When forming the balls, roll each ball in sesame seeds before deep-frying.

Add cayenne or red chilies to the batter.

Hiranya Garbanzos

Somewhat like a vegetable kugel, but with the added protein of garbanzos, this is a good winter main dish.

1¾ cups garbanzos
1 carrot, sliced
1 zucchini, sliced
1 cup peas
2 tablespoons butter
¼ cup fresh minced parsley
¼ teaspoon rosemary

1 teaspoon basil
1 celery stalk, sliced
2 tomatoes, chopped
½ cup whole wheat flour
salt and pepper

Soak the garbanzos overnight. Cook until they are tender. Add the carrot, zucchini, and peas to the beans and continue cooking until they are tender. Drain and mash the beans and vegetables together. While the garbanzos and vegetables are cooking, melt the butter in a skillet. Add the parsley, rosemary, and basil. Sauté for 1 minute, then add the celery and tomatoes. Sauté for 5 minutes. Mix the sautéed vegetables and the flour with the garbanzo mixture. Season to taste with salt and pepper. Place in a buttered baking dish. Bake in a 400° oven for 30 minutes. This recipe makes 6 servings.

Variation
Add grated cheese to the mixture before baking.

KIDNEY BEANS

Kidney beans have a beautiful color, and contrast well in salads. They may be marinated, and they may be used for *frijoles refritos* or bean patties (page 129). Add kidney beans to soups and stews.

Chili (Mexico)

1 cup kidney beans
2 cups water
1 bay leaf
2 teaspoons cumin
2 tablespoons olive oil
1 teaspoon oregano
1 stalk celery, sliced thin
1 green pepper, cut in chunks
2 cups chopped tomatoes
1 teaspoon coriander
½ teaspoon cinnamon

¾ teaspoon paprika
¼ teaspoon cloves
salt and pepper

Soak the beans overnight. Drain, and place in a pot with the water and bay leaf. Bring to a boil, then reduce to a simmer. Meanwhile, sauté the cumin in the oil in a large skillet for one minute. Add the oregano, celery, and green pepper and sauté for a few minutes. Add the tomatoes. Sauté for 2 to 3 minutes. Add the tomato mixture to the beans. Add the coriander, cinnamon, paprika, and cloves. Cover and simmer for 2 hours or longer on a low heat, until a thick sauce has formed and the beans are tender. Season to taste with salt and pepper.

Serve with rice or tortillas. This recipe makes 4 servings.

Variations
Add cayenne or red chilies to the oil.
Substitute pinto beans for kidney beans.

LENTILS

A green-brown variety of lentils is the most common, but there are also red lentils (mansoor dhal) and small green lentils available. Lentils are one of the shortest-cooking legumes. They do not require soaking, and firm lentils can be cooked in as little as half an hour.

Marinate lentils for antipasto platters and hors d'oeuvres. The French sometimes marinate lentils in a dressing prepared with walnut oil. Use in dhal and for vadas. Add lentils to soups and stews, and use for kedegree.

Lentil Burgers

The best of the burgers.

1 cup lentils
3 cups water
1 carrot, grated
1 celery stalk, sliced thin
½ cup bulgar or cracked wheat
2 tablespoons butter
salt and pepper
bread crumbs or breading mixture

Bring the lentils, water, carrot, and celery to a boil. Reduce the heat and simmer, uncovered, for 30 minutes. Stir in the wheat. Cover and simmer for about 20 minutes, until the water is absorbed. (Be alert that the mixture doesn't burn toward the end of cooking.) Mix in the butter. Season to taste with salt and pepper. Let the mixture cool until it can be handled, and has become firmer, Shape into burgers. Cover with bread crumbs or breading mixture. Fry in butter on both sides until golden.

Serve with nut gravy or on burger rolls. This recipe makes 10 to 12 burgers.

Lentil Loaf

1 cup lentils
3 cups water or broth
1 carrot, grated
1 celery stalk, cut fine
½ cup bulgar wheat
1 cup *fresh* bread crumbs, packed
4 tablespoons butter, melted
1 large tomato, chopped
salt and pepper

Bring the lentils, broth or water, carrot, and celery to a boil. Reduce the heat and simmer for 30 minutes. Add the bulgar wheat and simmer, covered, for 20 minutes, stirring occasionally, until all the water is absorbed. Be alert that the mixture doesn't burn. Mix the bread crumbs with the butter. Add to the lentil mixture. Add the tomato, and season to taste with salt and pepper. Place in a buttered loaf pan. Bake in a 350° oven for 1 hour.

Serve with tomato sauce or nut gravy. This recipe makes 4 to 6 servings.

LIMA BEANS

Dried limas can be used in the same manner as fresh limas when cooked. Add to succotash, or marinate and serve on antipasto platters or for mezethakia. Limas can be deep-fried or roasted, and may be used to prepare bean patties (page 129).

MUNG BEANS (KALAMATA BEANS OR MOONG DHAL)

Mung beans make excellent sprouts, and are used extensively in Chinese cooking. Add mung beans to soups and stews. Use split mung beans for dhal, and use either type in kedegree (page 130). Whole mung beans are available in health-food stores, and split mung beans may be found in Indian specialty shops.

NAVY BEANS AND WHITE BEANS

Add navy beans to soups and stews. Marinate for antipasto and mezethakia. The Greeks serve white beans simply dressed with olive oil.

Boston Baked Beans (USA)

As work, including cooking, was forbidden by the Puritans on the Sabbath, the early Bostonians would place their beans, along with Boston Brown Bread (page 222), in the oven on Saturday night, and the slow heat of the embers would gently cook them for Sunday dinner.

2 cups navy beans
3 medium tomatoes, pureed in the blender
½ cup molasses
½ cup packed dark brown sugar
1 tablespoon oil
½ teaspoon salt
¼ teaspoon cloves
dash mustard powder

Soak the beans overnight. Drain. Place the beans in a pot with water to cover and bring to a boil. Pour into a baking dish, making sure that the liquid covers the beans. Add the remaining ingredients and stir. Cover and bake for 5 hours in a 350° oven, checking every hour or so and replenishing the water so that it continually covers the beans.

After 5 hours, remove the lid. Add water to cover the beans once more, and bake uncovered for 1 to 1½ hours, until a little liquid remains as a thick sauce and the beans are a rich brown color.

The beans are traditionally served with Boston Brown Bread. They also go very well with cornbread. This recipe makes 6 servings.

Variation
Add a sliced celery stalk at the beginning of baking.

YELLOW OR GREEN SPLIT PEAS

Split peas are traditionally found in soup. They also may be used for vadas (page 71) and kedegree (page 130). The soft, smooth texture of cooked split peas adds natural thickening to stews.

PINTO BEANS

Pinto beans are used throughout the southern United States, and Central and South America. Use for bean patties (page 129). Add to soups and stews.

Frijoles Refritos (Mexico)

''Refried beans'' are served with rice, or in enchiladas, tacos, and other Mexican tortilla dishes.

¼ to ⅓ cup butter

2 teaspoons roasted cumin
3 cups cooked pinto beans
salt and pepper

Melt the butter in a skillet. Add the cumin and sauté for 1 minute. Add the beans and stir, mashing with a fork or potato masher while stirring. Remove after 5 to 7 minutes of frying and mashing. Season to taste with salt and pepper. This recipe makes 2 cups.

Variation

Replace pinto beans with black or kidney beans.

SOYBEANS

Many products are made from soybeans, including soy oil, soy flour, and bean curd. Soy milk and other dairy substitutes are produced from soybeans. For recipes of many dairy substitutes prepared from soybeans, see *The Oats, Peas, Beans and Barley Cookbook* by Edyth Cottrell (Woodbridge Press, 1974).

Cooking the beans themselves is a challenge. While they are loaded with nutrients, they are also hard to digest, and the taste is not particularly inspiring to many people. The goodness of soybeans can be derived from eating bean curd or by adding soy flour in small amounts to baked goods. (As soy flour is a part of our binding-powder egg substitute, it is present in most of the baked goods and many other dishes in this cookbook.) Soy grits, or finely broken-up soybeans, can be added to breakfast cereals and grain dishes.

For happy results with the beans themselves, one can cook them until very tender and mash or puree them, and add the puree to foods. Soybeans may also be deep-fried or roasted. For people who like soybeans, substitute them for navy beans in Boston Baked Beans, and for kidney beans in chili,

and marinate them for salads. Soybeans may also be cooked in tomato sauce.

Stewed Soybeans

Rather than serve soybeans plain, try this simple, flavorful method. It works well for other beans too.

1 cup soybeans
1 bay leaf
1 zucchini, sliced
1 carrot, sliced
1 stalk celery, sliced
1 green pepper, chopped
2 tomatoes, chopped
2 tablespoons fresh minced parsley
2 tablespoons butter
2 tablespoons whole wheat flour
1 tablespoon brown sugar *or* 2 teaspoons honey

Soak the soybeans overnight. Cook in plenty of water with bay leaf for 2 hours.

Have the soybeans just covered with water. Add the vegetables, tomatoes and parsley. Simmer, covered, for 1 hour.

In a small skillet, melt the butter. Add the flour and cook for 1 minute, stirring constantly with a whisk. Add the mixture to the soybeans and stir for a few minutes until thickened. Add the sugar or honey and season to taste with salt and pepper. This recipe makes 4 to 6 servings.

Soyburgers

1 cup soybeans
⅔ cup broth or water
1 carrot, grated
1 stalk celery, cut fine
1 tablespoon oil
1 medium potato, cooked and mashed
1 teaspoon dill seed
¼ cup soy flour
⅓ cup wheat germ or oats
salt and pepper

Soak the soybeans overnight. Cook for 2 to 3 hours until tender. Drain. Puree in a blender with the broth or water until smooth.

Sauté the carrot and celery in the oil for about 5 minutes. Add to the potato and mix. Add the dill seed. Add the soybean puree, soy flour, and wheat germ to the potato mixture. Season to taste with salt and pepper. Shape into patties. Fry the soyburgers in butter on both sides until golden brown, or broil on both sides.

Serve on burger rolls or with nut gravy. This recipe makes 10 burgers.

Variation

Place a slice of cheese on cooked soyburgers and place in the broiler for a minute to melt the cheese.

Soy Loaf

1 cup soybeans
¾ cup broth or water
1 carrot, grated
1 celery stalk, cut fine
½ green pepper, chopped
¼ cup butter
1 teaspoon dill seed
1 teaspoon basil
2 medium tomatoes, chopped
1 cup cooked bulgar wheat or other grain
½ cup toasted wheat germ
salt and pepper

Soak the soybeans overnight. Cook until tender. Drain. Puree in a blender with the water or broth until smooth. Sauté the carrot, celery, and green pepper in the butter with the herbs for 5 minutes. Add the tomatoes and cook for 3 more minutes. Mix together with the wheat and wheat germ. Season to taste with salt and pepper. Place in a buttered loaf pan and bake at 350° for 1 hour.

Serve with tomato sauce or nut gravy, or with béchamel sauce. This recipe makes 4 to 6 servings.

Bean Curd (Tofu or Dofu) (Oriental)

Bean curd can be found commercially in three types: firm, soft, and dried. Soft bean curd can be crumbled into Chinese-style stir-fried vegetables and fillings for won tons or spring rolls. The hard bean curd is cut into cubes and stir-fried or deep-fried and added to soups and vegetable mixtures.

Bean curd should be used when very fresh. It is highly perishable, and should be stored in the refrigerator, covered with water. Change the water every day if bean curd is held for a few days. Panir can be substituted if hard bean curd is unavailable.

A soft bean curd can be made at home by the following method. Lemon juice may be used to form the curd, but calcium lactate seems to work more successfully. It is available at pharmacies, where it is sold as a supplement for people with calcium deficiencies. The pills may be ground in a spice grinder or blender, or a mortar and pestle.

1 quart fresh soy milk prepared from soybeans (page 45)
1 to 3 teaspoons calcium lactate

Heat the soy milk in a double boiler or saucepan, stirring constantly. When it boils, add a teaspoon of calcium lactate. If it does not separate, add a second teaspoonful, and then a third. The "curds" will separate from the "whey." Drain through a muslin cloth or a fine strainer. Press the water out of the curd and let drain for a few hours. Refrigerate and use the same day, for best flavor, or hold covered with water overnight. This recipe makes about 1 cup.

Stir-fried or Deep-fried Bean Curd

Drain firm bean curd very well, by pressing a weight on it and allowing the water to drain off. Cut into cubes or rectangles. Stir-fry or deep-fry until lightly browned. If fried bean curd is added to a sauce and simmered, it will absorb the sauce and become spongy. Deep-fry a large rectangle of bean curd and use for a sandwich filling. Sprinkle with lemon juice.

Scrambled Bean Curd (China)

¼-inch piece fresh ginger, peeled and minced
2 teaspoons soy oil
2 large tomatoes, chopped
½ cup sattvic sauce (page 173)
3 cups crumbled soft bean curd (a triple or quadruple recipe for bean curd, above)
2 tablespoons soy or sesame-flavored oil
1 tablespoon cornstarch or arrowroot
¼ cup water

Sauté the ginger in the oil for 1 minute. Add the tomatoes and sauté for 2 or 3 minutes. Add the sattvic sauce and simmer, covered, for 20 minutes. Stir-fry the crumbled bean curd in the second amount of oil. Add to the sauce. Mix the cornstarch or arrowroot with the water. Add to the mixture and cook, stirring, until thickened. Add a little white pepper.

Serve over rice. This recipe makes 4 servings.

Variation
Add a little five-spice powder at the end of cooking.

Soups

There is a delightful old children's story, *Stone Soup,* about three resourceful soldiers who arrived in a village without provisions for a meal. They stood in the town square and announced their intention to make stone soup. The villagers gaped as they produced the special stones and placed

them carefully in a pot of water and busied themselves adjusting the temperature and sampling the flavor. "Ah," they would lament, "but the soup would be perfect if only we had a few carrots—or a potato—or just one cabbage . . . ," and the villagers, overcome by their curiosity, would run home to produce that one small item on which the success of the soup depended! The story ends with the soldiers and villagers sitting down to a meal of delicious soup.

Soups are indeed the best medium for such "something from nothing" treatment. All the little extras—the last few green beans, the tablespoon or two of barley left in the bag, and so forth, can find a place in the soup pot. As always, however, the quality and freshness of the ingredients will be reflected in the final product.

BROTHS AND STOCKS

A good stock, besides being the foundation of a good soup, can be used as the cooking water for grains, stews, and vegetable mixtures for extra flavor.

Basic Soup Stock

Soup stocks are essentially made from vegetables and herbs that are simmered in water. They are then strained out of the liquid, or they may be pureed into it. Vegetables that add particularly good flavor to stock are:

tomatoes
celery
kombu (kelp)
peas
watercress
parsley
green pepper

Broccoli and cauliflower tend to overwhelm soup stocks, and cabbage, if it is cooked more than half an hour, gives a sour flavor to stock.

A simple and economical method of preparing stocks is to keep a plastic bag in the vegetable bin and collect the edible scraps left from preparing the daily meals, such as spinach stems, carrot and zucchini ends, turnip and beet roots, and so forth. Every two or three days, prepare a soup stock by simmering them in water until tender and then straining them out. Two and a half cups of scraps will flavor one quart of water; however, for best flavor mix them with some whole sliced vegetables as well.

Diluted fresh vegetable juices aid in the preparation of soup stocks. Try carrot, tomato, or mixed green vegetable juices, mixed at a ratio of 3–5 parts water to 1 part juice.

The addition of a small amount of lemon juice, or replacing part of the water with sattvic sauce (page 173), will help add flavor to a stock.

Commercial broth powders and seasoned salts, found at health-food stores, can be used to add flavor. Check the ingredients on the label before purchasing, and do not use them as the sole flavoring ingredient for stocks. The only drawback in their use is that, though they can be delicious, it will be repetitive if they are used constantly. It is a lot of fun to use your creativity in selecting ingredients for stocks, and then adding a broth powder occasionally for a little extra flavor.

Vegetable Broth or Stock

½ cup peas
1 stalk celery, with leaves, sliced
¼ cup minced parsley or watercress
1 carrot, sliced
½ green pepper, sliced
4¼ cups water
salt

Bring all the ingredients to a boil. Cover and reduce the heat. Simmer until all the vegetables are tender, about 20 minutes. Strain out the vegetables, or puree them into the stock in a blender. If using for a plain broth, season to taste with salt. This recipe makes 1 quart (strained).

Vegetable Puree Stock

This is a basis for soup—it needs the extra flavoring from the soup ingredients, unless prepared with sattvic sauce or a broth powder.

1¼ cups steamed pureed vegetables (any or all of these—peas, carrots, potatoes, turnips, green beans)
3½ cups water or broth

Mix the ingredients together. Makes 1 quart.

Tomato Stock or Broth

Use rich, ripe tomatoes for the best flavor. This is delightful as a clear broth or as a soup base.

2 cups chopped tomatoes
2½ cups water
2 tablespoons minced fresh parsley
1 stalk celery with leaves, sliced
salt (celery salt is good)

Puree the tomatoes in the water in the blender. Combine all the ingredients in a pot. Simmer, covered, for 20 to 30 minutes. Strain if desired. If using as a plain broth, add salt to taste. This recipe makes 1 quart, unstrained.

Variations

Substitute watercress for parsley.
Substitute fresh tomato juice for tomatoes.
Substitute ½ cup sattvic sauce for water.

Sattvic Sauce Stock or Broth

Sattvic sauce stock is especially good for use in Chinese-style soups. If it is going to be served as a plain broth, use the additions in #2—it needs the flavor of vegetables to fill it out.

#1: Mix:
    ½ cup sattvic sauce (page 173)
    3½ cups water or vegetable broth
#2: Add to the above mixture:
    ¼ cup minced fresh parsley
    1 stalk celery with leaves, sliced
    ½ green pepper, sliced

Simmer for 20 minutes, then strain. Makes 1 quart.

Kombu Broth or Stock (Japan)

Kombu stock has a surprisingly delicate flavor, which makes it good for use in non-oriental soups as well as Japanese soups.

Also serve kombu stock over oriental noodles.

1 quart sattvic sauce broth or vegetable broth
2½-inch piece dried kombu (kelp)

Bring the broth and kombu to a boil. Reduce the heat and simmer for 5 minutes. Remove the kombu. It may be cut up and served with vegetables. This recipe makes 1 quart.

VEGETABLE SOUPS

A good vegetable soup needs slow simmering for all the flavors to blend. One to one and a half hours is usually sufficient, but the simmering can continue longer. Add the longer-cooking vegetables first, and reserve the shorter-cooking ones, such as peas and corn kernels, for the last 10 to 15 minutes of cooking, to retain their color and freshness. Broccoli and cauliflower tend to add an overly strong flavor to soups. Cabbage is great—but should not be cooked more than about 30 to 45 minutes.

Sautéing vegetables in butter or oil for a few minutes before adding them to a soup stock greatly enhances their flavor. Green herbs are almost essential for flavoring soups. They may be sautéed in butter or oil as well. Some cooks prefer to remove the herbs before serving the soup. This is unnecessary, unless the herbs are very large, but if it is preferred, they can be tied up in a piece of muslin or placed in a tea ball before adding.

Vary the textures of vegetable soups by slicing the vegetables for one soup, grating them for another, or pureeing the vegetables for another occasion.

Additions to Vegetable Soups

Grains may be added at the beginning of cooking. Remember that they will swell. Two to four tablespoons of grains for four to six cups of soup stock is sufficient. Allow enough time for the grains to cook, and in the case of wheatberries or rye, it may be best to soak them overnight before adding. In Europe, small amounts of farina (Cream of Wheat), semolina, and oats are added to soups, or may form their principal ingredient. These soups are quite thin, and bear no resemblance to the porridge associated with such cereals.

Beans of any kind may be used. Soak overnight if necessary, and remember that they will expand to 2 or 2½ times their uncooked volume. Allow enough time for the beans to cook, or partially precook them if necessary.

Milk or cream may be used to replace part of the stock toward the end of the cooking.

Butter can be added at the end of cooking as an enrichment. Use only 1 or 2 tablespoons and take care that the soup is not too oily.

Sour cream and hung yogurt can be passed at the table and added by the guests to vegetable soups—borscht is a primary recipient of such treatment. They can also be mixed into chilled soups.

Grated cheese may be stirred into soup, during the last minute of cooking, until melted and blended. Or pass grated cheese at the table to be added by the guests. Parmesan cheese is a favorite.

Bean thread noodles (see page 201).

Pasta may be added 10 to 15 minutes before the end of cooking. Fresh pasta may be added 6 minutes before the end of cooking.

Bean curd cubes, deep-fried or uncooked, may be added toward the end of cooking.

Gluten strips, deep-fried or pan fried, *vadas,* and *plain pakoras* may be added just before serving.

Thickeners: grated potato (cooked in the soup for 20 minutes at least)

cooked vegetable purees (to replace part of the broth)

fresh bread crumbs

barley or rice (to add a thicker effect)

a roux (added during the last few minutes of cooking)

Garnishes for Soup

tempura
crackers
croutons
minced parsley, watercress
thinly sliced lemons or limes
sprinkling of grated cheese
toasted sesame seeds, sunflower seeds
thin avocado slices

Soup au Gratin

Place vegetable soup in individual oven-proof bowls. Float a slice of toasted whole-grain bread in each bowl. Top the bread with grated cheese to cover the top of the soup. Place in the broiler until the cheese is melted and bubbly. Serve immediately.

Vegetable Soup

A good, basic vegetable soup which may be varied in hundreds of ways.

4 to 5 cups mixed vegetables, thinly sliced
2 tablespoons fresh parsley, minced
¼ teaspoon rosemary
½ teaspoon basil
1 bay leaf
2 tablespoons butter or oil
6 cups tomato or vegetable broth
1 tomato, chopped (if not using tomato broth)
salt and pepper

Sauté the vegetables and herbs in the butter for 5 minutes. Meanwhile, bring the broth to a boil. Add the vegetables to the broth. Cover and simmer for 1 or 2 hours. Season to taste with salt and pepper. Remove the bay leaf before serving. This recipe makes about 7 cups.

Barley Soup

A hearty European peasant soup.

¼ cup minced fresh parsley
¼ teaspoon rosemary
½ teaspoon basil
1 celery stalk with leaves, sliced
1 carrot, grated
1 tablespoon butter
5 cups stock or water
¼ cup barley
1 turnip, cut in small pieces
1 bay leaf
salt and pepper

Sauté the parsley, rosemary, basil, celery, and carrot in the butter slowly, for 10 minutes. Add the vegetables to the stock. Add the barley, turnip, and bay leaf. Bring to a boil. Cover and reduce heat. Simmer for 1½ to 2 hours. Season to taste with salt and pepper. This recipe makes about 6 cups.

Variation

Add chopped green pepper.

Cabbage Soup (Russia–Eastern Europe)

A flavorful stock is essential to this good, simple soup.

3 tablespoons butter
2½ to 3 cups shredded green cabbage
5 cups tomato or vegetable stock
salt and pepper

Sauté the cabbage in the butter for 5 to 7 minutes. Add the stock. Bring to a boil. Cover and simmer for about 30 minutes or a little longer, until the cabbage is tender. Season to taste with salt and pepper. This recipe makes about 7 cups.

Borscht (Russia)

Borscht can range from a cold beet soup to a hot, beet-based vegetable soup. For the cold soup, see the first Variation.

5 cups water or vegetable broth
¼ cup lemon juice
1 tablespoon sugar *or* 2 teaspoons honey
1 bay leaf
2½ cups grated beets
1 stalk celery, sliced
1 chopped tomato
1 large potato, cubed
1 cup shredded cabbage
salt and pepper

Combine all the ingredients in a pot. Simmer, covered, for 40 minutes to 1 hour, until all the vegetables are tender. Season to taste with salt and pepper. Remove the bay leaf before serving.

Serve with a spoonful of sour cream or hung yogurt in each bowl. This recipe makes about 7 cups.

Variations

Beet Borscht: Omit the cabbage and potato. Add ½ cup more grated beets. If desired, chill the finished soup. It may also be pureed in the blender, if desired. Serve with sour cream or hung yogurt; for a wild pink soup, blend the sour cream into the soup.

Cut the beets shoestring-style instead of grating them.

Spicy Borscht: Add 1 teaspoon roasted cumin, ⅛ teaspoon cloves, and ½ teaspoon cinnamon toward the end of cooking.

Minestrone (Italy)

Minestrone is a meal in itself—just add bread and a salad for a full dinner.

¼ cup garbanzos
¼ cup kidney beans
8 cups tomato broth, unstrained
1 bay leaf
2 tablespoons olive oil
½ teaspoon basil
½ teaspoon thyme
¼ teaspoon rosemary
½ cup shredded cabbage or spinach

½ cup sliced green beans
1 carrot, sliced
1 zucchini, quartered lengthwise and sliced
thin
½ green pepper, chopped
½ cup peas
1 cup noodles
salt and pepper
parmesan cheese (optional)

Soak the beans overnight, or precook for
1 hour. Drain. Bring to a boil in a large pot
with the tomato broth and bay leaf, then
reduce to a simmer. Heat the olive oil in a
wok or large skillet. Add the basil, thyme,
and rosemary, and sauté for 1 minute. Add
the vegetables, except the peas. Sauté for 5
minutes. Add to the broth. Cover the soup
and simmer for 1½ hours. Add the peas
and noodles. Simmer for 10 to 15 minutes
more. Season to taste with salt and pepper.
    Serve, if desired, with grated parmesan.
This recipe makes about 9 cups.

Variations
The ingredients of minestrone are flexible—
vary the beans and vegetables, and omit the
noodles if desired.

Turnip–Vegetable Rice Soup

A smooth, mellow-flavored soup.

4 cups water or broth
⅓ cup rice
2 tomatoes, chopped
1 carrot, sliced
1 cup cooked, mashed turnip
½ cup peas
2 tablespoons minced fresh parsley
1 tablespoon brown sugar *or* 2 teaspoons
honey
salt and pepper

    Bring the water or broth to a boil. Add
the rice, tomatoes, and carrots. Reduce
heat. Cover and simmer for 30 minutes.

Stir in the mashed turnip, peas, and parsley. Simmer another 20 minutes. Add the
sugar or honey. Season to taste with salt
and pepper. This recipe makes about 6
cups.

Variations
Replace the turnips with rutabagas.
    Replace ½ cup of the broth with heavy
cream, and add at the end of cooking.

Potage St. Germain (France)

For historical accuracy, it must be stated
that this soup was invented in St. Cloud
rather than in St. Germain. In any case, this
delightful pureed soup of peas and other
vegetables may be served either hot or
chilled. For the chilled version, omit the
butter.

3 cups peas
2 tablespoons butter
2½ cups water or broth
¼ cup thinly sliced radishes
2 cups packed shredded lettuce
1 celery stalk with leaves, sliced
1 tablespoon minced parsley
1 teaspoon crumbled dried mint leaves (1
tablespoon fresh)
½ cup heavy cream
salt and pepper

    Bring all the ingredients except the mint,
cream, and seasonings to a boil. Reduce
the heat, cover, and simmer until the vegetables are tender—about 15 minutes. Puree
the soup in a blender until smooth. Return
to the pot. Add the mint and cream. Heat
just to a simmer. Season to taste with salt
and pepper. This recipe makes about 6
cups.

Variation
Replace the cream with a thick mixture of
powdered milk and water.

Tomato Soup

The roux binder gives this soup smoothness. It may be omitted if you prefer a soup with the texture of fresh tomatoes.

3 cups chopped ripe tomatoes
1½ cups broth or water
1 tablespoon minced parsley
2 tablespoons butter
2 tablespoons flour
salt

Puree the tomatoes with the broth or water in a blender. Place in a saucepan with the parsley. Simmer, covered, for 20 to 30 minutes. Melt the butter in a small saucepan. Add the flour and cook for 1 minute, stirring constantly with a whisk. Add to the soup, beating with the whisk to remove lumps. Simmer, stirring, for 2 to 3 minutes to thicken. Season to taste with salt. This recipe makes 4 cups.

Variations

Sauté ½ teaspoon green herbs in the butter before adding the flour.

Blanch, peel, and seed the tomatoes before measuring if a perfectly smooth soup is desired.

Potato Soup

3 large potatoes
2 tablespoons butter
2½ cups stock
1 teaspoon dill weed
salt and pepper
2 tablespoons minced fresh parsley (optional)

Boil two of the potatoes until tender. While those potatoes are boiling, peel the third potato and cut into small cubes. Sauté in the butter until tender.

Drain, peel, and slice the boiled potatoes, and combine them with the stock and parsley in a blender until smooth. Return to the pot. Add the sautéed potatoes and the dill weed. Season to taste with salt and pepper. Heat to serving temperature.

Garnish with minced parsley. This recipe makes about 5 cups.

Corn Chowder

This "Manhattan-style" corn chowder is a real favorite—it is almost a stew.

1 potato
1 carrot, sliced thin
1 stalk celery, sliced thin
½ teaspoon thyme
½ teaspoon basil
⅛ teaspoon rosemary
2 tablespoons fresh parsley, minced
¼ cup butter
2 large tomatoes, chopped
4 tablespoons flour
3½ cups milk
2½ cups corn kernels
½ teaspoon paprika
salt and pepper

Boil the potato until tender. Cut into chunks.

While the potato boils, sauté the carrot, celery, herbs, and parsley in 1 tablespoon butter for 5 minutes. Add the tomatoes and cook for 5 minutes or more, until the vegetables are tender. Melt the remaining 3 tablespoons of butter in a pot. Add the flour and cook for 1 minute, stirring constantly with a whisk. Slowly add the milk. Beat with the whisk to remove any lumps.

Add the sautéed vegetables, potato, corn, and paprika. Bring to a simmer, stirring constantly. Simmer for 3 to 4 minutes, until the corn is tender and the soup is thickened. Remove from the heat and season to taste with salt and pepper. This recipe makes 4 to 6 servings.

Pumpkin Soup

Pumpkin soup can be prepared from any winter squash. Butternut squash gives a particularly attractive color.

2⅔ cups cooked, mashed pumpkin
2 cups milk or light cream
¼ teaspoon ground ginger
2 tablespoons butter
½ teaspoon salt
1½ tablespoons brown sugar or honey

Combine the pumpkin, milk, and ginger in a blender. Pour into a saucepan. Add the butter. Heat to serving temperature. Remove from the heat and add the salt and sugar or honey. This recipe makes 4 cups.

Variations

Curried Pumpkin Soup: Omit the ginger. Add ¾ to 1 teaspoon curry powder.

Vegan Variation: Replace the milk with broth or soy milk.

Won Ton Soup (China)

A real treat. Great for special occasions and with a Chinese-style meal.

won tons *uncooked* (page 67)
8 cups vegetable broth, boiling

Bring 6 quarts of water to a boil. Add a little salt to the water. When it boils, drop the won tons in. When the water boils again, add 2 cups of cold water to break the boil. Bring to a boil again and cook for about 6 minutes, until the wons tons are tender. (Check one first for tenderness.) Drain very gently.

Gently place the won tons in 5 or 6 individual bowls. Pour the boiling broth over them. This recipe makes 5 or 6 servings.

Variation

Add a handful of mung sprouts and shredded bok-choy or spinach leaves to the broth, and simmer for about 8 minutes before pouring over the won tons.

Sizzling Rice Soup (China)

The drama of sizzling rice soup is in its presentation. The last steps are performed at the table.

rice crust:
⅔ cup white rice
1⅔ cups water
oil for deep-frying

soup:
1 cup mung sprouts
½ cup snow peas
5 cups vegetable or sattvic sauce broth

Prepare the rice crust well ahead of time. Simmer the rice in the water, covered, for 10 minutes. Spread out in a thin layer—about 2 grains deep—on a buttered pan. Bake in a 250° oven for 1 hour. Place in the sun to dry for a few hours.

Shortly before serving time, prepare the soup by simmering the vegetables in the broth for 8 minutes. Break the rice crust into pieces and heat the oil for deep-frying. Place the soup in a tureen ready for serving; have another bowl ready to receive the rice crust, and cover a plate with paper towels.

Drop the rice crust into the oil. Call the family and friends to the table. Deep-fry the rice crust until just a hint of browning appears. Drain it on the paper towels for a few seconds and then transfer it to the bowl. Immediately bring the rice crust and the soup to the table. With one swoop, drop the rice crust into the soup, and listen to the sizzle. This recipe makes 4 to 6 servings.

Variation

The sprouts and snow peas can be replaced by thinly sliced celery and shredded cabbage.

CHILLED VEGETABLE SOUPS

Cold vegetable soups are excellent for summer meals. Remember that butter—which hardens when chilled—should not be used. Ingredients such as noodles and beans do not lend themselves gracefully to cold soups.

A simple method of preparing a chilled vegetable soup is to steam about twice as many sliced vegetables as the amount of soup desired (i.e., for 4 cups of soup, steam 8 cups of sliced vegetables). Puree the vegetables in a blender with yogurt or sour cream, and thin to the desired texture with broth. Add salt, pepper, and chopped fresh herbs. Powdered milk can be used instead of sour cream or yogurt, using a little more broth to thin the mixture.

Garnish cold soups with thin lemon and lime slices, mint leaves, parsley, watercress, and other fresh minced herbs, and thin slices of avocado. For a cooling effect, place an ice cube in each bowl. Besides the following suggested soups, serve Potage St. Germain and Beet Borscht chilled.

Avocado Soup

A rich cold soup. Use a flavorful broth for best results.

2 cups mashed ripe avocado (about 2 large avocados)
¼ cup lemon juice
1½ cups cooled vegetable broth
1 cup milk or part cream
seasoned salt

Combine the avocado, lemon juice, and broth in a blender. Add the milk and blend again. Season to taste with seasoned salt. This recipe makes 4 cups.

Variations

Add a handful of watercress leaves and blend.

Vegan Variation: Replace milk with a rich nut or soy milk.

Golden Avocado-Carrot Soup

2 cups mashed ripe avocado (about 2 large avocados)

¼ cup lemon juice
1¼ cups fresh carrot juice
1¼ cups milk or part cream
1 teaspoon basil
¾ teaspoon salt

Combine the avocado, lemon juice, and carrot juice in a blender. Add the milk and blend again. Add the basil and salt. This recipe makes 4 cups.

Variations

For a more golden color, blend in steamed carrots.

Vegan Variation: Replace milk with rich nut or soy milk.

Gazpacho (Spain)

Gazpacho, from Andaluz in southern Spain, is a liquefied salad—made entirely from uncooked vegetables. Very refreshing.

1 medium green pepper
3 cups chopped ripe tomatoes
¼ cup minced fresh parsley
½ cup chopped cucumber
½ cup lemon juice
2 teaspoons green herbs
½ cup water or broth
¼ cup olive oil
salt and pepper

Chop all the ingredients together very fine and season to taste with salt and pepper, or combine everything in a blender until smooth. Pour the gazpacho into individual bowls; place an ice cube in each bowl. Pass bowls of chopped green pepper, cucumber, and croutons at the table for people to add to the soup. This recipe makes 5 cups.

Variations

Add ½ cup fresh bread crumbs to the soup.

Add a little cream to the soup, omitting some of the water.

Cacik (Greece–Turkey)

A tangy, refreshing cucumber-yogurt soup. Preparation time is about 5 minutes.

2 cucumbers, peeled
2½ cups yogurt
2 tablespoons lemon juice
1½ teaspoons dill weed
2 teaspoons crumbled dry mint leaves *or*
    1½ tablespoons minced fresh mint
    leaves

Grate the cucumber and mix with the other ingredients, or combine everything in a blender.

For a beautiful presentation, strew a few whole mint leaves and some pomegranate seeds over the top. This recipe makes about 4½ cups.

CHILLED FRUIT SOUPS

Fruit soups, originally from Scandinavia, are served for light meals or for dessert. They can vary considerably, depending on the types of fruits used. A delightful soup can be prepared using only cherries—either the sweet or the sour variety. Here is a general recipe:

Fruit Soup

3 cups peeled, sliced mixed fruits (cherries, plums, mangoes, melons, apricots, peaches, grapes, small amount of berries)
1 cup water
¼ cup lemon juice
1 teaspoon cornstarch
¼ cup sugar *or* 3 tablespoons honey (approximate—adjust to the fruits)
1 cup pitted, halved cherries or sliced strawberries
whipped cream, sour cream, or yogurt

Puree the fruits, water, and lemon juice in a blender. Place in a saucepan, bring to a boil, and then reduce the heat. Simmer for 10 to 20 minutes until the fruit is tender. Mix the cornstarch with 2 tablespoons water until smooth. Add to the soup. Stir and simmer for 2 minutes. Stir in the sugar or honey and adjust to taste. Add the cherries or strawberries. Chill thoroughly.

Serve with spoonfuls of whipped cream, sour cream, or yogurt. This recipe makes about 4 cups.

Rose Hip Soup (Sweden)

An unusual summer lunch or dessert soup with a deep red color and tangy flavor.

1½ cups dried rose hips
5⅔ cups water
½ cup lemon juice
3 tablespoons cornstarch
1 cup sugar
whipped cream
slivered almonds

Soak the rose hips overnight in the water. Set aside ⅓ cup of the liquid and bring the rest to a boil. Reduce the heat and simmer for 10 minutes. Puree in the blender in small batches and strain. Return the strained liquid to the stove. Add the lemon juice. Bring to a simmer.

Mix the cornstarch with the reserved liquid until smooth. Add to the soup, stirring constantly, and cook for 2 to 3 minutes until thickened. Add the sugar and stir to dissolve.

Chill the soup thoroughly. Serve in individual bowls, topped with whipped cream and sprinkled with slivered almonds. This recipe makes about 6 cups.

Variation

Honey Variation: Replace sugar with ¾ cup honey and add ½ tablespoon cornstarch.

CREAM SOUPS

Cream soups are traditionally made by combining pureed vegetables with cream and stock. The following recipes are made with milk—they can even be prepared with nonfat or non-dairy milk. They have the advantage of being rich and filling, yet delicate and elegant. Some can be prepared quite quickly, in as little as 10 minutes.

The following recipes are thickened in the traditional manner with a flour-butter roux. Either unbleached white or whole wheat flour may be used. For a cream soup without flour, substitute Cream of Potato Soup (page 148) for the milk, flour, and butter.

If the traditional cream-broth base is desired, replace 3½ cups milk with 3 cups broth and ½ cup heavy cream.

Cream of Asparagus Soup

A beautiful, delicate green color and asparagus flavor are the characteristics of this soup.

1 pound asparagus
3½ cups milk
3 tablespoons butter
3 tablespoons flour
salt

Steam the asparagus until just tender. Drain. Slice off the tips and reserve. Puree the stalks with the milk in a blender. Strain. Reserve the pulp for some other use. Melt the butter in a large saucepan. Add the flour and cook for 1 minute, stirring constantly with a whisk. Slowly add the asparagus-milk, stirring constantly. Heat the soup to a simmer, stirring constantly. Add the asparagus tips. Remove from the heat, add salt to taste, and serve. This recipe makes 4 servings.

Cream of Carrot Soup

1½ cups grated carrots
4 tablespoons butter
3 tablespoons flour
3½ cups milk
2 teaspoons brown sugar or honey
⅛ teaspoon cinnamon (optional)
salt

Sauté the carrots in 1 tablespoon of the butter until tender, about 7 to 10 minutes. Melt the remaining 3 tablespoons of butter in a large saucepan. Add the flour and cook for 1 minute, stirring constantly with a whisk. Add the milk and beat with the whisk to prevent lumps. Add the carrots and the cinnamon (if desired). Bring the soup to a simmer, stirring constantly. Simmer for a few minutes, until the carrots are completely tender and the soup has thickened.

Remove from the heat and add salt to taste. This recipe makes 4 cups.

Cream of Cauliflower Soup

1⅔ cups cauliflower, cut fine
4 tablespoons butter
3½ cups milk
1 tablespoon fresh minced parsley
3 tablespoons flour
½ cup grated cheese
¼ teaspoon paprika
salt

Sauté the cauliflower in 1 tablespoon butter for 5 minutes. Melt the remaining 3 tablespoons butter in a large saucepan. Add the flour and cook for 1 minute, stirring constantly with a whisk. Slowly add the milk and beat with the whisk to prevent lumps. Add the cauliflower and parsley. Bring to a simmer, stirring constantly. Simmer until the cauliflower is tender. Add the grated cheese and the paprika. Stir for a minute until the cheese is melted. Remove from the heat and add salt to taste.

Garnish with minced parsley. This recipe makes 4 cups.

Variation

Vegan Variation: Omit the cheese. Slightly increase the amount of cauliflower, if desired.

Cream of Celery Soup

For best flavor, prepare the roux with whole wheat flour.

½ teaspoon thyme
½ teaspoon basil
1½ cups celery, with leaves, cut fine
4 tablespoons butter
3 tablespoons flour
3½ cups milk
1 bay leaf
celery salt

Sauté the thyme, basil, and celery in 1 tablespoon butter, until the celery is tender. Melt the remaining 3 tablespoons butter in a large saucepan. Add the flour and cook for 1 minute, stirring constantly with a whisk. Add the milk and beat with the whisk to prevent lumps. Add the bay leaf. Add the celery and bring the soup to a simmer, stirring constantly. Simmer until the celery is tender. Remove from the heat and season to taste with celery salt. This recipe makes 4 cups.

Cream of Corn Soup

4 tablespoons butter
3 tablespoons flour
3½ cups milk
2 cups corn kernels
2 tablespoons minced fresh parsley (optional)
¼ teaspoon paprika
salt

Melt the butter in a large saucepan. Add the flour and cook for 1 minute, stirring constantly with a whisk. Add the milk and beat with the whisk to remove lumps. Add the corn and parsley. Bring the soup to a simmer, stirring constantly, and simmer for 3 to 4 minutes or more until the corn is tender. Remove from the heat and season to taste with paprika and salt. This recipe makes 4 cups.

Cream of Potato Soup

Prepare potato soup, page 143, replacing the stock with milk or light cream.

Cream of Spinach or Watercress Soup

This soup can be prepared in about 10 minutes. Chard or other greens can replace the spinach or watercress. Watercress has singular merit—it adds a very special flavor to the soup.

3 cups washed, dried, packed leaves with stems removed
3½ cups milk
¼ cup butter
¼ cup flour
pinch nutmeg
seasoned salt

Combine the greens and the milk in a blender for 1 or 2 *seconds,* until the greens are chopped but not completely pureed. If you have no blender, chop the greens fine. Melt the butter in a large saucepan. Add the flour and cook for 1 minute, stirring constantly with a whisk. Add the greens-milk mixture. Beat with a whisk to prevent lumps. Heat to a simmer, stirring constantly. Simmer for 2 or 3 minutes, until the soup is thickened and the greens are cooked. Add the nutmeg, and season to taste with seasoned salt. This recipe makes 4 cups.

Cream of Tomato Soup

2 cups ripe tomatoes, chopped
1 cup water or broth
2 cups béchamel sauce (page 167)

Puree the tomatoes with the water or broth in a blender. Place in a saucepan and simmer, covered, for 20 minutes. Meanwhile, prepare the béchamel sauce. Slowly stir the sauce into the tomatoes, stirring constantly. Adjust the seasoning.

Garnish with minced parsley. This recipe makes 5 cups.

Variation

For a more textured soup, do not puree the tomatoes before cooking.

Cream of Vegetable Soup

Vegetables in a creamy tomato soup base.

1¾ cups fresh tomatoes pureed in the blender
1½ cups finely cut mixed vegetables (peas, corn, carrots, green beans, fresh limas, others)
3 tablespoons butter
1 teaspoon basil
4 tablespoons flour
2 cups milk
1 bay leaf
seasoned salt
pepper

Simmer the tomato puree and the bay leaf for 5 minutes. Add the vegetables, cover, and simmer for 10 to 15 minutes, until they are tender.

Melt the butter in a large saucepan. Add the basil and sauté for 1 minute. Add the flour and cook for a minute, stirring constantly with a whisk. Gradually add the milk, and beat with the whisk to prevent lumps. Bring to a simmer, stirring constantly, until thick. Add the tomatoes and

vegetables. Simmer for a minute. Remove from the heat. Season to taste with salt and pepper. Remove the bay leaf before serving. This recipe makes 4 cups.

Variation

Omit the tomatoes and the milk. Replace with 3 cups vegetable broth and ½ cup heavy cream. Steam the vegetables in ½ cup of the broth, simmer the basil and flour roux in the remaining broth, and add the cream just at the end.

Cream of Zucchini Soup

Seasoned salt is very important to this recipe; otherwise this smooth, gentle soup will be a bit bland.

1½ cups grated, drained zucchini
4 tablespoons butter
3 tablespoons flour
3½ cups milk
celery or seasoned salt
½ cup grated cheese

Sauté the zucchini in 1 tablespoon of the butter for 5 minutes. Melt the remaining 3 tablespoons butter in a large saucepan. Add the flour and cook for 1 minute, stirring with a whisk. Slowly add the milk, stirring constantly. Add the zucchini. Bring the soup to a simmer, stirring constantly. Simmer until the zucchini is tender and the soup is thickened. Season to taste with seasoned salt. Add the cheese and stir for 1 minute until it is melted and blended. This recipe makes 4 cups.

Variations

Add a little curry powder.
Vegan Variation: Omit the cheese.

Cheddar Cheese Soup

For the cheese-lovers of the world.

¼ cup binding powder (page 51)

3 cups milk
3 tablespoons butter
3½ cups cubed sharp cheddar cheese

Mix the binding powder into ½ cup of the milk until smooth. Pour into a large saucepan. Add the remaining milk and the butter. Heat, stirring constantly with a whisk, until the butter has melted and the mixture thickens. Stir in the cheese and cook, stirring constantly, just until it is melted and blended. Remove from the heat. Adjust the seasoning, and serve immediately. This recipe makes 5 cups.

Variation
Sauté 2 chopped tomatoes in the butter until mushy, and add to the soup.

BEAN SOUPS

When cooking bean soups, remember to:
1. Soak the beans overnight, if necessary.
2. Add salt *after* the soup is cooked—otherwise it toughens the beans.

Lentil or Split Pea Soup

1 cup lentils or split peas
6 cups water
1 bay leaf
2 tablespoons butter or oil
2 carrots, sliced
2 celery stalks, sliced
1 chopped tomato
salt and pepper

optional binder for lentil soup:
2 tablespoons flour
2 tablespoons butter

Bring the lentils, water, and bay leaf to a boil. Reduce the heat. Cover and simmer. While the lentils are simmering, sauté the carrots and celery in the butter or oil for 5 minutes. Add the tomatoes and cook for another 2 or 3 minutes. Add the vegetables to the beans. Continue to simmer, covered, until tender—about 1 to 1½ hours or more.

If you prefer your soup more smooth and thick, melt the butter in a small saucepan. Add the flour and cook for 1 minute, stirring constantly with a whisk. Add a little of the soup and mix in well; then return the entire mixture to the soup. Mix well and simmer for 2 to 3 minutes.

Season to taste with salt and pepper. This recipe makes 6 cups.

Variations
Use fresh bread crumbs, rather than the flour roux, to thicken the soup—it doesn't look as good, but it tastes wonderful.

Puree the soup in a blender.

Add other vegetables and green herbs.

Black Bean Soup

1 cup black beans
5 cups water
1 tomato, chopped
1 celery stalk, cut fine
1 bay leaf
1 tablespoon butter
1 teaspoon brown sugar or honey
salt and pepper
lemon juice
lemon wedges

Soak the beans overnight. Drain. Place in a pot with the water, tomato, celery, and bay leaf. Bring to a boil, reduce heat, cover, and simmer for 2 to 2½ hours until the beans are very tender. Remove the bay leaf. Puree the soup in a blender with the butter and sugar or honey. Season to taste with salt, pepper, and a sprinkling of lemon juice.

Garnish with lemon wedges. This recipe makes about 5 cups.

Yellow Split Pea Soup (Sweden)

This soup is traditionally served in Sweden on Thursday nights, accompanied by pancakes.

1½ cups yellow split peas
6 cups broth or water
1 bay leaf
1 teaspoon thyme
seasoned salt
pepper

Bring the split peas, water, and bay leaf to a boil. Reduce the heat, cover, and simmer for 2 hours or more, until the split peas have melted into the water. Stir occasionally. Add the thyme and season to taste with the seasoned salt and the pepper. This recipe makes about 6 cups.

Fasolada (Greece)

1 cup navy beans or other white beans
1 carrot, sliced
1 celery stalk, with leaves, sliced
½ teaspoon basil
¼ cup minced parsley
2 tablespoons olive oil
2 tomatoes, chopped
5 cups water
2 tablespoons lemon juice
salt and pepper

Soak the beans overnight. Drain. In a soup pot, sauté the carrot, celery, basil, and parsley in the olive oil for 5 minutes. Add the tomatoes and sauté for 2 to 3 minutes more. Add the water and the beans. Simmer, covered, for about 2 hours. Add the lemon juice and season to taste with salt and pepper. This recipe makes about 7 cups.

Refrito Soup

A soup with the flavor of *frijoles refritos.*

1 cup kidney or pinto beans
5 cups water or broth
1 large tomato, chopped
1 stalk celery, cut fine
1 bay leaf
1 tablespoon cumin

2 tablespoons butter
1 cup grated sharp cheese
salt and pepper

Soak the beans overnight. Drain. Place in a pot with the water or broth, tomato, celery, and bay leaf. Cover and simmer for 2 hours or more, until the beans are tender. Sauté the cumin in the butter for a minute. Add to the beans. Puree the soup in a blender. Return to the pot and bring to a simmer. Add the cheese and stir for a minute until melted and blended. Season to taste with salt and pepper, and serve immediately. This recipe makes about 5 cups.

Variations
Replace the beans with black beans.
Vegan Variation: Omit the cheese. Add a chopped green pepper before cooking, for more flavor.

DHAL

The word "dhal" means beans, but it is also a soup that is served daily throughout India. Different spicing is used with different beans. Here are two "general" versions.

Dhal #1 (India)

1 cup lentils, yellow split peas, or mansoor
    dhal
6 cups water
1 tablespoon ghee or oil
½ teaspoon black mustard seed
1 teaspoon each cumin, turmeric, salt
½ teaspoon coriander
⅛ teaspoon cloves

Bring the beans and water to a boil. Simmer for about 1 to 1½ hours for lentils, or 2 hours for split peas. Heat the ghee or oil in a small pot. Add the spices and salt, and sauté until the mustard seed dances. Remove from the heat. Add a little soup to the spices and stand back—it will sputter. When the sputtering subsides, mix and add the mixture to the soup. Beat with a whisk to break up the beans a little. This recipe makes about 6 cups.

Variations

Add cayenne or red chilies to the oil.

Add finely cut vegetables, such as tiny cubed potatoes, cut string beans, or carrots, to cook in the soup.

Puree the soup in a blender.

Dhal #2

1 cup yellow split peas, mansoor, split mung, or split urad dhal
6 cups water
2 tablespoons grated, toasted coconut
2 tablespoons ghee or butter
¼" piece fresh ginger, peeled and minced
1 teaspoon cumin seed
½ teaspoon coriander
1 teaspoon turmeric
¼ teaspoon cinnamon
1 teaspoon salt
lime juice
melted butter or ghee

Bring the beans and water to a boil. Reduce heat and simmer for 1½ to 2 hours, until the beans are tender. Add the toasted coconut. Heat the 2 tablespoons of ghee or butter in a small saucepan. Add the ginger and cumin seed and sauté for a minute, then add the remaining spices and salt. Sauté for 1 or 2 minutes. Pour a little soup into the spices, and stand back while it sputters. When the sputtering subsides, pour the mixture back into the soup.

To serve, pour into individual bowls. Top each bowl with a sprinkling of lime juice and a teaspoonful of melted ghee or butter. This recipe makes about 6 cups.

Variations

Add cayenne or red chilies to the butter.

Substitute non-dairy coconut milk for the water.

Salads

GREEN SALADS

Tossed green salads are daily fare for many, served either as part of a meal or as meals in themselves. For fresh, crisp green salads, wash the greens and vegetables just before preparing, and prepare just before serving.

To prepare lettuce for a salad, break off the leaves and rinse them thoroughly under running water in a colander or lettuce basket. A lettuce basket is the most convenient tool for washing and then drying lettuce.

You simply take the basket outside after rinsing the lettuce and twirl it around to shake off the moisture. Otherwise, use paper towels and pat dry.

Tear the lettuce leaves into small, bite-sized pieces. Slice leaves only when a shredded effect is desired. Have all the extras cut into bite-sized pieces. It is pleasant to have all the ingredients in a salad pre-sliced, rather than having to take a knife to your greens before eating.

Place all the ingredients in a salad bowl. The bowl may be made of any material ex-

cept plastic, which absorbs oil. Wooden and pottery bowls are aesthetically pleasing. (See the notes on salad bowls on page 6.) Just before serving, add the dressing and gently toss the salad. Remember that a dressing is meant to enhance the flavor of the greens—a light hand is in order.

Ingredients for Tossed Green Salads

LETTUCE: Try a variety of different lettuces—using two or three types in the same salad adds variety and color.

Iceberg lettuce is the most common variety of "head" lettuce. It is white to light green and comes in a tightly packed head. Select iceberg lettuce by weight rather than by size—a larger head may actually have spread-out leaves and contain less than a smaller, heavier head.

Romaine and other leaf lettuces have long, separated green leaves and wonderful flavor on their own. Colors vary from dark green to reddish.

Bibb lettuce is a dark green head lettuce.

Butter lettuce or Boston lettuce comes in a very loose-leafed head and has a particularly delicate texture.

Endive or chicory has prickly, curly leaves and may be added in small amounts with other lettuce leaves.

GREENS: In addition to or in the place of lettuce, try some of the following greens:
spinach

watercress (in small amounts)
parsley
dandelion and other wild greens
mustard greens—small amounts
shredded purple and green cabbage

OTHER ADDITIONS:
green herbs
sprouts (see below for directions)
carrots, sliced or grated
grated turnip, jicama, kohlrabi, celeriac, beets
sliced radishes
sliced tomatoes or cherry tomatoes
avocado slices
sliced Jerusalem artichokes
sliced green pepper
marinated vegetables
cubed cheese
cottage or ricotta cheese
sour cream or yogurt
seeds of all types: sesame, sunflower, pumpkin, caraway, etc.
chopped or slivered nuts
roasted almonds
croutons
roasted soybeans or garbanzos
small amounts of whole cooked grains
small amounts of raisins or chopped dried fruits
small amounts of cooked, cooled pasta
steamed chilled peas, green beans, beet cubes, okra slices, broccoli, asparagus spears, artichoke hearts, cubed potatoes and other vegetables

SPROUTING

Home sprouting can be easily accomplished in a number of ways, and with a variety of seeds and beans. Sprouters are available through health-food stores, but the home methods are relatively simple and inexpensive.

The steps involved in sprouting are:
1. Soak the beans or seeds overnight in cool water.

2. Drain them and set up an environment that is constantly moist, but not dripping wet, in a dark, airy place. Keep the environment in this condition for the few days it takes the sprouts to grow. The rest is accomplished by the sprouts themselves—harvest them just as they begin their acceleration toward planthood, and enjoy.

Different seeds and beans sprout in different spans of time. The range is generally 3 to 5 days. When the sprouts are ready to be harvested, they can be placed in the sun for an hour or two to develop a little chlorophyll, and then refrigerated. Use sprouts within a day or two of harvesting for maximum freshness. You can gauge the average amount of sprouts eaten by your household within a day or two, and start new batches timed to keep a constant supply in the house.

Most whole seeds and grains can be sprouted. Mung sprouts and alfalfa sprouts have the most general use and are easy to grow. Lentil sprouts are also simple to grow and delightful. Some of the other grains and seeds that can be sprouted are:

red clover
wheatberries
whole beans—all types
fenugreek
soybeans
mustard seeds—very sharp
brown rice
whole dried peas

Sprouting Methods

Method #1 (deluxe method for alfalfa sprouts): Make a frame and loosely stretch a piece of plastic mesh across it. Sprinkle the seeds, which have been soaked overnight, on the screen in an even layer. Place the screen on top of a moist towel and cover with a light, damp cloth. Sprinkle the cloth with a little water two or three times

a day to keep it moist, but not dripping. When the sprouts are ready, remove the top cloth and transfer the sprouts to a sunny area for 1 or 2 hours to develop a little chlorophyll. Peel them off the mesh and store in plastic bags in the refrigerator. Alfalfa sprouts will have developed little leaves when ready to be harvested.

Method #2: Place the seeds in a wide-mouthed jar and cover the top with screening or muslin, so that air can enter. Soak a layer of seeds to cover the bottom of the jar in water overnight. The next day, drain the water out through the screening or muslin.

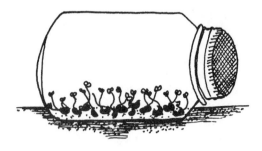

Water should not remain in a pool in the jar—the seeds should just be moist. Two or three times a day, fill up the jar with water and then drain it out. Store the jar in a dark, airy place. Continue until the sprouts are ready to be harvested.

Method #3: Place drained, soaked seeds on trays between layers of paper towels.

Ice-cube trays are ideal, because they won't rust. Sprinkle the paper towels three times a day with water to keep them moist, and store in a dark, airy place, until the sprouts are ready to be harvested. The same method can be applied to soaked, drained sprouts on towels spread in the bottom of orange crates, for making larger batches of sprouts.

Suggested Combinations for Salads

Spinach and mung sprouts with toasted sesame seeds

Lettuce-avocado-tomato-cubed cheese

Butter lettuce-spinach-cubed beets-tomato

Steamed green beans-celery-tomato-parsley

Lettuce-spinach-sprouts-sliced Jerusalem artichokes-slivered almonds

Leaf lettuce-grated carrots-shredded purple cabbage-cubed cheese

Salade Niçoise (France)

This lovely green salad from the Mediterranean is characterized by quartered tomatoes. Some traditionalists insist that a salade Niçoise can be prepared only from uncooked vegetables—which is fine by us. The following version is, if not the authentic, the traditional export which bears the name.

1 potato, boiled, peeled, and diced
6 radishes, thinly sliced
1 cup steamed, cooled green beans
2 or 3 tomatoes, quartered
3 cups torn greens (lettuce, spinach, etc.)
⅓ cup lemon-and-oil dressing (page 165), prepared with olive oil

Place the vegetables in a salad bowl. Pour the dressing over them and toss gently. This recipe makes 4 to 6 servings.

Variations
Add green herbs.

Add other steamed, chilled vegetables (asparagus tips would work well here) or uncooked vegetables. Anything goes, as long as the quartered tomatoes are present and accounted for.

Greek Salad (Greece)

In Greece this is called a rural salad, and makes use of both wild and cultivated greens in season.

5 cups torn greens
⅔ cups cubed feta cheese
2 or 3 sliced artichoke hearts (optional)
¼ to ⅓ cup lemon-and-oil herb dressing (page 165)

Place the greens, feta, and artichoke hearts in a salad bowl. Add the dressing and toss gently. This recipe makes 4 servings.

Variations
Add sliced cucumbers and green peppers.

Add cooked, cooled black beans.

Cole Slaw

From the Dutch: "Kool," meaning cabbage, and "sla," meaning salad.

2½ cups grated cabbage
1½ cups grated carrots
¾ cup cashew mayonnaise (page 170) plus 2 tablespoons lemon juice, or yogurt, or lemon-and-oil dressing (page 165)
salt and pepper

Mix all the ingredients together and season to taste with salt and pepper. Chill. This recipe makes 4 cups.

Variations
Add shredded beets, chopped cucumber, shredded zucchini, chopped green pepper, whole seedless grapes, pineapple cubes.

Add a tiny drizzle of honey.

A little fennel or anise seed gives an interesting flavor.

Carrot-Raisin Salad

2 cups grated carrots
¾ cup yogurt or cashew mayonnaise (page 170)
½ cup raisins
1 or 2 tablespoons honey

optional additions:
¾ cup diced pineapple
⅓ cup grated coconut
½ cup chopped walnuts

Mix all the ingredients together. Makes 3 cups.

Tomatoes Stuffed with Guacamole

Select firm, ripe tomatoes and cut off the tops. Carefully scoop out the inside pulp, leaving a case. Drain the cases and sprinkle them lightly with salt and pepper. Prepare guacamole (page 64) and add the chopped-up tomato pulp to it. Carefully fill each case and garnish with parsley, watercress, or cilantro sprigs.

Variations
Tomato cases can also be stuffed with corn and cottage cheese or other finely cut salads.

Avocado Salad

Slice avocados lengthwise. Remove the pit. Fill the hollows with:
#1: Lemon-and-oil dressing (page 165) or other light dressing.
#2: Grated vegetables; cover with a light dressing.
#3: Carrot and raisin salad, coleslaw, cucumber-tomato raita, or other light salads.
Sprinkle the avocados with lemon juice if they must stand more than a few minutes.

Beet Cups

Steam or bake whole beets. Carefully hollow out the insides, leaving a cup. Cool; fill the cup with grain salad, or cucumbers and sour cream, or another light salad.

Cucumbers with Yogurt, Dill, and Mint (Middle East)

Serve as part of mezethakia or as a small hors d'oeuvre or side salad. The mixture could also be added to a tossed green salad.

1 cup yogurt
½ teaspoon salt
¾ teaspoon dill weed
1 teaspoon crumbled, dried mint leaves *or* 1 tablespoon fresh minced mint
1 cucumber, peeled and sliced thin

Mix the yogurt gently with the salt, dill weed, and mint. Gently toss with the cucumber slices. Serve chilled. This recipe makes 4 servings.

Radish Salad

This little condiment salad was first seen prepared by a Mexican lady, and has since been found only in Chinese cookbooks. In any case, it would work well as part of Italian antipasto! You may want to add it to a tossed green salad, or serve it as a side salad.

2 cups grated radishes
2 tablespoons lemon juice
3 tablespoons oil (use sesame-flavored oil for Chinese meals)
salt and pepper

Mix radishes, lemon juice, and oil together and season to taste with salt and pepper. Chill. This recipe makes 2 cups.

RAITAS

Raitas are Indian preparations of raw or lightly cooked vegetables or bananas mixed with yogurt. They are for summer days, and for serving with hot, spicy foods. Raitas can be garnished with chopped nuts or with plain pakoras if desired. Chopped green chilies may be added if hotness is desired.

All of the following raitas serve 4 to 6 people.

Avocado Raita

2 cups yogurt
1 teaspoon roasted cumin
½ teaspoon salt
1 large avocado, cut into small pieces

Mix all the ingredients. Serve chilled or at room temperature.

Avocado-Watercress Raita

Add ½ cup finely chopped watercress to avocado raita.

Banana Raita I

¼ teaspoon cinnamon
⅛ teaspoon cloves
¼ teaspoon coriander
2 teaspoons sugar or honey
2 cups yogurt
2 ripe bananas, sliced thin

Gently mix the spices, and sugar or honey into the yogurt. Add the bananas. Chill.

Banana Raita II (cooked)

2 tablespoons oil
¼ teaspoon coriander
⅛ teaspoon cardamom
⅛ teaspoon ground ginger
½ teaspoon black mustard seed
¾ teaspoon salt
2 ripe bananas, sliced
2 cups yogurt
1 teaspoon sugar or honey

Heat the oil in a skillet. Add the spices and sauté until the mustard seed dances. Add the salt and the bananas. Cook, mashing the bananas with a fork, for 3 to 5 minutes, until they are mushy. Cool. Add the bananas to the yogurt. Add the sugar or honey. Mix and chill.

Cucumber Raita

1 cup cucumber, chopped and drained
2 cups yogurt
½ teaspoon salt
1 teaspoon roasted cumin

Mix the ingredients together.

Variations

Cucumber-Tomato Raita. Add 1 large chopped tomato and ¼ cup finely chopped cashews or almonds.

Potato Raita: Substitute 2 medium potatoes, boiled, peeled, and cubed, for the cucumber. Chill.

Eggplant Raita

4 to 5 tablespoons oil
¼ teaspoon black mustard seed
1 teaspoon cumin
1 medium eggplant, peeled and diced
¾ teaspoon salt
2 cups yogurt

Heat the oil in a skillet or wok. Add the mustard seed and cumin, and sauté until the mustard seed dances. Add the eggplant and sauté until tender, letting it brown a little. Cool. Toss the eggplant and salt with the yogurt. Chill.

Pumpkin or Squash Raita

Butternut squash or yams give a wonderful orange color to this raita.

1 cup cooked, cooled mashed pumpkin, squash, or yams
1 cup yogurt

½ teaspoon roasted cumin
½ teaspoon salt
1 teaspoon honey or sugar

Mix all the ingredients together. Chill.

COOKED VEGETABLE SALADS

A variety of cooked, cooled vegetables can be dressed with salad dressings and either mixed with uncooked vegetables and tossed green salads or served in their own right. Serve on beds of lettuce, greens, or sprouts in an attractive arrangement. For best presentation, the vegetables should be steamed until crisp-tender and still retain their bright colors. Beautiful large platters can be made containing these cooked vegetables and other small salads.

See Antipasto (page 72) and Mezethakia (page 73) for ideas.

Suggestions
Ratatouille served cold
Artichoke hearts with lemon-and-oil dressing
Wax beans and minced parsley with French dressing
Asparagus spears with cashew mayonnaise
Broccoli and cauliflower flowerets, mixed with slivered almonds and lemon-and-oil dressing
Green beans, peas, and uncooked red bell pepper slices with curried lemon-and-oil dressing
Broccoli spears with tahini dressing

MARINATED VEGETABLES

There are two methods of marinating: uncooked or lightly steamed vegetables may be soaked in the marinade, and vegetables may be cooked in the marinade itself. Marinated vegetables are at home in antipasto, or may be served as mezethakia or on summer salad platters. They may also be tossed into green salads. In any case, aim for beautiful color contrasts and arrangements.

Vegetables for marinating
zucchini and summer squashes
green beans
cucumbers (by method #1)
cauliflower flowerets
broccoli spears
sliced radishes (by method #1)
eggplant
asparagus spears
tomatoes (by method #1)
whole baby carrots
sliced carrots
beets
fennel stalks
artichoke hearts (by method #1)
whole artichokes (by method #2)
Jerusalem artichokes
lotus root

Marinated Vegetables #1

Steam all vegetables (except tomatoes, radishes, lotus root, cucumbers, and Jerusalem artichokes). Drain well. Place the dressing in a shallow bowl. Use lemon-and-oil dressing (page 165), with herbs if desired. Add the vegetables and toss to coat. Marinate for at least one hour, or all day. Stir occasionally to coat all surfaces. (Marinate beets separately—they tend to share their color with their neighbors.) Drain the vegetables slightly, if desired, before serving, or use the marinade as a salad dressing, as it has gained added flavor from the vegetables. Sprinkle the vegetables with fresh minced herbs.

Marinated Vegetables #2 (A La Grecque) (Greece)

½ cup olive oil
2 cups water
1 cup unsweetened apple juice or white grape juice

⅓ cup lemon juice
1 bay leaf
1 teaspoon salt
1 teaspoon dill weed
½ teaspoon oregano
½ teaspoon basil
a few peppercorns
1 pound cut vegetables

Combine all the ingredients except the vegetables in a pot. Bring to a boil, then reduce the heat. Add the vegetables (cook beets separately). Simmer, covered, until they are almost tender. Remove from the heat. Allow the vegetables to cool to room temperature in the marinade. Drain and serve at room temperature.

Russian Salad

1 cup each: steamed cubed beets, boiled
        cubed potatoes, steamed green beans
¾ cup cashew mayonnaise (page 170)

Mix all the ingredients together. Chill. Makes 3 cups.

Variation
Substitute lemon-and-oil dressing (page 165) for the cashew mayonnaise.

Potato Salad #1

Here is a light, bright version of the old classic.

6 potatoes
¾ cup cashew mayonnaise (page 170) or
        lemon-and-oil dressing (page 165)
¼ cup minced fresh parsley
1 small green pepper, cut small
½ cucumber, cut small
1 stalk celery, sliced thin
salt and pepper
paprika

Boil the potatoes until tender. Drain and cool. Peel if desired (it is not necessary to peel the potatoes). Mix all the ingredients

together gently. Season to taste with salt and pepper. Sprinkle paprika over the top. This recipe makes 6 servings.

Variations
Add mung or lentil sprouts, green herbs, sliced radishes, steamed cooled green beans, or sesame, sunflower, or pumpkin seeds.

Add ¼ cup toasted sesame seeds, and add 1 tablespoon curry powder to the dressing.

Potato Salad #2

A rich, creamy potato salad. The key to the special flavor and texture is to add the dressing while the potatoes are hot.

6 potatoes
vegetables as in Potato Salad #1
¾ cup lemon-and-oil dressing (page 165)
¾ cup sour cream
1 teaspoon dill weed
salt and pepper

Boil the potatoes until tender. Drain, and peel if desired. Place in a bowl. Pour the lemon-and-oil dressing over the potatoes. Let marinate for at least 1 hour, or all day. Stir occasionally so that the potatoes absorb all the dressing. When most or all of the dressing is absorbed, stir in the vegetables and sour cream. Add the dill weed and season to taste with salt and pepper. Chill. This recipe makes 6 servings.

Variation
Thick yogurt can replace the sour cream.

Artichoke Heart Salad

This simple and elegant salad was first encountered in a one-star restaurant in Albertville, France, where it was prepared with enormous artichoke hearts.

Place beds of lettuce on individual plates. On each plate place 2 large, cooked, cooled artichoke hearts. Fill the hollows with lemon-and-oil herb dressing (page 165). Serve at room temperature as a first course or as a salad course.

Artichoke Heart Salad with Yogurt

Serve as a small side dish.

1½ cups cooked artichoke hearts, cut into small pieces
1 medium tomato cut into small pieces
1 cup yogurt
½ teaspoon salt
½ teaspoon basil

Gently toss the ingredients together. Chill. Makes 2 or 3 servings.

Variation
For a more marinated effect, replace yogurt with 1 cup yogurt salad dressing (page 166).

Cauliflower-Guacamole Salad

A lovely presentation for a buffet table or summer meal.

Steam heads of cauliflower whole. Drain well and cool. Place upright on a bed of greens. Generously spoon guacamole (page 64) over the top of the cauliflower(s). Garnish with minced parsley.

Celeriac Salad (France)

Celeriac salad can be served on its own, mixed into tossed green salads, or served as part of an antipasto. It is a classic, with a very special flavor.

3 cups celeriac, coarsely grated or cut into matchsticks
¾ cup cashew mayonnaise (page 170) or lemon-and-oil dressing (page 165)

Blanch the celeriac for 1 minute. Drain well. Toss with the dressing. Marinate for 1 hour or more. Makes 3 cups.

BEAN SALADS

See marinated beans, page 128, for ideas for bean salads or beans to use in salads.

Three-Bean Salad

1 cup cooked, cooled kidney beans
1 cup cooked, cooled garbanzos
1 cup cooked, cooled green beans
¾ cup lemon-and-oil dressing (page 165)
¼ cup chopped celery
¼ cup chopped green pepper

Toss all the ingredients together. Marinate in the refrigerator, stirring occasionally to coat the beans. Makes 3 cups.

Variation
Five-Bean Salad: For a beautiful confetti version of the classic salad, use only ½ cup each of the kidney beans and garbanzos with ½ cup each cooked, cooled black beans and soybeans. For more color contrast, add a little chopped red bell pepper.

GRAIN AND PASTA SALADS

Whole cooked grains and cooked pasta can be mixed with vegetables and a salad dressing. Be sure to add crunchy vegetables for texture. Besides the old standbys of rice salad and macaroni salad, try using whole wheatberries or rye, bulgar wheat, and barley for added flavor and texture. Use whole-wheat noodles and artichoke and spinach noodles for color contrast.

Suggestions for Grain and Pasta Salads
Dressings:
  cashew mayonnaise
  sour cream and sour cream-based dressings
  cottage cheese-based dressings
  lemon-and-oil dressing

Additions:
sliced celery, green or red bell pepper, tomatoes, cucumbers

steamed, cooled beet cubes (to add pink
    color to the salad)
steamed, cooled peas or green beans
minced parsley or watercress
fresh or dried herbs
ricotta
grated carrots or beets
lentil, mung, alfalfa, or other sprouts
cubes of cheese, tofu, or panir
chopped nuts
sesame, sunflower, pumpkin, caraway, or
    poppy seeds
curry powder

Tabouli (Middle East)

Try taking tabouli on a picnic. It's great
stuffed in pita.

⅓ cup olive oil
⅓ cup lemon juice
1 cup finely chopped parsley plus 3 table-
    spoons dried crumbled mint, *or* ⅔ cup
    finely chopped parsley plus ½ cup
    finely chopped fresh mint
2 medium tomatoes, cut in small pieces
3 cups cooked, cooled cracked wheat or
    bulgar wheat
½ cup chopped green pepper
salt and pepper

Mix the olive oil and lemon juice. Mix
the remaining ingredients together and pour
the dressing over them. Mix well. Season
to taste with salt and pepper. Makes 4 to 6
servings.

Variations
Though not authentic, barley is a delicious
substitute for cracked wheat in tabouli.
    Add a few cooked, cooled garbanzos or
black beans.

Rice or Grain Salad

A basic formula with infinite potential for
variations.

2 cups cooked rice or other whole grains
1 tomato, chopped
1 stalk celery, sliced thin
1 green pepper, chopped
¼ cup minced parsley
½ cup cashew mayonnaise (page 170) plus
    ¼ cup lemon juice, *or* ⅔ cup lemon-
    and-oil dressing (page 165)
salt and pepper
½ teaspoon basil
½ teaspoon dill weed
2 to 4 tablespoons toasted sunflower seeds

Mix all the ingredients together. Season
to taste with salt and pepper. Marinate in
the refrigerator for at least 1 hour before
serving. Makes 4 servings.

Macaroni or Pasta Salad

Try preparing with a mixture of spinach
and whole-wheat macaroni for color contrast.

3 cups cooked macaroni or small noodles
1 celery stalk, cut thin
½ green pepper, cut into small pieces
1 tomato, chopped
¾ cup cashew mayonnaise (page 170) *or*
    lemon-and-oil dressing (page 165)
2 tablespoons minced parsley
2 tablespoons toasted sunflower seeds
salt and pepper

Mix all the ingredients together. Season
to taste with salt and pepper. Makes 4 to 6
servings.

MOLDED SALADS

The following is a basic formula. Agar agar
can be obtained from health-food stores.
The proportions given here are for agar
agar flakes, of which 1 tablespoon thickens
1 quart of water, marketed by Erewhon
Trading Company of Boston, Massachusetts. Different brands specify different

amounts—follow the directions given for thickening 1 quart liquid.

Molded Salad

1 quart clear vegetable or tomato broth, or diluted vegetable juice, or lightly sweetened lemonade
2 tablespoons lemon juice (unless using lemonade)
1 tablespoon agar agar flakes
2 cups cut or grated vegetables, uncooked or steamed and drained

Bring the liquid and the lemon juice to a boil. Add the agar agar. Reduce the heat and simmer for 5 minutes until the agar agar is dissolved. Add the vegetables. Adjust the seasoning. (Don't add ground pepper—it will sink to the bottom.) Pour into a rectangular pan. Chill to set.

To serve, cut into squares and remove with a spatula. Makes 8 to 10 servings.

Suggested Combinations

Grated carrot, green pepper strips, and drained pineapple chunks. Steamed asparagus tips and whole seedless grapes in lemonade. Chopped, drained cucumbers, tomatoes, and avocado slices. Cold beet borscht, served with sour cream.

Tomato Aspic

1 quart strained tomato broth
2 tablespoons lemon juice
1 tablespoon agar agar flakes

Prepare as above for molded salad. Serve with curried cashew mayonnaise on individual plates covered with butter lettuce. Makes 4 cups.

Iced "Salads"

On hot days, prepare tomato aspic or molded vegetable salad without the vegetables. Freeze in the same manner as fruit ice, page 306, and serve over tomato and avocado slices.

CHILDREN'S SALADS

These two salads for children were created by my grandmother, Fanny Sherman. So far, they have delighted two generations.

Candle Salad

Place a thick slice of pineapple with the core removed on a bed of lettuce, for the candle holder. For the candle, peel a banana and slice off one end. Fit it into the hole in the candle holder. For the flame, attach a cherry to the top of the banana with a toothpick.

Snowman Salad

Arrange cottage cheese on a bed of lettuce in the shape of a snowman. Use raisins for the eyes, mouth, and buttons, and use carrot slices to form the nose and the broom.

FRUIT SALADS

Fruit salads can be just about the most uplifting and attractive dishes ever served. Prepare fruit salads as close to serving time as possible. Sprinkle lemon juice over salads containing fruits which discolor when exposed to air, such as apples and bananas. Cut fruits into bite-sized pieces and remove all inedible parts, such as seeds, pits, and leaves. Use a melon baller for melons, and cube some of the fruits and cut others into rounds. Seedless grapes, small berries, or other small fruits can be added whole.

If using melon, hollow out the melon and use the shell as a bowl for the salad. Watermelons make beautiful containers for salads being served at large gatherings. Halved, scooped-out pineapples with the leaves still attached also make wonderful containers for fruit salads.

Dress fruit salads lightly, if at all. Add just a little sugar or honey if sweetening is necessary.

Fruit juices make good salad dressings.

For a main dish fruit salad, serve cottage cheese, ricotta, or yogurt over the fruit. For a cooling touch, serve with a fruit ice or a little ice cream.

Suggested Ingredients for Mixed Fruit Salads

Any fresh fruit, peeled, sliced, and cored as necessary
Additions:
Chopped dried fruit
grated coconut
mint leaves
sesame or sunflower seeds
chopped nuts
whole blanched almonds
cardamom
Dressings:
lemon juice or other fruit juices mixed with a little honey
lemon-and-honey dressing

yogurt
fruit-yogurt dressing
fresh fruit sauce
sour cream
cashew mayonnaise, plain or lightly curried

Fruit salads containing many types of fruits are often the best. Here are also some suggestions for more limited combinations:
oranges, bananas, and sliced dates
mangoes, papayas, and pineapples sprinkled with coconut
honeydew and cantaloupe balls with sliced strawberries, served with strawberry ice

Prasad Fruit Salad (India)

3 medium bananas
⅔ cup sliced pitted dates
⅓ cup grated coconut
2 tablespoons lemon juice
2 tablespoons honey
¼ teaspoon cardamom

Slice the bananas. Mix with the dates and coconut. Combine the lemon juice, honey, and cardamom. Toss lightly with the fruit. Serve at room temperature, plain or with heavy cream. This recipe makes 4 servings.

Avocado-Pineapple Salad

2 cups diced avocado (about 2 large avocados)
3 cups diced fresh pineapple (1 small pineapple)

Toss gently. Add grapefruit slices or grapefruit juice as a variation. This recipe makes 5 cups.

Ambrosia (USA)

A Southern dish, of which the simplest of many versions is sliced oranges sprinkled with coconut and powdered sugar.

2 seedless oranges, sectioned and with most
    of the membrane removed, sliced
2 bananas, sliced
1 cup cubed pineapple or mango
6 tablespoons grated coconut
2 tablespoons honey *or* ¼ cup confec-
    tioner's sugar

Toss the ingredients together. This recipe makes 3 or 4 servings.

Variation
Add chopped fresh mint.

Ambrosia Cream Salad

To Ambrosia, add:
2 tablespoons coconut
1 cup seedless grapes
1 tablespoon honey *or* 2 tablespoons con-
    fectioner's sugar
1 cup sour cream or thick yogurt.

Chill the mixture. Makes 4 servings.

Molded Fruit Salad

This basic formula uses agar agar, of which
a tablespoon thickens a quart of liquid. Follow the directions on the package for thickening 1 quart if they are different from
these.

4 cups fruit juice or lemonade
1½ tablespoons agar agar flakes
2 cups sliced fresh fruit, drained
honey or sugar to taste
½ to 1 teaspoon chopped mint leaves (op-
    tional)

Bring the fruit juice or lemonade to a
boil. Add the agar agar. Reduce the heat.
Simmer for 5 minutes to dissolve the agar
agar. Add the fruit and honey or sugar.
Pour into a rectangular pan or individual
cups. Chill to set. This recipe makes about
5 cups.

Salad Dressings, Sauces, and Chutneys

SALAD DRESSINGS

In the late eighteenth century, London
was graced by a Marquis d'Albignac, who
earned a comfortable livelihood solely by
running from house to house each evening
preparing the salad dressing! Few today (or
then, for that matter) would confine themselves to this singular talent, for salad
dressings—and great ones—are simple to
prepare. With the use of a blender, many
ingredients can be added to salad dressings,
and a great variety of dressings can be
achieved to enhance the daily fare.

The technique of enhancing a salad with
a dressing is just that—the dressing should
add flavor that enlivens the flavor of the
greens without overshadowing it. Use only
enough dressing to lightly coat the vegetables or fruits. Add just before serving and

toss lightly. To create your own dressings, try some of the following suggested ingredients. Some of the best dressings are the pure and simple. The base ingredients can be used alone as well.

Base
oil (Use any type except coconut, which hardens at room temperature. Vary mild, all-purpose oils with highly flavored oils such as olive and walnut. Sesame-flavored oil and ginger-flavored oil can also be used.)
yogurt
sour cream
cottage cheese, pureed in the blender
ricotta
cashew mayonnaise
thin tahini

Additions
lemon or lime juice
grated cheese
small amounts of honey
curry powder
pinch of cayenne
minced parsley or watercress
vegetable juices
nut butter
green herbs

mustard powder or seeds
fennel seed

Additions to Be Mashed or Pureed in the Blender
tomato
green pepper
watercress, spinach, parsley, cilantro, mint
cheese
bean curd
nuts
avocado
cooked beans
cream cheese
sesame, sunflower, or pumpkin seeds
steamed vegetables (broccoli is good)

Also see Taratoor Sauce (page 171) and Guacamole (page 64) for dressings.

Lemon-and-Oil Dressing

The basic dressing and marinade.

2 tablespoons lemon juice
¼ cup oil
¼ to ½ teaspoon salt
fresh pepper

Mix the ingredients together. See additions listed above for variations. Makes ⅓ cup.

Variations
Lemon-and-Oil Herb Dressing: Add 1 to 1½ teaspoons dried herbs or 1 to 1½ tablespoons minced fresh herbs. Basil and dill weed make a nice combination.

Lemon-Tomato Dressing: Add ½ tomato, and puree in a blender. Add 1 teaspoon honey for a sweet-and-sour dressing. Makes ½ cup.

Watercress or Spinach Dressing: Add a handful of washed, dried watercress or spinach leaves, and puree in the blender. Adds sharp flavor and beautiful green color to salads.

Tahini Dressing

3 tablespoons tahini
2 tablespoons oil (more if the tahini is
    thick)
1 tablespoon lemon juice
salt and pepper

Mix tahini, oil, and lemon juice together
with a sprinkling of salt and pepper. Makes
⅓ cup.

Lemon-and-Honey Dressing

A light, subtle dressing for vegetable or
fruit salads. It is successful only if used in
a very small amount—just enough to
awaken the flavors of the salad ingredients.

1½ teaspoons honey
¼ cup lemon juice

Mix well. Add a tiny pinch of cayenne if
desired. Makes about ¼ cup.

Cottage Cheese Creamy Salad Dressing

This is the basic creamy dressing for salads.
It can absorb many of the additions. Pureed
green pepper and green herbs are superb
additions.

⅓ cup cottage cheese
¼ cup oil
3 tablespoons lemon juice
salt and pepper

Puree all the ingredients in the blender
until smooth. Makes ½ cup.

French Dressing

To make a light, fresh facsimile of creamy
French dressing, add half a tomato to cottage cheese dressing and blend. Add green
herbs.

Creamy Avocado-Tomato Dressing

2 tablespoons oil
¼ avocado
¼ cup lemon juice
½ teaspoon basil
1 ripe tomato
¼ cup cottage cheese
salt and pepper

Combine all the ingredients in a blender.
Makes ½ cup.

Avocado Dressing

½ avocado
2 tablespoons lemon juice
3 tablespoons oil
salt and pepper

Mash the ingredients together with a
fork. Add green herbs if desired. Makes ½
cup.

Yogurt Dressing

Here are the proportions for another basic
dressing to which many ingredients may be
added.

2 tablespoons oil
⅓ cup yogurt
2 tablespoons lemon juice
1 teaspoon herbs
1 teaspoon honey (optional)

Mix all the ingredients together. Makes
½ cup.

Avocado-Yogurt Dressing

½ avocado
½ cup yogurt
2 tablespoons lemon juice
¼ teaspoon basil
¼ teaspoon dill weed
salt and pepper

Mash the avocado with a fork. Add the
remaining ingredients. Makes ¾ cup.

Variations
Add a little ground ginger and a little
honey.

Add, in a blender, a little green pepper or tomato.

Oil-free Salad Dressings

Replace the oil in any of the above recipes with vegetable juice or with half a tomato pureed in the blender.

Sour Cream Dressing

Use sour cream by itself, or mixed with herbs and whole yellow mustard seeds. Or substitute sour cream for cottage cheese, yogurt, and oil in any of the preceding dressings. Also see Sour Cream Dip or Dressing, page 64.

Cashew Mayonnaise Dressings

Replace the oil, cottage cheese, and yogurt in any of the above dressings with cashew mayonnaise (page 170). French dressing is particularly good when prepared in this manner.

Fruit-Yogurt Dressing for Fruit Salads

½ cup fruit juice (orange juice is good)
½ cup yogurt
1 tablespoon honey

Mix together and serve over fruit salads. Makes 1 cup.

Variations

Add a little cardamom, ground ginger, or minced mint leaves.

Replace the yogurt with sour cream.

Also dress fruit salads with:
fresh fruit sauce (page 284)
lemon juice and honey
cream cheese or ricotta thinned with fruit juice and honey, mixed with ground ginger
whipped cream, sour cream, or yogurt, sweetened with honey
fruit ices

SAUCES

Sauces dress up vegetables, grains, casseroles, crepes, burgers, stuffed vegetables, ad infinitum. They are particularly useful for dry dishes, such as nut and bean loaves. Sauces passed at the table are also a solution for families in which some members prefer their foods plain and others like them more dressed up.

An essential tool-of-the-trade for sauce-making is a whisk. It prevents (or removes) lumps, stirs, and beats. A wooden spoon is also good for stirring sauces gently.

Roux-based sauces are considered one of the fundamentals of western cookery, and are one of the first things children are taught to prepare in home economics classes. They may be prepared with unbleached white or whole wheat flour, and also with soy or chick-pea flour (though these will add flavor to the sauce—use only when herbs or strong-tasting ingredients will help mask their flavor). These sauces, though usually prepared with whole milk or even cream, can also be made with nonfat milk, and, for vegans, with soy milk. For *oil-free* and *flour-free* alternatives, see page 169, or Cottage Cheese Cream Sauce, also on page 169.

Bêchamel Sauce (or White Sauce or Cream Sauce)

Historical records have it that this classic sauce was invented by Orion, a chef in ancient Greece. It is the basis for so many sauces and so many dishes that it is helpful to memorize the proportions.

⅓ cup butter or ghee
¼ cup flour
2 cups milk
½ teaspoon salt
pinch nutmeg (optional)

Melt the butter in a saucepan. Add the flour and cook for 1 minute, stirring constantly with a whisk to eliminate all lumps. For best results, remove from the heat for a few minutes. Add the milk, stirring constantly. Return to the heat. Bring to a simmer, stirring constantly with the whisk. Do not boil. Simmer for a few minutes until thickened. Remove from the heat and add the salt and nutmeg. This recipe makes 2 cups.

Variations

For a less rich sauce, reduce the butter to ¼ cup. For other variations and Vegan variations, see page 169.

Bêchamel with Broth: Replace the milk with 1½ cups broth and ½ cup heavy cream.

Sauce Suprême: Replace ½ cup of the milk with cream.

Curried Bêchamel Sauce: Omit nutmeg and add 1 to 1½ teaspoons curry powder to the finished sauce.

Dark Bêchamel

Cook the flour and butter, stirring constantly, until the mixture turns golden brown. Remove from the heat for 5 minutes, then add the milk as above. The holding power of the flour is slightly reduced, but the taste is excellent.

Bêchamel-Herb Sauce

Omit the nutmeg in bêchamel sauce and sauté 1 teaspoon green herbs in the butter before adding the flour. Replace the salt with celery salt.

Mornay Sauce (France)

A light cheese sauce.

Add ½ cup grated Swiss or gruyere cheese to simmering bêchamel sauce. Stir constantly until the cheese is completely melted and blended. Remove immediately from the heat.

Cheese Sauce

Add 1¼ to 1½ cups grated cheese to simmering bêchamel sauce. Stir constantly until blended and melted.

Add ¼ teaspoon paprika and serve immediately.

Auroré Sauce (France)

Its name means dawn, for its dawn-pink color.

1 cup fresh tomato puree (tomatoes pureed in the blender)
milk
⅓ cup butter
¼ cup flour
salt

Simmer the tomatoes, covered, for 20 minutes. Measure, pour into a bowl, and add milk until there are 2 cups of liquid. Melt the butter in a saucepan and add the flour; cook for 1 minute, stirring constantly with a whisk. Add the milk and tomato liquid and bring to a simmer, stirring constantly with the whisk. Do not boil. Simmer a few minutes, until thickened, and remove from the heat. Add salt to taste.

Variation

Add ½ cup grated cheese to the finished sauce. Simmer, stirring constantly, just until the cheese is melted.

Nut Gravy

Here is a basic vegetarian gravy—delicious over stuffings, burgers, nut and bean loaves, or mashed potatoes. The flavor can be varied by the types of nuts employed. Pistachios contribute a beautiful green color. Roasted cashews and roasted almonds give excellent flavor.

2 tablespoons butter, ghee, or oil
3 tablespoons unbleached white or whole wheat flour

2 cups milk
1 cup ground roasted nuts or ground blanched pistachios
¾ teaspoon salt

Melt the butter, ghee, or oil in a saucepan. Add the flour and cook for 1 minute, stirring constantly with a whisk. Add the milk and beat with a whisk to prevent lumps. Add the nuts. Heat to a simmer, stirring constantly, and simmer until thickened. Remove from the heat and add the salt. This recipe makes 3 cups.

Variations

Add sautéed grated carrot, sliced celery, and minced parsley to the gravy.

Vegan Variation: Replace milk with soy or nut milk.

Pan Gravy

1 teaspoon thyme
2 tablespoons minced fresh parsley
½ green pepper, chopped
1 stalk celery, sliced thin
¼ teaspoon sage
5 tablespoons butter
¼ cup flour—unbleached white or whole wheat
2 cups broth or water
1 teaspoon salt
pepper

Sauté the thyme, parsley, green pepper, celery, and sage in 1 tablespoon of the butter until they begin to become tender. In a saucepan, melt the remaining 4 tablespoons butter. Add the flour and cook, stirring constantly with a whisk, until golden brown. (If using whole wheat flour, be especially alert not to burn.) Remove the mixture from the heat for 5 minutes. Add the broth or water and beat with a whisk. Add the sautéed vegetables and herbs. Return to the heat. Bring to a simmer, stirring constantly, and simmer until thickened.

Add the salt. Add a sprinkling of pepper. This recipe makes about 2 cups.

Oil-free and flour-free alternatives to roux sauces: The texture will differ, but the following procedure makes roux-based sauces available to those who wish to omit oil and/or flour from their diets:

In making béchamel sauce, omit the flour and butter. Mix 2 tablespoons arrowroot or cornstarch with ¼ cup of the milk. Return to the liquid. Heat the mixture to a simmer slowly, stirring constantly. Simmer until thickened. Add the salt and nutmeg.

Another alternative is to replace béchamel sauce with Cream of Potato Soup.

Cottage Cheese Cream Sauce

2 medium tomatoes
1½ cups cottage cheese
¾ teaspoon salt
1 tablespoon oil (optional)

Puree the tomatoes in a blender. Place in a saucepan and simmer, covered, for 5 minutes. Place all the ingredients in a blender. Puree. Makes 2 cups.

Use this cream sauce as a basis for all the béchamel sauce variations, or in all dishes calling for béchamel sauce.

Variation

Replace the tomatoes with ½ cup buttermilk or vegetable juice.

BUTTER SAUCES

Of all sauces, ghee, pure and simple, is superlative on steamed vegetables. Ghee and butter may be used interchangeably in the following sauces, but ghee will give the better flavor.

Ghee-and-Lemon Sauce

4 tablespoons melted ghee or butter
2 tablespoons lemon or lime juice

Mix well. Serve over vegetables or for dipping artichoke leaves. Makes ⅓ cup.

Variation
Add ½ teaspoon green herbs. (Dill weed and basil make a nice combination.)

Parsley Butter

1 tablespoon finely minced parsley
¼ cup melted ghee or butter

Mix together well. Use a blender if desired. Serve over vegetables or mashed potatoes. Makes ¼ cup.

Sauce Noisette (France)

½ cup ghee or butter
3 tablespoons ground nuts (hazelnuts and almonds are particularly good)

Combine the ingredients in a saucepan. Bring to a boil and cook until brown. Makes ½ cup.

Cream Cheese Hollandaise

A tart, creamy sauce for vegetables. At room temperature the sauce takes on a sour-cream-like texture, and is a delicious dip for artichokes.

½ cup melted ghee or butter
¼ cup lemon juice
½ cup softened cream cheese
½ teaspoon tarragon (optional)

Mix the ingredients together in a blender. Place in a saucepan. Heat to a simmer. The mixture will separate, but it doesn't matter. Rinse out the blender with hot water to heat. Just before serving, place the sauce in the blender and mix, then serve.

The sauce may be cooled to room temperature (do not heat after the simmering process), but do not chill or it will become solid. This recipe makes 1 cup.

Cashew Mayonnaise

Delightful on steamed, cooled vegetables, for dipping artichokes, in salads, and on sandwiches.

⅓ cup raw cashews
½ cup water
¼ teaspoon salt
¼ teaspoon paprika
⅔ cup mild-flavored oil
3 tablespoons lemon juice

Combine the cashews, water, and salt in a blender at high speed until completely pureed. Add the paprika. Reduce the blender speed to the lowest. Carefully remove the lid. While it is spinning, pour the oil into the mixture in a tiny, steady drizzle. When all the oil has been added, turn off the blender. Add the lemon juice, replace the cover, and return to high speed until the mixture is thick. Remove and chill to thicken more, or use as a sauce. This recipe makes about 1 cup.

Variations
Add curry powder.
Add minced parsley or green herbs.
Soy Mayonnaise: Replace the cashews with ⅓ cup soy flour. The flavor is not as good as when cashews are used, so use in salads or add herbs or curry powder to mask.

Tahini (Sesame Butter)

Tahini, sometimes called tahina or tehina, is featured in the cooking of the Middle East and also in that of Japan. It is used as a sauce for vegetables and grains, mixed into casseroles and desserts and in many other ways. In any case, it is very potent—a little goes a long way.
Grinder Method (Pure, thick tahini)
Put toasted sesame seeds through the finest blade of a meat grinder. Repeat the grind-

ing several times, if necessary, to produce a smooth paste.

Blender Method (thinner tahini)

Blend ½ cup toasted sesame seeds and ⅓ to ½ cup mild-flavored oil until smooth. Use the larger amount of oil for thin tahini. The oil and sesame seeds may separate a little during storage—just stir a bit if it happens.

Taratoor Sauce (Middle East)

½ cup tahini
¼ cup lemon juice
¼ teaspoon salt

Mix the ingredients well. Traditionally, taratoor is served on falafel sandwiches; it is also a versatile sauce that goes well with vegetables and salads, and can be mixed into casseroles and dips. Makes about ⅔ cup.

Variation

Add a little cayenne or powdered red chillies.

TOMATO SAUCES

Tomato sauces are the glory of Italy, where they range from cooked-all-day-and-then-some affairs to a simple sauce of tomatoes stewed with olive oil. In any case, the start of a good sauce is rich, red, ripe tomatoes. Use the Italian pear-shaped tomatoes, if available. Besides serving tomato sauce over pasta, you can cook vegetables in tomato sauce and serve the sauce as a main dish.

Tomato Sauce, Long-Cooking (Italy)

The rich flavor of this sauce is unsurpassed, and will be a pleasant surprise to those accustomed to cooking with a canned sauce base. It can be simmered all day on the lowest heat, or can be cooked on a medium-low heat in 2 to 3 hours. The final amount of sauce will depend on whether the cooking stops when the sauce is thick but still liquid, or whether it is cooked to a very thick paste with no separated liquid. If you prefer not to include the skins, blanch and peel the tomatoes before chopping.

1 green pepper, cut in small pieces
1 carrot, sliced
1 stalk celery, with leaves, sliced
2 teaspoons basil
1 teaspoon thyme
¼ cup fresh minced parsley
¼ cup olive oil
9 cups chopped ripe tomatoes
¾ cup water
2 bay leaves
1 teaspoon salt

Sauté the green pepper, carrot, celery, and herbs in the olive oil in a large pot for 5 minutes. Add the tomatoes, water, bay leaves, and salt. Cover and simmer on the lowest heat for 4 to 5 hours or more, or on a medium-low heat for 2 hours or more, until very thick. Stir occasionally. If the sauce is too tart, add 1 or 2 teaspoons sugar or honey. If it is too sweet, add a little lemon juice. This recipe makes 4 or 5 cups.

Variations

Add oregano.
Add zucchini.
Grate the vegetables.
For a sweet sauce, substitute 2 grated carrots for the celery and green pepper.
Substitute ½ cup sattvic sauce (page 173) for ½ cup water.

Tomato Sauce, Quick (Italy)

The flavor of a quickly cooked tomato sauce cannot have developed the richness of the slowly simmered version. This sauce, however, is quite good, and can be prepared when time is not available for the all-day one.

1 stalk celery, sliced thin
1 tablespoon minced fresh parsley
½ carrot, grated
½ green pepper, chopped
1 teaspoon basil
1 teaspoon thyme
2 tablespoons olive oil
4 cups chopped tomatoes
½ teaspoon salt
1 teaspoon brown sugar or honey (optional)
optional thickening:
up to ¼ cup powdered sunflower seeds, *or*
2 tablespoons flour
2 tablespoons butter

Sauté the celery, parsley, carrot, green pepper, and herbs in the olive oil for 5 minutes. Add the tomatoes and salt. Cover and simmer for ½ hour, stirring and mashing the tomatoes occasionally. Adjust the seasoning, adding the sugar or honey if the sauce is too tart. Add a little lemon juice if it is too sweet. To thicken, either add powdered sesame seeds until the desired thickness is achieved, *or* make a roux, as follows: Melt the butter in a small skillet. Add the flour and cook for 1 minute, stirring constantly with a whisk. Add to the simmering sauce and beat with the whisk. Simmer for 2 to 3 minutes until thickened. This recipe makes 4 cups.

Variations
See variations for long-cooking tomato sauce.
  Tomato-Cheese Sauce: Stir ½ cup grated cheese into finished tomato sauce. Simmer and stir for a minute until completely blended. Serve immediately.
  Oil-free Tomato Sauce: Eliminate the olive oil and cook all the ingredients together. To thicken quick-cooking tomato sauce, either use ¼ cup powdered sunflower seeds *or* dissolve 1 tablespoon arrowroot or cornstarch in a little water and add it to the finished sauce; simmer, stirring, for 2 to 3 minutes.

Mexican Tomato Sauce (Mexico)

For use on tacos, enchiladas, and tostadas.

To two cups quick-cooking tomato sauce or stewed tomatoes prepared without herbs, add:

¾ teaspoon paprika
pinch cloves
¼ teaspoon cinnamon
1 teaspoon sugar or honey
¼ teaspoon coriander
1½ teaspoons roasted cumin
1 tablespoon lemon juice

This recipe makes 2 cups.

Variation
For a "salsa picante," add cayenne, crumbled red chilies, or chopped fresh jualapeños.

Pesto (Italy)

An emerald green, flavorful sauce for pasta. Fresh basil makes it superlative, and the simplest pesto is prepared by grinding basil and olive oil together. A similar mixture, "Pistou," is prepared in southern France; it is added to vegetable soups at the table. For a pistou, omit the nuts, and pass at the table to add to minestrone or vegetable soup.

1 cup minced parsley
¾ cup fresh minced basil *or* ½ cup dried basil
1 teaspoon salt
¼ cup chopped walnuts or pine nuts
⅔ cup olive oil
¼ cup melted butter
½ cup grated parmesan or other cheese

Grind the herbs, salt, nuts, and cheese in a mortar and pestle. Add the oil and melted butter drop by drop. *Or* combine all the ingredients in a blender until smooth. This recipe makes 1½ cups.

Variations

Add more cheese or more nuts, or omit the nuts.

Vegan Variation: Omit the cheese. Slightly reduce the amount of oil, and replace butter with melted margarine.

Lentil Sauce

Lentil sauce is excellent over pasta or mixed with casseroles.

⅔ cup lentils
3⅓ cups broth or water
2 grated carrots
1 teaspoon thyme
1 teaspoon oregano
1 tablespoon oil
⅔ cup chopped tomato
2 tablespoons flour
2 tablespoons butter
salt and pepper

Bring the lentils and broth or water to a boil. Reduce heat, cover, and simmer. Meanwhile, sauté the carrots and herbs in the oil for 5 minutes. Add the tomatoes and cook for 3 more minutes. Add to the lentils. Simmer the mixture for 45 minutes.

Melt the butter in a small saucepan. Add the flour and cook for 1 minute, stirring constantly with a whisk. Add to the lentil sauce. Beat with a whisk. Simmer for 2 to 3 minutes, until thickened. Puree in a blender.

Season to taste with salt and pepper. This recipe makes about 4 cups.

Variation
Add water if a thinner sauce is desired.

Sattvic Sauce

A non-aged, nonfermented substitute for soy sauce. The flavor is not equal, but the color and added lift necessary for Chinese and Japanese-style foods will be supplied. It also adds flavor to soups and stews.

½ cup water
1 teaspoon blackstrap molasses
1 tablespoon lemon juice
1 teaspoon salt
¼ teaspoon grain coffee powder
½ teaspoon sugar or honey

Mix the ingredients together. Makes a little over ½ cup.

Sauce for Chinese-Style Foods

1 tablespoon arrowroot or cornstarch
½ cup water
½ cup sattvic

Mix the arrowroot or cornstarch in a little of the water. Add the remaining water and the sattvic sauce. Pour into stir-frying vegetables and stir for a minute to thicken. Makes 1 cup.

Variation
Add a little white pepper or five-spice powder.

Sweet and Sour Sauce (China)

1 tablespoon cornstarch or arrowroot
⅔ cup water
⅓ cup lemon juice
1 tablespoon sugar *or* 2 teaspoons honey

Mix the arrowroot or cornstarch in a little of the water. Add the remaining ingredients. Add to stir-frying vegetables and stir for a minute to thicken. This recipe makes 1 cup.

Variation
Replace water with part pineapple juice or tomato juice, or both.

Pineapple Sweet and Sour Sauce (Southeast and East Asia)

Excellent over stir-fried vegetables and grains. For a beautiful presentation, prepare stir-fried vegetables in this sauce and serve in a scooped-out pineapple shell.

2 cups chopped ripe tomatoes
1 cup pineapple, cut in small pieces
1 tablespoon brown sugar *or* 2 teaspoons
   honey
2 tablespoons lemon juice
½ teaspoon salt
½ cup water
1 tablespoon arrowroot or cornstarch
white pepper

Combine the tomatoes, brown sugar, pineapple, lemon juice, and salt in a saucepan with ¼ cup of the water. Simmer, covered, for 30 minutes, until the pineapple and tomatoes are tender. Mix the arrowroot or cornstarch into the remaining ¼ cup of water. Add to the sauce and stir for 2 or 3 minutes to thicken. Sprinkle with a little pepper. This recipe makes 1¾ cups.

Variation
Add a little chopped green pepper at the beginning of cooking.

Curry (India)

Here is one of the original forms of "kadi"—a light sauce to be served over rice. If desired, cook some finely cut vegetables in the sauce, or float plain pakoras in it after it has been cooked.

¼ cup ghee or butter
¼-inch piece fresh ginger, peeled and
   minced
½ teaspoon cumin
2 ripe tomatoes, chopped
2 tablespoons chick-pea flour or wheat flour
2 cups buttermilk
1 teaspoon salt
¼ teaspoon fenugreek
½ teaspoon turmeric
½ teaspoon coriander
⅛ teaspoon cloves

Heat the ghee or butter in a pot. Add the ginger and cumin, and sauté for 1 minute.

Add the tomatoes and cook for 3 to 4 minutes. Stir in the chick-pea flour. Beat with a whisk, and cook for 2 minutes, stirring constantly. Pour in the buttermilk. Add the salt and remaining spices. Bring to a simmer, stirring constantly with the whisk. Cover and simmer on a low heat for 20 minutes, stirring occasionally.

Serve over rice. This recipe makes a little over 2 cups.

Variations
Add cayenne or powdered red chilies to the ghee or butter.

For a thicker sauce, add 1 more tablespoon chick-pea flour.

CHUTNEYS

Chutneys originated in India, and some have migrated to England, where they have been adapted. Chutneys are intended to enhance and accompany a meal. A little is placed at the side of the plate and a small spoonful at a time is mixed with the main food. Chutneys are also used for dipping pakoras or vadas into, or for serving with samosas. Chutneys may be served with non-Indian meals, particularly when the food is mild and needs a strong contrasting flavor. Some chutneys go quite well with Mexican food.

Avocado-Coconut Chutney (India)

A quickly prepared, uncooked chutney.

1 cup mashed avocado (about 1 large avocado)
½ cup grated coconut
¼ cup lemon juice
¼ teaspoon salt
1 to 1½ tablespoons honey
½-inch piece fresh ginger, peeled and
   minced

Mix all the ingredients in a blender. Makes 1¼ cups.

Variations
Reduce the amount of coconut.
Add chopped green chilies.

Date Chutney (India)

1 tablespoon oil
¼ teaspoon black mustard seed
1 cup packed pitted dates
¼ teaspoon cardamom
¼ teaspoon salt
½ cup orange juice
¼ cup lemon juice
⅛ teaspoon cloves
¼ teaspoon coriander

Heat the oil in a saucepan. Add the mustard seed and sauté until it dances. Add the remaining ingredients. Cover and simmer for 10 minutes. Combine in a blender until smooth. Makes 1¾ cups.

Variations
Add ½ cup coconut.
Replace the orange and lemon juices with strong mint or hibiscus tea, for an inauthentic variation.

Coconut Chutney (India)

A pleasant surprise for those who associate coconut only with sweet dishes.

1 cup grated coconut
2-inch piece fresh ginger, peeled and sliced
½ teaspoon salt
3 tablespoons yogurt
2 to 3 tablespoons water
1 teaspoon oil
½ teaspoon black mustard seed
1 teaspoon urad dhal (optional)
pinch asafoetida (optional)

Combine the coconut, ginger, salt, and yogurt in a blender with enough water to grind to a paste. Heat the oil in a small skillet. Add the mustard seed and asafoetida and sauté until the mustard seed dances.

Add to the coconut and blend again. This recipe makes 1 cup.

Variation
Add cayenne or powdered red chilies to the oil.

Pineapple Chutney (India)

¼ cup ghee or butter
3 cups chopped pineapple, with its juice
¼-inch piece fresh ginger, peeled and minced
⅛ teaspoon cumin
1 cup brown sugar
⅛ teaspoon cardamom
½ teaspoon salt
⅛ teaspoon cinnamon
2 tablespoons lemon juice
⅓ cup golden raisins

Heat the butter in a large saucepan. Add the ginger and cumin, and sauté for 1 minute. Add the remaining ingredients. Cover and simmer for 1½ to 2 hours, until a jam-like texture is achieved. Stir occasionally.

Cool to room temperature for serving. This recipe makes 1½ cups.

Variation
Add cayenne or red chilies to the ghee or butter.

Plum Chutney

A westernized version of chutney. The fresh prunes are available in the late summer and early autumn. My brother likes to spread this chutney on burritos!

3½ cups pitted, halved fresh prunes (prune-plums)
1 cup golden raisins
⅓ cup water
⅓ cup lemon juice
1 cup brown sugar
2 teaspoons salt
2 teaspoons yellow mustard seed

½ cup slivered candied ginger *or* 1 tablespoon ground ginger

Combine all the ingredients in a large
saucepan. Bring to a boil, cover, and simmer for about 1 hour, until the mixture becomes jamlike. Cool to room temperature
for serving. Makes 2 cups.

Variation
Add cayenne or red chilies.

Mixed Fruit Chutney

Another anglicized version of chutney,
which can be prepared with anything from
apples to mangoes.

3½ cups mixed fruit, cut fine
½ cup golden raisins
¾ cup sugar
¼ cup water
¼ cup lemon juice
2 teaspoons salt
1 teaspoon coriander
2 whole cloves
2 teaspoons ground ginger
1½ teaspoons yellow mustard seed

Combine all ingredients in a large saucepan. Simmer, covered, for about 1 hour,
until the mixture becomes jamlike, stirring
occasionally.
Cool to room temperature for serving.
Makes about 1½ cups.

Variation
Add cayenne or red chilies.

Raisins and Rosewater (India)

Subtle rosewater-flavored raisins to serve
as a condiment.

¾ cup washed seedless raisins
1 cup water
1 teaspoon sugar or honey
1 teaspoon rosewater

Simmer the raisins in the water, covered,
for 20 minutes. Stir in the sugar or honey
and the rosewater. Cool to room temperature for serving. Makes 1 cup.

Tomato Chutney (India)

2 tablespoons oil
¼-inch piece fresh ginger, peeled and
    minced
1 teaspoon cumin
pinch cloves
½ teaspoon turmeric
1 teaspoon sugar or honey
½ teaspoon cinnamon
¼ teaspoon cardamom
½ teaspoon salt
2½ cups chopped ripe tomatoes
2 tablespoons water

Heat the oil in a saucepan. Add the ginger and cumin, and sauté for 1 minute. Add
the remaining ingredients. Cover and simmer for 30 minutes, until the tomatoes are
soft, stirring occasionally. Cool to room
temperature. Makes ¾ cup.

Variation
Add cayenne or red chilies to the oil.

Mint Chutney (India)

A cooling, emerald-green chutney that goes
particularly well with samosas.

1 cup packed fresh mint leaves
2 tablespoons lemon juice
1 tablespoon honey *or* 4 teaspoons sugar
½ teaspoon salt
2 tablespoons water

Combine all the ingredients in a blender
until smooth. Makes ½ cup.

Variation
Substitute parsley for mint.

Parsley Chutney

The nuts give this chutney a rich texture.

1½ cups coarsely chopped fresh parsley
½ cup raw cashews
1-inch piece fresh ginger, peeled and minced
½ teaspoon salt
1 or more tablespoons yogurt
2 tablespoons lemon juice

2 teaspoons honey

Combine everything in a blender until smooth. Add more yogurt, if necessary to blend. Makes about ½ cup.

Variations
Substitute cilantro for parsley.
Vegan Variation: Replace the yogurt with water.

Main Dishes, Sandwiches, and Stuffings

With today's lighter meals, there is often no one "main dish" to which all other foods on the table play second fiddle. A number of small dishes may be served to add up to a balanced and satisfying meal; they can be found throughout the hors d'oeuvres, soup, vegetable, salad, and grain and pasta sections. The labels are for the sake of cookbook organization, for the foods themselves have great flexibility in different meals. There are also many dishes which are meals in themselves.

The "main dishes" presented here are *mixtures* of vegetables, grains, nuts, and beans—dishes that are fairly balanced within themselves and need only a salad and perhaps a loaf of bread to be complete. By all means serve and enjoy them as often as desired, but in terms of menu planning remember that there is a great deal of flexibility in the construction of a meal, and one all-encompassing dish need not be relied upon every day of the week. Consult the menu plans on pages 20-23 for ideas.

CASSEROLES

A casserole in its original meaning is a large vessel with a lid, used for baking "casseroled" dishes. Today, casseroles are thought of as mixtures of partially pre-cooked food which are placed in a casserole dish and baked as the finishing touch. Consult the index for a full listing of the casserole recipes included in the book. Following are some suggestions for creating your own casseroles, as they are easy, very flexible, and can be improvised to include whatever is in the house at the moment. The skill is in creating harmonious and balanced compositions.

To create a casserole, place the foods in the casserole dish in layers, or mix the foods together and then place in the dish. Cover with a topping, and bake for about 30 minutes in a 350° oven.

Suggested ingredients
whole cooked grains
cooked noodles
stuffings
Chinese-style fried rice
saffron rice
lemon rice
pilau rice
bulgar pilaf
cooked beans
steamed or sautéed vegetables
vegetable stews
vegetable or bean purees
toasted nuts and seeds
fried bean curd cubes
fried gluten strips or ground gluten
fried panir cubes or crumbled panir
Toppings or mix-ins:
bêchamel and bêchamel-based sauces
cheese sauce
tahini (small amount)
sour cream
tomato sauce
grated cheese
ricotta or cottage cheese
Sprinklings for the top:
bread crumbs

chopped nuts and seeds
toasted wheat germ

Suggested Casserole Combinations
Spaghetti mixed with tomato sauce and a small amount of cooked lentils, covered with grated cheese.
Bulgar wheat pilaf mixed with garbanzos and bêchamel sauce, sprinkled with sesame seeds.
Sliced boiled potatoes covered with creamed spinach, topped with grated cheese and a sprinkling of bread crumbs.
Saffron rice covered with ratatouille and grated cheese.

Tamale Pie (Mexico)

Crust:
¾ cup cornmeal
2 cups water or broth
¾ teaspoon salt
2 teaspoons butter
1 cup grated sharp cheese
Filling:
chili (page 132)
1 cup corn kernels
1 cup or more sharp grated cheese

To make the crust, mix the cornmeal with 1 cup of the water. Bring the other cup of water to a boil. Add the cornmeal and the salt. Cook, stirring constantly with a whisk. When thick, remove from the heat and beat in the cheese. Pour the mush into a buttered 1-quart casserole dish. When it is cool enough to hold its shape, press it evenly over the bottom and sides of the dish to form a crust.

Mix the corn kernels into the chili. Pour the mixture into the crust. Sprinkle with the grated cheese. Bake in a 350° oven for 20 minutes, until the cheese is melted and bubbly, and the mixture is heated through. This recipe makes 4 to 6 servings.

Variations

Replace the cornmeal mixture with millet crust.

Omit the corn kernels.

Vegan Variation: Omit the cheese from the crust and topping.

Biryani (India)

Biryanis were introduced into India by the Moghuls. There are many types of biryanis—some sweet and some savory. For a festive occasion they can come to the table covered with gold or silver leaf—edible finely powdered real gold or silver, sometimes available in Indian specialty shops.

2 cups water (3 cups if using brown rice)
1 cup rice
⅛ teaspoon saffron
½ teaspoon salt
peas and potato curry (page 111)
1¼ cups yogurt
⅓ cup raw cashews, pistachios, or pine
   nuts
3 tablespoons raisins

Bring the water, salt, and saffron to a boil. Add the rice. Cover and simmer until the water is absorbed and the rice is tender. Spread the rice evenly in a buttered baking dish. Cover with the peas and potato curry. Spread evenly. Cover the curry with the yogurt. Sprinkle with the nuts and raisins. Bake in a 350° oven for 30 to 40 minutes, until the yogurt has set. This recipe makes 6 servings.

Variation

Substitute other vegetable curries for the peas and potato curry.

BURGERS AND LOAVES

The mixtures that form burgers and loaves are strikingly similar, if not absolutely the same. They both follow the same principle for preparation: Any mixture that tastes good, is good for you, is kind to the digestion, and—most important—*holds together,* goes. For loaves the mixture is pressed into a buttered loaf pan and baked; for burgers it is shaped into patties, rolled in breading mixture, and fried or broiled. While it is not very glamorous-sounding in theory, in practice it works, and with common sense in combining flavors, it works well.

Consult the index for a list of the burger recipes and loaf recipes contained in this cookbook. The following suggestions will help you create your own burgers and loaves. Just keep the fourfold principle in mind and the path will be smooth—and the meal a success.

Ingredients for Burgers and Loaves
Base:

cooked, cooled grains (grains which hold their individual shape, such as wheatberries, may have to be ground, or will necessitate the addition of more binding ingredients, such as nut butter, soy flour, or mashed potato)
crumbled bean curd
cooked lentils, split peas, or cooked mashed beans
ground sprouted wheat
vegetable purees, particularly potato
grated vegetables (will need a binding agent)
mixtures of ground nuts with grains, or vegetable or bean purees

Additions:

minced parsley
finely chopped sautéed vegetables
herbs and spices
ground or chopped nuts
toasted wheat germ
soy or chick-pea flour—small amounts
bran
béchamel sauce (loaves)

bread crumbs—fresh or dry
seeds
sprouts
grated cheese
farina and cornmeal
whole wheat flour

For loaves: Mix the ingredients. Press into a buttered loaf pan. Bake in a 350° oven for about 1 hour. Serve with tomato sauce or nut or pan gravy.

For burgers: Have the mixture cool enough to handle. Roll a handful of the mixture into a ball. Roll it in a breading mixture. The burger will hold together a little better after cooking. Fry in a well-buttered pan (oil can be used, but butter tastes better) on both sides until the breading mixture has browned and the burgers are heated through. Serve on burger rolls, or with a nut or pan gravy.

Nut Burgers (Sweden)

2 medium potatoes
2 cups roasted ground hazelnuts, almonds,
    or other nuts
1 tablespoon oil
1 teaspoon celery or seasoned salt

Boil the potatoes until tender. Drain and mash well. Mix all the ingredients together. When cool enough to handle, form into patties. Fry in butter on both sides until brown and crusty.

Serve with tomato sauce, gravy or on burger rolls. This recipe makes 8 to 10 burgers.

Nut Loaf

The flavor of nut loaf can be varied by the use of different nuts and grains. Walnuts and cracked wheat are a particularly good combination.

1 carrot, grated
1 stalk celery, sliced thin

2 tablespoons fresh minced parsley
1 tablespoon oil
2 cups cooked grains
2 cups roasted ground nuts
1 cup béchamel sauce (page 167)
1 teaspoon coriander
seasoned salt

Sauté the carrot, celery, and parsley in the oil for 5 minutes. Mix all the ingredients together. Season to taste with seasoned salt. Press into a buttered loaf pan. Spread evenly. Bake in a 350° oven for 30 minutes.

Serve with nut gravy or more béchamel sauce, or with tomato sauce. This recipe makes 4 to 6 servings.

Variations

Replace the béchamel sauce with auroré sauce (page 168).

Add 1½ cups grated cheese.

GLUTEN

Gluten is wheat protein, with the starch and bran removed. Preparing it for the first time can be a revelation—it is unique among foods.

Gluten has been used for centuries in China, and has been used in the west for preparation of "meat substitutes," because of its dense, chewy texture. The basic mixture can be cut into pieces and stir-fried, or can be used whole, or can be ground and added to casseroles, burgers, and other dishes. The important thing to remember is that gluten itself is very bland, and is also able to absorb the flavors of the foods it is cooked with. Cook it in a flavorful broth, and mix it with flavorful sauces and foods for best results. Gluten and bread take the same amount of time to prepare. You can reduce the time it takes to prepare gluten by using gluten flour in the recipe.

Gluten

4 cups whole wheat flour
1½ cups water
broth
2 tablespoons oil

Mix the flour and water together to form a dough. Knead vigorously on a floured board for 10 minutes to develop the gluten. Do not cut the time short. Cover the dough with cold water and soak for 1 hour.

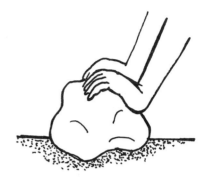

Place the dough in a colander under running lukewarm water (the temperature is for the sake of the hands—it can be cold

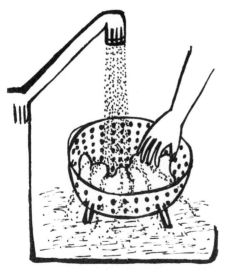

water). Work the dough with the hands, breaking off pieces and working each piece. The water will become milky as the starch is washed away. Continue working and rinsing until the water becomes almost clear—the process will take about 10 minutes. The remaining dough will be rubbery and spongy. Gather the gluten into a ball. Place in a flavorful broth to cover and add the oil. Simmer, covered, for 2 hours. Drain.

The gluten is now ready to be prepared for the food.

Stir-fried Gluten

Cut the gluten into strips. Drain well. Stir-fry in oil until lightly browned. Add to Chinese-style vegetable combinations, or to soups or vegetables.

Ground Gluten

Put gluten through the coarse blade of a meat grinder. Sauté the ground gluten in oil or butter and add to burgers, grains, casseroles, stuffings, or other dishes.

Gluten Cutlets

double recipe of gluten
½ recipe tempura batter (page 89)
breading mixture or bread crumbs
salt and pepper

Slice the gluten into ½-inch-thick pieces. Drain well. Dip the gluten pieces first in the tempura batter to coat lightly, then roll in the breading mixture to coat. (For better flavor, add a little salt and pepper to the breading mixture. You may also add some green herbs.) Fry the cutlets on both sides in ¼ inch of oil until browned.

Serve with nut or pan gravy. This recipe makes about 12 cutlets.

CHEESE DISHES

Welsh Rarebit

¼ cup binding powder (page 51)
1½ cups milk
3 cups cubed sharp cheese
2 tablespoons butter
dry mustard powder
toast
paprika
parsley or watercress

Mix the binding powder with ¼ cup of the milk until smooth. Add to the remaining milk and pour into a saucepan. Add the butter. Heat the mixture to a simmer, stirring constantly. When thick, add the cheese and stir until melted and blended. Season with a dash of dry mustard powder.

Place the toast on plates. Pour the rarebit over the toast pieces. Sprinkle a little paprika on top, and garnish with parsley or watercress. This recipe makes 4 servings.

Variation
Replace the mustard powder with ½ teaspoon curry powder.

Scottish Woodcock

A tomato version of rarebit.

1 cup cream of tomato soup (page 149)
2 cups cubed cheese
dry mustard powder
toast
toasted sunflower seeds

Heat the soup to a simmer, stirring constantly. Add the cheese and stir until it is melted and smooth. Add a dash of dry mustard powder.

Pour the mixture over the toast. Garnish with a sprinkling of the sunflower seeds. This recipe makes 4 servings.

Cheese Crepes (France)

crepes (page 231)
grated Swiss, gruyere, or other cheese

Fill crepes with a mound of grated cheese and fold up. Place in a buttered baking dish and sprinkle with more grated cheese. Dot with butter. Bake in a 350° oven for 15 to 20 minutes, until the cheese is melted and bubbly.

Variations
Place sautéed tomatoes inside the crepes with the cheese.

Place steamed asparagus tips inside the crepes.

Pizza (Italy)

A wide variety of vegetables that do not ordinarily find their way onto pizzas can be successfully incorporated by cooking them first in the sauce. Try a little cubed eggplant and winter squash for something new.

Crust:
1 tablespoon yeast
¼ cup warm water
3 tablespoons olive oil
1 teaspoon salt
1 cup warm water
2 cups unbleached white flour
2 cups whole wheat flour

Topping:
4 cups thick tomato sauce
3 cups or more sliced vegetables: green
    pepper, zucchini, eggplant, cauli-

flower, winter squash, etc.
mung sprouts (optional)
3 cups grated mozzarella cheese
basil
oregano

Mix the yeast with the warm water and let stand for 5 minutes. Add the oil, salt, remaining water and the flours. Mix, and knead on a floured board for about 5 minutes. Cover and let rise for 1½ hours or until doubled in bulk. Punch down.

Preheat the oven to 475°. Divide the dough in half. Spread out the dough on 2 baking sheets or pizza pans greased with olive oil. Don't roll out—spread and pinch with the hands to the desired size. Pinch a ridge around the edges of the dough to hold the filling. While the dough is rising and then being formed, cook all the vegetables except the sprouts and perhaps the green pepper in the sauce until almost tender.

Spread the sauce and the vegetables over the dough. Sprinkle the mung sprouts on top. Sprinkle the cheese over the filling. Sprinkle a little basil and oregano over the cheese. Drizzle a little olive oil on top. Bake for about 15 minutes on the lowest rack in the oven, until the crust is done. This recipe makes 2 medium pizzas.

Variations

For a plain cheese pizza, omit the vegetables.

Vegan Variation: Omit the cheese. For an interesting vegan pizza, replace the tomato sauce with pineapple sweet and sour sauce and green pepper, snow peas, and water chestnuts.

MEXICAN TORTILLA-BASED DISHES

There are many dishes which are variations on a theme of filling or topping tortillas with various combinations of the same ingredients. For a meal, serve two different types to each person, or serve one type and complete the meal with *frijoles refritos,* rice, and a salad.

Ingredients for Tortilla-based Dishes

tortillas or chapatis
frijoles refritos
Mexican-style tomato sauce
salad mix for Mexican foods (see below) or
     shredded lettuce
grated sharp cheese
sour cream
guacamole or avocado slices
steamed, drained spinach
chopped tomatoes, cucumbers, and green
     peppers

Salad Mix for Mexican Foods and Falafel

½ cup shredded lettuce
½ cup alfalfa sprouts
½ cup chopped cucumber

Mix together and serve in falafel sandwiches, tostadas, tacos, burritos, and so forth. Makes 1½ cups.

Enchiladas (Mexico)

tortilla dough (page 220)
2 cups or more Mexican tomato sauce
1 cup grated cheese
any of the enchilada fillings that follow

Roll out 12 tortillas. Place a little of the sauce in a shallow bowl. Quickly immerse each tortilla in the sauce, then fry on both sides in an ungreased skillet.

Place some of the filling on a fried tortilla. Roll it up. Place the filled tortillas side by side in an oiled baking dish, seam-side down. Pour the remaining sauce over

TOSTADA

the enchiladas. Sprinkle the cheese over them. Bake in a 350° oven for 20 minutes, until the cheese is melted. This recipe makes 12 enchiladas.

Fillings for Enchiladas (2 or 3 cups of filling is sufficient)

Cheese Enchiladas: grated cheese *or* grated cheese mixed with sour cream or ricotta

Spinach Enchiladas: steamed, chopped spinach mixed with sour cream or ricotta

Avocado Enchiladas: guacamole (page 64)

Refrito Enchiladas: *frijoles refritos* (page 134) topped with grated cheese *or* guacamole *or* steamed spinach and sour cream

or any mixture of the above ingredients.

Tostadas (Mexico)

For a party, distribute bowls containing the different fillings and let the guests construct their own. Roll out 12 tortillas. Fry them on both sides in ⅛ inch of oil until crisp. Drain on paper towels. To assemble the tostada, place a tortilla on a plate. Cover with the following layers, in order:

1. *frijoles refritos*
2. salad mix *or* shredded lettuce *or* alfalfa sprouts
3. Mexican tomato sauce
4. guacamole
5. grated cheese
6. sour cream
7. chopped tomatoes, cucumbers, and green peppers (optional)

Tacos (Mexico)

Tacos resemble tostadas, except that the tortillas are fried in a characteristic shape.

TACO

tortilla dough
fillings for tostadas (see above)

Roll out 12 tortillas. Gently fold each in half without breaking. Fry on each side in ¼ inch of oil, holding a fork or chopstick between the halves to leave a ½-inch gap between them. When they are crisp and hold their shape, drain on paper towels. Stuff with the filling ingredients desired (they do not have to be in any particular order) and cover the filling with a little Mexican tomato sauce. This recipe makes 12 tacos.

Flautas (Mexico)

These "flutes" are first filled and then fried until crisp. Try filling them with guacamole.

tortilla dough
any of the fillings listed on page 184, except salad mix and Mexican tomato sauce

Roll out the tortillas. Arrange 2 tortillas overlapping, as in the diagram. Place some

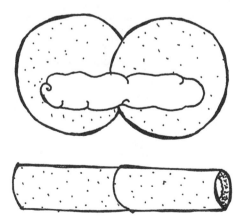

of the filling along one edge of the tortillas, leaving a small gap at each end. Roll up tightly, in the shape of a flute. Fry in ¼

inch of oil on all sides until crispy. Drain on paper towels. This recipe makes 6 flautas.

Burritos (Mexico)

For burritos, fillings are rolled up in soft tortillas. Wheat tortillas are particularly successful for burritos.

tortilla dough
any combination of the fillings listed on page 184

Roll out 12 tortillas. Fry in an ungreased pan for about 20 seconds on each side, until soft but cooked through. Roll up any (or all) of the fillings in the tortillas. Makes 12 burritos.

SANDWICHES

Sandwiches, those quick and portable meals, can be made in many vegetarian combinations—some eminently portable and others more suitable for meals at home. With the wide variety of breads that can be created, variety in sandwiches can be achieved with the use of different breads as well as the use of different fillings. Try preparing sandwiches in pita, the Middle Eastern pocket bread (page 211).

Suggested Ingredients for Sandwiches

> Spreads:
> cashew mayonnaise
> nut butters
> guacamole
> Besides lettuce:
> spinach leaves
> dandelion greens
> sprouts
> watercress

Suggested Sandwiches
Cucumber with cream cheese-herb spread.
Cashew butter, bananas, and honey on wheatberry bread.

Avocado, tomato, alfalfa sprouts, and cheese with cashew mayonnaise.

Soyburgers, sprouts, tomatoes, and cashew mayonnaise on burger rolls.

Deep-fried bean curd slices, spinach leaves, and tomato.

Falafel, salad mix and taratoor sauce on pita.

Cream cheese-orange spread on Boston Brown Bread.

Homos, sprouts, and tomato on pita.

Refrito burgers, lettuce, and guacamole on anadama bread.

Grainburgers, cashew mayonnaise, and tomato on herb bread.

Lentil loaf and French dressing on rye.

Melted cheese, tomatoes, and sprouts on cracked wheat bread.

Avocado slices, cream cheese, and toasted sunflower seeds on pumpernickel.

Avocado, tomato, and deep-fried bean curd slices on potato bread.

Grilled Cheese Sandwich

In the broiler:
Place cheese slices on a slice of bread. Place in the broiler for a minute until the cheese is melted. Top with a slice of bread toasted separately in the toaster.

In a skillet:
Place cheese between two slices of bread. Fry the sandwiches on both sides slowly in a little butter until the bread is golden brown and the cheese is melted.

Variations

Place guacamole, avocado slices, sprouts, French dressing, or sliced tomato under the cheese before *broiling*.

Broil open-faced, with sesame or sunflower seeds sprinkled over the cheese.

Frosted Sandwich Loaf

For large gatherings and celebrations, take 1 loaf of firm, non-crumbly bread. Slice it in 4 or 5 slices *lengthwise*. Spread fillings along each slice, varying the colors. Use smooth fillings, without loose ingredients which can fall out or cause a bumpy texture. Guacamole and cream cheese spreads are good, as are homos and soy spread. Reshape the loaf with the filled layers. Frost the loaf with a double or triple recipe for cream cheese frosting (page 282) or with cream cheese softened to a spreading consistency with milk. Decorate with nuts,

raisins, sliced dried fruit, pitted cherries, pineapple cubes, or minced parsley. To serve, slice and place on plates as a multi-layered sandwich.

Sandwich Spreads

homos
baba ganooj
sour cream dip or dressing
French dressing
cashew mayonnaise
nut butter

Soy Spread or Dip

1 cup soybeans
¼ cup lemon juice
2 tablespoons minced fresh parsley
up to ⅓ cup broth or water
1 medium green pepper
½ cup oil
1 teaspoon basil
salt and pepper

Soak the soybeans overnight. Cook until tender. Drain. Combine all the ingredients in a blender with just enough broth or water to puree the mixture thoroughly. Season to taste with salt and pepper.

Use as a sandwich spread, or thin a little and use as a dip. This recipe makes 2½ cups.

Cream Cheese-Herb Spread

This spread looks and tastes like some of the imported herbed cheeses; it is elegant for open-faced sandwiches and canapés. Ricotta may be used as a low-fat substitute for cream cheese, but the texture will not be quite as good.

1 cup (1 8-ounce package) cream cheese, softened
½ green pepper, chopped fine
1 teaspoon each: tarragon, basil, dill weed
¼ teaspoon salt
⅛ teaspoon curry powder

Mix all the ingredients well. Chill for at least 1 hour to allow the flavors to blend. This recipe makes 1 cup.

Cream Cheese-Orange Spread

1 cup (1 8-ounce package) cream cheese, softened
2 tablespoons honey
¼ cup chopped walnuts
1 teaspoon finely grated orange rind

Mix all the ingredients together. Makes a little over 1 cup.

Variations

Add chopped dates or other dried fruit.
Add chopped fresh pineapple.
Substitute ricotta for cream cheese.

STUFFINGS

The following stuffings may be used for stuffing vegetables, or may be eaten by themselves, as side dishes served with gravy or sauce. Stuffings also make nice ingredients for casseroles.

Many foods may be used for stuffing vegetables. Try some of the following dishes as stuffings:

creamed vegetables
Mexican-style corn for tomatoes and peppers
Chinese-style fried rice—good in winter squash
bulgar wheat pilaf
pilau rice
saffron rice
pilau-style saffron millet
soy spread or dip (for uncooked tomatoes and peppers)
baba ganooj for uncooked tomatoes
homos for uncooked tomatoes and peppers
vegetable purees

Breadcrumb Stuffing

The classic stuffing. Serve it by itself—with gravy, if desired. Whole-grain breads give it extra flavor and good texture. Perhaps prepare it for Thanksgiving, along with cranberry-orange punch, so that the low oven heat is utilized for more than one dish.

4 cups cubed bread
⅓ cup ghee or butter
2 tablespoons minced fresh parsley
1¼ teaspoons thyme
½ teaspoon sage
½ teaspoon rosemary

1 carrot, grated
3 cups thinly sliced celery
stock
salt and pepper
cabbage leaves

Spread the bread cubes on a baking sheet. Toast in a 350° oven until very dry. Cool. Meanwhile, melt the butter or ghee in a large skillet. Add the herbs and sauté for 1 minute. Add the carrot and celery, and sauté slowly for 10 minutes. Remove the vegetables from the heat. Toss in the bread cubes. Add just enough stock to moisten the bread. Season to taste with salt and pepper.

Butter a casserole dish. Line it with the cabbage leaves. Place the stuffing over the leaves. Do not pack. Cover and bake in a 225° oven for 3 hours or longer. This recipe makes 4 to 6 servings.

Variation

Replace the cabbage leaves with lettuce leaves.

Grain Stuffing

Vary the flavors and textures by varying the types of grains and nuts used. Roasted sliced chestnuts may be used instead of chopped nuts.

1 celery stalk, sliced
2 tablespoons minced fresh parsley
¼ teaspoon rosemary
2 tablespoons butter
2 cups cooked grains: rice, barley, bulgar
    wheat, etc.
½ cup pecan halves, coarsely chopped nuts
    or ¼ cup toasted sunflower seeds
seasoned salt

Sauté the celery, parsley, and rosemary in the butter until the celery is tender. Add the grains and nuts. Season to taste with seasoned salt. This recipe makes 2 cups.

Kasha Stuffing

For knishes and stuffed cabbage rolls.

1 stalk celery, sliced thin
½ green pepper, chopped
2 tablespoons butter
1⅓ cups broth or water
⅔ cup buckwheat
salt and pepper

Sauté the celery and green pepper in the butter until tender. Add to the broth or water. Toast the buckwheat in a dry skillet until it darkens slightly and smells nutlike. Add the broth or water, cover, and simmer until all the water has been absorbed. Season to taste with salt and pepper. This recipe makes 2 cups.

Potato Stuffing

Use this in piroshki, knishes, cabbage rolls, and pierogen.

2 large potatoes
1 cup shredded vegetables: carrot, zucchini, celery, green pepper (for piroshki, use mixed carrot and cabbage)
2 tablespoons butter
1 teaspoon caraway seeds
⅓ cup sour cream, ricotta, or cottage cheese
    (yogurt may be used if there is no
    cheese in the recipe)
2 tablespoons minced fresh parsley
seasoned salt
pepper

Boil the potatoes until tender. Drain, peel, and mash. While the potatoes are boiling, sauté the vegetables and parsley in the butter until tender. Mix all the ingredients together. Season to taste with seasoned salt and pepper. This recipe makes 2 cups.

Bread Crumbs and Breading Mixtures

Fresh bread crumbs are used in nut and bean loaves or burgers, and in soups and stews as a thickener.

To prepare, crumble fresh bread in a blender or by hand. Measure by packing lightly into a measuring cup. Fresh bread crumbs seem to combine wonderfully with beans. Try thickening a lentil soup with them.

Dry bread crumbs are used for coating burgers and other fried foods, in stuffings, and sprinkled on casseroles and vegetable dishes for a crunchy topping.

To prepare, grind very dry bread or crackers until fine. A blender or food processor may be used; or place the bread in a sturdy bag and pound with a hammer. (To dry out bread, place thin slices in a 300° oven and bake until dry.)

Breading mixtures: In addition to or instead of bread crumbs, the following ingredients can be used for coating burgers:

whole wheat flour
wheat germ (alone it can have a bitter flavor—mix with other ingredients for best results)

cornmeal
farina or semolina
Use in mixtures with other ingredients:
bran
sesame seeds
ground oats, barley, millet
ground nuts
ground sunflower or pumpkin seeds

For savory breading mixtures, add seasoned salt and green herbs.

Breading Mixture

This is a good all-around mixture that works very well.

½ cup whole wheat flour
½ cup wheat germ
½ cup dry bread crumbs

Mix the ingredients and use to coat burgers or fried foods. Makes 1½ cups.

Grains, Cereals, and Pasta

Some grains are refined or broken into pieces to make them more digestible. Other methods of refinement are simply intended to increase the shelf life of the product. The germ is removed from cornmeal and other grains because the germ will become rancid when exposed to the steel grinders in the mill, which heat up during use. Stone-ground cereals, on the other hand, can contain the germ, as those grinders remain

cool. Such grains and cereals can be obtained from health-food stores, or from small mills that specialize in stone-ground flours and cereals.

Records from the colonial days describe how cooks would choose their cereals according to what *type* of millstone a particular mill used—whether it ground "round" grains or "flat" grains. In light of such careful discrimination in the past, it is not

unreasonable at all to want one's staff of life ground in a whole and wholesome manner!

Store stone-ground cereals and grains in the refrigerator, in plastic bags or jars that seal out moisture.

Grain Burgers

Here are the basic proportions for grain burgers. Slightly different amounts of the binders—the soy flour and nut butter—may be necessary according to the texture of the particular grain. The firmer grains may require more.

1 carrot, grated
1 stalk celery, cut fine
2 tablespoons minced fresh parsley
1 tablespoon butter or oil
3 cups cooked, cooled grains
1 tablespoon soy flour
½ cup nut butter
seasoned salt

Sauté the carrot, celery, and parsley in the butter or oil until tender. Mix all the ingredients together. Adjust the nut butter and soy flour, if necessary, to shape the mixture into patties. Season to taste with seasoned salt. Fry on both sides in butter until golden brown.

Serve on burger rolls or with nut gravy. This recipe makes 10 to 12 burgers.

Variations

Add sesame or sunflower seeds.

Add cooked lentils or pureed beans. Roll the burgers in breading mixture before frying.

CEREALS

Cold Breakfast Cereals: There are two basic mixes for cold cereal that can be prepared at home. Both have infinite possibilities for variation. By preparing cereals at home, one can insure the freshness of the product and also regulate the sweetness. The first cereal, müesli, contains uncooked grains and nuts. The second, granola, contains toasted grains and nuts. If used often, both basic mixes can be prepared dried in a large amount and stored in the refrigerator, to be soaked or toasted as needed.

Müesli (Switzerland)

The original müesli was developed and served in the Bircher-Benner Clinic in Zurich in the late nineteenth century, as a way to encourage people to eat fruit. It was first called the "fruit diet," but as its fame spread it came to be known as simply "the diet." Today müesli is on the menu in most Swiss restaurants, and its original concept has been expanded to a method of preparing breakfast cereal mixes. The first recipe is a formula close to that of the original müesli, and next are suggestions for creating your own müesli breakfast cereal.

Swiss Bircher-Müesli

⅓ cup rolled oats
1 cup milk
¼ cup finely chopped almonds or hazelnuts

1 grated apple
1 tablespoon lemon juice
1 tablespoon honey (optional)

Soak the oats overnight in the milk, in the refrigerator. In the morning add the remaining ingredients. Serve with fruit. Makes 1 serving.

Müesli Variations

The basic principle of müesli is to soak cereals and grains overnight in milk to soften them, and then to mix in fruit and other ingredients just before serving. Soak dried fruits with the cereal to sweeten the mixture and to eliminate, partially or completely, the necessity of an added sweetening.

Ingredients: Soak 1 part cereal in 3 parts liquid overnight in the refrigerator.

rolled oats
millet flakes
rye flakes
rice flakes
wheat germ
bran
cracked wheat
milk
buttermilk
kefir
thin yogurt
soy milk
nut milk
raisins
chopped dates
chopped prunes
chopped dried apricots
chopped figs
other dried fruits

Add in the morning:
sesame, sunflower, or pumpkin seeds
chopped nuts
grated coconut
fresh sliced fruit

Add if desired:
honey

molasses
maple syrup
brown sugar

Granola

Here is a basic formula. The grains, nuts, and seeds, and their amounts, may be varied. The types and the amount of sweetening can be varied, or can be eliminated completely to allow the other ingredients to exhibit their own natural sweetness.

1½ cups rolled oats
1½ cups wheat germ
¼ cup sunflower seeds
3 tablespoons sesame seeds
¾ cup grated coconut
½ teaspoon salt
⅔ cup chopped nuts
¾ cup packed brown sugar
¼ cup ghee, melted butter, or oil
⅓ cup water or fruit juice

Mix the dry ingredients together. Mix the water and the ghee, melted butter, or oil, and add to the dry ingredients. Mix well. Scatter the mixture on a baking sheet. Toast in a 350° oven, stirring every five minutes, for 20 to 30 minutes until golden brown. Cool.

Serve with milk or yogurt. Store in the refrigerator in a jar or closed plastic bag. This recipe makes 7 cups.

Variations

Honey variation: Replace the brown sugar with ⅔ cup honey or maple syrup. Reduce the water or fruit juice to ¼ cup. Toast in a 325° oven.

Add a little cinnamon before toasting.

Add raisins or chopped dates after toasting.

Omit the sweetening, and increase the oil and water a little to moisten the ingredients.

Hot Breakfast Cereals: Most grains and cereals can be served for breakfast by cooking them in an increased amount of water to a soft, mushy consistency. Directions are given for each grain or cereal under its individual heading. The following additions can be applied to all breakfast cereals:

Cook in a mixture of milk and water, or in fruit juice.

Add a little cinnamon, cardamom, or other sweet spices.

Add sesame, sunflower or pumpkin seeds, or chopped nuts.

Add wheat germ, soy grits, or instant milk powder to cooking cereal.

Add raisins or chopped dried fruit to cooking cereal.

Add fresh sliced fruit or berries to finished cereal.

Serve with honey, maple syrup, molasses, or brown sugar *and* serve with butter, *and/or* serve with milk, cream, or nut milk.

INDIVIDUAL GRAINS AND CEREALS

Barley: Barley is an excellent addition to soups and stews, or for use in stuffings or grain salads. Replace cracked wheat in tabouli with barley. Replace rice in rice pudding with barley, using the proportions for brown rice. Add cooked barley in small amounts to bread dough. Use in grain stuffing (page 188) and grain burgers (page 190).

Barley may be ground into flour and toasted. Well-toasted barley flour is used as a grain coffee substitute (page 314).

Steamed Barley

1 cup whole barley
3 cups water or broth
½ teaspoon salt

Rinse the barley under running water. Bring the water and salt to a boil. Add the barley. Cover and reduce the heat. Simmer for about 1 hour, until all the water has been absorbed. Be alert during the last few minutes of cooking—barley tends to stick to the pot. This recipe makes 3½ cups.

Variation

Barley Breakfast Cereal: Use 4 cups of water instead of the 3 cups above.

BUCKWHEAT AND KASHA

Buckwheat is not really a member of the cereal family. It is found cracked and parched as "buckwheat groats," or kasha. Buckwheat may be ground into a flour, and roasted and ground to be added to grain coffee substitutes (see page 314). Use in grain burgers (page 190); also see kasha stuffing (page 188) to be used in knishes and stuffed cabbage rolls.

Buckwheat (Kasha)

2 to 2½ cups water or broth
1 cup buckwheat
½ teaspoon salt

Bring the water or broth to a boil. Meanwhile, toast the buckwheat in a dry pan until it darkens slightly and smells nutlike. Add the toasted buckwheat to the boiling water. Add the salt. Cover and reduce the heat to a very low temperature. Cook for 10 to 15 minutes, until the water is absorbed and the buckwheat is tender. This recipe makes 2½ to 3 cups.

Variations

To reduce the very strong flavor of buckwheat, substitute ½ cup cracked wheat for buckwheat.

Add to the cooking water: 1 finely sliced celery stalk, 2 tablespoons minced fresh parsley, and ½ green pepper, chopped and sautéed in 2 tablespoons butter.

Kasha Varnishkas (Jewish)

3 cups cooked kasha (preceding recipe)
1 cup cooked noodles
¼ cup butter
salt and pepper

Gently toss all the ingredients together. Season to taste with salt and pepper. Place in the broiler for a minute to brown the top. Serve with nut or pan gravy. This recipe makes 4 to 6 servings.

Mother K's Armenian Buckwheat

1 cup water
1 cup yogurt
1 cup buckwheat

Bring the water and yogurt to a boil. Meanwhile, toast the buckwheat until it darkens slightly and smells nutlike. Add the buckwheat to the boiling liquid. Cover, and turn off the heat. Let sit, without disturbing, for 15 minutes until the water is absorbed. This recipe makes 3 cups.

Variation
Cook buckwheat in the usual way. Stir in 1 to 2 cups yogurt after cooking.

CORNMEAL

Cornmeal is the staple grain of much of Central and South America. Look for stone-ground cornmeal, found in health-food stores. Store it in the refrigerator. Cornmeal may be added to baked goods, and to pie crusts and crackers for extra crunch. Use cornmeal as a breading mixture for burgers.

Cornmeal Mush

1 cup cornmeal
3 cups water
pinch salt

Mix the cornmeal with 1 cup of the water. Bring the remaining 2 cups to a boil. Mix the cornmeal into the boiling water. Add a pinch of salt. Bring again to a boil, then reduce the heat. Stir almost constantly until the mixture has thickened. A whisk is a good stirring tool, to prevent lumps. Serve as a breakfast cereal. This recipe makes about 3 cups.

Variation
Fried Mush: Drop large spoonfuls of cornmeal mush onto a buttered pan. Let cool and harden. When firm, fry on both sides in butter until lightly browned. Serve with maple syrup.

Polenta

The word *polenta* comes from the Latin "pulmentum," a staple of ancient Rome and an integral part of the rations for the Roman legions. It was a grain gruel, eaten like a porridge, or dried and hardened and eaten in cakes. Today it is a wonderful thick porridge made from a coarsly ground cornmeal bearing the name polenta, served in North Italy with tomato sauce. Polenta must be stirred constantly unless cooked in a double boiler.

1 cup polenta
2 cups milk
2 cups water or broth
salt and pepper

Mix all the ingredients together in a pot, with a sprinkling of salt and pepper. Bring to a boil, stirring constantly. Reduce heat and simmer, uncovered, stirring almost constantly for 1 hour, until thickened.
Serve with tomato sauce as a main dish. This recipe makes 3 cups.

Variations
Sprinkle with grated cheese after cooking.

Polenta may be cooked in up to 6 cups of liquid.

Vegan Variation: Replace the milk with water.

Fried Polenta: Prepare polenta and pour into a buttered pan, ½ inch thick. When firm, cut into squares or rounds. Fry on both sides in butter or olive oil until brown and crusty. Serve with tomato sauce.

Polenta and Cheese

3 cups cooked polenta
2 tablespoons butter
2 cups grated sharp cheese

Mix all the ingredients well. Preheat a buttered baking dish in a 350° oven. Pour in the polenta and bake for 20 to 30 minutes.

Serve with tomato sauce. Makes 4 to 6 servings.

Variation

Instead of baking, prepare as for fried polenta.

MILLET

Between 1456 and 1576 in Switzerland, the aldermen of Zurich made "millet journeys" to Strasbourg. They traveled nineteen hours to Strasbourg bearing an iron pot filled with hot millet to demonstrate that Zurich's residents could come to the aid of Strasbourg more quickly than the millet could cool in the pot.

The golden grain can be served as a breakfast cereal or a side dish. Millet is a wonderful addition to stews. Use millet for grain burgers (page 190). Millet can be ground into a flour and added to bread doughs. Add cooked whole millet in small amounts to bread dough.

Steamed Millet

3 cups water
1 cup millet
½ teaspoon salt

Bring the water, millet and salt to a boil. Cover and reduce the heat. Simmer until the water is absorbed. Stir several times during the cooking, and be especially alert during the last few minutes of cooking, as millet tends to stick to the pot. Makes 3½ cups.

Variations

Millet Breakfast Cereal: Use 4 cups of water instead of 3 cups.

Saffron Millet: The golden color and delicate flavor of millet is greatly enhanced by adding ⅛ teaspoon saffron to the cooking water.

Pilau-style Millet

This method of cooking makes the individual grains more distinct.

1 cup millet
2 to 4 tablespoons butter
3 cups boiling water or broth
½ teaspoon salt

Sauté the millet in the butter, stirring constantly, for 2 to 3 minutes. Add the boiling water or broth and the salt. Stir, cover, and reduce the heat. Simmer until all the water has been absorbed. This recipe makes 3½ cups.

OATS

The two "whole" oat varieties are rolled oats, which are simply oat grains that have been flattened by rollers, and scotch or steel-cut oats, which are whole oats cut into pieces. Oats are also ground into a flour (rolled oats can be ground in a blender at home) and added to baked goods. Oat flour may also be used as an egg substitute binder. Add oats to bread doughs, and use in müesli and granola as a base. In Europe, oats are cooked in small amounts in a flavorful broth and served as a soup.

Oatmeal Breakfast Cereal

3 cups water
pinch salt
1⅓ cups rolled oats

Bring the water and salt to a boil. Add the oats and stir. Cook, stirring almost constantly, until the mixture has thickened. Remove from the heat, cover, and let sit for a few minutes. Makes 4 servings. See the variations on page 191.

For scotch or steel-cut oats, cook in the same manner, using 1 cup oats and 4 cups water. Cook in a double boiler so that they do not have to be stirred constantly.

RICE

Rice was first cultivated in Asia, and there is evidence that it was introduced to the Western world by Alexander the Great. Rice, with its hundreds of varieties, is perhaps the most versatile grain. It certainly supports a large percentage of the world's population—no wonder such a life-giving substance is thrown over just-married couples for luck and prosperity. Rice can be ground into flour and used in baked goods and as a basis for puddings and breakfast cereals. Some of the available types of rice are:

Short-grain rice: Slightly sticky, good for rice puddings and rice molds.

Long-grain rice is a good general rice—firm, with separate grains. Used in Chinese-style cooking.

Brown rice comes in short and long-grained varieties—it is the short-grain

brown rice that has been very popular among health food enthusiasts. Brown rice is unhulled and contains more nutrients than white rice, but is also much harder to digest.

Basmati rice is a superior white rice, with a nutlike flavor and light, delicate texture. Basmati and its cousin, patna rice, are sometimes available in health-food stores and Indian specialty stores.

Glutinous rice is a special, somewhat sticky white rice used in Japanese-style cooking, found in Japanese specialty stores.

Wild rice is not a rice at all, but a type of grain first used by the American Indians, and still harvested by some tribes for sale.

Brown rice has long been preferred by natural foods users over the more refined white rice. We find that while it undeniably contains more nutrients, it is much harder to digest. Measurements are given in all recipes for the use of either type of rice, leaving the choice to you. However, we feel that the nutrients lost by the use of white rice can be made up for in other dishes in a meal, and that white rice—particularly basmati rice—is the preferable grain. Vary servings of white rice with other whole grains, such as barley or millet, during the week, and there is little overall loss.

Steamed White Rice—Any Type

1 cup rice
2 cups water or broth

Rinse the rice under running water. (Basmati rice particularly needs careful rinsing.) Bring the 2 cups of water to a boil. Add the rice. Stir once to distribute the grains, then cover and reduce the heat. Simmer for 20 minutes, until the water is absorbed and the rice is tender. This recipe makes 3 cups.

Steamed Brown Rice

3 cups water
1 cup brown rice

Rinse the rice under running water. Bring the rice and the 3 cups of water to a boil. Cover, reduce heat, and simmer for about 45 minutes, until the water is absorbed and the rice is tender. This recipe makes 3 cups.

Congee (China)

Serve as a breakfast gruel. In China it is sometimes served with deep-fried lima beans.

1 cup rice
5 cups water

Simmer until the water is absorbed. Makes about 5 cups.

Pilau-style Rice

1 cup rice
2 to 4 tablespoons butter or ghee
2 cups water (3 cups for brown rice)

Sauté brown or white rice in butter or ghee for 1 to 2 minutes. Bring the water to a boil; add rice, reduce heat, and simmer for 20 minutes, until water is absorbed. This recipe makes 3 cups.

Baked Rice

Baked rice has a particularly wonderful flavor when prepared with ghee.

¼ cup ghee or butter
1 cup rice
2 cups broth or water (3 cups for brown rice)
½ teaspoon salt

Melt the butter in a saucepan. Sauté the rice in it for 1 to 2 minutes. Add the broth or water and the salt. Pour the mixture into a baking dish. Cover and bake in 375° oven for 20 to 30 minutes for white rice and 40 to 50 minutes for brown rice, until the water is absorbed. This recipe makes 3 cups.

Variation
Stir sautéed vegetables in before baking.

Saffron Rice

Subtle and beautiful—goes with almost any meal.

Add ⅛ teaspoon saffron to the cooking water for pilau-style or steamed rice.

Pilau (India)

Pilaus are the glory of Indian rice preparations. Some are sweet, some savory, some spicy. Here is a mild, simple pilau.

1 cup rice
¼ cup ghee or melted butter
2 cups water (3 cups for brown rice)
½ teaspoon salt
⅛ teaspoon saffron
¼ cup roasted pecan halves
¼ cup blanched, toasted almonds
¼ cup golden raisins

Sauté the rice in the ghee or butter for 2 or 3 minutes. Add the remaining ingredients, water first. Bring to a boil, then cover and reduce the heat. Simmer until the water is absorbed and the rice is tender. This recipe makes 4 to 6 servings.

Variation
Add a little toasted coconut.

Chinese-style Fried Rice

1½ cups broth or water (2½ cups for brown rice)
½ cup sattvic sauce (page 173)
1 cup rice
3 tablespoons soy or sesame-flavored oil
¾ cup thinly sliced celery
¾ cup mung sprouts

Bring the broth or water and the sattvic sauce to a boil. Add the rice. Cover, reduce the heat and simmer until the water is absorbed and the rice is tender. Heat the oil in a wok or skillet. Sauté the celery for 5 minutes, then add the sprouts and sauté for 3 minutes more. Add the cooked rice. Sauté for 6 minutes, stirring constantly. Adjust the salt. This recipe makes 4 to 6 servings.

Variations

Add more vegetables.

Peel and mince a ¼-inch piece of fresh ginger. Add it to the oil with the celery.

Lemon Rice (India)

A tart, flavorful rice dish that goes especially well with tomato-based curries.

2 tablespoons ghee or butter
½ teaspoon cumin
1 cup rice
2 cups water (3 cups for brown rice)
½ teaspoon turmeric
½ teaspoon salt
½ cup cooked garbanzos
6 tablespoons lemon juice

Heat the ghee or butter in a saucepan. Add the cumin and sauté for 1 minute. Add the rice and sauté for 1 minute. Pour in the water. Add the turmeric, salt, and garbanzos. Stir, bring to a boil, then cover and reduce the heat. Simmer until all the water is absorbed and the rice is tender.

Gently fold in the lemon juice. Cover for 1 minute to allow the juice to be absorbed. This recipe makes 4 to 6 servings.

Variations

Add cayenne or flaked red chilies to the butter.

Omit the garbanzos, or, for a more substantial dish, add more garbanzos.

Substitute lime juice for lemon juice.

Add 2 more tablespoons ghee or butter.

Spanish Rice

Bulgar wheat or barley prepared in this manner is also delicious. Use the proportions for brown rice for barley.

3 cups ripe tomatoes, chopped
water or broth
1 cup rice
½ teaspoon salt
1 bay leaf
1 stalk celery, sliced
2 tablespoons fresh minced parsley
1 green pepper, cut in chunks
2 tablespoons olive oil
1 teaspoon paprika
salt and pepper

Puree 1 cup of the tomatoes in a blender. Place in a measuring cup and add water to equal 2 cups (3 cups for brown rice). Bring the mixture to a boil. Add the rice, salt, and bay leaf. Cover and reduce the heat. Simmer until the liquid is absorbed and the rice is tender. While the rice is cooking, sauté the celery, parsley, and green pepper in the olive oil for about 5 minutes, until tender. Add the other 2 cups tomatoes and continue cooking until the tomatoes are tender. Add the cooked rice and the paprika, and cook until all the liquid is absorbed. Season to taste with salt and pepper before serving. This recipe makes 4 to 6 servings.

Variation

Spanish Rice Casserole: Stir 1½ to 2 cups grated sharp cheese into Spanish rice. Place in an oiled baking dish and bake in a 350° oven for 30 minutes.

Baked Risotto (Italy)

Risottos—many different kinds—are the gift of Northern Italy. Here is a baked version of the famous rice dish.

¼ teaspoon saffron soaked in ¼ cup hot
    water

2½ cups broth or water (3½ cups for brown
    rice)
3 tablespoons butter
2 tablespoons minced fresh parsley
½ cup peas or asparagus tips
1¼ cups rice
1 teaspoon salt
pepper
2 cups grated mild cheese

Combine the saffron water and broth or
water in a saucepan and bring to a boil.
Meanwhile, sauté the parsley in the butter
for a few minutes. Add the rice and sauté,
stirring, for 1 minute. Add the boiling broth
and the salt to the rice. Cover, reduce the
heat, and simmer for 10 minutes (30 minutes for brown rice). Add the peas or asparagus tips and continue to simmer, covered,
until the water is absorbed and the rice is
tender.

Stir in the cheese. (Stop right here and
you have the traditional risotto a la Mil-
anese.) Place in a buttered baking dish.
Bake in a 350° oven for 25 to 30 minutes.
This recipe makes 4 to 6 servings.

Paella (Spain)

Paella is traditionally served in oval copper
pans. For a beautiful presentation, serve
paella as a main dish on an oval platter,
surrounded by whole cooked artichokes.
The Spanish use saffron lavishly in this
dish—up to 1 teaspoon can be added.

¼ to ½ teaspoon saffron, soaked in ¼ cup
    hot water.
2 cups water (3 cups for brown rice)
1 teaspoon salt
1 cup rice
⅓ cup peas
½ green pepper, cut into chunks
1 red bell pepper, cut into chunks
3 tablespoons olive oil
1 tomato, chopped

⅓ cup sliced cooked artichoke hearts
½ cup cooked garbanzos
2 tablespoons lemon juice

Bring the saffron water, water, and salt
to a boil. Add the rice, cover, and reduce
the heat. Simmer for 10 minutes (30 minutes for brown rice), and add the peas.
Cover and simmer until the water is absorbed and the rice is tender. Sauté the
green and red bell peppers in the olive oil
for 5 minutes. Add the tomato and continue
to sauté until the vegetables are tender.

Gently toss the peppers, artichoke hearts,
garbanzos, and lemon juice with the rice.
Adjust the seasoning. This recipe makes 4
to 6 servings.

Wild Rice

Wild rice may be mixed with long-grain
brown rice if desired.

¾ cup wild rice
3 cups water

Bring the water to a boil. Add the wild
rice. Cover, reduce the heat and simmer for
45 minutes to 1 hour, until the water is absorbed. Makes 3½ to 4 cups.

RYE

Whole rye is a delicious side dish, and
great in stuffings and casseroles. Though
best known for the rye flour into which it is
ground, whole rye has a very different flavor, mild and nutlike.

Steamed Rye

3 cups water
1 cup rye

Method #1:
Bring the rye and water to a boil. Reduce
heat, cover, and simmer for 1 hour or
more, until the water is absorbed.

Method #2:

Soak the rye overnight. Drain and proceed as above, using 2 cups water. Both methods make 2½ cups.

WHEAT PRODUCTS

Wheatberries are the basic wheat kernel. They are somewhat chewy, and each grain holds its individual shape after cooking. They may be sprouted. Cooked wheatberries may be used in casseroles and stuffings, or added to bread doughs. Cook in the same manner as rye. Unsoaked, they can take as long as 2 hours to cook. Soaked, they cook in 1¼ to 1½ hours.

Wheat bran, the outer layer of the wheat kernel, can be added to breads, crackers, and muffins. The bran may be toasted in a 325° oven for better flavor. Bran has a slightly drying influence on bread doughs, and should be used in small amounts. You may also add bran to hot cereals while they are cooking.

Bulgar wheat (burghul or ala) is used extensively in the cooking of the Middle East. It is wheat that has been partially cooked, and then dried and cracked into smaller pieces. It is a particularly flavorful grain, and combines well with beans and nuts. Use in casseroles, grain burgers, and stuffings.

Steamed Bulgar Wheat

2 cups water
1 cup bulgar wheat
½ teaspoon salt

Bring the water to a boil. Add the bulgar wheat, cover, and reduce the heat. Simmer for 20 minutes, until the water is absorbed and the wheat is tender.

Pilaf

2 cups broth or water
½ teaspoon salt
2 tablespoons minced fresh parsley
1 stalk celery, sliced
¼ cup butter
1 cup bulgar wheat
⅓ cup currants or raisins

Bring the broth or water and salt to a boil. Meanwhile, sauté the parsley and celery in the butter. Add the bulgar and sauté for 1 minute. Add the boiling liquid and the currants, cover, and reduce the heat. Simmer for 20 minutes, until the water is absorbed and the wheat is tender. This recipe makes 4 to 6 servings.

Variations

Add a little curry powder.
Add ¼ cup chopped nuts.
Stir in 1 cup yogurt after cooking.

Cous cous is an African wheat product, used extensively in Morocco. It is traditionally prepared in a couscousiere, two brass pots. One is placed on the fire and the other, which has holes in the bottom, rests over it. A flavorful stew is cooked in the bottom one, while its steam cooks the cous cous in the top pot.

Steamed Cous Cous

Cous cous can be prepared in a steamer, or in a colander that fits completely within a large pot.

1 cup cous cous
2 cups water
¼ cup olive oil (optional)

Soak the cous cous in the water with a light sprinkling of salt for 10 minutes. Drain and toss with the oil, if desired. Place the cous cous in the steamer or colander. Place in a pot above boiling water. Cover and simmer for 10 minutes, until the cous cous is tender. This recipe makes 3 cups (4 to 6 servings).

Cous Cous Breakfast Cereal

3 cups water
½ teaspoon salt
1 cup cous cous

Bring the water to a boil. Add the salt and cous cous. Cover and reduce heat. Simmer for 20 minutes, until the water is absorbed. Makes about 3 cups. See variations on page 191.

Sauté-style Cous Cous

Not quite as good as the traditional steamed method, but it will suffice if a steamer or the time to soak the grains is unavailable.

¼ cup butter or olive oil
1 cup cous cous
2 to 3 cups boiling broth or water
½ teaspoon salt

Melt the butter or heat the olive oil in a saucepan. Add the cous cous and sauté for 1 or 2 minutes. Add the water or broth and the salt. Cover, reduce heat, and simmer until all the water is absorbed—about 20 minutes. Makes about 3 cups.

Farina and semolina are very similar wheat products—farina is made from hard wheat and semolina is made from durum wheat. Both are usually served as breakfast cereals, but are served in a broth as soup in Europe, and are found in both main dishes and desserts in India. Use farina and semolina as breading mixtures for burgers.

Farina or Semolina Breakfast Cereal

2 cups water, or mixture of milk and water
½ teaspoon salt
½ cup farina or semolina

Bring the water to a boil. Add the salt. Add the cereal in small sprinklings, stirring constantly to avoid lumps. Simmer, stirring constantly (a whisk is good to keep the mixture smooth) until thickened. Remove from the heat, cover, and let sit a few minutes. See variations on page 191.

Wheat germ can be served as a cereal, added to hot cereals, used in müesli and granola, or added to baked goods. Wheat germ can also replace bread crumbs to top casseroles. Raw wheat germ occasionally has a bitter flavor. Toasted wheat germ has a nutlike flavor. Toast in a 325° oven until golden, stirring frequently.

Pasta is usually associated with Italy, where it is produced in literally hundreds of shapes and sizes. Noodles are also an integral part of the Chinese and Japanese cuisines, where they are served in broth. Whole-wheat pasta, and pasta containing spinach or artichokes, can be obtained from health-food stores. These pastas are not only more nourishing than the ordinary types, but also have a much better flavor and texture. Even better is homemade pasta, which is surprisingly easy to make. Once the basic technique is mastered, pasta can be whipped up quite quickly. Pasta-making machines are available that cut the dough into fancy shapes, but a sharp knife will suffice for the occasional noodle-maker.

Basic Noodles

2 cups unbleached white flour
½ to ⅔ cup water

Sift the flour. Add the water and mix to form a soft, non-sticky dough. Turn out on a floured board. Knead with one hand for 10 minutes, until completely smooth. Wrap the dough in plastic wrap and let rest for 10 to 30 minutes.

Divide the dough in four parts for easier handling. Roll out very thin on a well-floured board. Fold the dough over loosely

two or three times and cut off noodles the desired width. There will be about 1 pound of noodles.

To cook noodles (fresh or dried):

Bring 6 quarts of water to a boil. Add a teaspoon or more salt to the water, and, if desired, a little oil. (A teaspoon of oil will help keep the noodles separate and the water from boiling over.) When the water is boiling rapidly, drop 1 pound of noodles into it. Boil fresh noodles about 5 to 6 minutes, and dried noodles 8 to 10 minutes. The noodles should be at the point that the Italians call "al dente": they will be tender, but still offer a little resistance to the teeth.

Drain the noodles in a colander. Serve with:

- Butter, a little basil, and, if desired, parmesan cheese
- Tomato sauce and grated parmesan cheese
- Pesto
- Lentil sauce
- A mixture of sour cream and cottage cheese

Soy Noodles

These are the "preferred" homemade noodles—they are almost identical to regular noodles in flavor and in texture, but have the added nutrition of soy flour.

1 cup unbleached white flour
1 cup soy flour
½ cup (or slightly less) water

Prepare in the same way as basic noodles.

Pasta Verdi (Italy)

Puree 1 cup spinach leaves in a blender with ½ cup water. Strain out the spinach and use the green water to prepare basic, soy, or udon noodle dough.

Udon (Japan)

Prepare basic noodles with whole-wheat pastry flour. Cut into noodles ¾ inch wide.

Soba (Japan)

1 cup unbleached white flour
1 cup buckwheat flour
½ to ⅔ cup water

Prepare in the same way as basic noodles.

Bean thread noodles (Saifun or Sefun) are found in the cooking of China and Japan. They turn transparent when cooked, and can be quite a surprise for someone who unsuspectingly dips into a bowl of what looks like clear broth and comes up with a spoonful of clear noodles! Add bean thread noodles to Chinese or Japanese-style soups, or serve under stir-fried mixed vegetables. They come in bundles and must be cut to size.

To boil bean thread noodles, soak the bean threads in cold water for 20 to 30 minutes; add them to boiling broth for 5 minutes.

To make puffed bean threads, cut the noodles into pieces. Heat 2 tablespoons oil in a wok and add the dry noodles. Stir, and they will puff up. Use these as a bed for stir-fried vegetables.

Fettucine (Italy)

This dish is simple and very, very rich. Prepare it with homemade noodles, if possible. For color contrast, use half pasta verdi and half soy noodles for a green-and-white mixture called "straw and hay" by the Italians.

1 recipe noodle dough, cut in ¼-inch-wide
    noodles, *or* 1 pound dried noodles
¾ cup butter
¾ cup grated fresh parmesan cheese
½ cup heavy cream
salt and pepper

Cook the noodles al dente. Drain. While the noodles are boiling, cream the parmesan into the butter. Beat in the cream. Toss the noodles with the sauce until thoroughly coated.

Sprinkle with a little salt and pepper. Serve immediately. This recipe makes 4 servings.

Spaghetti

There is a wonderful whole-wheat spaghetti sold in health-food stores. It has a slightly nutlike flavor and a tiny bit of texture to it, which makes it more than just the bed for a sauce.

Cook spaghetti according to directions for noodles on page 201. Hold the spaghetti upright in the pot and gently push down, until the noodles in the water soften sufficiently for the noodles out of the water to be accommodated in the pot.

Serve spaghetti with:
- long-cooking tomato sauce and grated parmesan cheese
- pesto
- lentil sauce and parmesan cheese
- butter, with a little basil and parmesan

Macaroni and Cheese

This is one of those dishes which can be prepared simply and economically, or can be improvised to be quite rich and elegant. For best flavor, prepare it with whole-wheat macaroni.

3 cups cooked, drained macaroni
1 cup milk
2 tablespoons butter cut in small pieces
2 cups cubed cheese
salt and pepper
2 to 4 tablespoons bread crumbs

Toss the noodles, milk, butter, and cheese together. Sprinkle with a little salt and pepper. Place in a buttered baking dish and sprinkle with the bread crumbs. Bake in a 350° oven for 30 minutes. This recipe makes 4 servings.

Variations

Add 1 large chopped tomato.

Add 1 cup lightly steamed chopped spinach, or ½ cup steamed peas or asparagus tips.

Replace the milk with cream, or with béchamel sauce or one of the béchamel variations.

Manicotti (Italy)

The preparation of manicotti is involved, but ultimately it can be prepared in a quite acceptable amount of time. It looks very professional, and tastes divine.

1 pound soy noodle dough or pasta verdi
    (page 201)
4 cups ricotta
2 cups grated mozzarella
¼ cup binding powder
1½ teaspoons basil
⅛ teaspoon nutmeg
1½ teaspoons salt
3 to 4 cups tomato sauce
grated cheese for topping (optional)

Prepare the sauce. Prepare the noodle dough. While the dough is resting, prepare the filling: Mix the ricotta, mozzarella, binding powder, salt, basil, and nutmeg together. Roll out the dough and cut into ten 4-by-6-inch rectangles. Boil according to directions for boiled noodles on page 201. Drain very carefully. Run cold water over the drained noodles until they are cool enough to handle.

Gently spread the noodles out flat. Place an even layer of the filling along one long edge of each rectangle. Roll up the noodle to enclose the filling and form a tube. Place the tubes side by side in an oiled baking dish. Pour the tomato sauce over them. If desired, sprinkle with grated cheese. Bake in a 350° oven for 30 minutes. This recipe makes 10 manicotti (5 servings).

Lasagna (Italy)

For the best lasagna, prepare a flavorful, long-cooking sauce.

½ recipe for noodle dough *or* ½ pound lasagna noodles
3 cups tomato sauce
2 pounds spinach
3 cups ricotta
2 tablespoons binding powder
3 cups grated cheese

Wash the spinach well. Remove the stems. Steam slightly, drain thoroughly, and chop while draining.

Beat the binding powder into the ricotta.

Roll out the noodle dough. Cut into 9-inch-by-1½-inch noodles. Cook noodles according to the directions on page 201. Run cold water over them while draining until cool enough to handle.

Line up the ingredients. Place a layer of noodles in the bottom of an oiled rectangular baking dish. Cover them with layers, in order, of: 1½ cups ricotta, ½ of the spinach, and 1 cup each of first tomato sauce and then cheese. Lay down another layer of noodles and repeat.

Lay down the remaining noodles. Cover with the remaining tomato sauce and sprinkle the cheese on top. Bake in a 350° oven for 30 minutes.

To serve, cut in squares with a sharp knife. This recipe makes 6 to 8 servings.

Variations

Replace part of the spinach with grated zucchini or mung sprouts.

Vegan Variation: Omit the cheese and binding powder. Replace partially with crumbled bean curd. A nice lasagna can be made by replacing the cheeses with layers of spinach, lentil sauce, and tomato sauce.

Pierogen (Jewish)

1 recipe soy or basic noodle dough (pages 200-201)
2 cups mashed potatoes or potato stuffing (page 188)

Roll out the noodle dough on a floured board. Cut into 3-inch circles with the rim of a glass or a cookie cutter. Place a spoonful of filling on half of each circle. Fold the dough over, moisten the edges, and seal thoroughly. (Double-check the sealing—it is easy for these to fall apart during the cooking.) Let the pierogens dry for 2 to 3 hours on a floured board in the sun.

To boil: Drop each pierogen into 3 quarts of rapidly boiling salted water and boil for 8 minutes. Drain very gently.

To fry: Fry in ¼ inch of oil on both sides until golden brown.

Serve with sour cream. This recipe makes about 25 pierogen.

Ravioli (Italy)

Ravioli is an adventure to prepare for the first time. Sealing the edges very thoroughly, and handling the prepared raviolis gently, are the keys to success.

1 cup ricotta
¾ cup mozzarella
½ teaspoon salt
pinch nutmeg
2 tablespoons binding powder
soy, basic, or pasta verdi noodle dough
tomato sauce

Mix the ricotta, mozzarella, salt, nutmeg, and binding powder together.

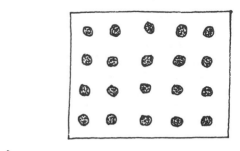

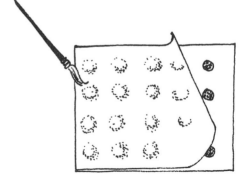

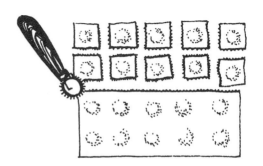

RAVIOLI

Divide the noodle dough into 2 pieces. Roll out each piece on a well-floured board into a 9-inch-by-11-inch rectangle. With moist hands, roll the filling into 20 little balls. Place on one of the rectangles 1 inch apart in rows—4 across and five down—with a ¾-inch edge around the outside. With a paintbrush, brush lines of water between each row and around the outside edge. Place the second rectangle of dough on top. Gently press down to seal between the rows and around the edges.

With a sharp knife or a pie edge trimmer, carefully cut down and across the rows to form the raviolis. Take each ravioli and make sure it is thoroughly sealed. Trim excess dough from the edges if necessary. Place on a floured tray and let dry in the sun for 2 to 3 hours.

Drop the raviolis into 3 quarts of boiling salted water in two batches. Boil for 8 to 10 minutes. Drain very gently in a colander.

Serve with tomato sauce. This recipe makes 20 large raviolis.

Noodles and Bean Curd (Japan)

Sometimes called "fox's noodles," since foxes are said to like bean curd.

1 quart kombu broth (page 139)
½ recipe for udon noodles (page 201)
2 teaspoons sugar or honey
bean curd cut into 20 1-inch cubes
oil for deep-frying

Deep-fry the bean curd until golden and crisp. Drain on paper towels and set aside. Cook the noodles according to directions on page 201. Drain. Bring the broth to a boil. Add the sugar or honey.

Place the noodles in 4 bowls. Cover with the broth. Place 5 pieces of bean curd on top of the noodles in each bowl. This recipe makes 4 servings.

Noodles and Tempura (Japan)

½ recipe for udon or soba noodles
1 quart boiling vegetable broth, sattvic sauce broth, or kombu broth
mixed vegetable tempura (page 89)

Cook the noodles according to the instructions on page 201. Drain and place in four bowls. Pour the boiling broth over them. Place pieces of tempura on top of the noodles in each bowl. This recipe makes 4 servings.

Breads, Rolls, Crackers, Biscuits, Muffins, Pancakes

YEASTED BREADS AND ROLLS

The one outstanding factor in baking yeasted bread is to simply *allow* the process to happen. Yeasts are living, growing organisms, and in preparing bread we simply set up the most supportive conditions for them to accomplish their work—which they will do in their own good time. For this reason, exact times cannot be given for rising.

Because different flours contain different amounts of moisture, exact measurements cannot be given. Approximations are within 15 minutes of time and 1 cup of flour, and it doesn't take long to develop a feel for the dough and to know just what it needs.

Before embarking on bread-baking, read about yeast on page 52. There are a variety of rising methods. The one we have found to be the most effective involves a first short rising of a sponge—a batter without the oil and salt, which retard the growth of the yeast. This first rising makes the loaves a little lighter than bread risen in the ordinary manner.

One further note: whole milk tends to slightly coat the yeast and inhibit its rising—not much, but a little. Nonfat powdered milk is good to use because it doesn't coat the yeast. It is also economical, and does not have to be scalded.

Complete instructions for bread-baking are given with the first recipe, which makes two loaves. The instructions in succeeding recipes are abbreviated.

Basic Bread

1 tablespoon (1 package) yeast
¼ cup lukewarm water
⅓ cup sugar *or* ¼ cup honey
2 cups milk, scalded and cooled to lukewarm, or reconstituted powdered milk, heated
3 cups unbleached white flour
3 to 3½ cups whole wheat flour
1 tablespoon salt
¼ cup melted butter or oil

In a pottery or glass bowl (anything but metal), mix the yeast with the water. Let sit for 5 minutes. Mix again. (A whisk is very useful for mixing the yeast.) Add the sugar or honey, the milk, and 3 cups of flour. Beat with a spoon until fairly smooth.

Cover with a cloth, and let rise in a warm, draft-free place for 45 minutes to 1 hour. The top shelf in a warm kitchen or a place near the pilot light on the stove can be used—or heat the oven for 1 minute, turn it off, and use that. It should be just warm.

Stir down the dough. Add the salt and the butter or oil, and stir in the remaining flour. Turn out on a floured board. Knead

for about 2 to 5 minutes. Kneading (see page 10 for the technique) developes gluten in the flour. This makes the bread more tight-grained. Though some cookbooks recommend 10 minutes of kneading, we like to knead just until the dough is no longer sticky. Add more flour as necessary. Place the dough in an oiled bowl. Cover, and return to the warm place. Let it rise until doubled in bulk. The rising takes

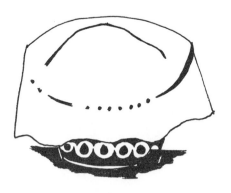

about 1½ to 2 hours—the longer time period for breads containing heavier flours. To test, insert two fingers deeply into the dough and remove. If the impression remains intact, the rising is done.

When the dough has doubled in bulk, literally punch it down with the fists to its original size. Then divide it in half. There are two basic types of loaves that can be formed: free-form, and in loaf pans. For

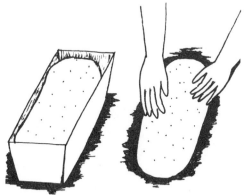

free-form loaves, shape into round, oval, or whatever shape is desired. Place the two loaves on an oiled baking sheet, far apart so that they will not touch when they rise.

Everyone has a favorite method of forming loaves for loaf pans. The simplest is just to mold the dough into an oval shape and place it in an oiled loaf pan. Another method is to roll out the dough into a rectangle. Roll up the rectangle jelly-roll style and tuck the ends under. Place in the loaf pan. A third method is to roll the dough into two large balls, and place the balls in a loaf pan. When the loaf is formed, cover and let rise in a warm place for 30 minutes.

Preheat the oven to 375°. Always place bread in a preheated oven. If the oven is cool and then heats up while the bread is in it, the yeast will leaven the bread furiously, spurred by the pleasant warmth, and then suddenly die when it is too hot for them to survive. This can make the top crust come off, or produce an uneven or incomplete rising.

If a light crust is desired, brush the tops of the loaves with milk. If a heavy crust is desired, place a pan filled with boiling water on the rack below the bread pans. Professional bakers' ovens have systems which inject steam into the oven for the purpose. If a medium crust is desired, do nothing. Free-form loaves will have more crust, as more of the surface is exposed to the oven heat.

Bake the loaves for 45 minutes, until done. To test for doneness, tap the top of a loaf. If it sounds hollow, it is probably done. Remove the loaf from the pan and tap the bottom. If it sounds hollow, the loaf is done.

Remove from the pan to cool. Bread fresh from the oven will be crumbly when sliced, so if possible, wait!

Store homemade bread in the refrigerator. It will not stay fresh as long as store-bought breads, which contain preservatives, so make it in batches that will last for only two or, at the most, three days.

Short Rising Method
If there is no time to prepare the sponge (the first, incomplete mixture), add *all* the flour, salt, and butter to the yeast/milk mixture. Proceed from there, omitting the 45 minutes-to-1-hour rising period, and go straight to the 1½-to-2-hour rising.

Vegan Variation
Bread may be prepared with water only, but it will be a little heavier and more crumbly.

Variations and Additions to Basic Bread
The heavier grains and flours will produce a heavier loaf. For best results, do not replace more than 2 or 3 cups of flour with a heavier flour.

Flour:
buckwheat flour (in small amounts)
rye flour

soy flour (in small amounts—½ cup is good)
millet flour (adds texture, but not flavor)
barley flour (toasted barley flour is delicious)
bran
wheat germ

Additions:
cooked grains and cereals (in small amounts; adjust the milk or water to accommodate the increased moisture)
raisins or currants
chopped dried fruit
chopped nuts
sesame, pumpkin, sunflower, poppy, and caraway seeds
milk powder (for extra nourishment)
herbs
grated cheese
granola or müesli cereal
molasses or maple syrup in place of sugar or honey

White Bread

Prepare basic bread, substituting unbleached white flour for whole wheat flour.

Raisin Bread

Add 1 cup of raisins to basic bread or any bread recipe (except rye, pumpernickel, and the other savory breads).

Rye Bread

Prepare basic bread, substituting for the flours:

2 cups unbleached white flour
2 cups rye flour
2 to 2½ cups whole wheat flour

Add 1 tablespoon caraway seeds after the first rising.

100% Whole Wheat or Rye Bread

Rye has no gluten in it, and a bread made with rye flour exclusively will be extremely dense and heavy. On the other hand, 100 percent whole wheat bread, though heavier than basic bread, has wonderful flavor and a good texture. You may prepare basic bread with exclusively rye or whole wheat flour, or, for extra lift, add 1 tablespoon yeast, ¼ cup lukewarm water, and a little extra flour.

Swedish Rye Bread (Sweden)

A fragrant, full-flavored bread.

2 tablespoons yeast
¼ cup lukewarm water
¼ cup molasses
1¾ cups lukewarm water
2 cups whole wheat flour
2 cups rye flour
2 to 2½ cups unbleached white flour
1 tablespoon finely grated orange peel
1 tablespoon salt
2 tablespoons oil
1 tablespoon caraway seeds
1 teaspoon anise or fennel seeds

Mix the yeast with the ¼ cup of water. Let stand 5 minutes. Stir again. Add the molasses, 1¾ cups water, and 3 cups of flour. Beat. Cover with a cloth and let rise in a warm place for 45 to 60 minutes.

Stir down. Add the remaining ingredients. Turn out on a floured board and knead about 5 minutes until smooth. Place in an oiled bowl, cover, and let rise until doubled in bulk, about 1½ to 2 hours.

Punch down. Divide in half. Form 2 round loaves. Place on an oiled baking sheet. Slash 3 diagonal gashes ½ inch deep on the top of each loaf with a sharp knife. Cover and let rise for 30 minutes.

Bake in a 375° oven for 45 minutes, until done. This recipe makes 2 loaves.

Anadama, or Cornmeal Bread (USA)

¾ cup water
¾ cup yellow cornmeal
2 tablespoons yeast
1¼ cup lukewarm water
¾ cup milk
¼ cup molasses
6 to 6½ cups flour—unbleached white or part whole wheat
¼ cup melted butter
2 teaspoons salt

Bring the ¾ cup of water to a boil. Add the cornmeal. Cook until thick, stirring constantly. Remove from the heat and cool to lukewarm. Mix the yeast with the remaining water. Let sit for 5 minutes. Mix again. Add the milk, molasses, cornmeal, and 2 cups flour. Mix well. Cover and let rise in a warm place for 45 to 60 minutes.

Stir down the batter. Add the butter, salt, and remaining flour. Knead on a floured board until smooth—about 3 to 5 minutes. Place in an oiled bowl, cover, and let rise in a warm place until doubled in bulk— about 1½ to 2 hours.

Punch down. Divide into 2 loaves, form, and place in buttered loaf pans. Cover and let rise for 30 minutes. Bake in a 375° oven for 45 minutes, until done. This recipe makes 2 loaves.

Sweet Corn-Raisin Bread

Prepare Anadama bread, replacing the molasses with ½ cup packed brown sugar or ⅓ cup honey. Add 1 cup raisins after the first rising. Replace ½ cup flour with ½ cup wheat germ. Form 2 round free-form loaves rather than bake in loaf pans. More flour may be necessary.

Granola Bread

2 tablespoons yeast
½ cup lukewarm water

⅔ cup packed brown sugar *or* ½ cup honey
1½ cups milk, scalded and cooled to luke-
    warm, or reconstituted powdered milk,
    heated (use 1¼ cups if using honey)
3 cups unbleached white flour
3 to 3½ cups whole wheat flour
¼ cup melted butter
2 teaspoons salt
3 cups granola (page 191)

Mix the yeast with the water. Let stand for 5 minutes. Mix again. Add the sugar or honey, milk, and 3 cups flour. Beat. Cover and let rise in a warm place for 45 to 60 minutes.

Stir down the batter. Add the remaining ingredients. Knead on a floured board for 3 to 5 minutes. Place in an oiled bowl, cover, and let rise until doubled in bulk, in a warm place—about 1½ to 2 hours.

Punch down the dough. Divide into two pieces and form them into loaves. Place in buttered loaf pans. Cover and let rise for 30 minutes.

Bake in a 375° oven for 45 minutes, until done. This recipe makes 2 loaves.

Variation
Add 1 cup raisins or chopped dates after the first rising.

Oatmeal Bread or Cracked Wheat Bread

Though the recipe is the same, these two breads have entirely different characters, and both are worth trying.

1 cup milk, scalded and cooled to luke-
    warm, or reconstituted powdered milk,
    heated
1 cup water
1 cup oats or cracked wheat
2 tablespoons yeast
½ cup lukewarm water
½ cup packed brown sugar *or* ⅓ cup honey
2½ cups unbleached white flour

2½ to 3 cups whole wheat flour
¼ cup melted butter or oil
1 tablespoon salt

Bring the milk and 1 cup water to a boil. Add the oats or cracked wheat, and cook until just slightly thickened—about 1 minute for oats, and 2 to 5 minutes for cracked wheat. Cool to lukewarm, uncovered.

Mix the yeast with the ½ cup of luke-warm water. Let stand for 5 minutes. Mix again. Add the oats or cracked wheat mixture, the sugar or honey, and 2 cups of flour. Beat. Cover and let rise in a warm place for 45 to 60 minutes.

Stir down the batter. Add the remaining flour, butter, and salt. Knead on a floured board for a few minutes. Place in an oiled bowl, cover, and let rise in a warm place for 1½ to 2 hours, or until doubled in bulk.

Punch down. Divide into 2 pieces, and form 2 loaves. Place in oiled loaf pans. Cover and let rise 30 minutes.

Bake in a 375° oven for 45 minutes, until done. This recipe makes 2 loaves.

Herb Bread

Make the following changes in basic bread recipe, page 206:

Replace the sweetening with 3 table-spoons sugar or 2 tablespoons honey. Replace the butter or oil with olive oil. Sauté 2 tablespoons minced fresh parsley, 2 teaspoons dill seed, 2 teaspoons basil, and 1 teaspoon rosemary in it before adding to the bread.

Form 2 oval loaves. Slash 3 diagonal gashes, about ½ inch deep, on the top of each loaf with a sharp knife.

Cheese Bread

A delicious bread for sandwiches and for toast.

2 tablespoons yeast

½ cup lukewarm water
3½ cups whole wheat flour
1½ cups milk, scalded and cooled to lukewarm, or reconstituted powdered milk,
heated
3 tablespoons sugar *or* 2 tablespoons honey
1 teaspoon salt
3 tablespoons melted butter or oil
2 cups grated sharp cheese
3 to 3½ cups unbleached white flour

Mix the yeast and the water. Let stand 5 minutes. Mix again. Add the milk, the sugar or honey, and 3 cups of the flour. Beat. Cover and let rise in a warm place for 45 to 60 minutes.

Stir down the batter. Add the remaining ingredients. Turn out on a floured board and knead for 3 to 5 minutes, until smooth. Place in an oiled bowl and let rise for 1½ to 2 hours, until doubled in bulk.

Punch down. Divide in half to form 2 loaves. Place in oiled loaf pans. Cover and let rise for 30 minutes.

Bake in a 375° oven for 45 minutes, until done. This recipe makes 2 loaves.

Variation

Cheese-Herb Bread: sauté the herbs listed for herb bread (page 210) in the butter before adding to the batter. For more flavor, substitute 2 cups rye flour for 1 cup each of the unbleached white and whole wheat flours.

Pumpernickel Bread

¾ cup water
¾ cup cornmeal
2 tablespoons yeast
1½ cups lukewarm water
2 tablespoons molasses
4 to 4½ cups whole wheat flour
2 tablespoons oil
1 tablespoon salt
1 tablespoon caraway seeds
2 cups rye flour

Bring the ¾ cup water to a boil. Stir in the cornmeal and cook for 1 minute, until thick. Remove from the heat and cool to lukewarm.

Mix the yeast with ½ cup of the lukewarm water. Let stand for 5 minutes. Mix again. Add the cornmeal, molasses, remaining water, and 2 cups of whole wheat flour. Beat. Cover and let rise for 45 to 60 minutes in a warm place.

Stir down the batter. Add the remaining ingredients. Turn out on a floured board and knead for 5 to 10 minutes, until smooth. Place in an oiled bowl, cover, and let rise in a warm place for about 2 hours, until doubled in bulk.

Punch down. Divide in half. Scatter cornmeal on an oiled baking sheet. Form 2 round free-form loaves. Place on the cornmeal. Cover and let rise for 30 minutes.

Bake in a 375° oven for 45 minutes, until done. This recipe makes 2 loaves.

Variation
For a darker loaf, mix 1 tablespoon grain coffee powder with the water.

Sesame Bread

Toast ⅔ cup sesame seeds. Grind to a powder in a blender. Add to basic bread (page 206) after the first rising. Press whole sesame seeds into the tops of the loaves after they are formed and before rising.

Pita (Middle East)

Sometimes called "Syrian bread," these breads are partially baked in a hot oven, then finished in the broiler, where they puff up and form a pocket in the bread. The final baking takes 1 to 2 minutes, and it is fun to watch them puff up.

1 tablespoon yeast
¼ cup lukewarm water
1 tablespoon sugar or honey

2 teaspoons salt
1 tablespoon oil
2 cups warm water
3 cups unbleached white flour
2 to 2½ cups whole wheat flour

Mix the yeast with the water. Let stand for 5 minutes. Mix again. Add the remaining water and the remaining ingredients. Turn out on a floured board and knead for 5 minutes to make a soft, smooth dough. Place in an oiled bowl, cover, and let rise for 1½ hours, until doubled in bulk.

Punch down. Divide the dough into 16 balls. Roll out each ball into a 5-inch circle. Cover and let rise for 30 minutes.

Preheat the oven to 500°. Bake the breads, 2 or 3 at a time, on the lowest shelf in the oven for 5 minutes. Remove from the oven and place in the broiler for 1 or 2 minutes, until brown and puffed up. Be very alert during this stage to not burn the breads. An assembly-line rhythm can be set up to keep some breads baking while others are broiling and then being transferred to a plate, so the process goes quickly.

Cool the breads. To serve for sandwiches, cut each bread in half and stuff with a sandwich filling. This recipe makes 16 individual pita breads.

Variation
Add ¼ cup sesame seeds to the dough for sesame pita.

Wheatberry Bread

A sweet bread, with the added texture of wheatberries.

1 tablespoon yeast
¼ cup lukewarm water
¾ cup brown sugar, packed
2 cups milk, scalded and cooled to lukewarm, or reconstituted powdered milk, heated
3 cups whole wheat flour
3 to 3½ cups unbleached white flour

1 tablespoon salt
¼ cup melted butter or oil
2 cups cooked wheatberries
½ cup wheat germ

Mix the yeast with the water. Let stand for 5 minutes. Mix again. Add the brown sugar, milk, and 3 cups flour. Beat. Cover with a cloth and let rise 45 to 60 minutes in a warm place.

Stir down the batter. Add the remaining ingredients. Turn out on a floured board and knead lightly for 2 to 3 minutes. Place in an oiled bowl. Cover and let rise in a warm place until doubled in bulk, about 1½ to 2 hours.

Punch down. Divide in half and form two loaves. Place in oiled loaf pans. Cover and let rise for 30 minutes.

Bake in a 375° oven for 45 minutes, until done. This recipe makes 2 loaves.

Honey Variation
Replace sugar with ½ cup honey. Reduce the milk to 1⅔ cups.

Kranzkuchen (Germany)

In some German villages on New Year's, godfathers give this bread to their godchildren. It comes in various versions—this is one of the fancier ones.

Dough:
1 tablespoon yeast
¼ cup lukewarm water
¾ cup sugar
1 cup milk, scalded and cooled to lukewarm, or reconstituted powdered milk, heated
¼ cup melted butter
1 teaspoon salt
4–5 cups unbleached white flour

Filling:
about ¼ cup melted butter
1 cup raisins
2 cups ground nuts
1 cup sugar

Glaze:

1 cup sifted confectioner's sugar
3 tablespoons chopped roasted nuts
2 tablespoons water
1 teaspoon finely grated orange rind

Mix the yeast with the water. Let sit for 5 minutes. Mix again. Add the sugar. Add the milk, butter, salt, and flour. Turn out on a floured board and knead lightly, for 2 or 3 minutes, until smooth. Place in an oiled bowl. Cover and let rise in a warm place until doubled in bulk—about 1½ hours.

Punch down the dough. Roll out in a 12-by-14-inch even rectangle. Cut into 3 long strips and brush each strip generously with butter. Mix the raisins, nuts, and sugar, and sprinkle them over the buttered dough strips. Roll up the strips from the wide end to form 3 long thin tubes. Pinch the edge closed on each strip and seal the ends.

Place the tubes side by side on an oiled baking sheet. Pinch the ends on one side together securely. Gently braid the tubes, and pinch the ends together. Tuck both ends under for a smooth appearance. Cover and let rise for 30 minutes. Brush the surfaces with milk.

Bake in a 350° oven for about 1 hour, until golden brown. Cool.

Mix all the ingredients for the glaze together. Spread on the cooled bread and allow to dry. This recipe makes 1 long braided bread.

Weihnachtstriezel (Germany)

A fruity, braided Christmas loaf.

1½ tablespoons yeast
¼ cup lukewarm water
2 cups milk, scalded and cooled to lukewarm, or reconstituted powdered milk, heated
⅔ cup sugar
¼ cup melted butter
1 cup raisins
2 tablespoons finely grated orange rind
6 to 6½ cups unbleached white flour
1 teaspoon salt
¾ cup blanched slivered almonds

Mix the yeast with the water. Let stand for 5 minutes. Mix again. Add the milk, sugar, and the remaining ingredients. Turn out on a floured board and knead lightly for 2 or 3 minutes. Place in an oiled bowl.

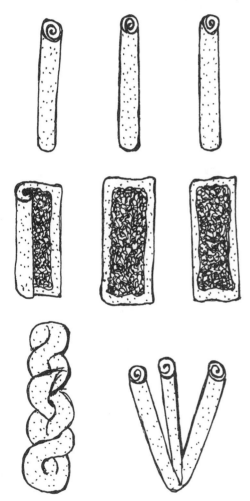

KRANZKUCHEN

Cover and let rise in a warm place until doubled in bulk, about 1½ hours.

Punch down the dough. Divide into three parts. Roll each piece into a long, thin, even tube. Place each tube on an oiled baking sheet. Pinch the ends together on one side. Carefully braid the three pieces. Pinch the ends together. Tuck both ends under for a smooth appearance. Cover and let rise for 30 minutes.

Bake in a 350° oven for about 1 hour, until golden brown.

Honey Variation
Replace the sugar with ½ cup honey. Reduce the milk to 1½ cups.

ROLLS

Dinner Rolls

Dinner rolls and other yeasted rolls can be made from bread recipes. One bread recipe will yield enough rolls to feed an army, so unless you have an army, cut the recipe in half. Cracked wheat bread makes particularly nice rolls.

½ bread recipe

Shape the rolls after the second rising, when the bread loaves would ordinarily be shaped. Cover and let them rise for 30 minutes. Unless otherwise specified, bake in a 375° oven for 20 to 25 minutes until done.

If desired, sprinkle the tops of rolls with sesame or sunflower seeds.

Variations
Burger Rolls (For lentil burgers, soyburgers, etc.): Roll the dough into 1½-inch balls. Flatten the balls on the bottom but leave the top rounded. Press sesame seeds into the tops, if desired.

Parkerhouse Rolls: Roll the dough into 1-inch balls. Flatten them and fold them in half.

Cloverleaf Rolls: Roll the dough into tiny balls. Place three balls in an oiled muffin cup to form a cloverleaf.

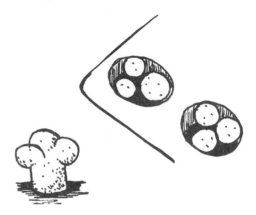

French-Style Rolls: Roll the dough into 1½-inch balls. Place on the baking sheet and flatten the bottom. Slash cross cuts into

FRENCH-STYLE ROLLS

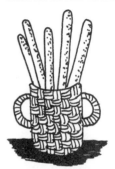

BREADSTICKS

the top of each roll with a sharp knife about ¼ inch deep. Place a pan of boiling water on the oven rack beneath the rolls to help give them a hard crust.

Bread Sticks: Roll out long, thin pieces of dough. Bake for only 10 to 15 minutes, until done.

Fan Tans: Roll out 10 thin rectangles, 4 inches by 5 inches. Stack them on top of each other, brushing each rectangle with butter before laying down the next one.

Fold in half from the wide end to form a 2-inch-by-5-inch rectangle. Cut out 3 rolls. Place, "fan"-side up, in oiled muffin cups. Repeat.

Bagels (Jewish)

Originally bagels were wide, thin rings of dough. They gradually became thicker, with a smaller hole, suitable for toasting or making sandwiches.

1 tablespoon yeast
1 tablespoon molasses
¼ cup lukewarm water
¾ cup lukewarm water
1 tablespoon oil
1 teaspoon salt
3 cups flour (unbleached white, whole wheat, or part rye)

Dissolve the yeast and molasses in the ¼ cup water for 5 minutes. Mix again. Add the remaining water, and the oil, salt, and flour. Turn out on a floured board and knead until smooth, about 5 minutes. Place in an oiled bowl. Cover and let rise in a warm place for 1½ hours, or until doubled in bulk.

Punch down. Divide into 12 pieces. Roll out each piece with the hands into a tube.

Join the ends to make a doughnut shape. Cover and let rise for 30 minutes.

Bring water to a boil in a saucepan. Drop each bagel into the rapidly boiling water for 1 minute. Remove with a slotted spoon and place on an oiled baking sheet.

Bake in a 400° oven for 15 to 20 minutes. This recipe makes about 12 bagels.

Variations

Add 1 teaspoon caraway or poppy seeds to the dough.

Sprinkle the tops with caraway, poppy, or sesame seeds.

Breakfast and Sweet Rolls: If preparing rolls for breakfast, you can make the dough the night before and leave it to rise overnight in the refrigerator, instead of the 1½-hour rising.

Basic Sweet Rolls

Prepare these rolls in any shape, and dress up as desired with raisins, chopped dried fruit, nuts, and seeds. Add a tablespoon of finely grated orange or lemon rind to the dough for a fruit flavor.

1 tablespoon yeast
¼ cup lukewarm water
¾ cup milk, scalded and cooled to luke-
    warm, or reconstituted powdered milk,
    heated
½ teaspoon salt
3 tablespoons melted butter or oil
½ cup packed brown sugar *or* ⅓ cup honey
3 to 3½ cups flour (unbleached white,
    whole wheat, or a mixture)

Mix the yeast with the water. Let stand for 5 minutes. Mix again. Add the milk and the remaining ingredients. Mix and turn out on a floured board and knead for 2 or 3 minutes until smooth. Place in an oiled bowl and let rise for 1½ hours, until doubled in bulk.

Punch down. Form into desired rolls. Cover and let rise on an oiled baking sheet for 30 minutes.

Bake in a 375° oven for 20 to 25 minutes, until golden brown. This recipe makes about 12 rolls.

Variations

Add 2 teaspoons cinnamon to the dough.

Add grated coconut to the dough, or sprinkle over it.

Cinnamon Rolls, Yeasted

1 recipe sweet roll dough (above)

Filling:
3 tablespoons melted butter
1 tablespoon cinnamon
¼ cup sugar
Glaze (optional)
½ cup confectioner's sugar

1 teaspoon finely grated orange rind
few drops water

After letting the dough rise until doubled in bulk, punch it down. Roll out on a floured board in a 6-by-10-inch rectangle. Brush the dough with the melted butter. Mix the sugar and cinnamon together and sprinkle it over the surface of the rectangle.

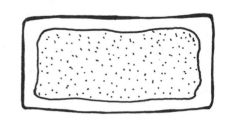

Roll up the dough tightly from the wide end to make a long, thin tube. Slice off 1-inch rolls. Place on an oiled baking sheet and cover. Let rise for 30 minutes.

Bake in a 375° oven for 20 to 25 minutes until golden. This recipe makes 12 rolls.

To glaze, cool slightly. Mix all the ingredients together and drizzle over the rolls.

Variations

See sticky buns, page 216.

Honey Variation: See sticky buns variation, page 216. These rolls tend to burn if prepared with a honey filling.

Cinnamon Rolls, Quick

The texture of these is not quite as good as that of the yeasted rolls, but they still are very good.

Dough:

3 cups flour (unbleached white, whole wheat, or half and half)
½ cup sugar
1 tablespoon baking powder
½ teaspoon salt
¼ cup melted butter or oil
1 cup yogurt
⅓ cup raisins

Sift the dry ingredients into a bowl. Add the melted butter and the yogurt. Mix lightly. Add the raisins. Roll out and proceed as for yeasted cinnamon rolls, above. This recipe makes 12 rolls.

Honey Variation

Replace sugar with ⅓ cup honey. Reduce the yogurt to ¾ cup.

Sticky Buns

¾ cup packed brown sugar
6 tablespoons melted butter
½ cup finely chopped pecans or walnuts
cinnamon rolls, unbaked (either of the previous recipes)

Mix the brown sugar, melted butter, and nuts together. Spread over the bottom of a 10-inch cast-iron skillet. Place the rolls in the skillet, touching one another. Cover and let rise 30 minutes (for yeast rolls).

Bake in a 350° oven for 25 to 30 minutes. Do not bake a moment past the time they are done.

Invert a large plate over the skillet. Reverse the skillet and plate, so that the rolls come out in a cake, covered with a sugar syrup and nuts. Pull off rolls from the cake to eat. This recipe makes 12 buns.

Variations

Honey Variation: Fill the buns with 3 tablespoons honey and 1 tablespoon cinnamon, mixed *with* the butter. Replace the brown sugar with ½ cup honey. Reduce the butter to 4 tablespoons (¼ cup). Be very careful not to overbake the rolls.

English Muffins

These muffins are fun to prepare—they are "baked" in a skillet.

1 tablespoon yeast
¼ cup lukewarm water
1 cup milk, scalded and cooled to lukewarm, or reconstituted powdered milk, heated
1 teaspoon salt
2 tablespoons sugar *or* 1½ tablespoons honey
2¾ to 3 cups flour
½ teaspoon baking soda dissolved in 1 tablespoon water
cornmeal

Mix the yeast with the water. Let stand for 5 minutes. Mix again. Add the milk, salt, sugar or honey, and flour. Mix well. The dough should be soft and slightly sticky. Do not knead. Cover and let rise in a warm place for 1½ hours, until doubled in bulk.

Beat in the baking soda and water. Scatter cornmeal on a tray. Drop the dough in 12 or 14 blobs, as round as possible, on the trays. Cover and let rise for 30 minutes. Fry the muffins in a well-buttered skillet on a low heat for about 5 minutes on each side, until browned. To serve, split in half with the tongs of a fork. Toast. This recipe makes 12 to 14 muffins.

Steamed Filled Buns with Aduki Paste (China)

Tender, light buns with a sweet aduki filling.

Buns:
1 tablespoon yeast
1 cup lukewarm water
3 cups unbleached white flour
½ teaspoon salt
1 tablespoon sugar or honey

Filling ("red bean sand"):
⅓ cup aduki beans
⅔ cup sugar *or* ½ cup honey
3 tablespoons oil

To make the dough, mix the yeast with ¼ cup water. Let stand five minutes. Mix again. Add the remaining water, the flour, and the salt. Mix and turn out on a floured board. Knead for 5 minutes. Place in an oiled bowl. Let rise, covered, in a warm place until doubled in bulk, about 1½ hours. While the dough is rising, cook the aduki beans until tender. Drain well.

Place the beans in a small saucepan with the sugar or honey and simmer for a few minutes, stirring constantly. Puree the mixture in a blender. Return to the saucepan. Boil for 5 minutes, stirring constantly. Gradually add the oil and cook until very thick, stirring constantly. Cool.

Punch down the dough. Divide into 12 balls. Flatten each ball. Roll the aduki paste, with oiled hands, into 12 balls. Place 1 ball on the center of each circle of dough. Bring up the dough and seal it thoroughly around the aduki paste. Gently roll the dough to form a ball again. Cover, and let rise for 30 minutes.

To steam, place a tray of the buns above boiling water in a steamer or pot. Cover the pot and steam the buns for 15 minutes. They should be somewhat glossy, but pure white in color. This recipe makes 12 buns.

UNLEAVENED BREADS

Unleavened breads—made without yeast or other leavening agents—are heavy, dense, and chewy. They may be prepared from any of the bread recipes, by making the following adjustments:

1. Omit the yeast.
2. Omit all the risings, though one can let the formed loaves rest for 1 hour before baking.
3. Knead the dough for 10 minutes before forming into loaves.

Real Good Bread

Real Good Bread was first sold in health-food stores in Berkeley, California. One of the original real-good-bread bakers recommends eating it warm with honey.

⅓ cup molasses or honey
¼ cup oil
1 cup warm water
2 cups graham flour
2 cups rolled oats
1 cup wheat germ
1 cup cornmeal
pinch salt

Mix the molasses or honey, oil, and water. Add the dry ingredients. Mix; then turn out on a floured board and knead for 10 minutes, until elastic. Shape into a loaf. Place on an oiled baking sheet and bake in a 350° oven for 1 to 1½ hours. This recipe makes 1 loaf.

INDIAN UNLEAVENED FLAT BREADS

These are flat, unleavened individual breads. In northern India they serve as edible utensils. One tears off a piece of bread and folds it around a morsel of food. One basic dough is used to prepare the breads. "Atta" flour, a grind prepared for these breads, is sometimes found in Indian specialty stores. Otherwise use whole wheat flour, or a blend with unbleached white flour.

Basic Dough for Chapatis, Puris, or Parathas

1¾ cups flour (whole wheat)
pinch salt
2 teaspoons melted butter, oil, or ghee
approximately ½ cup water

Mix the dry ingredients. Add the melted butter, oil, or ghee and enough water to make a soft, non-sticky dough. Knead on a floured board for 1 minute. Cover and let the dough rest for 10 to 30 minutes.

Variations

Omit the ghee, butter, or oil.

For a flaky, rich dough, use a total of 2 to 4 tablespoons ghee or melted butter.

For a golden dough, add a little turmeric.

For a bright green, delicately flavored bread, puree 1 cup of washed spinach leaves in a blender with the water for the dough.

Chapatis (India)

Chapatis are the basic bread of India. In Mexico they are served as "wheat tortillas," and can be used in Mexican tortilla-based dishes.

basic chapati dough (see above)

Pinch off pieces of the dough and roll into 1½-inch balls. Roll out each ball on a floured board into a 4 or 5-inch circle. Try to make each as round as possible. (Mothers in India chide their children's first attempts at chapati-making by exclaiming, "You make chapatis that look like a map of India!") Heat an ungreased skillet or griddle. In India a round, flat cast-iron griddle called a tava is used.

Method #1: Cook the chapatis on one side in a hot pan for 10 seconds. Flip and cook on the other side for 10 more seconds. Remove from the pan and hold the chapati directly over the flame for a second or two, using tongs or a spatula. Quickly, flip and place the other side over the flame for a second. The chapatis should puff up.

Method #2: Cook the chapatis in a hot ungreased pan, turning every few seconds. None should cook for more than 45 seconds.

Method #3 (4 to 6 very large chapatis): Roll out 4 or 6 very large chapatis instead of the 1½-inch balls. Cook by method #2. If you have a tava or a flat griddle, tilt the griddle and quickly push the chapatis' edges out over the flame for a second to puff up. To serve, fold in quarters; serve one to each person, under a cloth to keep it warm.

Keep finished chapatis under a cloth while the rest are cooking. If desired, brush with melted butter or ghee before serving, though that is not necessary. Leftover chapatis can be reheated in the toaster. This recipe makes about 15 small chapatis.

Puris (India)

Puris are light, deep-fried breads that puff up. Perfect puris are achieved by rolling them out very round, and by the pressing motion with a spatula described below. A fully puffed puri almost resembles a balloon.

basic chapati dough (see above)
oil or ghee

Roll out nearly perfect 4-inch circles of dough. Drop the puris, one at a time, into hot oil or ghee for deep-frying. Gently press each one flat to the bottom of the pot (do not try this in a wok—it is the wrong shape) with the flat part of a spatula and hold for 1 second, then release. This helps distribute the air evenly throughout the puri so that it will puff evenly. The puri should then rise to the top. Fry until golden on one side, then flip and fry on the other side for a few seconds. Drain on paper towels. The puris should be very tender, and they will lose some of their "puff." Keep prepared puris warm under a towel until all are cooked. Serve immediately. Makes 14 puris.

Parathas (India)

basic chapati dough (page 219)
ghee or melted butter

Roll the dough into 6 or 8 2-inch balls. Roll out each ball on a floured board into a 7 or 8-inch circle. Brush each paratha with ghee or melted butter. Fold in half. Brush

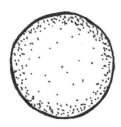

with ghee or melted butter and fold in half again. Gently roll out the folded paratha as thin as a chapati or puri. Fry on both sides in a generous amount of ghee or butter, until golden brown and crisp. Serve immediately. This recipe makes 6 to 8 parathas.

Variation

Stuffed Parathas: For a little added color and flavor, prepare a few parathas with each of the following fillings: ⅔ cup finely grated carrot, daikon radish, cauliflower or cabbage, or 1 cup minced spinach or watercress. Prepare parathas as described, sprinkling a little of the vegetables, coriander or garam marsala, and salt on each surface before folding.

Stuffed Chapatis

filling for samosas (page 65)
basic chapati dough (page 219)
yogurt
ghee or oil

Roll out 15 chapatis, as described on page 219. Place a spoonful of filling on half of each circle. Moisten the edges of the dough with yogurt or water, fold the dough in half, and seal the edges thoroughly. Fry in ¼ inch ghee or oil on each side until golden brown and crisp. Drain on paper towels.

Tortillas (Mexico)

These flat breads are prepared in Mexico by grinding dried corn and limestone together. The traditional cornmeal, "masa harina," is sometimes available in stores carrying Mexican specialties, and should be used without the addition of flour to prepare tortillas. In India they are served as "makki ki roti."

¾ cup yellow cornmeal
¾ cup unbleached white flour
approximately ⅓ to ½ cup water
½ teaspoon salt

Mix the ingredients in a bowl to form a soft, non-sticky dough. Knead on a floured board until smooth. Cover and let the dough rest for 30 minutes.

Divide dough into 12 balls. Roll out each ball into a thin circle on a floured board. To prepare plain tortillas, cook them in a hot, ungreased skillet for 20 to 25 seconds on each side. Serve warm with butter. This recipe makes about 12 tortillas.

Croutons

Croutons are great garnishes for soups and salads. Flavors can be varied by using different types of bread. Try making croutons from herb bread or cheese bread.

Cube bread. Scatter the cubes on a baking sheet and toast in a 325° oven until very dry.

Buttered Croutons

3 cups croutons
5 tablespoons butter

Melt the butter in a skillet and add the croutons. Stir for 5 minutes.

Herb Croutons

3 cups croutons
5 tablespoons olive oil
¼ teaspoon sage
¼ teaspoon rosemary
½ teaspoon thyme
½ teaspoon basil

Heat the oil. Add the herbs and sauté for a minute. Add the croutons and stir for 5 minutes.

QUICK BREADS

Quick breads are leavened with baking powder and/or soda rather than yeast, thus shortening their preparation time. Many quick breads are sweet, and contain fruit and nuts. They may be served for dessert or for snacks, or may accompany meals. Most may be served plain, or, at the most, with butter or cream cheese.

To make cupcakes or muffins from quick bread batters, place the batter in buttered muffin cups and bake in a 375° oven for 25 to 30 minutes, until done. Test for doneness using a toothpick, as for cakes. For Vegan quick breads, replace sour milk with water or soy milk mixed with a little lemon juice.

Applesauce Bread

1⅓ cups packed brown sugar
¼ cup butter
1¼ cups unbleached white flour
¾ cup whole wheat flour
2 tablespoons binding powder
1 tablespoon baking powder
½ teaspoon salt
1½ teaspoons cinnamon
1½ cups steamed, drained, mashed apples
¼ teaspoon cloves
½ cup raisins
½ cup chopped nuts

Cream the brown sugar and the butter. Sift the dry ingredients into the butter mixture. Add the apples and mix just until blended. Add the raisins and nuts. Pour into a buttered loaf pan. Bake in a 350° oven for one hour, until the loaf tests done. This recipe makes 1 loaf.

Honey Variation
Replace the brown sugar with 1 cup honey.

Persimmon Bread

Use fully ripe, California persimmons for this delicately flavored bread.

Prepare Applesauce Bread, the preceding recipe, with the following alterations: Replace the apples with 1½ cup persimmon pulp; replace the baking powder with 1 teaspoon baking powder and 1 teaspoon soda; omit the cloves. Bake in a 325° oven for 1¼ hours.

Banana Bread

¼ cup butter
1½ cups packed brown sugar

1½ cups unbleached white flour
¾ cup whole wheat flour
2 tablespoons binding powder
2 teaspoons baking powder
1 teaspoon soda
½ teaspoon salt
1½ teaspoons cinnamon
2 cups mashed ripe bananas
¾ cup chopped nuts

Cream the butter with the sugar. Sift in the dry ingredients. Add the mashed banana and mix just until blended. Add the nuts. Pour into a buttered loaf pan. Bake in a 350° oven for 1 hour, until done. This recipe makes 1 loaf.

Variations

Honey Variation: Replace the brown sugar with 1 cup honey.

Banana Apricot Bread: Add ½ cup chopped dried apricots, at the same time as the nuts. The tart flavor of the apricots complements the banana flavor.

Boston Brown Bread

A dense, sweet, moist loaf that is cooked by steaming. It can be prepared in a large can or a cylindrical mold, or, for a less authentic shape, in a casserole dish.

1 cup cornmeal
1 cup rye flour
1 cup graham or whole wheat flour
½ teaspoon salt
2 teaspoons soda
¾ cup molasses
1⅓ cups buttermilk
¾ cup raisins
½ cup chopped walnuts
1 tablespoon finely grated orange rind

Mix together the cornmeal, rye flour, graham flour, salt, and soda. Mix the molasses and buttermilk together and add to mixture. Add the raisins, nuts, and orange rind. Mix everything together well. Pour into a well-buttered can or mold. Cover tightly. (The batter should fill the container only ⅔ full.) Place the mold in a pan with 1 inch of boiling water. Place in a 350° oven and steam for 3 hours, replacing the water as it evaporates from time to time.

Cool and carefully remove from the mold. Serve with butter and cream cheese. This bread is traditionally served with Boston Baked Beans. This recipe makes 1 loaf.

Variation

Replace the buttermilk with sour milk or yogurt.

Cornbread

1½ cups unbleached white flour
1½ cups cornmeal
2 teaspoons baking powder
1 teaspoon soda
2 tablespoons binding powder
⅓ cup packed brown sugar
1 teaspoon salt
⅓ cup melted butter
1 cup buttermilk or sour milk
1 cup water

Mix the dry ingredients in a bowl. Add the melted butter, buttermilk or sour milk, and the water. Mix until blended. Pour into a buttered 9-inch-square pan. (For crusty cornbread, first heat the pan in the oven.) Bake in a 400° oven for 25 to 30 minutes, until golden.

Variations

Add chopped jalapeño peppers to the batter.

Honey Variation: Replace the brown sugar with ¼ cup honey.

Cranberry-Orange Nut Bread

A beautiful autumn bread, loaded with cranberries. Cranberries are somewhat elusive when being chopped with a knife, so place them in a blender in 3 batches and blend for 1 or 2 seconds.

¼ cup butter
1⅓ cups packed dark brown sugar
1½ cups unbleached white flour
¾ cup whole wheat flour
2 tablespoons binding powder
1½ teaspoons baking powder
¾ teaspoon baking soda
¾ teaspoon salt
1 tablespoon finely grated orange rind
½ cup orange juice
2½ cups chopped cranberries
¾ cup chopped walnuts

Cream the butter and brown sugar. Mix the dry ingredients and sift into the mixture. Add the orange rind, orange juice, and the cranberries. Mix. Add the nuts. Place in a buttered loaf pan. Bake in a 350° oven for 1 hour, until done. This recipe makes 1 loaf.

Honey Variation
Replace the brown sugar with 1 cup honey; omit the orange juice.

Date-Nut Bread

¼ cup butter
1¼ cups packed brown sugar
1½ cups unbleached white flour
¾ cup whole wheat flour
2 tablespoons binding powder
½ teaspoon salt
2 teaspoons baking powder
1 teaspoon soda
½ cup buttermilk or sour milk
½ cup water
1 cup chopped, pitted dates
1 cup chopped walnuts

Cream the butter and brown sugar. Sift in the dry ingredients. Add the buttermilk or sour milk and water, and mix just until

blended. Mix in the dates and nuts. Place in a buttered loaf pan. Bake in a 350° oven for 1 hour, until done. This recipe makes 1 loaf.

Honey Variation
Replace the sugar with 1 cup honey; reduce the sour milk and water to ¼ cup each.

Irish Soda Bread

The traditional method of preparing this bread is described first, but for texture we prefer the first variation listed, which is prepared in a pan and rises higher and lighter.

2½ cups unbleached white flour
1½ teaspoons baking powder
1 teaspoon soda
½ teaspoon salt
½ cup wheat germ
2 tablespoons sugar or honey
⅓ cup butter
1 cup buttermilk or sour milk
⅔ cup currants

Sift the flour, baking powder, soda, and salt. Add the wheat germ and sugar or honey. Cut in the butter and work with a pastry cutter or your fingers until the mixture resembles coarse meal. Add the buttermilk and currants, and mix into a soft dough. Knead lightly a few times. Place on a buttered baking sheet and form into a round loaf. With a sharp knife, slash a large "plus" sign across the top of the loaf, ¼ inch deep. Bake in a 375° oven for 25 to 30 minutes, until golden.

Serve warm with butter, cut in wedges. This recipe makes 1 small loaf.

Variations
Add 1 cup of water to the buttermilk. Stir to make a batter, pour into a buttered rectangular baking pan, and bake as above. Cut into squares to serve.

Pumpkin Bread

A moist, golden orange autumn loaf.

¼ cup butter
1½ cups packed brown sugar
1½ cups unbleached white flour
¾ cup whole wheat flour
2 tablespoons binding powder
¼ teaspoon salt
1½ teaspoons baking powder
1 teaspoon soda
1 teaspoon cinnamon
¼ teaspoon each: cardamom, cloves,
    ground ginger
2 tablespoons milk
1¾ cups cooked, mashed pumpkin

Cream the butter and the brown sugar. Sift in the dry ingredients. Add the milk and pumpkin. Mix just until blended. Pour into a buttered loaf pan. Bake in a 350° oven for 1 hour, until done. This recipe makes 1 loaf.

Honey Variation

Replace the brown sugar with 1⅓ cups honey, and omit the milk.

Zucchini Bread

The natural sweetness of zucchini enhances this moist loaf.

2 cups grated, drained zucchini
¼ cup oil or melted butter
1¼ cups packed brown sugar
2¼ cups whole wheat flour
2 tablespoons binding powder
½ teaspoon salt
2 teaspoons baking powder
1 teaspoon soda
1 teaspoon cinnamon
¼ cup milk

Mix the zucchini, butter or oil, and brown sugar. Sift in the dry ingredients. Add the milk and mix just until blended. Place in a buttered baking pan and bake in a 350° oven for 1 hour, until done.

Honey Variation

Replace brown sugar with 1 cup honey; omit the milk.

CRACKERS

Wheat Crackers

½ cup water
½ cup cracked wheat
¾ cup whole wheat flour
¾ cup unbleached white flour
¾ teaspoon salt
3 tablespoons oil
3 tablespoons yogurt
sesame or caraway seeds

Bring the water to a boil. Add the cracked wheat. Cook, stirring, until it becomes thick. Remove from the heat.

Sift the flours and salt into a bowl. Add the cracked wheat, oil and yogurt. Mix well. Roll out the dough on a floured board, about ⅛ inch thick. Cut out squares, rounds, or fancy shapes with cookie cutters or a knife. Place the crackers on an oiled baking sheet. Press sesame or caraway seeds into the crackers, if desired. Bake in a 350° oven for about 20 minutes, until browned very lightly. This recipe makes about 3 dozen 1½ by 2 inch crackers.

Variations

Vegan Variation: Replace the yogurt with water.

Wheat Chips: Prepare the dough and cut into small chips. Deep-fry in oil until golden brown. Drain on paper towels.

Canapé Crackers

For delicate, flaky crackers, prepare pastry pie crust (page 254). Roll out ⅛ inch thick on a floured board. Cut out fancy-shaped crackers with a knife or cookie cutters. If serving plain, without a spread, top with sprinklings of paprika, seasoned salt, and sesame or caraway seeds. Bake in a 375° oven for 10 to 15 minutes until golden brown. Cool.

For varied flavors, use the cheese and wheat germ and herb variations of pastry pie crust.

Tostaditas (Mexico)

To prepare these corn chips, prepare tortilla dough, page 220. Roll out small tortillas. Cut in fourths or eighths to form chips. Deep-fry until golden. Drain on paper towels.

Wheat Germ Sticks

2 cups whole wheat flour
1 cup wheat germ
¼ cup sesame seeds
½ cup dried grated coconut
1 teaspoon salt
¼ cup packed brown sugar
½ cup oil
1 cup yogurt

Mix the flour, wheat germ, sesame seeds, coconut, salt, and brown sugar in a bowl. Add the oil and yogurt. Mix to form a soft dough. Roll out on a floured board ½ inch thick. Slice into sticks ½ inch wide and about 4 inches long. Place the sticks on a buttered baking sheet. Bake in a 350° oven for 30 to 35 minutes, until golden. This recipe makes about 24 sticks.

Variations

Vegan Variation: Replace the yogurt with broth or water.

Honey Variation: Replace the brown sugar with 3 tablespoons honey.

Papadams (India)

Papadams are thin wafers made from bean flour. Though they cannot be prepared at home they are well worth mentioning. They may be purchased at Indian specialty stores in plain and spicy versions, and are great as a snack or with Indian meals. When cooked, tiny bubbles appear all over the surface of the wafer, and it curls slightly. Papadams may be fried in ghee or oil on both sides, or fried on both sides in a dry pan, or simply waved over a flame until done.

BISCUITS

Biscuits are quick to prepare. To insure success, handle the dough lightly and bake in a very hot oven. There are basically two kinds of biscuits: rolled and drop. Rolled biscuits look elegant, but we find that drop biscuits have a lighter texture. Biscuits tend to become hard if they are kept too long. It is best to bake them just before serving, and bring them to the table hot from the oven.

Rolled Biscuits

This recipe produces a full-flavored whole-grain biscuit. For the traditional kind, substitute unbleached white flour for the whole wheat flour and wheat germ.

½ cup wheat germ
1 cup whole wheat flour
½ cup unbleached white flour
½ teaspoon salt
1 tablespoon baking powder
¼ cup milk powder (optional)
2 teaspoons sugar or honey
⅓ cup butter
⅔ cup milk

Place the wheat germ in a bowl. Sift in the flours, salt, baking powder, and sugar or honey. Add the butter and work with the hands or a pastry cutter until the mixture resembles coarse meal. Add the milk. Mix, and knead a few times to make smooth.

Roll the dough out ½ inch thick on a floured board. Cut out biscuits with the rim of a glass or with a cookie cutter. Place on a buttered baking sheet and bake in a 450° oven for 8 to 10 minutes, until golden brown.

Serve hot, with butter. This recipe makes 18 to 20 biscuits.

Variations

Replace part or all of the wheat germ with: cornmeal, roasted barley flour, bran, millet flour, soy flour, or rice flour.

Add to the biscuit dough: grated cheese, or caraway, sesame, or poppy seeds.

Drop Biscuits: Add ⅓ cup milk to biscuit dough. Drop spoonfuls of the batter onto a buttered baking sheet.

Skillet Biscuits: Instead of baking, fry biscuits slowly in an ungreased skillet, for at least 5 minutes on each side, until browned.

Herb Biscuits: Add to biscuit dough 1½ teaspoons dried herbs *or* 2 tablespoons minced fresh parsley; substitute seasoned salt for salt.

Buttermilk Biscuits: Replace the milk with buttermilk. Replace the baking powder with 2 teaspoons baking powder and 1 teaspoon soda.

Cheese-Herb Pinwheels

dough for herb biscuits
melted butter
1½ cups grated sharp cheese

Roll out the dough in a 4-by-16-inch rectangle, about ¼ inch thick. Brush with melted butter. Sprinkle with the grated cheese. Roll up the dough tightly from the wide end to form a long tube. Slice off ¾-inch rounds. Bake as for biscuits.

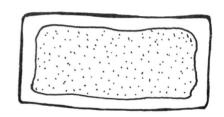

Vine Biscuits (Italy)

Bright purple biscuits! These are very hard and are meant to be eaten with (or dunked into) grain coffee or tea.

2½ cups unbleached white flour
1½ teaspoons baking powder
½ cup sugar
½ cup oil
1 tablespoon lemon juice, plus purple grape juice to equal ½ cup

Sift the flour and baking powder into a bowl. Add the sugar. Add the oil and grape/lemon juice. Mix to a soft dough. Roll into 1½-inch balls and place on a buttered baking sheet. Bake in a 375° oven about 20 minutes.

Cool very thoroughly before serving. This recipe makes 24 biscuits.

Scones (England)

2 cups unbleached white flour
2 teaspoons baking powder

1 teaspoon soda
½ teaspoon salt
¼ cup sugar *or* 3 tablespoons honey
¼ cup yogurt
¼ cup water
⅓ cup melted butter
⅓ cup raisins

Mix the dry ingredients together. Sift into a bowl. Add the yogurt, water, and melted butter. Add the raisins. Mix to form a soft dough. Either press into a buttered 8-inch cake pan (round) or roll out ⅓ inch thick and cut out biscuits, with a cookie cutter or the rim of a glass. Place biscuits on a buttered baking sheet. Bake in a 375° oven for 20 to 25 minutes for individual scones, or 30 minutes for the cake.

Cut the cake into wedges and serve warm with butter. This recipe makes 12 scones or 1 cake.

MUFFINS

To prepare successful muffins, have the oven preheated and the muffin tins buttered and ready before preparing the batter. Mix the batter quickly and with a light touch. Place the dry ingredients in a bowl, add the wet ones, and beat just until the dry ingredients are moistened—about 15 strokes are enough. If there are lumps, it is all right—overbeating will ruin the batter. Immediately after the batter is mixed, pour it into the muffin cups. It is all right to fill the batter up to the brim of the cups in these recipes. There is no need to use paper muffin cups—they pull off some of the crust, and if the cups are well buttered (butter works better than oil) the muffins will come out easily.

Place in the *hot* oven immediately after pouring, and bake just until golden brown. Remove muffins from the tin a few minutes after removing from the oven. Muffins be-

come hard if they are kept too long. It is best to bake them just before serving.

Quick-bread batters can be used for muffins. See page 221. For *Vegan* muffins, prepare with sour milk made from soy milk (page 45).

Muffins

Here is the basic muffin recipe that can be added to or altered to create your own original muffins.

1 cup whole wheat flour
1 cup unbleached white flour
1 teaspoon baking powder
¾ teaspoon soda
¾ teaspoon salt
⅓ cup sugar
1½ cups buttermilk or sour milk
¼ cup melted butter or oil

Sift the flour, baking powder, soda, and salt into a bowl. Add the sugar. Mix the buttermilk or sour milk and the oil. Pour over the dry ingredients. Beat 15 strokes. Pour batter into buttered muffin cups. Bake in a 400° oven for 20 minutes, until browned. This recipe makes 12 muffins.

Additions and Variations for Muffins

Honey Variation:
Replace sugar with ¼ cup honey. Reduce milk to 1⅓ cups.

Replace no more than ¾ cup flour with wheat germ, bran, barley or rice flour, or cornmeal.

Replace the unbleached white flour with whole wheat flour, or vice versa.

Replace the buttermilk or sour milk with fruit juice, water, thin yogurt, whole milk, or nonfat milk.

Add: granola cereal, raisins and chopped dried fruit, grated carrot, apple, zucchini, diced pineapple (reduce liquid), fresh berries or chopped fruit, sweet spices, mashed banana, chopped nuts, sesame, sunflower, or pumpkin seeds, carob chips, cooked grains or cereals.

Spice Muffins: Add ½ teaspoon each: cinnamon, allspice, ground ginger; add ¼ teaspoon each: nutmeg and cloves.

Orange Muffins: Mix 1 tablespoon finely grated orange rind in with the wet ingredients of basic muffins and replace ¾ cup of the milk with orange juice. If desired, add ⅓ cup toasted sunflower seeds.

Date-Nut Muffins: Add ⅔ cup chopped dates and ½ cup chopped walnuts to basic muffins.

Blueberry, Blackberry or Cranberry Muffins

All one's muffin desires fulfilled. The muffins are just a medium for the berries.

2 cups unbleached white flour
1 teaspoon baking powder
¾ teaspoon soda
¾ teaspoon salt
½ cup packed brown sugar
1½ cups sour milk or buttermilk
¼ cup melted butter or oil
1¼ cups blueberries or blackberries, *or* 1
    cup chopped cranberries

Sift the flour, baking powder, soda, and salt. Add the sugar. Mix the sour milk and the melted butter or oil, and add to the dry ingredients. Add the berries. Mix 15 strokes. Pour into buttered muffin cups. Bake in a 400° oven for 20 minutes, until done. This recipe makes 14 to 16 muffins.

Honey Variation
Replace sugar with ⅓ cup honey. Reduce milk to 1⅓ cups.

Bran Muffins

1 cup bran
½ cup packed brown sugar
1 cup unbleached white flour
¾ teaspoon soda
1 teaspoon baking powder
¾ teaspoon salt
1¼ cups buttermilk or sour milk
¼ cup melted butter or oil
½ cup raisins

Place the bran and sugar in a bowl. Sift the flour, soda, baking powder, and salt into the bowl. Mix. Mix the buttermilk or sour milk and the melted butter or oil; add to the dry mixture. Add the raisins. Beat 15 strokes. Pour into buttered muffin cups and bake in a 400° oven for 20 minutes, until done. This recipe makes 12 muffins.

Honey Variation
Replace sugar with ⅓ cup honey, molasses, or maple syrup. Reduce the milk to 1⅓ cups.

Cereal or Grain Muffins

Moist, textured muffins which can be made in a variety of flavors, using different grains and cereals. Try millet and cracked wheat.

1 cup cooked cereal or grains (any except
    wheatberries and rye)
¾ cup buttermilk or sour milk
¼ cup melted butter or oil
¼ cup packed brown sugar
1 cup unbleached white flour
¾ teaspoon salt
1 teaspoon baking powder
¾ teaspoon soda

Place the cereal in a bowl and mix with the buttermilk or sour milk and the butter or oil. Place the sugar in a bowl. Sift in the remaining dry ingredients. Add the cereal mixture and stir 15 strokes. Pour into buttered muffin cups and bake in a 400° oven for 20 minutes, until done. This recipe makes 12 muffins.

Honey Variation
Replace sugar with 3 tablespoons honey. Reduce the milk to ⅔ cup.

Banana-Nut Muffins

½ cup wheat germ
½ cup packed brown sugar
1½ cups unbleached white flour
1 teaspoon baking powder
1 teaspoon soda
¾ teaspoon salt
1 cup mashed ripe banana
¾ cup water
½ cup buttermilk or sour milk
¼ cup melted butter or oil
½ cup chopped nuts

Place the wheat germ and brown sugar in a bowl. Sift in the flour, baking powder, soda, and salt. Mix the banana, water, milk, and butter or oil together. Add to the dry ingredients. Add the nuts. Beat 15 strokes. Pour into buttered muffin cups. Bake in a 400° oven for 20 minutes, until done. This recipe makes 12 large muffins.

Variations

Add a little cinnamon or cardamom.

Honey Variation: Replace sugar with ⅓ cup honey and reduce water to ½ cup.

Banana-Apricot Muffins: Add ⅔ cup chopped dried apricots (will make about 2 more muffins).

Corn Muffins

1 cup cornmeal
1½ cups buttermilk or sour milk
¼ cup packed brown sugar
¼ cup melted butter or oil
1 cup unbleached white flour
1 teaspoon baking powder
¾ teaspoon soda
¾ teaspoon salt

Mix the cornmeal, buttermilk, sugar, and melted butter or oil. Sift the flour, baking powder, soda, and salt into a bowl. Add the cornmeal mixture. Beat 15 strokes. Pour into buttered muffin cups. Bake for 20 minutes in a 400° oven, until done. This recipe makes 12 muffins.

Honey Variation

Replace sugar with 3 tablespoons honey and reduce milk to 1⅓ cups.

Maple-Nut Muffins

1 cup unbleached white flour
1 cup whole wheat flour
¾ teaspoon soda
1 teaspoon baking powder
½ teaspoon salt
⅔ cup milk
1 cup maple syrup
¼ cup melted butter or oil
½ cup chopped walnuts

Sift the flours, baking soda, baking powder, and salt into a bowl. Mix the milk, maple syrup, and melted butter or oil together. Pour over the dry ingredients. Add the nuts. Beat 15 strokes. Pour into buttered muffin cups. Bake in a 400° oven for 20 minutes, until done. This recipe makes 12 muffins.

Oatmeal Muffins

1 cup rolled oats
1½ cups buttermilk or sour milk
⅓ cup packed brown sugar
¼ cup melted butter or oil
1 cup unbleached white flour
¾ teaspoon salt
1 teaspoon baking powder
¾ teaspoon soda
1 teaspoon cinnamon

Mix the rolled oats, buttermilk, and sugar. Add the melted butter or oil. Soak for 15 minutes. Sift the flour, salt, baking powder, soda, and cinnamon into a bowl. Add the oatmeal mixture. Beat 15 strokes. Pour into buttered muffin cups and bake in a 400° oven for 20 minutes, until done. This recipe makes 12 muffins.

Variations

Add ½ cup raisins or chopped dates.

Honey Variation: Replace sugar with ¼ cup honey or molasses; reduce the milk to 1⅓ cups.

PANCAKES

The Art of tossing a Pancake: This is a Thing very easy to a bold Hand, but which a timerous Person will never be able to do well; for such a one, she is to know that the first Thing to be done is to get rid of her Fear, and then a little Practise will make it quite familiar.

—Mrs. Martha Bradley, *A British Housewife* (circa 1770)

For best results, prepare the pancake batter at least an hour in advance (or the night before) and let it sit in the refrigerator. To fry a pancake, the pan should be just lightly buttered. Use a heavy skillet or a griddle. The pan should be hot enough so that a drop of water flicked on it sputters and dances. If it evaporates immediately, the pan is too hot—if it just sits there, it is too cold.

Pour the pancake batter into the skillet in circles. A three-inch circle is manageable for flipping. When bubbles form all over the surface of the pancake, it is ready to be turned over. Check to see that it is golden brown, not too pale. Flip with a spatula (or by quickly shaking the pan with the "bold Hand" of the British Housewife). The second side will cook in half the time of the first. The first batch may stick to the pan a little, but the succeeding batches will not. Add more butter to the pan as necessary. Do not stack the finished pancakes until they are brought to the table—the steam produced will make them soggy.

Serve pancakes with butter, honey, fruit sauce, maple syrup, yogurt or sour cream, fresh berries, or whatever is desired.

Basic Pancakes

1 cup whole wheat flour
1 cup unbleached white flour
2 tablespoons binding powder
½ teaspoon salt
1¼ teaspoons baking powder
¼ teaspoon soda
2 tablespoons oil or melted butter
1 cup buttermilk or sour milk
1 cup water

Combine all the ingredients in a blender, or beat together well. For best results, let sit in the refrigerator for at least 1 hour. (One can prepare the batter the night before, if desired.)

Fry as directed above. Makes 20 to 24 pancakes.

Variations and Additions

Replace the sour milk or buttermilk with water, preferably mixed with a little lemon juice; fruit juice; thin yogurt; soy or nut milk mixed with a little lemon juice; or milk.

Replace no more than ¾ cup flour with cornmeal, wheat germ, buckwheat flour, bran, soy flour (no more than ¼ cup), or barley, millet, or rice flour.

Replace the unbleached white flour with whole wheat flour, or vice versa.

Add to the batter: raisins or chopped dried fruit; grated coconut; mashed banana (reduce the milk); carob chips; sesame, sunflower, or pumpkin seeds; grated carrot, apple, or zucchini; persimmon pulp (reduce the milk); chopped nuts; soy grits; sweet spices.

Fruit Pancakes: Add 2 cups thinly sliced apples, bananas, or drained peaches or apricots, *or* 1½ cups blueberries, blackberries, or chopped cranberries to the batter just before cooking.

Vegetable Pancakes: For a lunch or dinner main dish, add 2 cups minced or shredded vegetables to the batter just before cooking. If desired, blend in the blender for 1 second, just to insure that the vegetables are fine enough, but not to puree them. Fry small pancakes and serve them with cheese sauce, sour cream, or other sauces.

Raised Buckwheat Pancakes

Whole milk is usually used in the preparation of these raised pancakes. However, we have found that unless raw milk is used, the flavor can be spoiled. Hence we have substituted powdered milk, to be added just before cooking.

1 teaspoon yeast
¼ cup lukewarm water
1½ cups buckwheat flour
½ cup unbleached white flour
1 tablespoon molasses
2 cups lukewarm water
⅔ cup milk powder
½ teaspoon salt

Mix the yeast with the ¼ cup water. Let stand for 5 minutes. Mix again. Add the flours, molasses, and 2 cups water (a blender works well). Let stand overnight at room temperature in a container with high sides. The next morning, beat in the milk powder and salt. Fry according to directions on page 000. This recipe makes about 24 pancakes.

Crepes (France)

"Crepe" is simply the French word for pancake. It is usually associated with the delicate, wafer-thin pancakes which are elegantly wrapped around vegetable or dessert fillings. Here is a basic recipe. See index for main dish crepes, dessert crepes, and cheese crepes.

2 cups milk
1¾ cups unbleached white flour
½ teaspoon salt
2 tablespoons binding powder
2 tablespoons oil or melted butter

Combine the ingredients in a blender, or beat well. Let the mixture rest in the refrigerator for at least 1 hour.

To fry, heat a crepe pan or an 8-inch frying pan. Coat it lightly with melted butter. Pour a little batter in the center of the pan, and immediately lift the pan and swirl it around to distribute batter over the bottom in a thin layer. Replace the pan on the heat. After 30 seconds, gently check the bottom of the crepe (the top will not form bubbles). When the crepe is golden brown, carefully flip with a spatula and fry until golden brown. Continue preparing the crepes one at a time in this manner. This recipe makes about 10 crepes.

Variation

Swedish Pancakes: Roll up whipped cream and berry sauce in the crepes and dust lightly with confectioner's sugar. (Lingonberries are used in Sweden.)

Blintzes (Jewish)

Blintzes are specially prepared crepes wrapped around a sweet cheese filling. They may be served either as a main course or for dessert.

crepe batter (see above)
1 cup cream cheese (1 8-ounce package)
2 cups ricotta
½ cup sugar *or* ⅓ cup honey
2 tablespoons binding powder
¾ teaspoon cinnamon

optional topping:
fresh sliced strawberries, blueberries, or fruit sauce

Prepare the crepes in a 10-inch skillet, frying on one side only. The top side will be firm and non-sticky.

To prepare the filling, mix the cream cheese, ricotta, sugar or honey, and binding powder. Add cinnamon and beat until smooth. Place a crepe, cooked side up, on

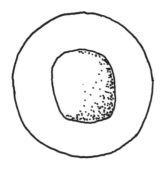

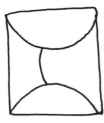

a plate and put a large spoonful of the filling in the center. Gently bring up the two opposite edges of the crepe over the filling, then bring up the remaining two edges to form a rectangular "package." Be careful not to break the crepe.

Fry on both sides in plenty of butter until golden brown, turning very gently. Serve topped with fruit and sour cream, or sour cream alone. This recipe makes 8 to 10 blintzes.

Note to those accustomed to preparing blintzes with baker's cheese: Baker's cheese is made with a large amount of rennet, and therefore we have substituted ricotta.

Jonnycakes (USA)

Jonnycakes are from Rhode Island, the name coming possibly from "Shawnee cakes," or more believably, from "Journey cakes." They were first prepared by the Narragansett Indians. If Rhode Island white cap cornmeal is available, you can prepare the absolutely real thing.

½ teaspoon salt
1 cup cornmeal
1 teaspoon sugar or honey (optional)
1 cup boiling water
½ cup milk or water

Mix the salt, cornmeal, and sugar or honey. Make a well in the center. Pour the boiling water into the well. Beat with a whisk to make smooth. Add the cold milk or water, and beat to make a thick, smooth batter.

Fry like small pancakes in plenty of butter. Jonnycakes take longer to cook than ordinary pancakes. Make sure they are brown and crusty before flipping, or they will fall apart in mid-air. Keep thinning the batter as necessary with milk or water, as the cornmeal will swell. This recipe makes 12 cakes.

Cornmeal Pancakes

1 cup cornmeal
½ teaspoon salt
¼ cup brown sugar

1 cup boiling water
⅔ cup unbleached white flour
1 teaspoon baking powder
½ teaspoon soda
2 tablespoons binding powder
½ teaspoon salt
2 tablespoons oil or melted butter
1 cup milk

Mix the cornmeal, salt, and brown sugar. Pour the boiling water over the mixture and beat with a whisk until smooth. Sift in the flour, baking powder, soda, binding pow-der, and salt. Add the oil or melted butter and the milk. Beat until smooth. Fry according to the directions for pancakes on page 230. This recipe makes 16 to 18 pancakes.

Variation

Honey Variation: Replace brown sugar with 3 tablespoons honey, added with the oil or butter and milk.

For other pancakes, see Latkes, Bocoles, and Dosas.

Fruits

Selection: For wholesomeness and the best flavor, select, if possible, tree-ripened, unsprayed, undyed fruit grown with natural fertilizers (compost). For the sake of freshness, buy fruit that is in season. Fruits shipped across country or imported have probably been picked unripe and allowed to ripen in shipping—often with the encouragement of chemical gases.

Select fruit that is unwithered, without browned bruise spots. Check the stem ends for mold. Fruit grown without the use of pesticides may have some superficial marks left by insects, but these will not affect the quality of the fruit.

Storage: With the exception of bananas, all fruits can be stored in the refrigerator. Apples should be stored separately from carrots, as the interaction of their chemical compositions may spoil their flavors. You may wish to have a fruit bowl out for snacks.

Preparation: Peel or wash and slice fruit just before serving. Rinse under running water, without soaking. Fruits such as apples, bananas, and avocados discolor quickly when their sliced surfaces are exposed to air. A sprinkling of citrus juice, particularly lemon juice, will help them maintain their fresh color.

Fruit Fool

Fold fresh, finely cut fruit or berries, or cooked, chilled fruit sauce, into an equal amount of sweetened whipped cream. Mound up in individual bowls. Chill thoroughly before serving.
Suggested fruits for fruit fool:

> berry sauce (page 285)
> mango sauce (page 285)
> fresh fruit sauce (page 284) of raspberries and peaches
> fresh chopped pineapple
> fresh crushed strawberries
> whole blueberries and chopped apricots

Molded Fruit Dessert

A variety of flavors can be achieved by using different fruits and fruit juices. The basic recipe here uses agar agar flakes. (One tablespoon of agar agar thickens one quart of liquid. Check the directions on the package—if they differ, go by the directions for thickening 1 quart, and add a little more to accommodate the juice from the fruits.)

4 cups fruit juice or lemonade
1½ tablespoons agar agar
2 cups sliced fruit, whole berries, or seedless grapes
¼ cup sugar *or* 3 tablespoons honey (or to taste)
½ to 1 teaspoon chopped mint (optional)

Bring the fruit juice to a boil. Stir in the agar agar. Reduce the heat and simmer for 5 minutes to dissolve the agar agar. Add the fruit and sweetening to taste. Add the mint, if desired. Pour into a bowl or individual bowls. Chill to set. Serve plain or with yogurt, whipped cream, or sour cream. This recipe makes from 8 to 10 molded desserts.
Suggestions for molded fruit desserts:

- Orange juice with whole strawberries and pineapple cubes.
- Lemonade with avocado slices and well-drained grapefruit slices.
- Cherry juice with mixed fruits.
- Orange juice with melon balls and grated coconut.

Variations
Add whole blanched almonds or grated coconut to molds.
Add whole mint leaves for a decorative effect.

Fruit Fritters

tempura batter (page 89)
4 to 5 cups thinly sliced apples, banana chunks, cubed drained pineapple, or pineapple rings

Dip the fruit pieces, one at a time, into the tempura batter. Deep-fry until golden. Drain on paper towels. Sprinkle with confectioner's sugar and serve warm. This recipe makes 4 servings.

Stewed Fruit

For best results, use dried fruits or a mixture of fresh sliced fruits and dried fruits. Simmer them in water to cover until tender. Add sweetening if desired (with dried fruits added, sweetening is unnecessary). Serve with some of the cooking water for breakfast, or with cottage cheese, sour cream, or yogurt for a light lunch. Try stewing figs in apple juice, or stewing prunes and fresh apricot halves together.

DRIED FRUIT

Dried fruits are wonderful natural candies and snacks. They may be added to baked goods, or stewed and added to breakfast cereals, fruit salads, and other desserts of various kinds. Soaking dried

fruits overnight in water or fruit juice helps make them more digestible, but to gain the full nutrients of the fruit, the soaking water should also be taken. (It can be heated as a hot drink.) Because of the concentrated sugars in dried fruits, they can partially—and sometimes totally—replace sugar or honey in desserts. Select the unsulphured, untreated dried fruits available in health-food stores. Sometimes fruits are treated to keep them very soft. Health-food stores also have wider selections of dried fruits than do regular supermarkets. Besides the standard raisins, dates, and prunes, try dried pineapple, cherries, pears, and mangoes for starters. There is at least one person on the planet who swears that dried cantaloupe is the most delicious dried fruit around.

Dried Fruit Purees

Dried fruit purees can be used as a substitute for sugar or honey in some desserts, and as a natural frosting for cakes and cookies. Also use for jam. The flavor and sweetness are highly concentrated.

Method #1: Grind soft, pitted, dried fruits to a paste in a meat grinder.

Method #2: Steam pitted, dried fruits in a little water until tender. Puree through a food mill or sieve, or in a blender.

INDIVIDUAL FRESH FRUITS

Apples: Apples may be served uncooked or cooked, and may be juiced for a delicious sweet juice. Dried apples are available and make a chewy snack. Apple slices served with slices of cheese is a classic dessert.

Use one of the more tart varieties, such as Granny Smith, for cooking, and either the tart varieties or the sweet ones, such as Golden Delicious, for eating. Select very firm apples, without bruise spots or withered skins. Sprinkle apple slices with lemon juice if they must stand for more than a few minutes, to prevent discoloration.

Baked Apples Plain

Core apples. Place in a baking dish, with a little water to prevent scorching. Cover and bake in a 350° oven for about 30 minutes, until tender.

Baked Apples Fancy

6 large apples
⅓ cup chopped walnuts
⅓ cup raisins
¼ cup packed brown sugar *or* 3 tablespoons honey or maple syrup
1 teaspoon cinnamon
¼ cup boiling water or apple juice
butter

Core the apples. Mix the nuts, raisins, sugar or honey, and cinnamon together. Stuff the center of each apple with the mixture. Place the apples vertically in a baking dish. Pour the apple juice or water into the dish. Dot the apples with butter. Cover and bake in a 350° oven for about 30 minutes until the apples are tender. Baste with the cooking liquid.

Serve warm, with cream or ice cream if desired. This recipe makes 6 servings.

Variation
Replace the raisins with chopped dates.

Mandarin Apples or Bananas (China)

Meltingly soft with a hard candy coating, these Chinese delicacies are prepared in three steps. The fruit is coated with batter and deep-fried; then it is dipped into a boiling candy coating; then it is plunged into ice water to harden the coating. The technique is to perform all the operations quickly. Set up the oil, candy coating, and ice water in a row, with separate utensils for each.

2 tablespoons black sesame seeds or poppy
    seeds
¼ cup water
oil or ghee for deep-frying
1½ cups white sugar
½ cup packed light brown sugar
4 cups thinly sliced apples or 5 cups bananas in ½-inch chunks
crisp tempura batter (page 89)

Heat the oil in a pot. In a second pot, combine the white and brown sugars, water and sesame seeds. Boil for 5 minutes, then reduce the heat to a simmer. Fill a bowl with cold water and place plenty of ice cubes in it.

Dip the fruit slices one at a time into the tempura batter. Drop into the oil and deep-fry a few at a time until crisp and just faintly golden. With a separate spoon, transfer the deep-fried fruit to the sugar mixture. Swirl it around to make sure it is thoroughly coated. Remove from the syrup and drop into the ice water. Let sit for at least 5 seconds. With a separate utensil, remove the fruits from the ice water. The candy coating should be hard. If it is not,

the sugar syrup was not boiled long enough, or—less likely—the water isn't icy enough.

Repeat in small batches. Work quickly, as the sugar syrup may burn (if it does, make a new syrup). This recipe makes 4 to 6 servings.

Apricots: A seasonal summer fruit, an apricot must be completely ripe to exhibit its sweet flavor and juicy texture. The flavor of many non-organically grown apricots is disappointing—try to obtain naturally grown fruit if possible. Select soft, unshrivelled fruits with red-orange coloring on yellow, with no green spots. When fresh apricots are juiced they produce a thick sauce, which can be mixed with other fruit juices. The nectar we are familiar with is cooked. Apricots may be stewed and sometimes can be substituted for peaches. Dried apricots add a wonderful tart flavor to dishes.

Avocados: Rich, buttery avocados are found in many combinations mixed with vegetables and green salads. Mix avocados into fruit salads, or slice them lengthwise, remove their pits, and stuff with finely cut fruit salad or fruit ice. Select avocados that are soft all over, but not collapsing and mushy. Unripe avocados may be ripened by placing them in a paper bag. Sprinkle sliced avocados with lemon juice to help prevent discoloration. Storing opened (even mashed) avocados with their pits also helps maintain their color. Use mashed avocado like butter as a spread for bread, or add it to ice cream.

Bananas: Bananas are an especially versatile fruit. They may be added to most fruit dishes. They may be mashed and added to baked goods and pancakes. Use bananas for fruit fritters and for pakoras. Select bananas with peels that are all yellow and flecked with brown or black spots. Avoid green-skinned, unripe bananas.

Baked Bananas

4 ripe bananas
butter
½ cup orange juice
3 tablespoons brown sugar
¼ cup grated coconut (optional)

Slit the bananas in half lengthwise. Arrange cut side up in a buttered baking dish. Pour the orange juice over them. Sprinkle with the brown sugar. Optionally, sprinkle with coconut. Bake in a 375° oven for 15 to 20 minutes.

Serve warm. This recipe makes 4 servings.

Variation

Honey Variation: Honey tends to burn when baked in this recipe. For best results, omit the sugar and, after the bananas have been baked, drizzle with 2 tablespoons honey.

Banana Curry (India)

Serve banana curry as a main or side dish with an Indian meal.

1½ cups yogurt
2 tablespoons ghee or butter
¼ teaspoon black mustard seed
4 bananas, cut in ½-inch pieces
½ teaspoon cardamom
½ teaspoon cinnamon
1 teaspoon coriander
½ teaspoon salt
2 tablespoons sugar or 1½ tablespoons honey

Slowly heat the yogurt to serving temperature. Do not simmer or boil.

While the yogurt is heating, heat the ghee or butter in a skillet. Add the mustard seed and sauté until it dances. Add the bananas, spices, and salt. Sauté for 5 to 7 minutes until the bananas are tender. Add the bananas and sugar or honey to the yogurt. Serve immediately. This recipe makes 4 servings.

Variation

Add cayenne or flaked red chilies to the butter.

Also see Mandarin Apples or Bananas, page 236.

Berries: Most berries are seasonal summer fruits, with cranberries making their entrance in the autumn. Add berries to pancakes, baked goods, and—with the exception of cranberries, which must be cooked—

to fruit compotes, fruit fool, and fruit salads. Berries, though they can be added to so many dishes, are superlative served alone, sweetened lightly with honey or confectioner's sugar. When berries are juiced they produce a thick sauce, which may be diluted with thinner fruit juices.

Cherries: There are a number of varieties of cherries, ranging in color from white to a rich dark red. There is a variety of sour cherry which must be stewed and sweetened, but most cherries are wonder-

fully sweet. Cherry juice is marvelous. Cherries may be prepared in the manner of berries when their pits have been removed. A darning needle or a small paring knife can be used to pit cherries. Dried cherries are good for snacks, though it is difficult to remove their pits for cooking.

Dates: Dried dates are well known as a snack, a candy, and a natural sweetening. Dried dates are pulverized to make date sugar. Occasionally fresh dates will appear on the market, although they are rare outside their places of origin (usually in the Middle East) They are best enjoyed pure and simple.

Figs: Fresh, ripe figs are delicious plain or with cream. They are found in both a dark purple-black variety and a green variety. Choose soft, unbruised figs. Ripe figs

tend to burst open, and their juices may ferment slightly. Dried figs are delicious plain or stewed.

Grapes: Use seedless grapes for cooking and salads, and all varieties may be eaten

plain. Grape juice can be prepared in a blender, or without the use of any special tools.

Grapefruit: Pink grapefruits tend to be sweeter than the yellow variety, and Texas Ruby Reds are the best for sweetness and juiciness. To eat a grapefruit plain, cut it in half. Use a grapefruit spoon with a serrated edge to cut out the sections, or cut around

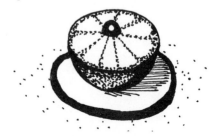

the skin and the sections with a paring knife; eat the sections with a spoon. Grapefruits can be sectioned like oranges, but the white portion, which is quite bitter, tends to cling to the sections. Juice grapefruits on a citrus juicer.

Broiled Grapefruit

1 grapefruit
2 teaspoons brown sugar

Cut the grapefruit in half. Sprinkle with the brown sugar. Place in the broiler for a minute until the sugar is melted and bubbly. Serve for breakfast. Makes 1 or 2 servings.

Variations

Honey Variation: Honey tends to burn, so drizzle it over the grapefruit after broiling.

Guavas: Sweet tropical fruits which can be eaten plain or stewed.

Kiwi Fruit (Chinese Gooseberries): Peel the green, fuzzy skin off a kiwi and enjoy the pink-red fruit. It has a flavor that seems to be an indescribable blend of two or three fruits.

Lemons and Limes: The juice of lemons and limes is indispensable for enhancing the flavors of other foods. Lemon or lime juice may be used as a substitute for salt. The juice is added to milk to sour it and assist in leavening baked goods, and is

used as an agent vital in the preparation of panir and bean curd. Add finely grated lemon rind to baked goods, frostings, and candies. Use unsprayed, undyed fruit, if possible, for this purpose. Lemon peel may also be candied for use in fruitcakes and desserts.

Mangoes: Sweet, juicy mangoes grow in tropical areas. Completely ripe, they are divine, but they can taste like turpentine when unripe. Select mangoes that are quite

soft. The skins may be yellow-orange or green. Mangoes have a large pit which may be sucked on to remove the fruit from the fibers. The fruit which can be sliced off may be added to fruit compotes, or can make a delicious drink combined with milk and a little honey in a blender.

Melons: Melons are served uncooked, either plain or in fruit salads and compotes. They may be juiced for a somewhat watery juice. To select a ripe melon, see that it has a fragrance, and then press the end where the stem has been cut off. If it is soft, the

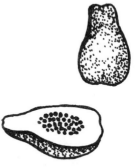

melon is probably ripe. With the exception of watermelons, melons can be halved and the seeds removed. The hollow is a convenient place to tuck fresh berries, fruit salad, or ice cream. Scoop out melons with a melon baller for salads. Use hollowed-out watermelon halves as bowls for large amounts of fruit salad.

Nectarines: A cross between a peach and a plum, the nectarine can be used in the same manner as peaches for cooking, or eaten plain and simple.

Oranges: Oranges were first grown in Asia. If Christopher Columbus truly said, as we all learned in grade school, that the world was "round, like an orange," it is due to the fact that exactly 50 years before

he set sail, the first orange tree was brought to Europe from China as a gift for the wife of King Charles III of France. It was up-rooted and replanted during several later changes of power, but eventually found its home in the gardens of Versailles, where it lived for 400 years.

Seedless navel oranges are the best variety for eating plain. Other seeded varieties are better for juicing. Try juicing a blood orange for its red juice. Finely grated orange rind can be used as a flavoring for baked goods, frostings, and other desserts. It can also be candied for fruitcakes. Use orange juice for cooking and baking liquids. To eat, section the orange and remove as much of the white part as possible.

Peaches: Peaches are seasonal summer fruits. To remove the fuzzy skin for cooking, blanch the fruits and peel. However, enough of the fuzz can often be removed by washing and then rubbing vigorously with a towel. Add peaches to all fruit salads and cooked fruit combinations. A cooked peach nectar can be prepared.

Pears: Winter pears can be quite hard and still be ripe, while summer pears should

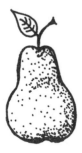

be soft and juicy. Sprinkle pear slices with a little lemon juice if they must stand more than a few minutes. Pear slices served with cheese slices is a classic dessert.

Baked Pears Plain

Halve pears lengthwise. Remove the stems and seeds. Place in a baking dish with a little water to keep from scorching. Bake in

a 350° oven for about 1 hour, covered, until tender.

Baked Stuffed Pears

Other nuts and dried fruits may be mixed for the stuffing, but the suggested ones work particularly well with the pears.

4 ripe pears
⅓ cup pine nuts
⅓ cup finely chopped dried apricots
½ cup orange juice
butter
honey

Halve the pears lengthwise. Remove the stem and the seeds, leaving a small hollow in each pear. Combine the pine nuts, apricot pieces, and ¼ cup orange juice in a blender until smooth. Place a spoonful in the hollow in each pear. Place the pear halves in a baking dish and pour the remaining orange juice over them. Dot with butter. Cover and bake in a 350° oven for about 1 hour, until tender.

Remove from the dish and drizzle with a little honey. This recipe makes 4 servings.

Persimmons: California persimmons, originally imported from Japan, are large, soft, and mushy compared to the smaller, more astringent eastern U.S. varieties. They

must be ripe to offer their sweet, mild flavor, as unripe persimmons can be sour. Ripe persimmons are usually quite soft. Peel and eat the flesh with a spoon. The pulp can be added to bread or cake batter, and foods containing persimmons are best baked at a low heat—about 325°. The pulp is a natural sauce for fruit salads and ice cream.

Pineapples: A tropical citrus fruit, the pineapple can be juiced in the blender, and it can be crushed and added to baked goods. Pineapple skins can be hollowed and used as bowls for fruit salad or sweet-and-sour vegetables. Pineapple can be cubed and added to stir-fried vegetable combinations. Use pineapple for fruit fritters, and for all fruit compotes, fruit fool, and other desserts. Also, use pineapple cubes in kebabs.

To select a ripe pineapple, sniff to see if it has a fragrance. Next, pull on a leaf. If it comes out fairly easily, the pineapple is probably ripe. To eat, carefully slice away the skin. Remove the core of the pineapple, which is quite fibrous and tough in most cases, and cut slices or chunks of the remaining fruit.

Plums: Plums are best ripe and eaten plain. They may be cooked, and make a wonderful chutney. Plums come in many colors, from golden yellow to a purple-black fresh prune that comes in during the late summer and early fall. Most other varieties are seasonal summer fruits.

Pomegranates: In Greek mythology, six pomegranate seeds eaten by Persephone caused the events responsible for the changing of the seasons. Pomegranate seeds are beautiful sprinkled in fruit salads. To eat a pomegranate, peel and remove the clusters of seeds from the white membrane. The red outer covering is eaten, and the inner seeds may be eaten or discarded. Po-

megranates may be halved and juiced on a citrus juicer; you may also squeeze a whole pomegranate and roll it around on a hard surface to soften it, then poke a hole in the skin and suck out the juice. Be very careful not to break the skin while rolling—pomegranate juice stains!

Rhubarb: The stalks of the rhubarb are edible, but the leaves contain a large amount

of oxalic acid and should be avoided. Rhubarb is sliced, cooked, and sweetened. If it is young, simply slice it crosswise. If it is older, peel it like celery and then slice.

Tangerines: Tangerines may be served in the same manner as oranges. The juice is especially sweet and delicious.

242

THE RECIPES

Cakes, Pies, and Pastries

CAKES

Eggless cakes follow somewhat different rules of construction than ordinary cakes. See the section on eggless baking, page 50, to understand the principles behind the ingredients in the following cakes, and for the recipe for binding powder. For those who are new to cake-baking, complete instructions are given with the first recipe to guide you step-by-step through the procedures. To adjust recipes for high altitude areas, see page 13 for some hints.

Sweet quick breads can be served as moist, fruity cakes quite successfully. They may be served plain, or iced with a simple cream cheese frosting. Your own cakes may be created with some of the suggested variations and additions on page 244.

White Cake

The basic cake, with two 8-inch layers.

⅔ cup butter
2 cups white or light brown sugar
3 cups unbleached white flour
½ cup whole wheat flour
2 tablespoons binding powder (page 51)
2 teaspoons baking powder
½ teaspoon soda
½ teaspoon salt
1 cup sour milk or buttermilk
1 cup water

Preheat the oven to 350° (325° if using glass pans). Prepare 2 8-inch baking pans

by spreading a thin coating of butter over the bottom and sides of each pan. Sprinkle a few pinches of flour on the bottom of each pan and shake it to distribute. (In Europe, bread crumbs are used instead of flour.)

Cream the butter and sugar together thoroughly. (Have the butter at room temperature for easy handling.) Mix the dry ingredients—the flours, binding powder, baking powder, soda, and salt—and sift them into the butter-sugar mixture. Pour in the milk and the water. Mix just until the ingredients

are blended together, and no more. (Forget about the 400–600 strokes that ordinary cakes receive.)

Pour the batter into the cake pans. The pan should be no more than ⅔ full, and the batter should be no less than 1 inch deep and no more than 1½ inches deep in the pan for best results.

Place in the oven. Cakes baked on the upper racks will take less time than those baked on the lower racks, as heat rises. Do not open the oven door more than absolutely necessary. The oven loses heat when the door is opened, and sudden drops in temperature may cause the cake to fall. Try not to poke or jiggle the cake during baking—these sharp movements can also cause the untimely collapse of a beautifully rising cake.

Bake for about 35 minutes. Check after 30 minutes, but sometimes a cake can take as long as 40 minutes.

A cake is done when:

1. A toothpick or knife is inserted in the center and comes out clean, without any batter clinging to it.
2. The top of the cake is lightly browned and the sides shrink slightly away from the sides of the pan.
3. When pressed lightly, the cake feels fairly solid underneath and springs back when the touch is released.

Gently remove the cakes from the oven and place them on a trivet or rack to cool. After 15 or 20 minutes, run a knife around the edge of the pan to loosen the cake from the sides. Invert a plate over the cake pan. Turn the whole thing over to release the cake onto the plate. If the cake, despite gentle prodding around the sides with a knife, refuses to release its grip on the pan,

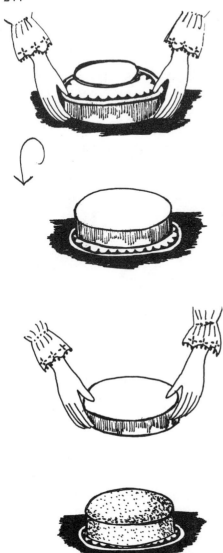

invert it on the plate and cover it with a cold, damp towel. Wait three minutes, then tap all over the bottom of the pan, through the towel, to release the cake.

If a cake does break or crumble while being removed, it can almost always be mended and disguised with frosting. There are few cakes that cannot be made to look beautiful with a little help from frosting and decorations. Wait until the cake is thor-oughly cool before frosting it. If a cake is for a party and there is a tight cooking schedule, it may be baked the night before and stored, covered, in the refrigerator.

Variations and Additions

Bake cakes in different-shaped pans.

Flours: Cakes can be made with 100 percent whole-wheat pastry flour, or with 100 percent unbleached white flour. Do not prepare cakes from 100 percent enriched bleached white flour, as they will rise unevenly. Carob flour may be added as a chocolate flavoring, but do not replace more than ¾ cup flour with carob in a standard cake recipe.

Flavorings: Finely grated orange or lemon rind, grain coffee powder. *Sweet spices:* Cinnamon, cloves, ginger, mace, nutmeg, allspice, cardamom. The flavor of the spices will be slightly stronger in the batter than in the baked cake.

Fruit: Add up to 2 cups of whole blueberries, chopped raspberries or strawberries, chopped cranberries, mashed banana, or grated drained apples, carrots, or zucchini to a standard cake batter. Reduce or eliminate the liquid in the recipe. Add the fruits first, then add any liquid as necessary.

Add about ½ cup chopped dried fruits or raisins.

Nuts and seeds may be added without any alterations.

Melted butter or oil may be substituted for butter. Reduce the liquid slightly. The texture of the cake will be more dense.

Vegan Variations: Replace the buttermilk, sour milk, or milk with fruit juice or with water, nut, or soy milk mixed with a little lemon juice. Cakes made with water or fruit juice may be a little crumbly.

Honey Variations are given with each cake where the alteration is possible. Maple syrup or light molasses may be substituted for honey. See also Honey Cake, below.

Cupcakes: Fill buttered muffin cups ⅔ full of cake batter. Bake in a 375° oven for about 25 minutes, until done.

Honey Cake

¾ cup butter
1½ cups honey
3 cups unbleached white flour
½ cup whole wheat flour
3 tablespoons binding powder (page 51)
1½ teaspoons baking powder
½ teaspoon soda
½ teaspoon salt
½ cup milk

Cream the butter and honey. Sift the dry ingredients into the butter-honey mixture. Add the milk and stir just until the ingredients are blended. Bake in a 350° oven for about 35 minutes, until done. This recipe makes 2 8-inch layers.

Variation

Honey Spice Cake: Add 1½ teaspoons cinnamon and ½ teaspoon each cloves, ground ginger, and nutmeg to the dry ingredients, and decorate the top of the cake with whole blanched almonds before baking. This cake is sometimes served on Hannukah.

Nut Cake

A subtle added flavor and texture.
Add to the batter of White Cake or Honey Cake:

¾ cup roasted, ground nuts
2 teaspoons grain coffee powder

Bake in a large rectangular pan at 350° for about 35 minutes. For an optional topping, sprinkle nut-crunch topping (page 284) over the batter after 25 minutes of baking, and bake for another 15 minutes.

Poppy Seed Cake

Add 2 tablespoons poppy seeds to batter for White Cake or Honey Cake (or to Orange Cake; try an Orange-Poppy Seed Cake with Caramel Frosting, page 284).

Lady Baltimore Cake

Lady Baltimore cake is traditionally made from 3 layers of white cake. Either make two layers of white cake, as the recipe calls for, or make a double recipe of white cake and bake it in 3 9-inch round pans. After baking, spread buttercream frosting (page 282) over each layer and the top. Sprinkle ⅓ cup each chopped figs and raisins, and ⅔ cup chopped nuts, on each layer and over the top.

Variations

Replace some of the chopped figs and raisins with chopped dried pineapple or cherries.

Honey Variation: Replace frosting with Honey-Cream Frosting, page 282.

Orange Cake

⅔ cup butter
2 cups sugar
3 cups unbleached white flour
½ cup whole wheat flour
3 tablespoons binding powder (page 51)
2 teaspoons baking powder
½ teaspoon soda
½ teaspoon salt
1 cup orange juice
1 cup milk
2 tablespoons finely grated orange rind

Cream the butter and sugar. Sift the dry ingredients into the butter-sugar mixture. Add the orange juice, milk, and grated orange rind. Mix just until blended. Pour into 2 8-inch buttered, floured cake pans. Bake in a 350° oven for about 35 minutes.

Variations

Honey Variation: Replace sugar with 1¾ cups honey; reduce the orange juice and milk to ¼ cup each.

Lemon Cake: Prepare Orange Cake, substituting ¾ cup water, ½ cup lemon juice, and ¾ cup milk for the liquid. Replace the orange rind with 4 teaspoons finely grated lemon rind. The extra lemon juice causes this cake to rise very high, so 2 9-inch baking pans must be used. For a *Honey Variation*, replace the liquid with 3 tablespoons each water and milk, and 2 tablespoons lemon juice.

Carob Cake

Butter the pans well for this rich moist cake.

⅔ cup butter
2¼ cups packed brown sugar
1 cup carob powder
3 cups unbleached white flour
3 tablespoons binding powder (page 51)
2 teaspoons baking powder
½ teaspoon soda
½ teaspoon salt
1 teaspoon grain coffee powder (optional)
1 cup buttermilk or sour milk
1 cup water

Cream the butter and the brown sugar. Sift the dry ingredients into the butter mixture (the carob powder may make you cough—sift quickly). Add the sour milk or buttermilk and the water. Mix just until blended. Pour into the cake pans and spread evenly. Bake in a 350° oven for about 30 to 35 minutes.

Frost with German Frosting (below) for German Carob Cake, or with carob fudge frosting or mocha frosting. This recipe makes 2 8-inch layers.

Variation

Honey Variation: Replace brown sugar with 1¾ cups honey; reduce the sour milk and the water to ½ cup each.

German Frosting

1¼ cups light brown sugar, packed
¾ cup cream or rich milk
1 tablespoon butter
¾ cup dried grated coconut
1 cup chopped, roasted cashews or walnuts

Combine the sugar, cream and butter in a saucepan. Bring to a boil, stirring constantly, and cook for 5 minutes, to the soft ball stage. Remove from the heat and cool for 10 to 15 minutes.

Beat in the nuts and coconut. Cool to lukewarm. Spread half of the mixture on each cake layer and place one layer over the other. Keep the cake at room temperature (if it is chilled the frosting will become like hard candy). This recipe covers 2 8-inch layers.

Variation

For the "ultimate cake," Carob Cake with German Frosting may be covered with coffee-flavored sweetened whipped cream just before serving.

Marble Cake

½ recipe for White Cake or Honey Cake
½ recipe for Carob Cake

Drop alternate spoonfuls of the two batters into a buttered, floured, 10-by-14-inch pan. Swirl a spoon through the batters once or twice to achieve a marbled effect.

Bake in a 350° oven for 30 to 35 minutes, until done.

Mocha Cake

⅔ cup butter
2 cups packed brown sugar
3 cups unbleached white flour
½ cup carob powder
2 teaspoons baking powder
½ teaspoon soda
½ teaspoon salt
3 tablespoons grain coffee powder
1 cup sour milk or buttermilk
1 cup water

Cream the butter and the brown sugar. Sift the dry ingredients into the butter-sugar mixture. Add the sour milk or buttermilk and the water. Stir just until blended. Pour into two buttered, floured 8-inch cake pans. Bake in a 350° oven for about 35 minutes, until done. This recipe makes 2 8-inch layers.

Variations
   Honey Variation: Replace sugar with 1½ cups honey; reduce the sour milk and the water to ¼ cup each.
   Mocha Spice Cake (sometimes called "Egyptian Cake"): Add to the dry ingredients in Mocha Cake: 2 teaspoons cinnamon, ½ teaspoon cloves, and ½ teaspoon ground ginger.

Coconut Cake

Prepare with dried coconut if fresh coconut is unavailable. If using a fresh coconut, replace as much of the milk as possible with the coconut liquid.

¼ cup butter
1¾ cups sugar
2 cups unbleached white flour
½ cup whole wheat flour
2 tablespoons binding powder (page 51)
½ teaspoon salt
2 teaspoons baking powder
½ teaspoon soda
1¾ cups grated coconut
⅓ cup sour milk or buttermilk
⅓ cup water
1 teaspoon finely grated lemon rind

Cream the butter and the sugar. Sift the dry ingredients (except the coconut) into the butter-sugar mixture. Add the coconut and add the sour milk or buttermilk, the water, and the lemon rind. Mix just until blended. Pour into two buttered, floured 8-inch cake pans. Bake in a 350° oven for about 35 minutes, until done.

Frost with coconut frosting. For a tropical cake, place crushed pineapple and mango slices between the layers.

Variations
   Honey Variation: Replace the sugar with 1¼ cups honey; reduce the buttermilk and water to 3 tablespoons each.
   Orange-Coconut Cake: Replace the lemon rind with 2 tablespoons finely grated orange rind; replace the water with orange juice.

Sour Cream Spice Cake

½ cup butter
2 cups packed brown sugar
1½ cups sour cream
½ cup water
3 cups unbleached white flour
½ cup whole wheat flour
3 tablespoons binding powder (page 51)
1 teaspoon grain coffee powder
½ teaspoon salt
1½ teaspoons baking powder
1 teaspoon soda
1½ teaspoons cinnamon
½ teaspoon *each:* cloves, ground ginger, nutmeg, cardamom

Cream the butter and brown sugar. Add the sour cream and beat until smooth. Add the water. Sift the dry ingredients into the sour cream mixture. Mix just until blended. Pour into two buttered, floured 8-inch cake pans and bake in a 350° oven for about 35 minutes, until done. This recipe makes 2 8-inch layers.

Variations

Honey Variation: See Honey Spice Cake, page 245.

Vegan Variation: Replace the sour cream with soy milk mixed with a little lemon juice.

Banana Cake

⅔ cup butter
2 cups sugar
2 cups mashed ripe bananas
2½ cups unbleached white flour
½ cup whole wheat flour
2 tablespoons binding powder (page 51)
2 teaspoons baking powder
½ teaspoon soda
½ teaspoon salt
⅔ cup milk

Cream the butter and sugar. Add the mashed bananas and beat until smooth. Sift the dry ingredients into the banana mixture. Add the milk and mix just until blended. Pour into two 8-inch buttered, floured cake pans. Bake in a 350° oven for about 35 to 40 minutes, until done. This recipe makes 2 8-inch layers.

Variation

Honey Variation: See Banana Bread, page 221.

Carrot Cake

⅓ cup butter
1¾ cups packed brown sugar
2 cups grated carrots
2½ cups unbleached white flour
½ cup whole wheat flour
2 tablespoons binding powder (page 51)
2 teaspoons baking powder
1 teaspoon soda
½ teaspoon salt
1½ teaspoons cinnamon

¼ teaspoon each: nutmeg and cloves
½ cup sour milk or buttermilk
½ cup water

Cream the butter and brown sugar. Add the carrots and beat. Sift the dry ingredients into the carrot mixture. Add the sour milk or buttermilk and the water, and mix just until blended. Pour into two 8-inch buttered, floured pans and bake in a 350° oven for about 35 minutes. This recipe makes 2 8-inch layers.

Variations

Add walnuts to the cake batter.

Honey Variation: Replace the brown sugar with 1¼ cups honey; omit the sour milk or buttermilk and the water entirely.

Cheesecake, Baked

1½ tablespoons arrowroot or cornstarch
¾ cup milk
2 cups cream cheese (2 8-ounce packages)
1 cup sugar
¼ teaspoon finely grated lemon rind
1 9-inch unbaked crumb crust (page 257)
1¼ cups sour cream
crushed fruit, berries, or fruit sauce (optional)

Mix the arrowroot or cornstarch into the milk. Place in a blender with the cream cheese, sugar, and lemon rind, and blend until smooth. Pour the mixture into the crust. Bake in a 350° oven for 45 to 60 minutes, until the top is lightly browned in a few places.

Chill the cheesecake. When it is cool, cover the top with the sour cream. If desired, cover the sour cream with berry sauce, lightly sweetened berries, crushed pineapple, pitted halved cherries, or other fruit. This recipe makes one 9-inch pie.

Variation

Honey Variation: Replace the sugar with ⅔ cup honey, and use only ⅓ cup milk.

Cheesecake, Unbaked

1 teaspoon agar agar flakes*
¾ cup water
¼ cup powdered milk
2 cups cream cheese (2 8-ounce packages)
1 cup sugar
¼ teaspoon finely grated lemon rind
1 9-inch pre-baked crumb or granola crust
1¼ cups sour cream

Bring the water to a boil. Sprinkle in the agar agar. Stir, reduce the heat and simmer for 5 minutes to dissolve the agar agar. Place the water in a blender and combine with the cream cheese, sugar, powdered milk, and lemon rind. Blend until smooth.

Pour into the crust. Chill to harden. Top with sour cream, and if desired, with the fruit toppings suggested for baked cheesecake. This recipe makes one 9-inch pie.

Variation

Honey Variation: Replace the sugar with ⅔ cup honey; increase the agar agar by ½ teaspoon.

Blue Lotus Cheesecake

2 bananas
½ cup water
2 teaspoons agar agar flakes*
2 cups cream cheese (2 8-ounce packages)
⅓ cup honey
½ cup sour cream
¼ teaspoon finely grated lemon rind
9 chopped pitted dates
1 9-inch pre-baked granola or crumb crust

Slice the bananas thin and press lightly into the crust. Bring the water to a boil and sprinkle in the agar agar flakes; stir, and

reduce heat. Simmer for 5 minutes to dissolve the agar agar. Place the agar agar mixture in the blender, along with the cream cheese, honey, sour cream, lemon rind, and dates. Blend until the mixture is completely smooth.

Pour the mixture into the crust. Chill to a firm texture. This recipe makes one 9-inch pie.

Yogurt-Lemon "Cheesecake"

Yogurt produces a light, fluffy cake with a special flavor and texture.

1 crumb crust, unbaked
3 cups yogurt
3 tablespoons cornstarch
½ cup sugar
1½ teaspoons finely grated lemon rind

Line a 9-inch pie pan with the crust mixture. Combine all the ingredients for the filling in a blender until smooth (or mix the cornstarch with a little of the yogurt and beat in the remaining ingredients). Pour into the crust. Bake in a 350° oven for 50 to 60 minutes, until the top is lightly browned in a few places.

Chill to harden. The filling will sink slightly. This recipe makes one 9-inch pie.

Variation

Honey Variation: Replace the sugar with ⅓ cup honey; reduce the yogurt to 2⅔ cups.

Fruitcake

Vary the color by using either light or dark brown sugar or different proportions of unbleached white and whole wheat flour. See the recipe for fresh candied fruit peel, page 299.

¾ cup raisins
2 cups chopped mixed dried fruit
2 cups apple juice

---

* This measurement is for agar agar flakes which thicken 1 quart of liquid with 1 tablespoon of agar agar. If the package directions call for *more* agar agar to thicken 1 quart, use 1 more teaspoon agar agar in the cheesecake.

3¼ cups flour, whole wheat or part un-
      bleached white
2 cups packed brown sugar
1 teaspoon soda
2 teaspoons baking powder
1½ teaspoons cinnamon
1 teaspoon each cardamom and cloves
1 cup candied orange or lemon peel
2 cups chopped mixed nuts
pecan halves

Soak the raisins and dried fruit overnight
in the apple juice.

Sift the dry ingredients into a bowl. Add
the apple juice and dried fruit, the candied
peel, and the mixed nuts. Stir until blended.
Pour into two 5 by 9 inch buttered, floured
loaf pans. Decorate the tops with the pecan
halves. Bake in a 300° oven for 1¼ hours
until done. This recipe makes 2 9-inch
fruitcakes.

Variations
Replace the candied fruit peel with
chopped dried fruit.

Replace the cardamom with ground ginger.

Gingerbread

¼ cup butter
⅔ cup packed brown sugar
⅔ cup molasses
1½ cups unbleached white flour
1 cup whole wheat flour
2 tablespoons binding powder (page 51)
2 teaspoons soda
¼ teaspoon salt
1½ teaspoons cinnamon
1½ teaspoons ground ginger
1 cup water

Cream the butter and sugar. Beat in the
molasses. Sift the dry ingredients into the
molasses mixture. Add the water and mix
until blended. Pour into a buttered loaf pan
and bake in a 350° oven for about 1 hour,
until done.

Serve with whipped cream or hung yogurt, and/or applesauce. This recipe makes
1 loaf.

Variation
Honey Variation: Replace the brown
sugar with ½ cup honey; reduce the water
to ⅓ cup.

Mexican Cornbread Dessert (Mexico)

Prepare cornbread, page 222. Top with
whipped cream and fruit salad, sweetened
fresh berries or berry sauce, or crushed
pineapple and raisins. Sprinkle with pine
nuts.

Shortcake (Strawberry, Blueberry, or Peach)

One of the most beautiful cakes in exis-
tence.

3 cups unbleached white flour
1 cup whole wheat flour
1 cup sugar
1 tablespoon baking powder
1 teaspoon soda
1 teaspoon salt
1 cup butter
1⅓ cups milk
1 quart berries *or* 4 cups sliced peaches
1 cup heavy cream
sugar or honey

Sift the dry ingredients into a bowl. Cut
in the butter and work with the hands or a
pastry cutter until the mixture resembles
coarse meal. Stir in the milk to make a soft
dough. Press evenly into two 8-inch round,
buttered, floured cake pans, and bake in a
425° oven for 25 to 30 minutes, until done.
Cool thoroughly.

If using strawberries, slice half of them,
reserving the most beautiful strawberries to
be used whole. Sweeten the fruit with a little honey or sugar. Whip the cream until it
stands in soft peaks.

Place one layer of cake on a plate. If the top is very rounded, trim it flat. Spread half the whipped cream over it, and cover with half the fruit (use the sliced strawberries). Place the second layer on top. Spread with the remaining whipped cream and top with the remaining fruit in a pretty design. This recipe makes one 8-inch shortcake.

Variations

Cover the first layer with blueberries or peaches and cover the second layer with whole strawberries, for a double fruit shortcake.

Honey Variation: Replace the sugar in the cake with ¾ cup honey; reduce the milk to ⅓ cup.

Pineapple Upside-Down Cake

This exquisite cake is prepared in a 10-inch cast-iron skillet with a cast-iron handle.

Pineapple covering:
1 small pineapple
¼ cup butter
¾ cup packed dark brown sugar
10 or 12 pecan halves
Cake:
1½ cups unbleached white flour
½ cup whole wheat flour
2 teaspoons baking powder
½ teaspoon salt
1 cup sugar
2 tablespoons melted butter
½ cup sour milk or buttermilk
½ cup water

Peel the pineapple. Slice thin. Remove the core from each slice with an apple corer or a paring knife.

Melt the butter in a 10-inch cast-iron skillet. Add the brown sugar and stir for a minute. Remove from the heat. Arrange five pineapple slices, overlapping, in a circular pattern in the bottom of the skillet. Cut the remaining slices in half, and arrange along the sides of the skillet, cut side down. Place a pecan half in the center hole of each pineapple slice.

To make the cake, sift all the dry ingredients into a bowl. Add the melted butter, water, and sour milk or buttermilk. Mix just until blended. Pour the cake batter over the pineapple design. Spread evenly. Bake in a 350° oven for 40 to 45 minutes, until done.

Let the cake cool for 5 minutes. Very gently loosen it with a knife. Invert a plate over the top of the skillet. Reverse the skillet and plate to release the cake onto the plate. If any pineapple slices slip off in the unmolding, simply put them back in place.

Serve warm with whipped cream. This recipe makes one 10-inch cake.

Variation

Peach Upside-Down Cake: Replace the pineapple with peach slices, and arrange overlapping in a pinwheel formation in the center and along the sides. Omit the pecans.

Ra Æblekage (Denmark)

This "raw applecake" is known for the natural flavors and sweetness of its ingredients. Use a sweet variety of apple, such as Golden Delicious. As the name implies, the cake is served unbaked. However, it can also be sweetened and baked.

⅓ cup sesame seeds
1 cup finely chopped nuts
1 cup grated coconut
4 cups coarsely grated apples
¼ cup packed brown sugar *or* 3 table-
    spoons honey (optional)

Toast the sesame seeds, nuts, and coconut separately. If desired, toss the apples with the sugar or honey. Spread half the apples in an attractive serving dish. Sprinkle with half of the toasted sesame seeds, coconut, and nuts. Place a second layer of apples in the dish and sprinkle with the remaining nuts and seeds. Chill.

Serve with yogurt or whipped cream. This cake can be served for breakfast as well as for dessert. This recipe makes 6 to 8 servings.

Variation

To bake, toast only half the nuts and seeds. Sprinkle the toasted nuts and seeds over the first layer and the untoasted nuts and seeds on top. Bake in a 375° oven for 20 to 25 minutes.

Cardamom Tea Cake (Sweden)

¼ cup butter
1¼ cups sugar
2 cups unbleached white flour
½ cup whole wheat flour
2 teaspoons baking powder
½ teaspoon soda
1½ teaspoons cardamom
½ teaspoon salt
⅔ cup sour milk or buttermilk

⅔ cup water
nut-crunch topping (page 284)

Cream the butter and the sugar. Sift the dry ingredients into the butter mixture. Add the sour milk or buttermilk and the water, and stir just until blended. Pour into a buttered, floured, 8-by-12-inch rectangular pan and bake in a 350° oven for 20 minutes. Gently open the door and sprinkle the nut-crunch topping on top. Continue baking for another 10 to 15 minutes until done. This recipe makes 1 rectangular cake.

Variation

Honey Variation: Replace the sugar with ¾ cup honey; reduce the water and milk to ⅓ cup each.

Blueberry-Sour Cream Tea Cake

A rich, not-too-sweet offering for summer.

⅓ cup butter
1⅓ cups packed light brown sugar
1 cup sour cream
2½ cups unbleached white flour
½ cup whole wheat flour
1 teaspoon soda
2 teaspoons baking powder
1 teaspoon salt
2 tablespoons binding powder (page 51)
¾ cup water
2½ cups blueberries
nut-crunch topping (page 284) (optional)

Cream the butter and brown sugar. Beat in the sour cream until smooth. Sift the dry ingredients into the sour cream mixture. Add the water and mix until blended. Gently fold in the blueberries. Pour into two 8-inch round buttered, floured cake pans. Bake for 25 minutes. Gently open the door and sprinkle on the nut-crunch topping. Continue baking for another 10 to 15 minutes, until done. This recipe makes 2 8-inch layers.

Variation

Honey Variation: Replace the brown sugar with ¾ cup honey; reduce the water to ⅓ cup.

Pflaumen Kuchen (Germany)

A beautiful plum crumbcake.

½ cup butter
1 cup sugar
2½ cups unbleached white flour
½ cup whole wheat flour
1 tablespoon baking powder
½ teaspoon salt
½ teaspoon nutmeg
1 tablespoon finely grated lemon rind
½ cup milk
2 pounds ripe purple plums, halved and pitted

Cream the butter and sugar. Sift the dry ingredients into the butter mixture. Add the lemon rind and milk. Mix until blended. Press the mixture into a 9-inch round buttered spring-form cake pan. Arrange the plums in concentric circles, overlapping, on top of the dough. Press lightly into the dough to hold them securely.

Bake in a 350° oven for about 1 hour. Cool the cake, and gently lift it out and transfer it to a plate. If the plums are tart, drizzle with a little honey. This recipe makes one 9-inch cake.

Variation

Honey Variation: Replace the sugar with ¾ cup honey; reduce the milk to ¼ cup.

German Apple Torte

This cake looks quite professional, served in squares for dessert or with tea.

Filling:
3 cups apples, peeled, cored and chopped very coarsely
⅓ cup raisins
¼ cup sugar
½ teaspoon cinnamon

Cake:
1¾ cups unbleached white flour
½ cup whole wheat flour
2 tablespoons binding powder (page 51)
1 tablespoon baking powder
¾ cup sugar
½ teaspoon salt
½ cup butter
⅓ to ½ cup milk
confectioner's sugar for topping

Steam the apples in a little water until soft. Drain very well. Mix in the raisins, sugar, and cinnamon.

While the apples are steaming, sift the dry ingredients for the cake into a bowl. Cut in the butter and work with the fingers or a pastry cutter until the mixture resembles coarse meal. Add just enough milk to make a crumbly dough. Crumble half the dough into the bottom of a buttered, 9-inch square pan. Spread evenly to cover the bottom. Spread the apple mixture evenly over the dough. Crumble the remaining dough evenly over the apple mixture to completely cover it. Bake in a 325° oven for 40 to 45 minutes. Turn the heat off and let the cake sit in the cooling oven for another 10 minutes, until the top is golden brown.

When the cake is cool, sift a little confectioner's sugar over the top. Bring to the table already cut in squares, to reveal the filling.

Variation

Honey Variation: Replace the sugar in the filling with 3 tablespoons honey. Drain the apples once again after the honey has been added, just before spreading on the cake. Replace the sugar in the cake with ½ cup honey and omit the milk.

Swedish Pancake Cake (Sweden)

crepes (page 231)
sweetened whipped cream
fresh berries or berry sauce (page 285)

Pile the crepes, spreading whipped cream
and fruit on each crepe, to form a cake.
Chill thoroughly. To serve, cut in wedges
like a cake.

Variation

Replace the whipped cream with sweetened
ricotta for a firmer, less rich filling.

Welsh Cakes (Wales)

Little buttery skillet cakes that are served
in Wales for dessert.

½ cup butter
1 cup sugar
1 cup unbleached white flour
1 cup whole wheat flour
¾ teaspoon baking powder
¼ teaspoon soda
½ teaspoon salt
½ teaspoon nutmeg
½ cup currants or raisins
½ to ⅔ cup milk

Cream the butter and sugar. Sift the dry
ingredients into the butter mixture. Add the
currants and enough milk to make a fairly
firm dough. Roll out dough on a floured
board, ⅓ of an inch thick. Cut out circles
with the rim of a glass or cookie cutter.

Fry the cakes at a low heat on an ungreased griddle or skillet for about 5 minutes on each side, until golden brown. This
recipe makes 12 cakes.

Variation

Honey Variation: Replace the sugar with
¾ cup honey; omit the milk. Fry very
slowly, being alert not to burn the cakes.

PIES: THE CRUST

There is a wide range of crusts and fillings available for pies. Different types of
pie require different types of treatment—
some are baked and some are not, some are
double-crust and some are single-crust, and
so forth. We will begin by describing how
to construct a double-crust pie, using a pastry pie crust—the basic pie. Some of the
procedures used apply to all types of pies,
so if pie-baking is a new experience, please
read the instructions carefully before embarking on the recipe that appeals to you.

Pastry Pie Crust

This is the basic flaky pie crust. To insure
success, always handle the dough as little
as possible, have the cold ingredients *cold,*
and have the oven *hot.* The flakiness is
caused by a cold crust coming into contact
with a high heat.

This recipe makes enough crust for a 9-inch
double-crust pie, with a little left over. You
can use the leftover dough to make pastry
canapé crackers (page 224).

2 cups unbleached white flour
½ teaspoon salt
⅔ cup chilled butter
5 to 5½ tablespoons ice water

Sift the flour and salt into a mixing bowl. Cut the butter into small pieces and work in with the fingers or a pastry cutter until the mixture resembles coarse meal. If using the fingers work quickly, so that the body temperature does not warm the butter. Add the ice water. Stir with a fork; then, with the hands, gather the mixture into a ball that just holds together. Do not knead or otherwise work the dough.

Wrap the dough in plastic wrap or waxed paper and chill for about 6 hours. One can hasten the process by placing in the freezer for 1 hour instead. You may also simply prepare the dough the night before and let it chill overnight.

Remove the dough from the refrigerator or freezer and let it sit at room temperature for 15 to 30 minutes, so it can be rolled out without unnecessary manipulation. Lightly

butter a 9-inch pie pan. Divide the dough in half. Roll one of the halves out on a floured board, until it is ⅛ inch thick and 2 inches wider than the diameter of the pie

pan. Be careful that the dough does not stick to the board, picking it up once or twice during the rolling and changing its position slightly. Check to see that there is still enough flour on the board. When rolling out, roll away from the body rather than "wringing it out" by rolling back and forth.

To transfer the pie dough to the pan, either roll the dough loosely around the

rolling pin and then unroll it in the pan, or roll it out initially on floured waxed paper and reverse it over the pie pan, and peel off the waxed paper. Gently press the crust into place in the pan, filling in the bottom edge. Mend any tears in the crust with patches of pie dough. Trim the crust so that it just hangs over the edges of the pan.

Place the desired filling in the crust. Roll out the remaining pie dough in the same manner as the bottom crust and place it over the filling. Trim the crust evenly

around the outside edge so that it slightly overlaps. There are pie-edge trimmers that do this in fancy patterns. Otherwise, seal by pressing the edges together with the tongs of a fork to leave a fluted design, or pinch in even ridges for a ripple effect. Use a little water, if necessary. Prick the top crust with a knife or fork in a few places to serve as air vents. If it is a fruit pie, you may want to place a baking sheet on the rack below the pie to catch any filling that

might leak out during the baking. However, be careful not to block heat circulation.

Lattice Crust

A lattice crust can be formed by weaving strips of dough in a lattice formation over the top of the pie to serve as a top crust. Seal the edges and trim as indicated above.

Pre-baked Single Pastry Pie Crust

To pre-bake a single crust, use half the recipe for pastry pie crust. Roll out and press into a pan as directed. Trim the edges and decorate as indicated for sealing, though here it is simply for appearance. Either prick the crust in a few places with a fork, or weight down the crust with dry beans or small clean pebbles, as the Europeans do. Bake for 9 to 12 minutes in a 450° oven, until delicately browned.

Partially Baked Crust

When a recipe calls for a partially baked crust, prepare a single crust as above and bake in a 450° oven until it begins to be crisp but does not brown—about 6 to 8 minutes.

Other Variations and Additions to Pastry Pie Crust

Replace 1 cup of unbleached white flour with whole wheat pastry flour. A pie crust can be made from 100 percent whole wheat pastry flour, but it will be difficult to work with—you may have to press it into a pan by hand rather than rolling it out. The best method for rolling it out is the waxed paper method.

Replace ½ cup flour with wheat germ or cornmeal.

Add: ½ cup grated sharp cheese, 2 tablespoons sesame seeds, and 2 teaspoons green herbs (for vegetable pies).

Replace the water with ice-cold broth for vegetable pies.

Oil Crust

The advantage of an oil crust is that it contains half the amount of oil that a pastry crust does, and it is unsaturated oil rather than butter. Otherwise, it is not flaky and does not roll out well, so it is recommended only for those people who wish to reduce their oil intake.

2 cups unbleached white flour
½ teaspoon salt
6 tablespoons oil
3 tablespoons cold water or milk

Sift the flour and salt into a bowl. Beat the oil and water or milk until creamy. Pour over the flour and mix lightly with a fork until blended. Divide in half. Roll out by the waxed paper method, or simply crumble into the pan and press. Bake in the same manner as a pastry crust. This recipe makes two 9-inch crusts.

Crunchy Oil Crust for Vegetable Pies

A flavorful pie crust with a crunchy texture.

1½ cups unbleached white or whole wheat pastry flour
1 teaspoon seasoned salt
½ cup wheat germ
2 tablespoons sesame seeds
3 tablespoons olive oil
3 tablespoons mild-flavored oil
3 tablespoons ice water

Sift the flour and salt into a bowl. Add the wheat germ and sesame seeds. Beat the oils and water together until creamy. Pour over the flour and mix lightly with a fork until blended. Roll out by the waxed paper method, or crumble into a pan and press. This recipe makes two 9-inch crusts.

Variations

Replace ½ cup unbleached white flour with rye flour.

Replace the oils with 6 tablespoons sesame-flavored oil.

Use the herb and cheese variations for pastry crust, page 254.

Crumb Crust

Crumb crusts are used for single-crust pies and for cheesecakes. Vary the flavor by varying the crackers or cookies. To obtain the fine texture necessary, crush the crackers or cookies in a blender in small batches, or grate on a fine grater.

1½ cups cracker or cookie crumbs, crushed fine
⅓ cup melted butter
¼ cup packed brown sugar

Mix all the ingredients. Press evenly into a buttered 9-inch pie pan. To pre-bake the crust, bake in a 350° oven for 10 to 12 minutes, until lightly browned. This recipe makes one 9-inch crust.

Variations
Replace ¼ to ½ cup crumbs with ground nuts.

Honey-Crumb Crust: Use 3 tablespoons honey and 3 tablespoons melted butter or ghee with the crumbs.

Granola Crust

Granola crust is usually used for single-crust pies, but it can be used as a crumble topping to form a double-crust pie. Double the recipe if the topping is desired.

½ cup chopped nuts
⅔ cup rolled oats
⅔ cup wheat germ
½ cup grated coconut
¼ teaspoon salt
¼ cup whole wheat flour
3 tablespoons brown sugar
2 tablespoons melted butter or oil
3 tablespoons water

Mix the nuts and dry ingredients to-gether. Add the oil and water and gently toss to coat the dry ingredients. Press into a 9-inch buttered pie pan. Since granola crusts tend to bake quickly, a shiny metal pie pan is a better choice than a quick-bak-ing glass or dull metal one. To pre-bake, bake in a 350° oven for about 20 minutes, until lightly browned. This recipe makes one 9-inch crust.

Variation:

Honey Variation: Replace the sugar with 2 tablespoons honey; reduce the water to 2 tablespoons.

Rice Flour-Nut Crust

¾ cup rice flour
¾ cup ground walnuts or other nuts
¼ cup brown sugar
¼ cup oil or melted butter

Mix all the ingredients together well. Press into a buttered 9-inch pie pan. To pre-bake, bake in a 350° oven for 20 to 30 minutes. This recipe makes one 9-inch crust.

To prepare a fruit pie, fill an unbaked crust with the fruit filling. Cover the pie with an inverted identical pie pan. Bake in a 350° oven for 1 hour.

Variation

Honey Variation: Reduce the oil to 2 ta-blespoons and replace the brown sugar with 2 tablespoons honey.

Millet Crust

A great crust for vegetable pies and for Tamale Pie, page 178.

1½ cups cooked millet
¾ teaspoon seasoned salt
½ cup grated cheese
¼ cup toasted wheat germ
2 tablespoons sesame seeds

Mix all the ingredients together well. When cool enough to keep its shape, spread the mixture over a buttered pie pan or 1-quart casserole dish. This recipe makes one crust.

Variation

Vegan Variation: Omit the cheese.

FRUIT PIES

Almost all fresh fruits can be used in fruit pies, and small amounts of dried fruit can be mixed in as well. To create your own mixed fruit pies, follow the directions for Berry Pie, page 259, using finely cut mixed fruit. Suggested combinations:

strawberry-blueberry
mango-banana
cherry-peach
cherry-plum-pear
raspberry-peach
pear-raspberry-peach
apple-pear-raisin
peach-banana-date
apricot-pineapple

If desired, a little yogurt or sour cream can be mixed into the filling.

Fill the crust just before baking so that it doesn't have a chance to get soggy.

Apple Pie

Nothing beats apple pie hot from the oven. Here are two ways to prepare this favorite, one with a pastry crust and the other with a granola crust.

5 cups thinly sliced apples, peeled or un-peeled
⅓ cup sugar *or* ¼ cup honey
2 teaspoons lemon juice
¼ teaspoon cinnamon
1 tablespoon arrowroot or cornstarch
1 tablespoon butter

For deep dish 9" pie — 6½ c. sliced apples raisins

With a pastry crust:

Line a 9-inch pie pan with the crust.

Mix all the ingredients for the filling except the butter. Pour into the crust. Dot with the butter. Place the second crust on top. Seal and prick in a few places with a fork or knife. Bake in a 450° oven for 10 minutes, then reduce the heat to 350° and continue baking for 45 minutes, until the crust is golden.

Serve warm with ice cream or slices of sharp cheddar cheese.

With a granola crust:

Prepare a double recipe of granola crust, page 257. Press half of it evenly into a 9-inch pie pan.

Steam the apples for about 5 minutes, until they start to become tender. Drain well. Melt the butter. Mix all the ingredients for the filling and place in the crust. Sprinkle the top with the remaining granola mixture. Bake in a 350° oven for 30 to 40 minutes, until the crust is lightly browned.

Serve hot with whipped cream or ice cream.

Variations

Add ⅓ cup raisins.

Replace 1 or 2 cups of the apples with other sliced fruits.

Berry or Cherry Pie

4 cups ripe berries or ripe pitted cherries
2 tablespoons arrowroot, cornstarch, or quick-cooking tapioca
⅔ cup sugar
1 tablespoon butter, melted
2 teaspoons lemon juice
pastry pie crust

Line a 9-inch buttered pie pan with half of the crust.

Mix all the ingredients for the filling. If using quick-cooking tapioca, let the mixture soak for 15 minutes. Pour the filling in the bottom crust. Place the second crust on top, seal, and prick in a few places with a knife or fork. Bake in a 450° oven for 10 minutes; then reduce the temperature to 350° and bake for 45 minutes, until the crust is golden.

Variation

Honey Variation: Replace the sugar with ½ cup honey and add ½ tablespoon of the arrowroot, cornstarch, or tapioca.

Peach or Apricot Pie

pastry pie crust
5 cups sliced peaches or apricots, blanched and peeled if desired
⅔ cup packed brown sugar
¼ teaspoon cinnamon
2 teaspoons lemon juice
1 tablespoon arrowroot or cornstarch
1 tablespoon butter

Line a 9-inch buttered pie pan with half the pie dough.

Mix the fruit, sugar, cinnamon, lemon juice, and arrowroot or cornstarch. Pour into the bottom crust. Dot with butter. Place the second crust on top, seal, and prick in a few places with a fork or knife. Bake for 10 minutes in a 450° oven, then lower the temperature and bake at 350° for 45 minutes, until the crust is golden. This recipe makes one 9-inch pie.

Variations

Honey Variation: Replace brown sugar with ½ cup honey; add 1 tablespoon cornstarch or arrowroot.

Use a double granola crust; bake for 30 to 40 minutes in a 350° oven.

Rhubarb Pie

pastry pie crust
4 cups rhubarb, cut in ¾-inch pieces
1½ cups sugar

¼ cup unbleached white flour
1 tablespoon butter

Line a 9-inch buttered pie pan with half the dough.

Mix the rhubarb, sugar, and flour together. Let sit for 15 minutes. Place the rhubarb mixture in the crust. Dot with the butter. Place the second crust on top, seal, and prick in a few places with a knife or fork. Bake in a 400° oven for 10 minutes. Lower the temperature to 350° and bake for another 45 minutes, until golden. This recipe makes one 9-inch pie.

Variation

Honey Variation: Replace the sugar with ¾ cup honey; increase the flour to ⅓ cup. Honey and rhubarb taste somewhat bitter together.

Strawberry-Rhubarb Pie: Replace 2 cups of rhubarb with 2 cups sliced strawberries.

Pumpkin Pie

When the filling is baked in the crust, the crust always seems to be soggy. Here we pre-bake the crust and cook the filling separately, and they coexist happily.

3 tablespoons arrowroot or cornstarch
½ cup milk or cream
2¾ cups cooked, pureed pumpkin
1 cup light brown sugar
⅛ teaspoon salt
2 tablespoons butter
1 teaspoon cinnamon
¼ teaspoon nutmeg
¼ teaspoon ginger
⅛ teaspoon cloves
1 pre-baked pastry pie crust

Mix the arrowroot or cornstarch with the milk or cream. Add all the other ingredients for the filling and mix (a blender may be used). Heat the filling slowly in a saucepan, stirring constantly. Simmer until

thickened. Pour the filling into the crust. Chill to harden.

Serve with whipped cream. This recipe makes one 9-inch pie.

Variation

Honey Variation: Replace the sugar with ¾ cup honey; add ½ tablespoon cornstarch or arrowroot. Reduce milk to ⅓ cup.

Fruit-Yogurt Pie

double recipe for granola pie crust
2 cups thinly sliced apples
⅓ cup raisins
1 cup yogurt
½ banana
3 tablespoons sugar
5 pitted dates

Line a buttered 9-inch pie pan with half the granola crust.

Steam the apples for about 5 minutes. Drain well. Place in the crust with the raisins. Combine the yogurt, sugar, half banana, and dates in a blender until smooth. Pour the mixture over the apples and raisins. Sprinkle the remaining crust over the filling, covering it completely. Bake in a 350° oven for 30 to 40 minutes, until the crust is golden brown. Chill.

Variations

Omit the sugar for natural sweetness alone.

Honey Variation: Replace the sugar with 2 tablespoons honey.

Mince Pie (England)

1 double pastry crust
2 cups coarsely chopped apples
1 cup raisins
¼ cup chopped dates
¼ cup chopped figs
⅔ cup packed brown sugar
¼ cup chopped prunes

¼ cup candied orange rind
1 teaspoon finely grated lemon rind
¼ cup lemon juice
⅓ cup orange juice
2 tablespoons arrowroot or cornstarch
¼ teaspoon cloves
½ teaspoon cinnamon

Line a buttered 9-inch pie pan with half the pie dough.

Mix all the ingredients for the filling together. Place in the pie crust. Place the second crust on top. Seal, and prick in a few places with a knife or fork. Bake in a 450° oven for 10 minutes; then reduce the heat to 350° and continue baking for 45 minutes, until the crust is golden.

Variations

Replace the arrowroot or cornstarch with tapioca. Let the filling mixture sit for 15 minutes before placing in the crust.

Honey Variation: Replace the brown sugar with ½ cup honey; add ½ tablespoon arrowroot, cornstarch, or tapioca.

Unbaked fruit pies can be created by filling a single pastry or other pie crust with a mixture of about 3 cups sliced, fresh juicy fruit with 1½ cups fruit sauce. Use berry sauce (page 285) for best results, as it contains a little cornstarch to give the mixture body. Chill thoroughly and top with a layer of sweetened whipped cream.

Suggested combinations:
• sliced strawberries with blueberry sauce
• blueberries mixed with blueberry sauce
• Peach Melba pie: sliced peaches with raspberry sauce and whipped cream

Hung Yogurt Pie

Hung yogurt pies are quite flexible—mixtures of sweetened hung yogurt and fresh fruit. Here is a basic formula.

2 cups hung yogurt (page 42)

¼ cup honey
¼ teaspoon finely grated lemon rind
½ cup berries or chopped, juicy fruit
1 pre-baked crumb crust or granola crust
½ to 1 cup sliced fruit

Mix the hung yogurt, honey, lemon rind, and chopped fruit together. Add more sweetening if necessary. Spread evenly in the crust. Arrange the sliced fruit over the top. Chill.

Variations

Add grated coconut to the yogurt; sprinkle chopped nuts on the top.

Replace the hung yogurt with ricotta.

Replace the hung yogurt with shrikhand.

TARTS

Tarts are basically single-crust fruit pies. They are baked in spring-form cake pans so that they can be removed from the pan for serving. Hence, it is very important to line the crust evenly and completely, and to have no holes, uneven patching, or thin spots. Here are three beautiful and elegant French fruit tarts.

Apple Tart (France)

1 uncooked pastry pie crust
1 cup applesauce
2 cups thinly sliced apples
3 tablespoons sugar
1 tablespoon melted butter
1 tablespoon lemon juice
1 teaspoon cornstarch

Line a buttered 9-inch spring-form cake pan with the pie crust. Spread the applesauce evenly over the bottom of the crust.

Mix the apples with the sugar, butter, lemon juice, and cornstarch. Arrange the apples in concentric circles around the outside edge. Fill the center with another concentric circle, or with a nice design. Bake in a 375° oven for 45 to 50 minutes. Cool thoroughly, and gently transfer from the pan to a plate. This recipe makes one 9-inch tart.

Variation

Honey Variation: Replace the sugar with 2 tablespoons honey.

Strawberry Tart (France)

1 pre-baked pastry pie crust (baked in a buttered 9-inch spring-form pan)
1 tablespoon arrowroot or cornstarch
1 cup heavy cream
1 tablespoon butter
3 tablespoons sugar *or* 2 tablespoons honey
1 quart strawberries, evenly sized, with good color
glaze (see page 263)

Gently remove the cooled crust from the cake pan and transfer it to a plate.

Mix the arrowroot or cornstarch with half the cream. Place in a saucepan with

the remaining cream, the butter, and the sugar. Heat slowly, stirring constantly with a whisk until thickened. Cool slightly, and spread the mixture evenly over the bottom of the crust. Stud the cream filling with the strawberries, stem end down. Chill while preparing the glaze.

Spoon a little of the glaze over each strawberry to coat. Chill the tart until the cream filling and the glaze are cool. This recipe makes one 9-inch tart.

Variation
Replace the cream filling with 1 cup sweetened ricotta.

Apricot Tart (France)

1 pre-baked pastry pie crust (baked in a buttered 9-inch spring-form pan)
1 tablespoon arrowroot or cornstarch
1 cup heavy cream
1 tablespoon butter
3 tablespoons sugar *or* 2 tablespoons honey
8 ripe apricots
glaze (see page 263)

Cool the crust and carefully transfer it from the pan to a plate.

Mix the arrowroot or cornstarch with half the cream. Pour into a saucepan, add the butter and sugar or honey, and heat, stirring constantly with a whisk, until thickened. Cool slightly, and spread the mixture over the bottom of the crust. Drop the apricots into rapidly boiling water for 3 minutes. Drain. Gently peel off the skins. Cut the apricots into perfect halves and remove the pits. Carefully cover the cream mixture with apricot halves—arrange them around the outside edge first and then work inward. Chill while preparing the glaze.

Spoon a little of the glaze over each apricot to coat. Chill the tart to set the cream filling and the glaze. This recipe makes one 9-inch tart.

Variation
Replace the cream filling with 1 cup sweetened ricotta.

Glaze for Tarts

Sugar glaze:
⅓ cup steamed, pureed apricots
1 tablespoon lemon juice
¼ cup sugar

Place all the ingredients in a saucepan. Bring to a boil and boil for 5 minutes.

Honey glaze:
⅓ cup steamed, pureed apricots
3 tablespoons honey
1 tablespoon lemon juice
1 tablespoon water
2 teaspoons cornstarch

Mix the cornstarch into the ingredients until smooth. Heat the mixture, stirring constantly, until it is thickened.

CREAM PIES

Pre-baked pie crusts can be filled with any of the cornstarch-based puddings in the Puddings section. Chill, and top with whipped cream. Or try the following rich-rich pies.

Carob Cream Pie

3 tablespoons cornstarch or arrowroot
½ cup water
2 cups heavy cream
¾ cup packed brown sugar
2 tablespoons butter
½ cup carob powder
1 pre-baked pie crust (any type)
¾ cup heavy cream (for topping)

Mix the arrowroot or cornstarch into the water until dissolved. Place in a saucepan with the heavy cream, brown sugar, butter, and carob powder. Heat, stirring constantly, until the mixture has thickened. Do not boil. Pour the carob mixture into the crust. Chill to harden.

Whip the cream until stiff. Spread it over the pie.

Variations
Honey Variation: Replace the sugar with ½ cup honey; reduce the water to ¼ cup and add ½ tablespoon cornstarch or arrowroot.
Vegan Variation: Replace the water and cream with nut milk; omit the cream topping.
Mocha Cream Pie: Add 1½ teaspoons grain coffee powder and 1 tablespoon or more confectioner's sugar to the whipped cream topping.

Triple Decker Cream Pie

The ultimate cream pie.

1 pre-baked crumb or pastry pie crust
½ recipe Carob Cream Pie filling (see above)
½ recipe Butterscotch-Coconut Pudding (page 289)
¾ cup heavy cream
1½ teaspoons grain coffee powder
1 tablespoon or more confectioner's sugar

Prepare the carob cream pie filling. Spread it over the bottom of the crust. Chill to set.

Prepare the butterscotch-coconut pudding. When the carob cream filling is set, spread the butterscotch-coconut pudding over it. Chill to set.

Just before serving, whip the heavy cream until stiff. Add the grain coffee powder and confectioner's sugar. Spread the whipped cream over the pie. This recipe makes one 9-inch pie.

Banana Cream Pie

3 tablespoons arrowroot or cornstarch
¼ cup water
1 cup heavy cream
1 tablespoon butter
⅓ cup packed brown sugar
1 cup mashed ripe bananas
1 pre-baked pie crust (granola, pastry, or crumb)
¾ cup heavy cream (for topping)

Mix the arrowroot or cornstarch with the water to dissolve. Place in a saucepan with the heavy cream, butter, sugar, and bananas. Heat slowly, stirring constantly with a whisk until thickened. Do not boil. Pour into the crust. Chill to harden.

Whip the cream until stiff, just before serving. Sweeten with a little confectioner's sugar or honey. Spread over the pie. This recipe makes one 9-inch pie.

Variations

For a tropical pie, cover the whipped cream with crushed pineapple and mango slices. Sprinkle with a little coconut.

Honey Variation: Replace the sugar with ¼ cup honey; add 1 teaspoon cornstarch or arrowroot.

Coconut Cream Pie

3 tablespoons arrowroot or cornstarch
2¼ cups heavy cream
1 cup sugar
3 tablespoons butter
2 cups grated coconut, fresh or dried
1 pre-baked pie crust (granola, pastry, or crumb)
¾ cup heavy cream (for topping)

Mix the arrowroot or cornstarch into ¼ cup of the cream. Pour into a saucepan. Add the remaining cream, sugar, butter, and coconut. Heat, stirring constantly, until thickened. Do not boil. Pour into the crust. Chill to harden. Just before serving, whip the cream until stiff. Sweeten with a little confectioner's sugar or honey. Spread over the pie. This recipe makes one 9-inch pie.

Variations

Honey Variation: Replace sugar with ¾ cup honey; reduce the cream to 2 cups and add ½ tablespoon cornstarch or arrowroot.

Vegan Variation: Replace the cream with coconut milk. Omit the cream topping, and top with fruit.

See "tropical pie" variation under Banana Cream Pie.

Ice Cream Pie

Fill a single, pre-baked crumb or granola crust with ice cream, and add:

sliced fresh fruit
chopped nuts
carob chips
dessert sauces
honey
persimmon pulp
candies
fruit sauce
grated coconut
granola
whipped cream
maple syrup
praliné

Freeze the mixture to harden.

Banana Ice Cream Pie

An ice cream sundae in a pie.

1 pre-baked crumb or granola crust
1 or 2 bananas, sliced thin
2 cups softened banana or fruit ice cream
½ cup caramel sauce (page 287)
chopped nuts
grated coconut
whipped cream (optional)

Cover the crust with sliced bananas. Spread the ice cream evenly over the bananas, and pour the cooled caramel sauce over the ice cream. Sprinkle with chopped nuts and coconut. Freeze just to firm the ice cream. If desired, top with whipped cream.

Fruity Ice Cream Pie

1 cup sliced peaches, berries, or fruit salad
1 pre-baked granola or crumb pie crust
2 cups fruit ice cream, softened
½ cup fresh fruit sauce (page 284), berry sauce (page 285), or other fruit sauce
chopped nuts
grated coconut
whipped cream (optional)

Spread the fruit evenly over the crust. Cover with an even layer of ice cream. Pour the fruit sauce over the ice cream and spread evenly. Sprinkle with nuts and coconut. If desired, top with whipped cream.

PASTRIES

Baklava (Greece)

Nut-filled layers of flaky filo pastry.

4 cups ground walnuts, or a mixture of ground walnuts, pistachios, and pine nuts
½ cup sugar
2 teaspoons cinnamon

¾ cup butter
¾ cup mild-flavored oil
1 pound filo pastry (24 sheets)
chopped pistachios (optional)
Syrup:
2½ cups sugar
1¼ cups water
2 tablespoons lemon juice
3 tablespoons honey
few drops rosewater

Mix the ground nuts with the sugar and cinnamon.

Melt the butter. Mix with the oil, and brush a 12-by-14- or 16-inch pan with the butter-oil mixture. (A broiling pan can be used if it has shallow sides; cover it with foil to smooth out the grooves.)

Lay 1 sheet of filo pastry flat. Brush with the butter-oil. It does not have to be coated completely; just make certain that most of the area has some oil on or near it. Lay down another sheet and brush with butter-oil again. Repeat until 4 sheets are on the pan. Sprinkle 1 cup of the nut mixture over the pastry. Lay down 4 more sheets of the pastry, with butter-oil brushed between them. Repeat, laying down 1 cup of nut mixture and four sheets of pastry, until the nut mixture is gone. Lay down the remaining 4 sheets of pastry and pour any remaining butter-oil over the top.

Score the top layer ¼ inch deep with a knife, making 2½-inch-wide diamond shapes, to guide later cutting. Sprinkle a little water on it to make the dough lie flat. Bake in a 300° oven for 1 to 1¼ hours, until the pastry is just a very pale gold—not browned.

While the baklava is cooling, prepare the syrup by boiling the sugar, water, and lemon juice together for 5 minutes. Cool for a few minutes. Stir in the honey and rosewater. Pour over the baklava. If desired, sprinkle the top of the baklava with pistachios. Let the baklava cool and soak in the syrup for at least 1 hour before serving.

Cut into diamond shapes and serve. This recipe makes approximately 30 2½-inch baklava.

Fruit Cobbler

Cobblers are quick and easy to prepare, delicious served warm with ice cream or whipped cream. Try a cherry or blueberry cobbler. The fruit may be placed either over or under the dough.

Dough:
2 cups unbleached white flour or whole wheat pastry flour
¼ cup sugar
1 tablespoon baking powder
½ teaspoon salt
⅓ cup butter
4 to 6 tablespoons milk

Topping:
4 cups berries, pitted cherries, sliced peaches, or apricots
¾ cup sugar or to taste
2 tablespoons arrowroot or cornstarch
1 tablespoon lemon juice
¼ cup water

To prepare the dough, sift all the dry ingredients into a bowl. Cut in the butter, and work with the fingers or a pastry cutter until the mixture resembles coarse meal. Add milk to make a soft dough.

To prepare the topping, bring all the ingredients to a boil.

At this point, you may either press the dough into a buttered baking dish or a 10-inch cast-iron skillet, top it with the fruit, and dot with butter; or pour the fruit into a buttered baking dish or cast-iron skillet, and press the dough evenly over the fruit. Bake in a 425° oven for 30 minutes.

Variations

Honey Variation: Replace the sugar in the dough with 3 tablespoons honey; reduce the milk slightly, and replace the sugar in the filling with ½ cup honey. Add ½ tablespoons arrowroot or cornstarch.

For *Rhubarb Cobbler,* use the filling for Rhubarb Pie, page 259.

Fruit Crisp

Apple filling:
5 cups thinly sliced apples (peeled or unpeeled)
⅓ cup packed brown sugar *or* ¼ cup honey
½ teaspoon cinnamon
½ cup raisins
1 tablespoon butter

Berry, cherry, peach, or apricot filling:
4 cups berries, pitted cherries, sliced peaches, or apricots
½ to ¾ cup sugar *or* ⅓ to ½ cup honey
2 tablespoons cornstarch
1 tablespoon lemon juice

Rhubarb filling:
filling for Rhubarb Pie, page 259.

Topping:
¾ cup unbleached white or whole wheat flour
½ cup ground nuts
¼ cup wheat germ
½ teaspoon salt
⅓ cup butter
1 to 2 tablespoons milk

(granola pie crust may also be used)

Mix all the ingredients for the desired filling together and pour into a buttered baking dish.

Combine the dry ingredients for the crumble topping in a bowl. Cut in the butter and work with the fingers or a pastry cutter until the mixture resembles coarse meal. Add the milk and crumble with the fingers. Crumble the topping over the fruit.

Bake in a 350° oven for 30 to 40 minutes, until the topping is lightly browned, and the fruit is tender. Serve warm with ice cream or whipped cream.

DESSERT CREPES

Prepare crepes (page 231) and fill or top with any of the following ingredients:

fresh berries
sliced peaches, mangoes, bananas, apricots, or other soft juicy fruits
fruit sauces
dessert sauces
honey
maple syrup
fruit salad
ambrosia and ambrosia cream salads
diced pineapple
shrikhand
butterscotch-coconut pudding
caramel sauce
ice cream
ricotta
hung yogurt
whipped cream
sour cream
banana pudding
carob pudding
carob sauce

Additions, or sprinklings for the top:
chopped nuts
carob chips
grated coconut
granola cereal
praliné
confectioner's sugar

Suggested Dessert Crepes

Crepes stuffed with sliced strawberries and sweetened ricotta, sprinkled with confectioner's sugar.

Crepes stuffed with ice cream and sliced bananas, and covered with carob sauce.
Crepes stuffed with mango slices, whipped cream, and slivered almonds.
Crepes stuffed with ambrosia salad and covered with lemon sauce.

DOUGHNUTS

Doughnuts, as they were originally prepared in Holland, had no hole in the center. It was the Dutch immigrants in colonial America who conceived of the idea of punching a hole to allow the oil to cook the inside. Doughnuts may also be formed into a cruller, a piece of braided dough 3 or 4 inches long.

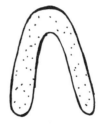

To prepare successful doughnuts:
1. Keep the dough fairly plain and add sweetness in the embellishments after the doughnuts have been cooked. The more sugar or honey (and the more butter) the dough contains, the more oil it will absorb.
2. For best texture, handle the dough as little as possible.
3. To facilitate light handling, have the butter at room temperature.
4. Chill and dry the doughnuts for about 15 minutes before frying, so that they will absorb less oil. (The air dries the dough a little—don't go at them with a towel.)

5. Deep-fry doughnuts for 2 or 3 minutes at high heat, turning them over once during the frying if necessary.

Frostings for Doughnuts

a glaze made of confectioner's sugar with
    a few drops of water
honey
cake frostings
dried fruit purees
confectioner's sugar with a few drops of
    maple syrup
plain confectioner's sugar (place the sifted
    sugar in a bag, drop in the doughnuts
    one at a time, and gently shake to
    coat)
Roll *frosted* doughnuts in:
grated coconut
ground nuts
granola cereal
praliné
crushed cookies
sesame or ground sunflower seeds

Cake Doughnuts

1½ cups unbleached white flour
1½ cups whole wheat pastry flour
1 cup sugar
2 teaspoons baking powder
½ teaspoon soda
½ teaspoon salt
2 tablespoons binding powder (page 51)
¼ teaspoon cinnamon
¼ teaspoon nutmeg
3 tablespoons melted butter or oil
¾ cup milk
ghee or oil for deep-frying

Mix the dry ingredients and sift into a bowl. Add the melted butter and milk. Mix to blend. Roll dough out on a floured board, ¼ inch thick. Cut out rounds with cookie cutters or the rim of a glass. Cut out the hole in the middle with a bottle-top. For best results, chill the doughnuts for about 15 minutes before frying.

Deep-fry for about 3 minutes, turning once, until golden brown. Drain on paper towels. Serve plain, or with the suggested frostings (see above). This recipe makes 18 to 20 doughnuts.

Variation

Honey Variation: Replace sugar with ¾ cup honey. Reduce the milk to ⅓ cup.

Raised Doughnuts

1½ tablespoons yeast
¼ cup lukewarm water
¾ cup milk, scalded and cooled to luke-
    warm, or reconstituted powdered milk,
    heated
⅔ cup sugar
2 tablespoons butter or oil
1½ cups whole wheat pastry flour
2½ cups unbleached white flour
½ teaspoon allspice

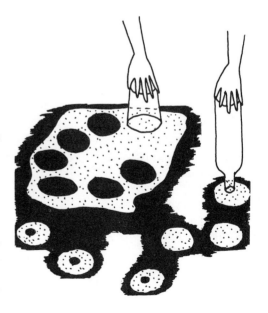

Mix the yeast with the lukewarm water. Let stand for 5 minutes. Mix again. Add the milk, sugar, oil, flour, and allspice. Mix in and knead for 2 to 3 minutes. Place in an oiled bowl and cover; let it rise in the refrigerator overnight, or let it rise in a warm place for 1½ hours, until doubled in bulk.

Punch down. Roll the dough out on a floured board, ¼ inch thick. Cut out rounds with a cookie cutter or the rim of a glass. Cut out the middle hole with a bottle-top. Cover and let rise in a warm place for 30 minutes.

Deep-fry on both sides until golden, for about 3 minutes altogether. Drain on paper towels. Frost with one of the frostings suggested on page 268. This recipe makes 18 to 20 doughnuts.

Variations

Honey Variation: Replace the sugar with ½ cup honey; reduce the milk to ⅓ cup.

Vegan Variation: Replace the milk with water or soy milk.

Filled Doughnuts, or Berliners

Roll out the dough for raised doughnuts ⅛ inch thick. Cut out rounds, but do not cut holes in them. Place a spoonful of dried fruit puree (page 235) in the center of a round. Moisten the edges and place another round on top. Seal together thoroughly. Cover and let rise for 30 minutes. Deep-fry as usual. While they are warm, coat with confectioner's sugar.

Cottage Cheese Doughnuts (Switzerland)

1 cup unbleached white flour
1 cup whole wheat pastry flour
¼ teaspoon salt
2 teaspoons baking powder
¼ cup butter
½ cup plus 1 tablespoon milk

Filling:
¾ cup cottage cheese
2 teaspoons milk
⅓ cup sugar
1 tablespoon binding powder (page 51)
½ teaspoon cinnamon
¼ cup ground almonds
¼ cup raisins
confectioner's sugar
cinnamon

Combine the dry ingredients for the dough in a bowl. Cut in the butter and work with the fingers or a pastry cutter until the mixture resembles coarse meal. Add the milk. Work until the dough holds together in a ball. Roll out the dough on a floured board, ⅛ inch thick. Cut out rounds with a cookie cutter or the rim of a glass.

To make the filling, combine the cottage cheese, milk, sugar, binding powder, and ½ teaspoon cinnamon in a blender until smooth. Place in a bowl and add the ground nuts and the raisins.

Place a spoonful of the filling in the center of a round. Moisten the edges and place another round on top. Seal the edges very thoroughly. Press the edges with the tongs of a fork for a fluted design. Deep-fry on both sides until golden. Drain on paper towels.

Roll doughnuts in confectioner's sugar mixed with a little cinnamon. This recipe makes 12 to 16 doughnuts.

Variation

Honey Variation: Substitute 3 tablespoons honey for the sugar, and omit the milk from the filling.

Dutch New Year's Doughnuts

A variation on the doughnuts served on New Year's in Holland. These are like little puffs of fruitcake.

2 cups unbleached white flour
½ cup sugar

1 teaspoon baking powder
½ teaspoon soda
¼ teaspoon salt
1 teaspoon cinnamon
¼ teaspoon each: ground ginger and mace
⅛ teaspoon cloves
½ cup milk
1½ tablespoons melted butter
¾ cup grated apple
grated rind of 1 lemon
⅓ cup raisins
½ cup chopped dried fruit
confectioner's sugar

Sift the dry ingredients into a bowl. Add the milk, melted butter, grated apple, and lemon rind. Stir in the raisins and dried fruit. Deep-fry spoonfuls of the batter slowly, until golden. Check one to see if it is cooked through. If not, make the spoonfuls smaller and fry more slowly.

Drain on paper towels and roll in confectioner's sugar. Makes about 2 dozen donuts.

Variations

Honey Variation: Replace the sugar with ⅓ cup honey; reduce the milk to 3 tablespoons.

Vegan Variation: Replace the milk with water.

Loukoumathes (Greece)

Deep-fried puffs in honey sauce.

Puffs:
1¾ cup yogurt
2 cups unbleached white flour
¼ cup lemon juice
pinch salt
1 teaspoon finely grated lemon rind
Sauce:
1 cup honey
⅔ cup warm water
1 tablespoon lemon juice
¼ teaspoon cinnamon

Combine all the ingredients for the puffs in a blender, or beat until smooth. Let stand at room temperature for 2 hours.

Mix all the ingredients for the sauce together. Drop spoonfuls of the batter into hot ghee or oil. They will swell during the cooking, so do not crowd. Cook until browned. Drain on paper towels. Check one to see that it is cooked through. If not, fry smaller spoonfuls a little more slowly.

Just before serving, place in a bowl. Pour the sauce over them and serve at once. The puffs should not soak in the sauce. This recipe makes 6 to 8 servings.

Gulab Jamun (India)

A quick version of "rose fruit," and a very special dessert. Very good for holidays.

2 cups non-instant milk powder
¾ teaspoon baking powder
½ - ⅔ cup whole milk
3 tablespoons unbleached white flour
sugar cubes (optional)
Syrup:
2 cups water
1 cup sugar
pinch saffron
a few crushed cardamon seeds
few drops rosewater

To prepare the syrup, bring the water, sugar, cardamom, and saffron to a boil. Reduce heat to a simmer. Mix the milk powder, flour, and baking powder in a bowl. Add the whole milk and mix to a sticky dough. With clean hands, roll some of the dough into 1-inch balls. Drop a few of the balls into heated ghee or oil. Fry very slowly, taking about 5 minutes for each ball to become golden brown. The balls will swell, so do not crowd them. Stir occasionally so that all sides will brown—if they brown a little unevenly it does not matter. Drain on paper towels.

Continue rolling balls and deep-frying them. Add milk to the dough when it starts to dry out. It is important that the dough stay soft and sticky, or the balls will be hard. Roll out the balls just before frying to insure softness.

Add the rosewater to the syrup, and drop a few of the balls into the syrup as it simmers. They will almost double their size, so do not crowd them. Cover and simmer very gently for 10 minutes. Very gently move them with a slotted spoon to a bowl, and cover with a little of the syrup. Continue with the remaining fried balls. An assembly line can be set up, with some frying while others are simmering.

When all the balls are done and are in bowls, pour the remaining syrup over them. Allow to soak at room temperature for an hour or even an afternoon. Serve at room temperature. This recipe makes 25 to 30 galub jamuns.

Note: The gulab jamuns should be meltingly soft. If they are hard on the inside, they were either cooked too quickly, or the dough was too dry when the balls were made.

Variation

Chop sugar cubes into small pieces. When forming the balls, place a tiny piece of sugar cube in the center. It will melt during frying.

Jalebis (India)

Deep-fried spirals of translucent pastry coated with a sweet syrup. Versions of jalebis are found in the Middle East as well as in India. A little practice is required to make perfect spirals; in the meantime, abstract patterns are perfectly acceptable.

Batter:
3 cups unbleached white flour
¼ teaspoon saffron soaked in ¼ cup hot water

1 tablespoon baking powder
¼ cup yogurt
1¾ cups water

Syrup:
1 cup water
1¾ cups sugar
few drops rosewater

Combine all the ingredients for the batter in a blender, or beat until smooth. Let stand at room temperature for 2 hours.

Heat oil or ghee for deep-frying. In another pot, combine the water and sugar for the syrup. Bring to a boil and boil for 5 minutes, until the syrup thickens slightly. Reduce the heat to a simmer.

Place a plain round nib on a pastry tube. Hold the nib shut and fill the bag with batter. Pipe the batter in spirals into hot oil. The batter will run out of the tube, without having to be forced. If it is too difficult to pipe spirals, just pipe abstract patterns. When the jalebis are golden brown, remove and drain on paper towels.

Drop the jalebis, a few at a time, into the simmering syrup. Add the rosewater with the first batch. Simmer for 2 or 3 minutes. Make sure the jalebis are coated with the syrup. Remove and let dry on a plate. This recipe makes about 40 jalebis.

Sweet Samosas (India)

Deep-fried pastries with a sweet nut filling.

Prepare samosas, page 65, substituting the following filling for the vegetable filling:

1½ cups ground almonds or other nuts
½ cup non-instant milk powder
1 cup sugar
2 to 3 tablespoons milk

Mix the ingredients to form a mixture that just holds together when squeezed. Squeeze 25 to 30 balls to fill the samosas.

Cookies

Preparing cookie dough is relatively simple. It is the baking that requires special alertness and attention.

Ovens usually heat unevenly to some degree. If the oven is noticeably hotter toward the back, the cookie sheet may have to be turned around once during the baking to make sure that all the cookies are done at the same time. If you are baking cookies on two racks, place the racks far apart so that there is room between for heat to circulate. The middle rack, however, generally has the best heat distribution. Cookies baked higher in the oven will bake more quickly than those on a lower rack, because heat rises.

Distribute cookies over the entire cookie sheet. Heat is drawn to where the cookies are, and if they are all on one end they may get a double dose of heat and burn.

Place cookies on thoroughly cooled baking sheets. If the sheets are hot, the bottoms of the cookies may burn. Wait between each batch for the baking sheets to cool—it is only a matter of a few minutes.

Remove the cookies immediately from the baking sheets with a spatula when they are done. Eggless cookies tend to stick to the sheet if they are cooled on it. Remove

them even if soft and fragile, and allow to cool and harden on a plate. Do not stack cookies that are cooling or otherwise allow them to touch. Cookies that cool together stay together.

There are various types of cookies. Many can be prepared from the same basic dough.

Rolled cookies are prepared from a fairly firm dough. Roll out the dough on a well-floured board ⅛ to ¼ inch thick, and cut

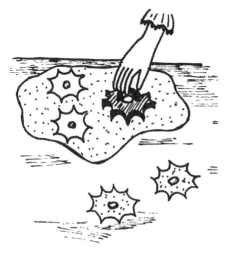

out with cookie cutters. A knife may be used to cut fancy shapes, and the rim of a glass makes good round cookies. Rolled cookies hold their shape during baking and do not spread out very much.

Drop cookies are prepared from a thick, sticky batter that is dropped in teaspoonfuls

on a buttered baking sheet. The cookies spread out during the baking, so place them 1½ inches apart on the baking sheet to allow for expansion.

Refrigerator cookies are prepared from a stiff dough, as rolled cookies are. Roll the dough into a cylinder of the diameter desired for the cookies. Wrap it in waxed paper or plastic wrap and chill in the refrigerator for 6 to 12 hours to become very firm. When ready to bake, slice off cookies ⅛ to ¼ inch thick, and bake. Refrigerator cookies are easy to prepare for large gatherings and celebrations, or when the cookies must be prepared in advance.

Bar cookies (which include brownies) are baked in rectangular or square baking

pans, and then cut into squares when cooled.

Molded and pressed cookies are formed in beautiful molds that leave picture impressions in the cookies of little windmills, people, and so forth.

Variations and Additions for Cookies

Basic cookies, such as butter cookies and oatmeal cookies, are especially receptive to additions. Though honey variations are listed for cookies, cookies prepared with honey generally do not have a very good texture, and often have a strong flavor. As it is advised throughout this cookbook not to use honey in cooked foods, it is advised here doubly, for reasons of flavor and texture as well as for those of health.

Additions:
  carob chips
  granola cereal
  raisins or currants
  grated coconut
  grain coffee powder
  soy grits (small amounts)
  sesame, sunflower, or pumpkin seeds
  chopped or halved nuts
  chopped dried fruit
  finely grated lemon or orange rind
  milk powder
  sweet spices: cinnamon, cardamom, nutmeg or mace, ground ginger, cloves, allspice
• Substitute molasses or maple syrup for honey.
• Substitute wheat germ for ½ cup of the flour.
• Substitute whole wheat pastry flour for unbleached white flour, or vice versa.

Butter Cookies

Tender and buttery, these cookies may be served as is, or use as a base for some of the additions listed previously. They may be prepared as rolled cookies, refrigerator cookies, or just formed into patties with the hands.

2½ cups butter
2¼ cups sugar, white or packed brown
4⅓ cups flour
1 teaspoon baking powder
½ to ¾ cup milk

Cream the butter and sugar together. Sift in the flour and baking powder. Add milk to make a soft dough. (Make fairly firm for rolled cookies.) Shape into ⅛-inch-thick cookies by the desired method. Place on a buttered baking sheet. Bake in a 350° oven for 12 to 15 minutes, until lightly golden. Remove immediately with a spatula and transfer to a plate to harden and cool. This recipe makes 4 dozen cookies.

Variations

Honey Variation: Replace the sugar with 1½ cups honey; omit the milk. Chill the mixture to harden before forming cookies.

Carob-Chip Cookies: Add 1 cup or more carob chips.

Raisin Cookies: Add 1 cup or more raisins.

Oatmeal Cookies

Try preparing oatmeal cookies with pecan halves and chopped dates, for something really special.

½ cup butter
1¼ cups packed brown sugar
1 cup unbleached white flour
1 teaspoon baking powder
1 teaspoon cinnamon
¼ teaspoon cloves
¾ teaspoon ginger
3 cups rolled oats
¾ cup milk
½ cup chopped nuts (optional)
1 cup raisins or chopped dates

Cream the butter and brown sugar. Sift the dry ingredients into the butter-sugar mixture. Add the oats and the milk. Stir until blended. Add the nuts and raisins and stir. Drop spoonfuls of the batter onto a buttered baking sheet 1½ inches apart. Bake in a 350° oven for 12 to 15 minutes. Transfer immediately to a plate to cool and harden. This recipe makes 2½ to 3 dozen cookies.

Variations

Honey Variation: Replace the sugar with 1 cup honey; omit the milk.

Vegan Variation: Replace the milk with water or nut milk.

Banana-Oatmeal Cookies

½ cup butter
1¾ cups packed brown sugar
2 cups mashed ripe bananas
3 cups rolled oats
1 cup whole wheat flour
1 teaspoon baking powder
½ cup wheat germ
½ teaspoon salt
¾ teaspoon cinnamon

Cream the butter and sugar. Add the bananas and beat until smooth. Add the oats. Sift in the remaining dry ingredients. Mix well. Chill the dough for an hour.

Drop spoonfuls of batter on a buttered baking sheet 1½ inches apart. Bake in a 350° oven for 12 to 15 minutes. Remove immediately to a plate to cool and harden. This recipe makes 3 dozen cookies.

Nut Butter Cookies

Prepared with nut butter made from roasted cashews, these cookies are sublime. The recipe has always been tested with nut butter made by the blender method. While other types of nut butter may work as well, the results are assured by preparing one's own as a first step.

3 cups homemade nut butter (page 47)
2 cups whole wheat flour
½ cup milk
2½ cups packed brown sugar
1 teaspoon baking powder

Mix all the ingredients together well. Shape into flat, round cookies and place on a buttered baking sheet 1 inch apart. Bake in a 350° oven for 12 to 15 minutes, until golden brown. Immediately transfer the cookies to a plate to cool. This recipe makes 4 dozen cookies.

Variation

Vegan Variation: Replace the milk with water or nut milk.

Granola Cookies

2 cups unbleached white or whole wheat
    pastry flour
1 cup packed brown sugar
3 cups granola cereal
1 teaspoon baking powder
½ cup milk
½ cup melted butter

Mix the flour, sugar, granola, and baking powder together. Add the milk and melted butter. Mix well. Shape into round, flat cookies. Bake for 12 to 15 minutes in a 350° oven until golden. This recipe makes 2½ dozen cookies.

Variations

Add raisins or chopped dates.

Honey Variation: Replace the brown sugar with ¾ cup honey; omit the milk.

Vegan Variation: Replace the milk with soy milk or water.

Ranger Cookies

½ cup butter
1½ cups packed brown sugar
1½ cups rolled oats
¾ cup grated coconut
1 cup whole wheat flour
1 teaspoon baking powder
¼ teaspoon salt
4 tablespoons milk or water

Cream the butter and brown sugar. Add the oats and coconut. Sift remaining dry ingredients into the mixture. Add the milk or water. Mix well.

RANGER COOKIES

Roll the dough into 1-inch balls. Place them 1 inch apart on a buttered baking sheet. Press down the middle of each cookie with a fork to flatten it and leave a striped pattern. Bake in a 350° oven for 12 to 15 minutes, until golden brown. Immediately transfer the cookies to a plate to cool. This recipe makes 2½ dozen cookies.

Variation

Honey Variation: Replace the sugar with ¾ cup honey; omit the milk or water. Chill the mixture until firm before forming the cookies.

Wheat Germ Cookies

2 cups wheat germ
2 cups whole wheat flour
2 cups packed brown sugar
1 teaspoon baking powder
½ cup melted butter
1 tablespoon finely grated orange rind
½ cup milk

Mix the dry ingredients together. Add the melted butter, orange rind, and milk. Mix well. Shape into flat, round cookies and place on a buttered baking sheet. Bake in a 350° oven for 12 to 15 minutes until golden. Move the cookies immediately to a plate to cool. This recipe makes 2 dozen cookies.

Variation

Honey Variation: Replace the brown sugar with 1½ cups honey. Omit the milk. Chill the mixture until firm before forming into cookies.

Coconut Macaroons

Delicate, chewy, pure sweet coconut.

1 cup white sugar
1½ to 1¾ cups non-instant milk powder
2 cups grated coconut (dry)
2 tablespoons unbleached white flour
2 tablespoons melted butter
1 cup milk

Combine the sugar, milk powder, and coconut in a bowl. Add the flour. Add the butter and milk. The batter should be quite sticky, but not liquid. Add more milk powder if necessary. Drop spoonfuls of the batter on a buttered baking sheet 1½ inches apart. Bake in a 350° oven for 15 to 20 minutes, until the edges are golden brown and the tops are lightly browned. Very gently transfer the cookies to a plate to cool as soon as they are removed from the oven. This recipe makes 2 dozen cookies.

Note: If the centers fall out of the cookies when they are removed from the pan, the batter was too liquid.

Christmas Almond Balls

Little melt-in-your-mouth cookies from Raymond Farm. The dough can also be pressed into a pan and baked in the same way as Scotch shortbreads. For a pretty effect, shape the cookies like crescent moons instead of little balls.

1 cup butter
1 cup light brown sugar
2¼ cups unbleached white flour
¼ teaspoon salt
1⅓ cups ground almonds
3 tablespoons milk or water
confectioner's sugar

Cream the butter and brown sugar. Sift in the flour and the salt. Add the almonds and the milk. Mix well. Chill for 1 hour or more.

Roll into 1-inch balls. Bake in a 300° oven for 20 to 25 minutes. Remove and roll in confectioner's sugar while warm. This recipe makes 4 dozen cookies.

Variations

Substitute hazelnuts or walnuts for almonds.

Honey Variation: Replace the brown sugar with ¾ cup honey; omit the milk.

Speculatius (Holland-Germany)

Speculatius originated in Holland and are now traditional Christmas cookies in Germany, where they are pressed into windmill molds before baking. Here they are rolled out and cut with cookie cutters.

½ cup butter
1½ cups packed brown sugar
½ cup ground almonds
2½ cups whole wheat flour
1 teaspoon baking powder
¼ teaspoon cloves
¼ teaspoon ground ginger
¼ teaspoon mace
1½ teaspoons cinnamon
6 tablespoons milk

Cream the butter and brown sugar together. Beat in the almonds. Add the dry ingredients to the almond mixture. Add the milk and mix well. Chill the dough for at least 1 hour.

Roll out ⅛ inch thick on a floured board. Cut out cookies with the rim of a glass or with cookie cutters and place on a buttered baking sheet. Bake in a 350° oven for 10 to 12 minutes, until golden brown. This recipe makes 4 dozen cookies.

Variation

Honey Variation: Replace the brown sugar with ½ cup each of honey and molasses. Omit the milk.

Lemon Cookies

These may be prepared as rolled or as refrigerator cookies.

½ cup butter
1⅔ cups sugar
2¾ cups unbleached white flour
½ teaspoon baking powder

⅓ to ½ cup milk
1 tablespoon finely grated lemon rind

Cream the butter and sugar. Sift the flour and baking powder into the butter mixture. Add the the milk and lemon rind to make a fairly stiff dough. Chill for at least 1 hour.

Roll out on a floured board ⅛ inch thick. Cut out cookies with the rim of a glass or with cookie cutters and place on a buttered baking sheet. Bake the cookies in a 350° oven for 10 to 12 minutes. Remove the cookies immediately to a plate to cool. Cool thoroughly. Frost with the following glaze.

Lemon Glaze:
1½ cups confectioner's sugar
1 teaspoon finely grated lemon rind
1½ to 2 tablespoons water

Mix together and spread on the cookies. Allow the glaze to dry. Makes about 4 dozen glazed cookies.

Variation

Vegan Variation: Replace the milk in the dough with water.

Gingerbread People

¼ cup butter
½ cup packed brown sugar
½ cup molasses
2¼ cups whole wheat pastry flour
½ teaspoon baking powder
1 teaspoon cinnamon
1 teaspoon ginger
¼ teaspoon salt
3 to 4 tablespoons water

Cream the butter and brown sugar. Beat in the molasses. Mix the dry ingredients and add. Add the water to make a dough that just holds together. Roll into a ball, cover with waxed paper or plastic wrap, and chill in the refrigerator for at least 1 hour.

Sculpt gingerbread people, or roll out the dough ⅛ inch thick on a floured board and cut out the people with a knife or cookie cutter. Cut out a paper pattern and lay it on the dough to guide the cutting, if desired. Punch a hole in the top if the cookies are to be hung from the Christmas tree. Carefully transfer the people to a buttered baking pan and bake in a 350° oven for about 10 minutes.

Cool the cookies thoroughly. To decorate, make a glaze of confectioner's sugar and a few drops of water. Use a thin paintbrush to apply it. Also use the glaze as glue to affix raisins for the eyes and buttons. This recipe makes 8 to 10 large "people."

Gingersnaps

¼ cup butter
1 cup packed brown sugar
¼ cup molasses
2 tablespoons binding powder (page 51)
2 cups whole wheat pastry flour
2 teaspoons soda
1 teaspoon cinnamon
¾ teaspoon ground ginger
¼ teaspoon cloves
½ teaspoon salt
½ cup water
granulated sugar

Cream the butter and sugar. Beat in the molasses. Mix all the dry ingredients ex-

cept the granulated sugar and add to the molasses mixture. Add the water and mix. Roll the dough into 1-inch balls. Roll the balls in the granulated sugar and place on a buttered baking sheet 1½ inches apart. Bake for 8 to 10 minutes in a 350° oven. Move the cookies immediately to a plate to cool and harden. This recipe makes 2½ dozen cookies.

BAR COOKIES

Carob-Nut Brownies

1 cup packed brown sugar
¾ cup unbleached white flour
¾ cup whole wheat flour
2 tablespoons binding powder (page 51)
6 tablespoons carob powder
1½ teaspoons baking powder
¼ teaspoon salt
⅓ cup melted butter or oil
¾ cup water
¾ cup chopped walnuts

Sift the dry ingredients into a bowl. Add the melted butter or oil and the water. Mix until blended. Add the nuts and mix in. Pour into a buttered, floured 9-inch square cake pan. Bake in a 350° oven for 25 to 30 minutes, until done.

Cool thoroughly and cut into squares. This recipe makes about 16 brownies.

Variation

Honey Variation: Replace the sugar with ¾ cup honey; reduce the water to 2 tablespoons.

Scotch Shortbread

Rich and buttery, and very, very easy to make. Use high-quality unsalted butter for best results.

1¼ cups butter (at room temperature)
1 cup light brown sugar
2½ cups unbleached white flour
½ teaspoon salt

Cream the butter and the sugar. Sift in the dry ingredients. Mix until blended. Press evenly into a buttered 10 by 14-inch pan, about ¼ inch thick. Bake in a 300° oven for 20 to 25 minutes. Do not allow the mixture to brown, or it will harden.

Cool thoroughly, and cut into squares.

Fig or Date Bars

Filling:
1½ cups chopped figs or dates, packed
⅔ cup apple juice
½ cup sugar
2 tablespoons lemon juice
Dough:
1¾ cups unbleached white or whole wheat
    flour
½ cup ground nuts
½ cup wheat germ
2 tablespoons binding powder (page 51)
½ teaspoon salt
2 tablespoons brown sugar
⅓ cup melted butter
2 tablespoons milk or water

Simmer the ingredients for the filling, covered, for 10 minutes. Mash to a smooth paste.

Combine all the dry ingredients for the dough in a bowl. Add the melted butter and the milk or water. Mix to a crumbly dough with the fingertips. Press half the dough evenly into a buttered 9-inch square pan. Spread the fruit filling evenly over the dough. Sprinkle the remaining dough over the filling to completely cover it.

Bake in a 400° oven for 20 to 25 minutes, until lightly browned. Cool thoroughly and cut into squares. This recipe makes about 16 bars.

Variation

Honey Variation: Replace the sugar in the filling with ⅓ cup honey and reduce the apple juice to ⅓ cup; replace the sugar in the dough with 1½ tablespoons honey and reduce the milk to 1 tablespoon.

Sesame Squares

¾ cup butter
1 cup packed brown sugar
½ teaspoon baking powder
¼ teaspoon salt
½ cup toasted sesame seeds
1 cup unbleached white or whole wheat
    pastry flour

Cream the butter and the sugar. Add the sesame seeds and the dry ingredients. Press into a buttered large (10 by 14-inch) rectangular pan, ¼ inch thick. Bake in a 350° oven for about 20 minutes. Be careful not to let the mixture burn.

Cool thoroughly and cut into squares.

Variation
Replace the sesame seeds with coarsely chopped toasted sunflower seeds.

Molasses Bars

When prepared with sugar, these are bar cookies. When prepared with honey, they are cakelike.

¼ cup butter
½ cup packed brown sugar
½ cup molasses
1¾ cups whole wheat pastry flour
½ teaspoon cardamom (optional)
¼ teaspoon soda
½ teaspoon finely grated orange rind
1 cup slivered almonds
1 tablespoon water

Cream the butter and the sugar. Beat in the molasses. Mix the dry ingredients and add to the molasses mixture. Add the water and mix well. Mix in the orange rind and the almonds. Press into a buttered 9-inch square pan to ¼ inch deep. Bake for 15 to

20 minutes in a 375° oven, until lightly browned.

Cool thoroughly and cut into 2-by-1-inch rectangles.

Variation

Honey Variation: Replace the sugar with ⅓ cup honey; omit the water. Bake in a 350° oven for 20 to 25 minutes.

Frostings

Frostings are very flexible, and many ingredients can be brought into play to enhance a cake.

First, there are those cakes which need no frosting at all. Quick breads and other fruity cakes can be served plain, or with a light fruit sauce such as applesauce. Whipped cream, sour cream, and hung yogurt may also be served over individual slices of such cakes. A simple procedure is to place a paper doily on an unfrosted cake, sift powdered sugar over it and then carefully remove the doily to leave the lacy pattern traced by the sugar. Dried fruit purees can also be used to give a naturally sweet "non-frosting" frosting.

Spectacular cakes can be made by spreading a rich substance between the layers and then covering the cake with unsweetened whipped cream. Some good fillings are:

dried fruit purees
barfi (spread before it hardens)
halvas
marzipan
praline mixture (while it is soft)
carob fudge, caramel fudge, or date fudge
Also try tucking pieces of sliced fruit between cake layers. Spread a frosting on the cake, and then press in an even layer of sliced bananas, crushed pineapple, pitted cherries, and so forth. Place the second layer on top.

CAKE DECORATIONS

Decorating cakes leaves endless room for creativity—and will surely be appreciated by the viewers (for a minute or two at least).

As a first step, cakes can be baked in different shaped pans and assembled decoratively. For a heart, use one round pan and one square pan of the same size. Cut the round cake in half and arrange as shown in the diagram. For a rabbit, bake three round cakes—two of equal size and one a little smaller. Cut one of the larger cakes in half and arrange as shown in the diagram.

Muffin cups, cast-iron skillets, and pots with oven-proof handles can all be brought into play to produce different shapes and sizes.

To frost a two-layer round cake, apply the frosting with a flat knife or a rubber spatula. Spread an even layer of frosting on the top of one layer. Place the second layer on top of it. Brush away any crumbs on the plate. First frost the sides, applying the frosting in a circular motion and then smoothing by stroking upward. Next, apply the frosting to the top. For a glossy finish, dip the knife in water and lightly run it over the frosting. Always frost cakes with whipped cream at the last minute, or no more than an hour or two before serving, for best results.

To decorate cakes with a pastry tube, first apply a ''base coat'' of frosting, as smoothly and evenly as possible. Allow the frosting to dry. (If using whipped cream, continue the decorating immediately.) The frosting to be used in the pastry tube should be very smooth and spreadable, without any nuts, coconut, or other additions that could jam the tube. Buttercream frosting and stiff whipped cream are the best frostings to use for this purpose. If the designs seem to melt after being applied, the frosting is too thin. If it is impossible to squeeze the frosting through the tube, it is too thick.

Different colored frostings can be used to create designs. Color frostings yellow with saffron, or orange with completely pureed dried apricots. Wash out the pastry bag between applications of different colors. Bright-colored fruit juices, such as cherry juice (or even a tiny bit of beet juice—who's to know?) can also be used in the preparation of frostings.

Canvas pastry bags with detachable nibs are easiest to handle, and are used by professional bakers. Place the desired nib on the bag, then fold the sides of the bag halfway down, as if turning it inside out. Fill with frosting, and unfold the top part of the bag. Now twist the bag shut down to the level of the frosting. Apply the frosting by twisting the bag to squeeze it out with one hand, guiding the nib steadily along the cake with the other hand. With a little experimentation, many designs can be created without any special techniques. For more elaborate cake-decorating, almost every community sponsors cake-decorating classes through continuing education programs or community centers.

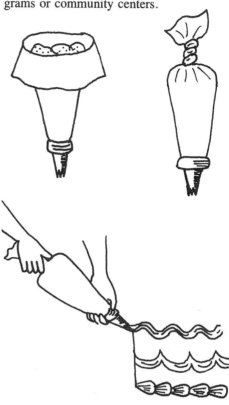

Various fruits and nuts can be used to decorate cakes. Create flowers, borders, and other designs out of fresh sliced fruits, dried sliced fruits, and whole or slivered nuts. Halved pistachios make green leaves, dried apricots can be sliced for orange petals, whole raspberries and halved pitted cherries make red accents, raisins and currants can be used to form designs. Try using golden almonds for petals and designs. Sprinkle grated coconut, ground nuts, seeds, and praliné for backgrounds.

Marzipan can be sculpted into figures and flowers. The marzipan itself can be colored with saffron, or can be painted with thin frostings. Fresh flowers (check to make sure they are a nonpoisonous variety) can be used to garnish cakes or surround cakes on a plate. Also use carob chips and candies to form designs.

FROSTINGS

There are five basic frostings from which many different flavors can be created. They also work quite successfully by themselves. They are buttercream, honey-cream, cream cheese frosting, hung yogurt frosting, and whipped cream. Once these basic frostings are mastered, almost all other frosting flavors are available to the cook.

Buttercream Frosting

We have added non-instant milk powder to the traditional buttercream frosting to give it more body and creaminess.

½ cup butter (at room temperature)
1 pound confectioner's sugar, sifted
½ cup non-instant milk powder
3 to 4 tablespoons milk

Cream the butter with the sugar and milk powder as completely as possible. Beat in the milk until the desired consistency is achieved, adding more milk to make it thinner and less to make it thicker. (The mixture will harden if it sits—thin with milk to the desired texture if this happens.) This recipe makes 2 cups.

Variation
Vegan Variation: Replace the milk with soy or nut milk.

Honey-Cream Frosting

½ cup butter, at room temperature
1 cup honey
1 cup non-instant milk powder

Cream the butter and honey thoroughly. Beat in milk powder to the desired consistency. (Honey-cream frosting hardens rather

quickly—prepare just before applying to the cake.) This recipe makes 2 cups.

Hung Yogurt Frosting

2 cups hung yogurt (page 42)
4 to 6 tablespoons honey

Mix the ingredients thoroughly, adding honey to attain the desired sweetness and consistency. This recipe makes 2 cups.

Variations
For a thicker consistency, add sifted confectioner's sugar instead of honey.
Use shrikhand (page 293) as a frosting.

Cream Cheese Frosting

Cream cheese frosting is quite flexible in its preparation—all's fair that renders the cream cheese spreadable and sweet.

With honey:
2 cups softened cream cheese (2 8-ounce packages)
¼ to ½ cup honey
With sugar:
1¾ cups softened cream cheese
¼ cup milk or cream
1 cup sifted confectioner's sugar

Beat the ingredients together until smooth. This recipe makes 2 cups.

Variation
For a non-sweet frosting for quick breads, mix softened cream cheese with milk to the desired consistency.

Whipped Cream

1 cup (½ pint) heavy cream

Always whip cream just before serving. For best results, chill the bowl and the whisk or eggbeater. Beat the cream briskly with an eggbeater, or whip with a whisk according to the instructions on page 12.

For spooning onto cakes, stop when the cream stands in soft peaks. For a firmer frosting, whip until the mixture stands stiff. Do not proceed any further—it will turn to butter. This recipe makes 2 cups.

Sweeten whipped cream, if desired, with 2 tablespoons honey or 3 to 4 tablespoons confectioner's sugar, *after* the cream has been whipped.

Lemon or Orange Frosting

Add 2 tablespoons finely grated orange rind or lemon rind to any of the preceding frostings except whipped cream.

Coffee Frosting

Add 2 teaspoons grain coffee powder to buttercream, honey-cream, or sweetened whipped cream frostings.

Mocha Frosting

Add 2 teaspoons grain coffee powder and a little prepared carob beverage powder (usually mixed with milk) to buttercream, honey-cream, or sweetened whipped cream frostings.

Coconut Frosting

Mix the desired amount of coconut into one of the preceding frostings, or frost the cake with any frosting and then sprinkle grated coconut all over it and press in lightly.

Nut or Granola Frosting

Frost a cake with one of the base frostings and sprinkle ground nuts, granola cereal, or praliné all over it, and press in lightly.

Apricot Frosting

A naturally sweet frosting with a delicate flavor and color. The proportions of the fruit to the cream cheese or hung yogurt can be altered to give a more distinct flavor, if desired.

¾ cup dried apricot puree (page 235)
1⅔ cups softened cream cheese or hung yogurt

Mix the ingredients together well. Add a little honey if a sweeter frosting is desired. This recipe makes 2 cups.

Variation
Replace the apricot puree with date puree.

Banana-Date or Fig Frosting

1 cup mashed ripe bananas
⅓ cup melted butter or ghee
⅓ cup pitted dates or figs, packed
1 to 1½ cups non-instant milk powder
3 tablespoons honey
1 teaspoon cinnamon

Combine all the ingredients in a blender until smooth, using 1 cup of the milk powder. Chill to harden. If the frosting is still not thick enough, beat in milk powder until the desired thickness is achieved.

Date Frosting

1½ cups chopped, pitted dates, packed
½ cup fruit juice or water
⅓ cup butter
½ cup honey
1½ cups non-instant milk powder

Combine the dates, water or juice, and butter in a saucepan. Simmer, covered, until the dates are soft and the mixture is thick, about 10 to 15 minutes. Puree in the blender with the honey, and chill. Beat in milk powder until the desired consistency is achieved. This recipe makes about 2 cups.

Carob Fudge Frosting

Prepare this frosting in advance, as it can take several hours to cool and thicken.

3 cups sugar, white or packed brown
⅓ cup carob powder
⅓ cup butter
1 cup milk or light cream

Combine all the ingredients in a saucepan. Bring to a boil. Boil until the mixture reaches the soft ball stage—about 5 minutes. Cool the mixture at room temperature until it is thick enough to spread. Beat, and spread on a thoroughly cooled cake. Keep the frosted cake in the refrigerator until ready to serve. This recipe makes a little over 2 cups.

Caramel Frosting

2 cups caramel sauce (page 287)
confectioner's sugar
non-instant milk powder

Chill the caramel sauce. Beat in equal amounts of confectioner's sugar and milk powder until the mixture is of the desired consistency. (No precise proportions can be given because caramel sauce tends to be different from one time to the next, depending on its preparation.) Beat until creamy. Try sprinkling toasted chopped cashews on a cake covered with caramel frosting. This recipe makes 2 cups.

Nut-Crunch Topping for Tea Cakes

1 cup chopped nuts
½ cup packed dark brown sugar
2 tablespoons melted butter

Mix all the ingredients together. Gently sprinkle on a cake 15 minutes before the baking is completed.

Dessert Sauces and Fruit Sauces

Fresh Fruit Sauce

The only sauce one needs to know for ice creams and fruit salads—pure, fresh fruit.

2 cups pitted cherries, berries, sliced strawberries, finely cut peaches, apricots, mangoes, or peeled persimmons (at least 2 fruits combined)
2 tablespoons honey *or* 3 tablespoons sugar
2 to 3 tablespoons lemon juice

Puree all the ingredients in a blender. The best combinations are made from a mixture of berries with sliced fruit. Try raspberries and peaches for the classic Melba combination. This recipe makes 1½ cups.

Applesauce

4 cups cored, sliced apples, peeled or unpeeled
⅓ cup raisins
½ to 1 teaspoon cinnamon
sugar or honey to taste

Place the apples in a saucepan, in ½ inch of water. Simmer, covered, about 15 to 20 minutes, until the apples are soft. Mash, or puree in the blender, until the apples are smooth. Add raisins, cinnamon, and sweetening to taste. This recipe makes about 2 cups.

Variation

Add cranberries, pears, or other fruits.

Pear Sauce

6 ripe pears, cut in small pieces, peeled or unpeeled

¼ cup water
½ teaspoon cinnamon
¼ teaspoon ground ginger
2 tablespoons brown sugar *or* 1 tablespoon honey

Place the pears and the water in a saucepan. Simmer, covered, until soft—about 30 minutes. Drain off the water. Add the cinnamon, ginger, and the sugar or honey. Mash, or puree in a blender. This recipe makes about 3 cups.

Banana Sauce

Simple ingredients, prepared in 5 minutes— yet this sauce has a special flavor that seems to speak of some secret ingredient. It is great over ice cream.

¼ cup ghee or butter
2 cups mashed bananas
¼ cup honey
2 tablespoons lemon juice
1 teaspoon cinnamon

Melt the butter or ghee in a skillet. Add the bananas and sauté for 5 minutes, mashing them as you cook. Sprinkle the lemon juice over the bananas while cooking. When the bananas are tender, remove from the heat and cool for a few minutes. Add the

cinnamon and honey, and mix well. This recipe makes 2 cups.

Apricot, Peach, or Mango Sauce

3 cups chopped and crushed ripe apricots, peaches, or peeled mangoes
¼ cup water
2 tablespoons lemon juice
¼ to ½ cup sugar *or* 3 to 6 tablespoons honey

Steam the fruit in the water, covered, for about 10 to 15 minutes, until very soft. Add the lemon juice and sugar or honey to taste. Puree in a food mill or a blender. This recipe makes about 1½ cups.

Variation

Add a tiny amount of cardamom or cinnamon.

Berry or Cherry Sauce

A thickened sauce that becomes somewhat glossy and firm if chilled, making it a nice topping for cheesecake.

1½ cups whole blueberries, blackberries, raspberries, or sliced strawberries, or halved and pitted cherries
½ cup water
3 to 4 tablespoons sugar
1 tablespoon lemon juice
1 tablespoon arrowroot or cornstarch

Steam the berries or cherries in the water, covered, for 10 minutes, until tender. Add the sugar and lemon juice. Dissolve the cornstarch or arrowroot in 2 tablespoons water. Add to the sauce and simmer, stirring, for a few minutes until thickened.

Serve over ice cream, blintzes, or pancakes. This recipe makes 1½ cups.

Variation

Replace the sugar with 2 to 3 tablespoons honey.

Cranberry Sauce

Cranberry sauce is served as an accompaniment to main dishes. Try serving it with nut or bean loaves, or with gluten cutlets on Thanksgiving.

1½ cups sugar
1½ cups water or part orange juice
1 teaspoon finely grated orange rind
1 pound (4 cups) cranberries

Combine the sugar, water, and orange rind in a saucepan. Boil for 5 minutes. Add the cranberries and return to a boil for 5 to 7 minutes, until the skins pop and the berries are tender.

Chill thoroughly so that the sauce will jell slightly. This recipe makes about 3½ cups.

Honey-Cranberry Sauce

The combination of honey and cranberries tastes slightly bitter.

1 cup honey
1 cup water or part orange juice
1 teaspoon finely grated orange rind
1 pound (4 cups) cranberries

Bring the water to a boil. Add the cranberries and orange rind. Cover and simmer for 5 to 7 minutes, until the cranberries are tender. Remove from the heat and cool for a few minutes. Add the honey. This recipe makes about 3½ cups.

Rhubarb Sauce

Rhubarb sauce is delicious plain or over ice cream.

8 cups rhubarb, cut in 1-inch pieces
¼ cup water
1½ cups sugar

Place the rhubarb in a saucepan with the water. Cover and simmer for 15 minutes.

Add the sugar and simmer for 5 minutes more. This recipe makes 4½ cups.

Variation

Honey Variation: Place the rhubarb in the top of a double boiler and cook, without water, for 20 minutes, until tender. Remove from the heat, cool a few minutes, and stir in ¾ cup honey. The flavor of rhubarb and honey together is somewhat bitter.

Orange Sauce

3 tablespoons butter
1½ tablespoons cornstarch
½ cup water
1 cup orange juice
½ teaspoon finely grated orange rind
2 tablespoons sugar
pinch salt

Melt the butter in a saucepan. Mix the cornstarch into the water until smooth. Add to the butter along with the orange juice, orange rind, and sugar. Bring to a simmer, stirring constantly with a whisk. Simmer for a few minutes until thickened. Add a pinch of salt.

Serve warm over ice cream, crepes, or pancakes. If chilled, the sauce will be like a light pudding. This recipe makes 1½ cups.

Variation

Honey Variation: Replace the sugar with 1½ tablespoons honey.

Lemon or Lime Sauce

1½ tablespoons cornstarch
1¼ cups water
¼ cup lemon or lime juice
1 teaspoon finely grated lemon or lime rind
3 tablespoons butter
⅔ cup sugar
pinch salt

Dissolve the cornstarch in ¼ cup of the water. Combine all the ingredients in a saucepan. Bring to a simmer, stirring constantly with a whisk. Simmer for a few minutes until the butter is melted and the mixture is thick.

Serve over ice cream, pancakes, or crepes. If the sauce is chilled it will be like a light pudding. This recipe makes 1½ cups.

Variation

Honey Variation: Replace the sugar with ⅓ cup plus 1 tablespoon honey; add ½ tablespoon cornstarch.

Raisin Sauce

¾ cup seedless raisins
3 tablespoons packed brown sugar
2 tablespoons butter
¼ cup lemon juice
1½ cups water
1½ tablespoons cornstarch

Combine the raisins, sugar, butter, lemon juice, and 1¼ cups of the water in a saucepan and bring to a boil. Cover, reduce heat, and simmer for 20 minutes.

Mix the cornstarch with the remaining ¼ cup of water. Stir into the mixture and simmer, stirring, until the sauce thickens. Puree in a blender if desired.

Serve warm over puddings and ice cream. This recipe makes about 2 cups.

Variation

Honey Variation: Replace the sugar with 2 tablespoons honey. Add the honey after the mixture is cooked and has cooled for a few minutes.

Carob Sauce

¾ cup water
1 cup packed brown sugar
⅓ cup carob powder
2 tablespoons butter
⅓ cup milk powder

Combine the water, brown sugar, carob powder, and butter in a saucepan. Bring to a boil. Reduce the heat and simmer for 5 minutes, stirring frequently.

Cool to lukewarm and beat in the milk powder. Serve warm or cold over ice cream or puddings, or use to prepare carob beverages. This recipe makes about 1½ cups.

Variation

Honey Variation: Replace the sugar with ⅔ cup honey. If the sauce is too thin, thicken it by beating in more milk powder.

Caramel Sauce

Preparing caramel sauce is an adventure. It looks as if it is not going to come out right—the butter separates from the sugar, the sugar masses together in the cream—and then, at the very last moment, it is transformed into a smooth, creamy sauce. Try it over toasted almond ice cream.

⅓ cup ghee or butter
2 cups white sugar
1 cup heavy cream

Melt the butter in a saucepan with high sides. Add the sugar. Cook on a medium heat, stirring constantly, until the sugar turns brown. (The butter will separate from the sugar at this point.) Remove from the heat for a few minutes. Pour in the cream, and stand back. The cream will bubble up and the sugar will turn into a solid mass. When the bubbling subsides, return the mixture to a low heat. Stir and simmer about 5 minutes, until the sugar melts to form a smooth sauce. Strain the sauce to remove the few chunks of hardened sugar that inevitably remain in the bottom of the pot (the chunks can be sprinkled on ice cream like candy).

Serve the sauce warm over ice cream, puddings, or crepes. This recipe makes 2 cups.

Quick Caramel Sauce

2 cups packed dark brown sugar
1 cup cream (heavy or light)
2 tablespoons butter

Bring the ingredients to a boil. Boil for 5 minutes. This recipe makes 2½ cups. (Do *not* use this sauce to make Caramel Frosting or Caramel Fudge Balls.)

Caramel Syrup

¾ cup packed dark brown sugar
2 teaspoons butter
¼ cup water.

Bring all the ingredients to a boil. Boil to the soft ball stage (about 5 minutes).

Use for preparing caramel popcorn, apples, and candies. This recipe makes ½ cup.

Puddings

CORNSTARCH OR ARROWROOT PUDDINGS

Puddings thickened with arrowroot or cornstarch thicken somewhat during cooking, and then complete their thickening in the refrigerator. They may be prepared with anything from heavy cream to nonfat milk to a non-dairy milk, such as soy milk. In

any case, mix the arrowroot or cornstarch thoroughly with part of the milk, until

smooth, before adding to the entire mixture. The pudding base (milk, cornstarch or arrowroot, and sugar) may be combined until smooth in a blender before cooking.

Puddings may be prepared in a saucepan or, for the cautious or those who do not wish to stir the mixture constantly, in a double boiler. A whisk is a good tool for stirring the puddings and preventing lumps.

Cornstarch and arrowroot-thickened puddings can be used as fillings for cream pies, or they can be frozen like ice cream.

Carob Pudding

5 tablespoons arrowroot or cornstarch
3½ cups milk
¼ cup carob powder
¾ cup packed brown sugar
2 tablespoons butter

Mix the cornstarch or arrowroot with ½ cup of the milk until smooth. Place in a saucepan with the remaining ingredients. Bring the mixture to a simmer, stirring constantly with a whisk. Simmer until the mixture thickens.

Pour into individual bowls or a large bowl. Chill to thicken. Serve with whipped cream, if desired. This recipe makes 4 cups.

Variations

Honey Variation: Replace the brown sugar with ½ cup honey.

Mexican Carob Pudding: Add 1 teaspoon cinnamon to carob pudding.

Banana Pudding

2½ cups milk
¾ cup sugar
2 tablespoons butter
2 cups mashed ripe bananas
3½ tablespoons arrowroot or cornstarch
⅛ teaspoon salt

Combine all the ingredients in a blender, or beat well. Pour into a saucepan and bring to a simmer, stirring constantly with a whisk. Simmer until thickened. Pour into individual bowls and chill.

Serve with whipped cream, if desired. This recipe makes 5 cups.

Variations

Honey Variation: Replace the sugar with ½ cup honey; reduce the milk to 2¼ cups.

Add a little cinnamon or cardamom.

Add chopped dates or dried apricots when heating the mixture.

Butterscotch-Coconut Pudding

5 tablespoons arrowroot or cornstarch
3½ cups milk
1⅓ cups packed dark brown sugar
1 tablespoon blackstrap molasses
1 cup grated toasted coconut
2 tablespoons butter

whipped cream (optional)
chopped roasted cashews (optional)

Mix the cornstarch with ½ cup of the milk. Pour into a saucepan with the remaining ingredients. Heat, stirring constantly with a whisk, to a simmer. Simmer until thickened. Pour into cups and chill.

Serve with whipped cream, if desired, sprinkled with chopped roasted cashews. This recipe makes 5 cups.

See Orange Sauce and Lemon or Lime Sauce (page 286) for other cornstarch-thickened puddings.

STEAMED PUDDINGS

Steamed puddings are cooked slowly in the oven. The pudding is placed in a mold, and the mold is placed in a pan of boiling water. They are very festive, and ideal for holidays. Puddings may be steamed in a pudding mold or in a tight-lidded casserole dish. Butter the mold or dish very well so that the pudding can be unmolded easily.

Steamed Date Pudding

⅓ cup butter
1 cup packed brown sugar
¼ cup toasted wheat germ
1 cup whole wheat pastry flour
1½ teaspoons baking powder
½ teaspoon soda
1 cup milk
1 cup pitted chopped dates, packed
1 cup chopped walnuts (optional)

Cream the butter and brown sugar. Add the wheat germ. Sift the dry ingredients into the mixture. Add the milk and mix. Stir in the dates and nuts. Place in a well-buttered 1-quart mold or casserole dish. Cover.

Place the mold in a pan. Pour in boiling water until it is ⅓ of the way up the sides of the mold. Place in a 350° oven and steam for 2 hours, replacing the water occasionally as it evaporates.

Carefully unmold onto a plate. Serve hot, with heavy cream. This recipe makes 4 to 6 servings.

Variation

Vegan Variation: Replace the milk with fruit juice or soy milk.

Christmas Pudding

1½ cups grated carrots
1 cup raisins
1½ cups grated apples
1¼ cups whole wheat pastry flour
¾ cup packed brown sugar
½ teaspoon cinnamon
pinch cloves
⅛ teaspoon nutmeg
1½ teaspoons baking powder
2 tablespoons binding powder (page 51)
½ teaspoon salt

Place the carrots, raisins, and apples in a bowl. Sift in the dry ingredients. Mix well. Place in a well-buttered 1-quart mold or casserole dish. Cover. Place in a pan with boiling water reaching ⅓ of the way up the sides of the mold. Carefully place in a 350° oven. Steam for 1½ hours, replenishing the water occasionally as it evaporates.

Carefully remove the pudding from the pan, and unmold on a plate. Serve with caramel sauce or with heavy cream. This recipe makes 4 to 6 servings.

BAKED PUDDINGS

Indian Pudding (USA)

Indian pudding is a New England specialty, prepared in many variations from the basic ingredients of cornmeal and molasses.

½ cup cornmeal
5 cups milk
⅓ cup molasses
⅓ cup packed brown sugar
⅔ cup raisins
1½ teaspoons cinnamon
½ teaspoon ground ginger
2 tablespoons butter

Mix the cornmeal with the milk. Pour into a saucepan or a double boiler and bring to a boil, stirring constantly. Reduce the heat and simmer, stirring constantly, for 15 minutes (if using a double boiler, stir frequently, but not constantly), until somewhat thickened. Add the molasses and stir for 2 to 3 minutes more. Add the remaining ingredients and stir until the butter is melted. Place in a buttered baking dish. Bake in a 350° oven for about 1 hour, until a dark brown skin has formed on the pudding.

Serve hot with heavy cream or ice cream. This recipe makes 6 servings.

Variations

Honey Variation: Replace the brown sugar with ¼ cup honey or with ¼ cup molasses.

Vegan Variation: Replace the milk with soy milk or water.

Bread Pudding

Use whole grain bread for a fuller flavor.

4 cups cubed bread
3 cups milk or half-and-half
1 medium apple, chopped
¼ cup melted butter
¼ cup chopped dates
¼ cup raisins
1 teaspoon cinnamon
1 cup packed brown sugar

Place the bread in a bowl. Pour the milk over it and soak for 15 minutes. Add the remaining ingredients to the bread mixture and place in a buttered baking dish. Place the baking dish in a pan filled with boiling water. Bake for 45 minutes in a 350° oven.

Serve warm, with cream if desired. This recipe makes 4 to 6 servings.

Variations

Honey Variation: Replace the brown sugar with ⅔ cup honey, and reduce the milk to 2⅔ cups.

Vegan Variation: Replace the milk with soy milk.

Baked Rice Pudding

Rice is a wonderful medium for puddings. Use short-grain rice, brown or white, for best results. This is a light, fruit-flavored version of the old classic.

3 cups milk
⅓ cup pitted dates
¾ cup dark brown sugar, packed
½ teaspoon cinnamon
pinch nutmeg
2 cups cooked rice
⅓ cup raisins

Mix the milk, dates, sugar, and spices in a blender until smooth. Place the rice and raisins in a buttered baking dish. Add the milk mixture and stir gently. Bake in a 350° oven for about 1 hour, until a light-brown skin has formed on the top.

Serve warm or cold. This recipe makes 4 to 6 servings.

Variations

Blend 1 ripe banana into the milk before adding to the rice.

Replace part of the milk with cream.

Sprinkle the cinnamon on the top instead of mixing it in.

Honey Variation: Replace the sugar with ½ cup honey; reduce the milk to 2⅔ cups.

Vegan Variation: Replace the milk with soy milk.

Simple Rice Pudding

Here is the simple "milk rice" of Europe. In Yugoslavia a rice pudding such as this, mixed with sweet fruits, is offered to guests as a welcome. (Barley may be substituted for rice; for barley, use the proportions given for brown rice.)

1½ cups water (use 2¼ cups for brown rice)
¾ cup short-grained rice
4 cups milk
1 cup sugar (white or light brown)
½ teaspoon cinnamon
⅓ cup raisins

Bring the water to a boil. Add the rice, cover, and simmer on a low heat until all the water is absorbed. Add 1 cup of milk. Simmer until it is absorbed. Repeat this procedure twice, until 3 cups of milk have been used. Add the remaining cup of milk and the sugar, cinnamon, and raisins. Simmer until the mixture is thick. Serve warm or cold. This recipe makes 6 servings.

Variations

Replace 1 cup of the milk with cream.

Add fresh sliced fruits after the pudding has been cooked and cooled.

Honey Variation: Replace the sugar with ¾ cup honey; reduce the milk to 3½ cups.

Vegan Variation: Replace the milk with soy milk.

Khir (India)

A rich, sweet, spiced rice pudding.

¾ cup uncooked rice
⅛ teaspoon saffron
5½ cups milk (6½ cups for brown rice)
1 cup cream
⅔ cup sugar
¼ teaspoon cinnamon
¼ teaspoon cardamom

⅛ teaspoon ground ginger
few drops rosewater

Combine the rice, saffron and 1½ cups of the milk (2¼ cups for brown rice) in a saucepan. Simmer, stirring frequently, until the milk is absorbed. Add the milk and the cream one cup at a time, simmering until one cup is absorbed before adding the next one. With the last addition of milk, add the sugar, cinnamon, cardamom, and ginger. Simmer until a thick sauce has formed. Remove from the heat and beat with a whisk to smooth out the mixture a little. Beat in a few drops of rosewater.

Pour into individual cups and chill. If desired, sprinkle a few chopped pistachios on top of each serving. This recipe makes about 3 cups.

Variations

Add chopped dates or raisins to the mixture.

Honey Variation: Replace the sugar with ½ cup honey; add it after the pudding has been cooked, and has cooled for a few minutes.

Vegan Variation: Replace the milk with soy milk.

Danish Rice Pudding (Denmark)

1½ cups cooked, cooled rice
3 tablespoons honey *or* ¼ cup sugar
⅓ cup blanched slivered almonds
¼ cup raisins
¼ teaspoon ground ginger
¼ teaspoon cardamom
1 fruit (apple, banana, pear, peach, mango, etc.), cut in small pieces
1 cup heavy cream

Combine the rice with the honey or sugar, almonds, raisins, spices, and fruit. Whip the cream until stiff and fold into the rice mixture.

Chill thoroughly before serving. This recipe makes 4 to 6 servings.

Variation

Omit the raisins and serve with raisin sauce (page 287).

Orange Rice (Sweden)

The oranges give the rice a very special sweet flavor. Tangerines also work very well in this dish.

⅔ cups sugar
3 or 4 oranges
1½ cups cooked, cooled rice
1 cup heavy cream

Peel and section the oranges. Remove and discard as much of the white portion as possible. Cut the sections into small pieces. Mix with the sugar and chill for 1 hour in the refrigerator (do not skip this step—it allows the orange flavor to permeate the sugar). Mix the oranges into the rice. Whip the cream until stiff and fold into the rice mixture.

Chill before serving. This recipe makes 4 to 6 servings.

Honey Variation: Replace the sugar with ⅓ cup honey.

Variations

Replace the oranges with cubed pineapple.

Tapioca

1 cup pearl tapioca
4 cups milk
⅓ cup sugar *or* ¼ cup honey
1 cup fruit sauce
1 teaspoon finely grated lemon rind
1 tablespoon lemon juice

Soak the tapioca overnight in 2 cups of the milk, in the refrigerator.

Place in a double boiler with the remaining milk. Simmer, stirring frequently, until the mixture is thick, for 1 hour or more. Add the sugar or honey, the fruit sauce, and the lemon rind. Cool the mixture. Add the lemon juice.

Serve at room temperature or chilled. This recipe makes 6 servings.

Variations

Add sliced fresh fruit or fresh berries.

For a lighter texture, fold in whipped cream after the mixture is cool.

Shrikhand (India)

3 cups hung yogurt (see page 42)
⅛ teaspoon saffron, soaked in ⅓ cup hot water
½ cup honey
few drops rosewater

Mix all the ingredients together gently. Place in small cups or bowls and chill. This recipe makes 4 servings.

Candy

The cooking term used most often in candymaking is the "soft ball stage." The soft ball stage is the point at which sugar has reached a temperature between 234°

and 240° F. and forms a syrup that will harden when cooled. The syrup reaches the soft ball stage after about 5 to 7 minutes of boiling. The surface will usually have a mixture of large and small bubbles. To make the soft ball test, drop a little of the syrup into a cup of cold water. The drops will hold their shape instead of dispersing in the water. They will feel rubbery to the touch. The drops may not hold the perfect shape of balls, but there will be an obvious difference from a syrup that simply dissolves in the water.

SIMPLE CANDIES

Serve the following foods as candies:

sweetened nut butter
dried fruits
dried fruit puree (grinder type), rolled in ground nuts or dried grated coconut
sweetened cream cheese, formed into balls and rolled in ground nuts or coconut
mixtures of raisins, nuts, sunflower seeds, and pumpkin seeds

Stuffed Dates

Slit dates lengthwise and carefully remove the pits. Replace the pits with a single blanched almond, a dab of marzipan, or cream cheese. Roll the dates in dried grated coconut.

Bliss Balls

Bliss balls are quite flexible—mixtures of dried fruits, nuts, and coconut ground to a paste and rolled into balls. A meat grinder does the best job of mixing and grinding the ingredients, but a small electric grinder, and sometimes a blender, can be used. Here are two versions of the candy:

Bliss Balls #1
½ cup raisins
½ cup pitted dates or figs
½ cup nuts
¼ cup sunflower seeds
¼ cup grated coconut
½ banana, for a soft candy (optional)

Grind all the ingredients to a smooth paste. Roll into balls and roll the balls in grated coconut. (A little oil on the hands helps in rolling the balls.) This recipe makes 16 to 20 balls.

Bliss Balls #2
½ cup non-instant milk powder
¼ cup chopped nuts
¾ cup pitted dates
¼ cup grated coconut
¼ cup honey
3 tablespoons butter

Grind all the ingredients together. Roll into balls and roll the balls in grated coconut. This recipe makes about 20 balls.

Nut Brittle

The secret of preparing nut brittle is to remove the mixture from the heat the moment the sugar melts, and spread it on the tray with lightning speed.

1½ cups white or light brown sugar
1½ cups coarsely chopped nuts, raw or
    roasted

Place the sugar in a saucepan on a medium heat. Stir constantly until the sugar melts. Be careful not to burn it. Add the nuts, remove from the heat, and immediately spread on a large (9 by 12-inch) buttered pan with the back of a wooden spoon. Allow the mixture to harden. Break into pieces.

Note: The saucepan will look impossible to clean, but a little soaking in hot water will easily remove the sugar residue.

Variations

Sesame Brittle: Replace the nuts in nut brittle with 1 cup sesame seeds. (Unhulled sesame seeds—the brown type—are occasionally bitter in this dish. Try to use the white, hulled sesame seeds.)

Praliné: Smash nut brittle to a coarse powder and use to decorate cakes and sprinkle on ice cream.

Marzipan

Marzipan is great for sculpting into figures and flowers for cake decorations. It also can be used as a rich filling between the layers of cakes.

2 cups blanched almonds
¾ cup confectioner's sugar
1 tablespoon lemon juice
¼ cup non-instant milk powder
few drops rosewater
2 to 3 tablespoons water

Grind the almonds to a completely smooth paste. Mix the paste and the other ingredients together.

For candy, form into balls. Roll in grated coconut, if desired. This recipe makes about 1¾ cups.

Variation

Honey Variation: Replace the sugar with ⅓ cup honey; omit the water.

Barfi (Long-cooking) (India)

A rich milk candy, made from khoa, or boiled-down milk. The quick version follows this recipe, but try this traditional method of preparation at least once for its superior flavor.

½ gallon whole milk
⅔ cup sugar
2 tablespoons water
¼ teaspoon cardamom
few drops rosewater
⅓ cup chopped almonds or pistachios
⅓ cup grated coconut (optional)

To prepare the khoa, bring the milk to a boil, stirring frequently. Boil on a medium-high heat for 1½ to 2 hours, stirring frequently, and toward the end constantly, until the mixture forms a very thick paste that pulls slightly away from the sides of the pan. Cool.

Mix the sugar, water, and cardamom together. Boil to the soft ball stage. Add the sugar syrup to the khoa. Return the mixture to the stove and cook for about 10 more minutes, stirring constantly, until very thick. Add the rosewater. Pour into a buttered 9-inch square pan. Sprinkle with the nuts and, if desired, the coconut. Chill until very firm. Cut into small squares. Makes 25 squares.

Note: For those accustomed to quick barfi, this isn't quite as firm.

Barfi (Quick-cooking)

Quick barfi is quite good, and as the name implies, quickly prepared. Try to use fresh, non-instant milk powder. The milk powder sometimes has a faintly bitter quality, which must be masked by the large quantity of nuts in the recipe and the addition of dried fruit.

⅓ cup butter or ghee
¾ cup sugar
¾ cup milk or part cream
¼ teaspoon cardamom
4 to 4½ cups non-instant milk powder
1 cup chopped almonds, pistachios, or roasted cashews
optional additions: raisins, chopped dates, chopped dried pineapple, grated coconut

Melt the butter or ghee in a saucepan. Add the sugar and mix. Remove from the heat. Add the milk and cardamom. Gradually beat in the milk powder, being careful not to cause lumps. Add the nuts and any other desired additions.

Spread the mixture in a buttered 9-inch square pan. Chill to harden. Cut into small squares. Makes 25 squares.

Variations

Replace the milk with cream.

Decorate the top with dried fruits and nuts.

Add saffron soaked in a little hot water to the mixture.

Honey Variation: Replace the sugar with ½ cup honey; reduce the milk to ⅓ cup.

Carob Fudge

The most important part of fudgemaking is to be sure that the mixture reaches the soft ball stage, so that it will harden properly when cooled.

4 cups packed dark brown sugar
⅔ cup carob powder
¼ cup butter
1⅓ cups milk or cream
1 cup chopped nuts (optional)

Combine all the ingredients except the nuts in a saucepan. Bring to a boil. Boil until the mixture reaches the soft ball stage, about 5 to 7 minutes. Remove from the heat. Cool to lukewarm without stirring or handling. Beat until creamy, then beat in the nuts. Pour into a buttered 9-inch square pan. Chill. Cut into 25 fudge squares.

Date Fudge Balls

1½ cups chopped pitted dates, packed
⅓ cup butter
½ cup water
2½ cups non-instant milk powder
½ cup honey
coconut

Combine the dates, butter, and water in a saucepan. Simmer, covered, for 10 minutes.

Puree the date mixture and honey in a blender. Place in a bowl and beat in the milk powder. Chill the mixture. Roll into balls with oiled hands. Roll the balls in the coconut. This recipe makes 20 to 25 fudge balls.

Caramel Fudge Balls

Try rolling these in roasted ground cashews. Exact proportions cannot be given, as caramel sauce tends to vary slightly in consistency each time it is made.

2 cups caramel sauce (page 287)
1 to 1½ cups non-instant milk powder
1 to 1½ cups confectioner's sugar
¾ cup chopped nuts
grated coconut
ground nuts

Chill the caramel sauce. Beat in milk powder and confectioner's sugar until the mixture is stiff enough to hold its shape. Add the nuts. Roll into balls with oiled hands. Roll the balls in grated coconut and ground nuts. Chill. Makes 20 to 25 balls.

Tahini Fudge

For real tahini lovers only. The proportions may need to be altered slightly, due to the different consistencies of tahini.

¾ cup tahini
2 cups non-instant milk powder
¼ cup honey
¼ cup milk

Beat all the ingredients together thoroughly. Spread ¼ inch thick in a buttered 8-inch square pan. Chill to harden. If the mixture is too thin, add more milk powder. Cut into tiny squares. Makes 25 fudge squares.

HALVA

Halvas are a cross between a pudding and a candy. They are found in different forms throughout the Middle East and India. The following halvas are from India. On special occasions they are coated with gold or silver leaf—finely powdered edible gold or silver pressed into a foil, sometimes available in Indian specialty stores.

Farina Halva (India)

¼ cup ghee or butter
¾ cup farina (cream of wheat)
2 cups water or milk
⅛ teaspoon saffron soaked in ¼ cup hot water
¾ cup sugar
½ teaspoon cinnamon
½ teaspoon cardamom
⅓ cup golden raisins
few drops rosewater (optional)

Melt the ghee or butter in a saucepan. Add the farina and fry slowly, stirring constantly, for about 10 minutes, until slightly darkened. Add the water or milk and the saffron water. Beat well. Add the sugar, cinnamon, and cardamom. Cook until very thick, stirring constantly. Remove from the heat. Mix in the raisins and, if desired, the rosewater.

Mound on a plate and serve warm. Makes 6 servings. Halva can also be spread in a buttered rectangular pan, chilled to harden, and cut into squares.

Variations

Add chopped almonds or pistachios.

Honey Variation: Replace the sugar with ½ cup honey.

Nut Halva (India)

Prepare nut halva from roasted almonds, cashews, or, for a beautiful color, from blanched, peeled pistachios.

1 cup nuts
2 cups milk
1 cup sugar

Combine the nuts and milk in a blender until smooth, or grind the nuts and add them to the milk. Pour into a saucepan. Bring to a boil. Add the sugar. Simmer, stirring constantly, for about 30 minutes, until very thick. Pour into a buttered tray and chill until firm. Makes 4 to 6 servings.

Variation

Honey Variation: Replace the sugar with ¾ cup honey, and add it after the mixture has been cooked until thick. Continue cooking until the mixture thickens again.

Vegan Variation: Replace the milk with soy milk.

Coconut Halva (India)

This takes time, but the result is worth it.

½ cup ghee or butter
1 cup grated coconut
4 cups milk
1 cup heavy cream
¾ cup sugar

¼ to ½ teaspoon ground cardamom
few drops rosewater
chopped pistachios (optional)

Melt the butter in a large saucepan. Add the coconut and cook on a medium heat, stirring constantly, for about 5 minutes. Add the milk and the cream. Bring to a boil, stirring constantly. Add the sugar. Reduce the heat to a low boil, and cook for 1½ to 2 hours, stirring frequently until the mixture has the texture of a very thick pudding. Stir constantly during the last part of the cooking, when the mixture is quite thick, to avoid scorching.

Add the cardamom and rosewater, and pour into a buttered 9-inch square pan. Sprinkle with pistachios, if desired. Chill until firm. Makes 4 to 6 servings.

Variations

Add raisins with the rosewater and cardamom.

Honey Variation: Replace the sugar with ½ cup honey, and add it when the mixture is very thick. Continue cooking until it thickens again.

Carrot Halva

After it has been tried once, carrot halva becomes a very popular sweet. The bright orange color makes it particularly attractive. The contrast of the orange with a garnish of green chopped pistachios and gold foil is very special.

½ cup ghee or butter
3 cups finely grated carrots
4 cups milk
1 cup sugar
¼ to ½ teaspoon cardamom
few drops rosewater
chopped pistachios (optional)

Melt the ghee or butter in a saucepan. Add the carrots and cook, stirring constantly, for 10 minutes, until the carrots are slightly mushy. Add the milk and sugar. Bring to a boil, stirring constantly. Reduce the heat to a low boil and cook for 1½ to 2 hours, stirring frequently, until the mixture is very thick. Stir constantly toward the end of the cooking when the mixture is thick, to avoid scorching.

Add the cardamom and rosewater. Mound on a plate. Decorate with chopped pistachios. This recipe makes 6 to 8 servings.

Variations

Replace 1 cup of the milk with cream.

Honey Variation: Replace the sugar with ¾ cup honey, and add after the mixture is very thick. Continue cooking until it thickens again.

Louisiana Pralines (USA)

A famous candy from the South, sold in New Orleans.

1 cup white sugar
1 cup packed dark brown sugar
1 cup heavy cream
2 cups coarsely chopped pecans

Combine the sugars and cream in a saucepan. Bring to a boil, stirring constantly. Boil for about 5 to 7 minutes, to the soft ball stage. Remove from the heat and cool to lukewarm. Beat until creamy. Add the nuts. When cool enough to shape, form 1½-inch patties. Place on a buttered tray to cool and harden. This recipe makes about 20 pralines.

Variation

Replace the pecans with chopped walnuts or blanched and roasted chopped almonds—not authentic, but good.

Mysore Pak (India)

A creamy, fudgelike candy that is high in protein, due to its chick-pea flour base.

1 cup sugar
⅓ cup water
1½ cups melted ghee or butter
¾ cup chick-pea flour
⅛ teaspoon cardamom
slivered nuts (optional)

Boil the sugar and water together for 5 minutes to make a thick syrup.

Place ½ cup of the ghee or butter in a saucepan. Add the chick-pea flour and fry together on a low heat, stirring constantly, for 10 minutes. Gradually add the sugar syrup, stirring constantly, and cook for 1 minute. Add the remaining ghee or butter, a spoonful at a time, mixing in thoroughly before adding the next spoonful, until all is added. Cook for 5 to 10 minutes more, stirring constantly, until the mixture takes on a spongy appearance and sticks together in a mass, pulling away from the sides of the pan.

Pour into a buttered 9-inch square pan. Decorate with slivered nuts, if desired. After the mixture cools for a few minutes, slice into squares. Cool to harden (the mixture will harden quite quickly) at room temperature. This recipe makes 25 small squares.

Laddus (India)

These crumbly, high-protein sweets melt in the mouth.

¾ cup plus 2 tablespoons ghee or melted butter
2 cups chick-pea flour
½ cup ground almonds
2 cups confectioner's sugar
½ teaspoon cinnamon

Melt the butter or ghee in a saucepan. Add the chick-pea flour and cook, stirring constantly, on a low heat for 15 to 20 minutes or longer, until slightly darkened.

Remove from the heat. Stir in the nuts, confectioner's sugar, and cinnamon. When cool enough to handle, squeeze into 1-inch balls. The ball should just barely hold together. This recipe makes 3 dozen balls.

Variations

If desired, toast the chick-pea flour in a 325° oven for a few minutes before cooking, to remove some of its characteristic flavor.

Add more ground nuts.

Add grated coconut.

Sesame Halvah

1½ cups sesame seeds
½ cup honey
3 tablespoons melted ghee or butter

Toast the sesame seeds and grind to a coarse powder in a blender. Mix in the honey and butter. Press into a buttered pan and chill to harden. Cut into squares, or, with oiled hands, roll the mixture into balls. Chill. Makes about 20 pieces.

Variations

Add a little cardamom, cinnamon, or anise.

Replace some of the sesame seeds with pine nuts and/or pistachios.

Candied Flowers

Delicate cake decorations. The first test of this recipe was made with spring violets picked in the woods of Switzerland, by the shores of Lake Lucerne.

1 tablespoon water
½ cup sugar
drop rosewater
rose petals or violets

Bring the water and sugar to a boil, stirring constantly, and cook to the soft ball stage. Add the rosewater. Carefully dip rose petals or whole violets (stem and leaves et al.) into the mixture. Carefully spread to dry on a plate dusted with confectioner's sugar.

Old colonial recipe for candied rose petals: Sprinkle rose petals with sugar and rosewater and place in the sun. When dry, turn over and repeat the procedure on the other side.

Candied Citrus Peel

Preparing citrus peel is a labor of love for a special fruitcake or other baked dessert. Use the peels of unsprayed, undyed fruit, if possible.

2 cups orange or lemon peel, with the white part removed, cut in ¼-by-½-inch pieces
1 quart water
1 tablespoon salt

Mix the salt into the water. Soak the peel overnight in the mixture. Drain, and rinse in clear water.

Sugar method:
2 cups sugar
½ cup water

Bring the sugar and water to a boil. Boil for 5 minutes. Add the peel and simmer for 20 minutes. Cool in the syrup. Drain in a colander. Spread the fruit peel in a pan and dry in the sun all day. If desired, roll in confectioner's sugar before using.

Honey method:
1 tablespoon cornstarch
¼ teaspoon lemon juice
1 cup honey

Mix the cornstarch and lemon juice into the honey until smooth. Bring to a boil. Boil for 5 minutes. (The mixture may be foamy—be careful that it doesn't boil over.) Reduce the heat, add the peel, and simmer for 20 minutes. Drain in a colander. Spread the fruit peel in a pan and dry in the sun all day. Roll in confectioner's sugar, if desired, before using.

Rasgulla (India)

Not quite a candy, this classic Bengali sweet defies western classifications. The ingredients are simple—it is the technique that makes the transformation of milk, sugar, and water into this special dessert.

panir made from 1 gallon of milk, by the lemon juice method (page 44)
1½ teaspoons unbleached white flour
pinch baking powder
2½ cups water
2½ cups sugar
1 or 2 drops rosewater

Hang the panir for 2 hours. Spread the flour and baking powder on a board. Knead the panir on the board until it feels slightly sticky and oily. Roll it into smooth ½-inch balls, with no cracks. Bring the sugar and water to a boil. Boil for 5 minutes, then reduce heat and simmer for 15 minutes. Remove ⅓ of the syrup and set it aside in a bowl to cool.

Gently drop the panir balls into the remaining simmering syrup. They will swell to double their size, so do not crowd them. Prepare in two batches, if necessary. Cover and gently simmer for 10 minutes. Remove the cover and simmer for 10 more minutes. The balls should be soft, spongy, and very delicate.

Remove the balls very gently with a slotted spoon, and place in the cooling syrup. Let them soak and cool to room temperature. If desired, you may soak them for a few hours before serving. This recipe makes 4 small servings.

Variation
Substitute farina for the flour.

Ice Creams, Ices, and Ice Cream Sundaes

ICE CREAM

The earliest ice creams were perhaps sweetened creams and syrups poured over fresh snow (which is still great—try pouring maple syrup or sweet heavy cream over fresh clean snow). Water ices were prepared in Eastern Europe in the fifteenth century, and a recipe for "cream ice" can be found in *The Experienced English Housekeeper,* published in 1769. In the United States, Mrs. Alexander Hamilton and Dolly Madison helped popularize the sweet. Earlier, George Washington's records show the "purchase of a machine for preparing ice cream."

The following recipes can be made at home in the freezer, without having to use a churn. "Still-frozen" ice creams have a slightly different texture from those which are churn-frozen, but they can still be scooped, or can be frozen in a mold and unmolded to make a spectacular dessert. Once the basic technique is mastered, the whole field of different flavors is opened.

Still-frozen ice creams need an emulsifier to prevent the formation of large crystals of ice. Here, agar agar flakes are employed. Agar agar is available at most health-food stores, and is simple to use. Mixtures can also be cooked and thickened with arrowroot or cornstarch to keep crystals from forming. Milk powder is employed to give ice cream a smooth, creamy texture, and because agar agar does not dissolve well in whole milk.

It is best to whip the cream until it stands in soft peaks, rather than until stiff. Very stiffly whipped cream sometimes gives ice cream a buttery texture.

How to freeze ice cream: Ice cream freezes in approximately 6 hours. The time can be 1 hour more or less, or even 2 hours, depending on the freezer, the type of container the ice cream is in, and the actual temperature of the mixture when it is placed in the freezer. For quick freezing, have the mixture cold and freeze it in shallow containers.

Freeze the mixture until semi-solid. Stir to distribute the ingredients—the nuts and additions tend to sink to the bottom. Freeze again until the desired texture is achieved. Try not to freeze it too long—don't prepare ice cream a day in advance. It can become solid occasionally, and trying to melt it back to the desired texture usually results in a mixture of part melted and part rock-solid ice cream.

If the ice cream is frozen in a mold, dip the mold in hot water for 1 or 2 seconds, and then unmold onto a plate. *All the recipes, unless otherwise indicated, yield a little over 1 quart.*

Note: These recipes have been prepared with the type of agar agar which thickens 1 quart of liquid with 1 tablespoon of agar agar flakes. It is distributed by Erewhon Trading Company of Boston, Massachusetts. If the package directions for your agar agar state that more flakes are necessary to thicken 1 quart of liquid, *double the amount of agar agar in the recipe.*

Flavors and Additions for Ice Cream

Honey, sugar, and maple syrup all work well as sweeteners in ice cream. There is no advantage to any one of them over the others, except for preference. (We have generally favored honey, particularly in the fruit recipes.)

   dried fruit puree
   carob powder
   finely chopped dried fruit
   crushed fresh fruit (large pieces will
      freeze solid)
   minced mint leaves
   chopped nuts
   sunflower or pumpkin seeds
   crushed praliné
   cardamom
   granola cereal
   grain coffee powder
   finely grated lemon or orange rind
   grated coconut
   carob chips
   cinnamon

Note to Vegans: Try preparing frozen yogurt (page 305) with nut or soy milk instead of yogurt. Also try the ices on pages 306-307. Ice cream can be made from nut or soy milk more successfully by the churn method than by the still-frozen method. One is simply making "ice milk." Look up churn-frozen ice cream recipes in any standard cookbook and substitute a non-dairy milk for the cream and milk in the recipe. Or experiment on your own by sweetening the milk and making any of the suggested additions, and then freezing it in an ice cream maker.

Carob Ice Cream

2 cups water
½ cup carob powder
½ cup packed brown sugar *or* ⅓ cup honey
1 tablespoon agar agar flakes
1½ cups milk powder
1 pint heavy cream

Bring the water and carob powder to a boil; if using sugar, add it to the mixture. Add the agar agar and reduce the heat. Simmer for 5 minutes, until the agar agar is dissolved. Cool. When lukewarm, beat in the milk powder; if using honey, beat it in as well.

Whip the cream until it stands in soft peaks. Gently fold in the carob mixture. Place in a 1-quart bowl or mold. Freeze according to directions on page 301.

Mocha Ice Cream

2 cups water
⅓ cup carob powder
5 teaspoons grain coffee powder
½ cup sugar *or* ⅓ cup honey
1 tablespoon agar agar flakes
1 cup powdered milk
1 pint heavy cream

Bring the water, carob powder, and grain coffee powder to a boil; if using sugar, add it as well. Add the agar agar and reduce the heat. Simmer for 5 minutes, until the agar agar is dissolved. Cool the mixture. Pour it into a blender and blend in the milk powder; if using honey, blend it in now.

Whip the cream until it stands in soft peaks. Gently fold in the mocha mixture. Place in a 1-quart mold or bowl, and freeze according to the directions on page 301.

Coffee Ice Cream

2 cups water
1 tablespoon agar agar flakes
2½ tablespoons grain coffee powder
⅓ cup packed brown sugar *or* ¼ cup honey
1 cup milk powder
1 pint heavy cream

Bring the water to a boil. Add the agar agar and reduce the heat. Simmer for 5 minutes, until the agar agar is dissolved. Add the grain coffee powder. Cool the mixture to lukewarm. Place in a blender and add the sugar or honey and the milk powder. Blend until smooth. Cool a little more.

Whip the cream until it stands in soft peaks. Gently fold in the coffee mixture. Freeze in a 1-quart bowl or mold according to the directions on page 301.

Variation

Coffee Crunch Ice Cream: Add 1 recipe for praliné (page 294) before freezing.

Maple-Nut Ice Cream

1½ cups water
1 tablespoon agar agar flakes
1 cup maple syrup
1½ cups milk powder
½ cup chopped nuts
1 pint heavy cream

Bring the water to a boil. Add the agar agar flakes. Reduce the heat and simmer for 5 minutes, until the agar agar is dissolved. Add the maple syrup. Cool to room temperature. Place in a blender and add the milk powder; blend until smooth. Add the nuts—do not blend.

Whip the cream until it stands in soft peaks. Gently fold the maple mixture into the cream. Place in a 1-quart mold or bowl and freeze according to the directions on page 301.

Nut Ice Cream

Try preparing this dessert with toasted almonds, and serving it with caramel sauce.

1 cup water
1 teaspoon grain coffee powder
½ cup honey *or* ¾ cup packed brown sugar
1 tablespoon agar agar flakes
1 cup toasted almonds, cashews, walnuts, hazelnuts, or blanched pistachios
¾ cup milk powder
1 pint heavy cream

Bring the water and grain coffee powder to a boil; if using sugar, add it to the mixture. Add the agar agar. Reduce the heat and simmer 5 minutes for the agar agar to dissolve. Cool to lukewarm. Place in a blender and blend in the milk powder; if using honey, add it as well. Add the nuts and blend for *3 seconds,* so that they are finely chopped, but not completely pulverized.

Whip the cream until it stands in soft peaks. Gently fold in the nut mixture. Place in a 1-quart mold or bowl, and freeze according to the directions on page 301.

Berry or Cherry Ice Cream

¾ cup water
1 tablespoon agar agar flakes
2 cups blueberries, sliced strawberries, crushed raspberries or blackberries, or halved, pitted cherries
⅓ cup honey *or* ½ cup sugar
¾ cup milk powder

2 tablespoons lemon juice
1 pint heavy cream

Bring the water to a boil. Add the agar agar and reduce the heat; simmer for 5 minutes, until the agar agar is dissolved. If using sugar, add it now. Cool. Combine in a blender with the berries or cherries, the milk powder, and lemon juice. If using honey, blend it in as well.

Whip the cream until it stands in soft peaks. Gently fold in the berry or cherry mixture. Place in a 1-quart bowl or mold and freeze according to the directions on page 301.

Peach, Apricot, or Mango Ice Cream

1 cup water
1 tablespoon agar agar flakes
3 cups peeled, chopped peaches, apricots, or mangoes
½ cup honey *or* ¾ cup sugar
½ cup milk powder
2 tablespoons lemon juice
1 pint heavy cream

Bring the water to a boil. Add the agar agar. Add the fruit (and the sugar, if used), reduce the heat, and simmer for 5 minutes, until the agar agar is dissolved. Cool the mixture. Place in a blender with the milk powder; if using honey, add it now. Blend until smooth. Blend in the lemon juice.

Whip the cream until it stands in soft peaks. Gently fold in the fruit mixture. Place in a mold or bowl and freeze according to the directions on page 301.

Fruit Salad Ice Cream

For best results use mixtures of juicy, flavorful fruits, such as berries and peaches.

1 cup fruit juice
1 tablespoon agar agar flakes
¾ cup sugar *or* ½ cup honey

3 cups finely cut fruit salad
¾ cup milk powder
2 tablespoons lemon juice
½ cup grated coconut (optional)
1 pint heavy cream

Bring the juice to a boil. Add the agar
agar. Reduce heat and simmer for 5 minutes, until the agar agar is dissolved. If using sugar, add it now. Cool to lukewarm.
Place the mixture in a blender. Add the
fruit, and milk powder, and blend until
smooth; if using honey, blend it in as well.
Blend in the lemon juice. Stir in the coconut.

Whip the cream until it stands in soft
peaks. Gently fold in the fruit mixture.
Place in a mold or bowl and freeze according to the directions on page 301.

Banana Ice Cream

Fresh banana ice cream has a very special
flavor completely unlike the commercial
banana ice creams.

1½ cups water
1 tablespoon agar agar flakes
½ cup honey *or* ¾ cup sugar
1½ cups mashed ripe bananas
1 cup milk powder
1 pint heavy cream

Bring the water to a boil. Add the agar
agar. Reduce the heat and simmer for 5
minutes until the agar agar is dissolved. If
using sugar, add it now. Cool the mixture.
Place in a blender with the mashed bananas
and milk powder. If using honey, blend it
in. Blend until smooth.

Whip the cream until it stands in soft
peaks. Gently fold in the banana mixture.
Place in a 1-quart mold or bowl and freeze
according to the directions on page 301.

Variation
Add ½ cup chopped nuts.

Date Ice Cream

Prepared without any extra sweetening, but
the flavor is very rich.

2 cups water
1½ cups pitted dates, packed
1 tablespoon agar agar flakes
1 cup milk powder
1 pint heavy cream
½ cup chopped nuts (optional)

Bring the water and dates to a boil. Add
the agar agar. Reduce the heat and simmer
for 5 minutes, until the agar agar is dissolved. Cool the mixture. Place in a blender
with the milk powder. Blend until smooth.
Strain the mixture.

Whip the cream until it stands in soft
peaks. Gently fold in the date mixture. Add
the nuts, if desired. Place in a 1-quart mold
or bowl and freeze according to the directions on pabe 301.

Avocado Ice Cream

A pale green, mellow ice cream.

1½ cups water
1 tablespoon agar agar flakes
⅓ cup honey *or* ½ cup sugar
1 cup milk powder
1½ cups mashed ripe avocados
3 tablespoons lemon juice
1 pint heavy cream

Bring the water to a boil. Add the agar
agar. Reduce the heat and simmer for 5
minutes. If using sugar, add it now. Cool.
Place in a blender. Add the milk powder
and avocados and blend until smooth. If using honey, blend it in as well. Add the
lemon juice and blend again.

Whip the cream until it stands in soft
peaks. Gently fold in the avocado mixture.
Place in a 1-quart mold or bowl and freeze
according to the directions on page 301.

Ricotta Spumoni (Italy)

3 cups ricotta
½ cup heavy cream
½ cup honey *or* ¾ cup sugar
1 tablespoon finely grated orange rind
1 cup sliced cherries or strawberries
¾ cup coarsely chopped pistachios
¼ cup raisins
½ cup grated coconut
walnut halves

Beat the ricotta, heavy cream, honey or sugar, and the orange rind together. Mix in the strawberries or cherries, pistachios, raisins, and coconut. Pour into individual cups or into a mold. Decorate the tops with walnut halves. Freeze for about 6 hours, until firm. This recipe makes 4 to 6 servings.

Frozen Yogurt

To be completely smooth and creamy, frozen yogurt must be prepared in a churn-type ice cream freezer. The following still-frozen recipe produces a delicious dessert with the texture of a sherbet or an ice. Sweeten to taste according to the sweetness of the fruit and the tartness of the yogurt.

¾ cup fruit juice or water
1 tablespoon agar agar flakes
2½ cups crushed fresh juicy fruit
1 tablespoon lemon juice
⅓ to ½ cup honey *or* ½ to ¾ cup sugar
3 cups very thick yogurt

Bring the juice or water to a boil. Add the agar agar. Reduce the heat and simmer for 5 minutes. Add the fruit, lemon juice, and sugar or honey. Blend until smooth. Cool.

Gently fold the mixture into the yogurt. Freeze according to the directions for ice on page 306. This recipe makes about 5 cups.

Quick Yogurt Sherbet

A good snack or quick dessert, these mixtures have a texture somewhere between a sherbet and a smoothie. Serve immediately after preparation.

Freeze fruit juice or fruit sauce in ice cube trays. Place some of the frozen cubes in a blender with yogurt just to cover. Blend just until smooth. Serve immediately. Add a little honey or sugar to the mixture if desired.

Variations

Freeze small amounts of berries or slices of juicy fruits to add to or replace the fruit juice.

Sweeten with chopped dates or raisins blended into the mixture.

Banana Freeze

Freeze peeled ripe or slightly overripe bananas. Put through a juicer or the fine grater on a food processor, or puree in a blender. Serve immediately.

Variation

For a popsickle, cut off one end of a banana and carefully place a stick in it. Freeze. For a fancy popsickle, dip the banana in carob sauce and roll it in ground nuts before freezing.

ICES

Ices have a slightly more crunchy texture than ice creams. These homemade fresh fruit ices have the flavor of pure, sweet, fresh frozen fruit—which is what they basically are. Agar agar flakes are used to prevent large crystals of ice from forming. Please see the important note about agar agar on page 301 before embarking on any of the recipes. Serve ices plain, over fruit salads, or in the center of a halved, seeded melon.

How to freeze ices: Pour the mixture for the ice into a bowl, or into ice cube trays with the separators removed. Freeze until semi-solid. Beat with a whisk or an electric mixer to break up the ice crystals. Beat again every half hour until the mixture has reached the desired frozen consistency. The beating helps to refine the texture of the final product. Total freezing time will be approximately 6 hours.

Berry or Cherry Ice

1 cup water
1 tablespoon agar agar flakes
3 cups sliced strawberries, whole blueberries, crushed blackberries or raspberries, or pitted, halved cherries
2 tablespoons lemon juice
⅓ cup honey *or* ½ cup sugar

Bring the water to a boil. Add the agar agar. Reduce the heat and simmer for 5 minutes, until the agar agar is dissolved. Cool to lukewarm. Place in a blender with the fruit, lemon juice, and honey or sugar. Blend until smooth. Freeze according to the directions above. This recipe makes about 6 cups.

Orange Ice

3 cups fresh orange juice
1 teaspoon agar agar flakes
2 tablespoons lemon juice
1½ tablespoons honey *or* 2 tablespoons sugar

Bring 1 cup of the orange juice to a boil. Add the agar agar. Reduce the heat and simmer for 5 minutes, until the agar agar is dissolved. Cool to lukewarm. Add the remaining orange juice, lemon juice, and honey or sugar. Freeze according to directions above. This recipe makes about 5 cups.

Lemon Snow

2¾ cups water
½ cup lemon juice
1 teaspoon agar agar flakes
⅓ cup honey *or* ½ cup sugar

Bring the water to a boil. Add the agar agar flakes. Reduce the heat and simmer for 5 minutes, until the agar agar is dissolved. Cool to lukewarm.

Add the lemon juice and honey or sugar. Freeze according to the directions above. This recipe makes about 5 cups.

Variation
Lemon-Mint Ice: Replace the water with mint tea.

Peach, Apricot, or Mango Ice

¾ cup water
3 cups sliced peeled peaches, apricots, or mangoes
3 tablespoons lemon juice
1 tablespoon agar agar flakes
⅓ cup honey *or* ½ cup sugar

Bring the water, fruit, and lemon juice to a boil. If using sugar, include it in the mixture. Add the agar agar flakes. Simmer for 5 minutes, until the agar agar is dissolved. Cool the mixture. Pour it into a blender and puree. If honey is used, blend it in as well. Freeze according to the directions above. This recipe makes about 8 cups.

Rhubarb Ice

A tart and refreshing ice. Add a little more sugar or honey if a very sweet ice is desired. Sugar tastes better here.

4 cups rhubarb, cut in 1-inch pieces
1¼ cups water
2 teaspoons agar agar flakes
⅓ cup honey *or* ¾ cup sugar

Bring the rhubarb and water to a boil. Reduce the heat and simmer, covered, for 15 minutes. Add the agar agar and simmer for another 5 minutes. If using sugar, add it. Cool the mixture to lukewarm. If using honey, stir it in. Puree in a blender. Freeze according to the directions on page 306. This recipe makes 5 cups.

Pineapple Ice

1¾ cups water
1 tablespoon agar agar
¾ cup sugar *or* ½ cup honey
3 cups crushed pineapple
¼ cup lemon juice

Bring the water to a boil. Add the agar agar. Reduce the heat and simmer for 5 minutes, until the agar agar is dissolved. If using sugar, add it at this point. Cool to lukewarm. Place in a blender with the pineapple and lemon juice. If using honey, blend it in. Blend for 1 or 2 seconds. Freeze according to the directions on page 306. This recipe makes 5 cups.

Rose Hip Ice

Prepare rose hip soup (page 146) and freeze according to the directions on page 306. This results in 6 cups of an unusual, rich red ice.

Herb Tea Ices

Subtly-flavored ices can be created from herb teas. Serve herb tea ices in the hollow part of a halved melon or over fruit salads.

3¾ cups strong herb tea
2 teaspoons agar agar flakes
¼ cup lemon juice
sugar or honey to taste

Bring the tea to a boil. Add the agar agar. Reduce the heat and simmer for 5 minutes. Cool the mixture to lukewarm. Add the lemon juice and sweetening to taste (make slightly sweeter than desired—freezing diminishes the sweetness). Freeze according to the directions on page 306.

ICE CREAM SUNDAES

Sprinkle, pour, or arrange over or around scoops of ice cream:
chopped dried fruit
sliced fresh fruit
fresh fruit sauce
berry or cherry sauce
rhubarb sauce
sunflower or pumpkin seeds
lemon sauce
maple syrup
crushed or whole brownies
raisins
grated coconut
granola cereal
praliné
crushed candies
orange sauce
carob sauce
honey
mint leaves
ambrosia salad
prasad fruit salad
crushed or whole cookies
whipped cream
caramel sauce
carob chips

Banana Split

Split a banana in half lengthwise. Place in a dish. Place scoops of ice cream between the banana slices. Top with nuts, a sauce, and whipped cream.

Brownie Sundae

Cover a brownie with a scoop of ice cream and carob sauce. Top with whipped cream.

Coupe Jacques

Cover ice cream with fruit salad. Top with fresh fruit sauce and whipped cream.

Coupe Melba

Cover a scoop of ice cream with a blanched, peeled peach half. Top with fresh fruit sauce prepared from raspberries, and whipped cream.

Coupe Denmark

Cover ice cream with hot carob sauce, nuts, and whipped cream.

Coupe Hawaii

Top ice cream with pineapple slices, bananas, sliced oranges, and mangoes. Sprinkle with grated coconut.

Ice Cream Sodas

Place 2 or 3 scoops of ice cream in a glass and fill the glass with carbonated mineral water.

Parfaits

Place layers of ice cream and crushed fresh fruit and/or fruit sauce in a tall glass. Top with whipped cream.

Beverages

JUICES

There are three types of machines that extract the juice from fruits and vegetables:

Juicers, or *juice extractors,* are for vegetables and for some fruits. Look for juicers which separate the pulp from the juice, rather than mixing the two together.

Citrus juicers come in both hand and electric varieties. They are used for oranges, grapefruits, lemons, and limes, and also work for pomegranates.

Blenders juice a very limited amount of juicy fruit, by pureeing the fruit so that the juice can be strained out.

Fresh juices are a joy. They are delicious and very nourishing, and it is fun to create new combinations. Fresh juice should be prepared just before serving for optimum freshness. Some vegetable and fruit juices are suitable for drinking "straight," while others, either because they have a very strong flavor or because very little juice can

be extracted from their source (such as spinach or parsley) or because they are very thick, are more suitable for mixing with other juices. The "base" juices are those which may be served alone, or into which small amounts of other juices may be mixed.

Base Juices:
- carrot
- apple
- beet
- watermelon
- tomato (very thick and rich)
- grape
- cherry
- pineapple
- zucchini (somewhat thin and mild-flavored)
- grapefruit
- orange
- cucumber

Juices to be added in small amounts to the base juices:
(This is a partial list, mentioning some of the more popular juices. Most fruits and vegetables can be juiced.)
- celery
- spinach and greens
- apricot, peach, mango (very thick)
- green pepper
- lemon
- fennel
- berry (very thick)
- parsley
- pomegranate
- lime
- pear

Some suggested juice combinations:
- carrot-apple
- carrot-green pepper, with a little cream
- tomato-zucchini-celery
- apricot-pineapple
- apple-pineapple-beet
- carrot-beet
- carrot-spinach-watercress
- pineapple-orange-coconut milk
- orange-grapefruit
- cherry-blueberry-orange

Grape Juice

Remove grapes from their stalks and place in a blender. Blend to a mush. Strain through a sieve. Serve immediately. Fresh grape juice, even when refrigerated, tends to taste less fresh even after an hour.

Pineapple Juice

Peel a pineapple and cut into small pieces. Place in a blender. Blend to a mush. Strain through a sieve.

Tomato Juice

12 medium tomatoes, chopped
1 celery stalk with leaves, sliced
2 tablespoons fresh minced parsley
½ teaspoon or more celery or seasoned salt
½ teaspoon or more sugar or honey (optional)

Puree the tomatoes in a blender. Place in a saucepan with the remaining ingredients. Simmer, covered, for 30 minutes. Season to taste. Strain out the celery and chill. This recipe makes 1 quart.

Peach, Apricot, or Mango Nectar

3 cups crushed peaches, apricots, or mangoes
1 tablespoon lemon juice
1 to 1½ cups water
sugar or honey to taste

Combine the fruit, lemon juice, and 1 cup water in a blender. Simmer about 10 minutes. Add sugar or honey to taste. Add more water to thin, if necessary. Chill. This recipe makes 2 to 2½ cups.

Cranberry Juice

3½ cups water
3½ cups cranberries
1 tablespoon lemon juice
½ cup orange or apple juice
⅓ to ½ cup sugar *or* ¼ to ⅓ cup honey

Bring the cranberries and the water to a boil. Simmer for 5 to 7 minutes, until the skins pop. Mash lightly and strain. Mix in the remaining ingredients, with sweetening to taste. Chill. This recipe makes 1 quart.

Cranberry-Orange Punch

1 grapefruit
whole cloves
1 quart fresh cranberry juice
1 quart fresh orange juice

Wash the grapefruit. Stud it lightly with cloves. Place in a baking pan and bake in a 200° oven for 3 hours. Cool to room temperature.

Mix the juices together and pour into a punchbowl. Just before serving, place the grapefruit in the punchbowl. If the punch seems to be getting too spicy, remove the grapefruit or add more juice. This recipe makes ½ gallon.

Lemonade or Limeade

2 tablespoons lemon or lime juice
1 teaspoon or more honey
1 cup water

Mix the lemon juice and honey in a glass. Add the water and stir well.

Variations

For mint lemonade, replace the water with mint tea.

Serve lemonade hot.

DAIRY BEVERAGES

Basic Milkshake

¾ cup ice cream
½ cup milk

Combine in a blender or shake in a tightly closed jar.

Additions to Milkshakes

(Puree the additions in a blender, if necessary.)
   juicy fruits
   bananas
   chopped dried fruits
   ground nuts and seeds
   carob sauce or carob drink powder
   fruit sauces
   grated coconut
   sweet spices

Banana Milkshake

½ cup milk
½ cup ice cream
1 large banana

Combine all the ingredients in a blender.

Fruit Milkshake

½ cup ice cream
¼ cup milk
1 cup fruit salad or sliced juicy fruit

Combine all the ingredients in a blender.

Carob, Coffee, or Mocha Milkshake

¾ cup carob, coffee, or mocha ice cream
½ cup milk

Combine in a blender or shake in a tightly closed jar.

Smoothies

Here are the basic proportions for preparing smoothies. Buttermilk or kefir can replace the yogurt.

1½ cups yogurt
½ cup or more sliced juicy fruit (banana makes a good base for adding other fruits)
honey or sugar to taste

Combine all the ingredients in a blender. This recipe makes 2 servings.

Variations

Replace fresh fruit with fruit sauce.
Add a pinch of saffron soaked in a little hot water.
Suggested smoothies: banana, banana-strawberry, mango, blueberry-peach.

Fruit Frappé

For something very special, try a mango frappé.

½ cup milk
1 cup finely cut juicy fruit or banana
honey or sugar to taste

Combine all the ingredients in a blender.

Variations

For additions, see additions to milk-shakes, page 310.
Vegan Variation: Replace milk with coconut or nut milk.

Sweet Saffron Lassi (India)

Lassi is a cool yogurt- or buttermilk-based beverage from India. To make lassi even more cooling, omit the water from the recipe and place 4 or 5 ice cubes in the blender. Blend at high speed until it is completely smooth—just finely crushed ice and the yogurt or buttermilk.

1½ cups yogurt
½ cup water
2 tablespoons honey
1 to 2 drops rosewater (optional)
pinch saffron soaked in 1 tablespoon hot water

Mix the ingredients well. This recipe makes 2 cups.

Variation

Replace the yogurt with buttermilk.

Salt Lassi (India)

This version is cooling on a hot day.

1½ cups yogurt or buttermilk
1 teaspoon roasted cumin
½ cup water
½ teaspoon salt

Mix the ingredients together well. This recipe makes 2 cups.

Orange-Grapefruit Lassi (India)

juice of 1 orange
juice of 1 grapefruit
1 cup yogurt
1 to 2 tablespoons honey

Freeze the juices in an ice cube tray and combine with the remaining ingredients in a blender. Or simply mix all the ingredients, without freezing the juices. This recipe makes 2 servings.

Koldskål (Denmark)

1 pint buttermilk
¼ cup honey
¼ cup lemon juice
½ cup heavy cream
1 lemon, sliced thin

Beat the buttermilk, lemon juice, and honey together until frothy. Whip the cream until stiff and fold into the buttermilk mixture. Garnish with lemon slices. This recipe makes 5 or 6 servings.

Amrit (India)

A nice beverage to drink at bedtime.

2 cups milk
1½ tablespoons honey
pinch cinnamon
pinch cardamom
pinch saffron soaked in 1 tablespoon hot water

Combine all the ingredients in a sauce-pan, and heat. This recipe makes 2 cups.

Variation

Vegan Variation: Replace the milk with soy milk.

Carob Milk

Prepared carob powders that dissolve into milk are available at health-food stores. If they are unavailable, try this method.

1 cup milk
2 to 4 tablespoons carob sauce (page 287)

Mix well. Serve hot or cold. For a Mexican touch, add a dash of cinnamon.

Variation

Vegan Variation: Replace the milk with any non-dairy milk.

Tahini Milk

1 cup milk
1 tablespoon tahini
1 tablespoon honey

Mix all the ingredients together well.

Variation

Vegan Variation: Replace the milk with any non-dairy milk.

Almond Milk

A delightful beverage, found in both classical Indian and French cooking.

½ cup blanched almonds
2 cups milk
1½ tablespoons honey

Combine the ingredients in a blender. If desired, let chill and soak in the refrigerator. Strain out the almond meal through a fine muslin cloth. This recipe makes 2 cups.

Variation

Vegan Variation: Use non-dairy nut milk prepared with almonds instead of this recipe. Blend in a teaspoon or more of mild-flavored oil to make it richer.

TEAS

Spice Tea (India)

A lovely after-dinner beverage. If a caffeine-free black tea is available in the local health-food store, use it for this recipe.

2 cups milk
2 cups water
¼ teaspoon cinnamon
⅛ teaspoon cardamom
⅛ teaspoon ground ginger
⅛ teaspoon saffron
dash nutmeg
4 teaspoons caffeine-free black tea leaves or mild herb tea leaves, such as vervain
4 to 5 tablespoons sugar *or* 3 to 4 tablespoons honey

Bring the milk, water, and spices to a boil. Remove from the heat. Add the tea and steep for a few minutes. Add the sugar or honey, strain out the tea leaves, and serve. This recipe makes 1 quart.

Variations

Replace the milk and water with ½ cup heavy cream and 3½ cups water.

Vegan Variation: Replace the milk with nut or soy milk. You may want to use more milk than water, to make it richer.

Herb Tea

Most herb teas can be prepared in the following manner.

1 cup boiling water
1 rounded teaspoon herbs

Pour the boiling water over the herbs. Let steep for 1 to 5 minutes, depending on the strength desired. Strain and serve.

Herb teas have been used since the beginning of time for their medicinal value. It might be interesting (and wise) for the cook to read a book on herbal medicine to find out some of the physiological effects of different teas. Though trying to cure illness should be left to the experts, you will want to be aware of which teas are enlivening and stimulating to the nervous system, and which teas tend to make one drowsy. For instance, you would not want to drink chamomile as a pick-me-up in the morning, for it would be more enjoyed as a soothing before-bed beverage.

We have left such discussions to the experts, and have listed some of the teas commonly served for their flavor as well as for their effects. Herb tea mixtures, or tisanes, can also be created, and many good blends can be found in health-food stores.

Anise: Crushed anise seeds make a licorice-flavored tea.

Chamomile: There are two types of chamomile: true chamomile (*matricaria chamomilla*) and Roman chamomile (*anthemus nobilis*). The first is said to have greater health-giving effects. It is a light, sweet, golden tea.

Clove: Simmer a small amount of whole cloves in water for 15 to 20 minutes for a spicy tea.

Clover: Both red and white clover blossoms can be gathered and dried for a light tea.

Dandelion root: Scrub, grind, and roast it as a coffee substitute.

Fennel: The tea is prepared from the seeds, and has a light licorice flavor.

Ginger root: Slice, peel, and boil it for a tea.

Ginseng: Long used for its medicinal effects, this herb is associated with the orient, but it grows wild in the United States. In fact, at one point it was exported from Canada to China. George Washington recorded, "In passing over the mountains I met a number of persons and pack horses going in with ginseng." Ginseng root can be found in a whole root or in a powdered form. It should be boiled for 15 minutes. Mu tea is a common blend that contains ginseng.

Hibiscus blossoms: A tart, red tea.

Lemon balm or Melissa: Brew the leaves for tea.

Lemon grass: A refreshing, lemon-flavored tea.

Linden flower: Very light and mild tea.

Mint tea: Spearmint and peppermint are some of the most common herb teas.

Raspberry leaf tea: A fruit flavored tea fabled as promoting fertility.

Rose hips: A tart, dark red tea. Steep rose hips for 10 minutes or longer for their full effect.

Saffron: Add a pinch of saffron to water and boil until the water turns golden.

Sassafras: A bark that makes an orange-brown, root-beer-flavored tea.

Strawberry leaf: A delicate, fruit flavored tea.

Vervain or verbena: A light, mild tea.

If you are new to herb teas, try some of the following teas and branch out from there. These teas are generally available, and are very popular.

Mint

Rose hip

Chamomile

Lemon grass

Hibiscus blossoms

Besides the herbs and spices above, orange

peel can be cut into small pieces and dried to make a light, subtle tea, or to be added to tisanes.

GRAIN COFFEE SUBSTITUTES

Grain beverages stand up well in their own right, without being considered a substitute for anything. Postum (originally developed by Mr. Kellogg for his health-food sanatorium in Battle Creek, Michigan!) is available in supermarkets, and other grain mixtures can be found in health-food stores.

Grain beverages can be made at home, in many variations. You may wish to experiment and come up with your own "house blend."

Grain Beverage

¾ cup barley
1 tablespoon carob powder
2 tablespoons wheatberries

Toast the barley and wheatberries until dark brown in a dry pan. Grind the grains to a powder in a blender. Toast again until dark. Remove from the heat and cool for a few minutes. Add the carob powder.

To prepare the beverage, pour 1 cup boiling water over 1 tablespoon grain powder. Steep for a few minutes. Strain. Serve with honey or sugar and milk or cream.

Variations

Add or substitute buckwheat, bran, or dandelion root (ground and roasted) for the grains or carob.

Change the proportions of barley to wheatberries.

Index